Whitefella Dreaming

Meinen lieben Freunden
Midi und Hannes
zur Erinnerung an
einen netten Tag
im Sanctuary
Eure Barbara

The authorised biography of
William Ricketts

For Midi and Hannes,
with best wishes from
Peter Brady
24th Feb 1995

Whitefella Dreaming
The authorised biography of William Ricketts

Published by:
Preferred Image PO Box 155
Olinda Victoria Australia 3788

With the assistance of the

Shire of Lillydale
and the
Victorian Conservation Trust

Design consultant: John Boucher
Editorial consultants: Robert D. Croll and Jonathon Barnsley
Typeset in Bembo by Axiom Typesetting and Graphic Services Pty Ltd
139 Charles Street, Abbotsford, Victoria 3067.
Printed by McPherson's Printing Group
Mulgrave, Victoria
Wholly produced in Australia
First published 1994

National Library of Australia Cataloguing-in-Publication data:
    Brady, Peter, 1958–
    Whitefella Dreaming
    Includes index
    ISBN 0 646 15862 7.
    1. Ricketts, William. 2. Sculptors – Australia – Biography.
    3. Sculpture, Australian. [4.] Aborigines, Australian, in art.
    I. Title
730.92

Contents

Acknowledgements

This book is dedicated to my wife, Marguerite, whose help and support made it possible. Without her, there would not have been a book.

To the rest of the many hundreds who helped, advised, contributed and encouraged, I am truly grateful. This has been a huge combined effort. I thank the following in particular:

The Victorian Conservation Trust Trustees and employees, past and present, in particular the Director, Warwick Forge, for his initial gamble. Special thanks to Sanctuary employees, Paul Bennett, Marlene Benson, Suzanne Boutsis, Barry Horsburgh, Bet Kennedy, Joan Munro and Olivia Rich.

The Shire of Lillydale's Councillors, staff and rate payers, whose material assistance in the early stages and ready financial assistance at the publishing stage was invaluable. Special thanks to Linda Leckie, whose capacity for patience when introducing me to computers was amazing.

The editors and staff, past and present, of the Melbourne *Age*, *Argus*, *Herald*, *Sun* and *Truth*, the Adelaide *Advertiser* and *News*, the *Australian*, the *Centralian Advocate*, *Free Press*, the *Lillydale Express*, the *New York Times*, the *Knoxville News-Sentinel*, the *Australasian*, the *Australian Women's Weekly*, *Woman's Day*, the *Woman's Day and Home*, *Woman's Day with Woman*, *People*, *Pix*, *Bank Notes*, *Simply Living*, *Time* and the *Australian Home Beautiful*, for their foresight to record Bill's history as it happened and, variously, access to their libraries and permission to use the material contained therein.

The librarians of Shire of Lillydale library, the State Libraries of Victoria and South Australia, the National Library in Canberra and Cheryl McNamara of the Australian Archives in Darwin. The Trustees and staff of the Sydney Museum of Applied Arts and Sciences [especially Jai Patterson], the State Gallery of South Australia, the National Gallery of Victoria, the National Gallery in Canberra and the Shepparton Gallery.

Peter Timms [*Australian Studio Pottery and Porcelain Painting*] and Michael Jones [*Prolific in God's Gifts*] for allowing me to quote freely from their excellent books.

The private citizens who gave their time, memories and energy, with special thanks to Dorothy Atkinson, Douglas Baglin, Helene Burns, Bet Cromb, the Crow family, Martin and Mrs Dalwitz, Helen and Chris Dixon, Peter and Margaret Dormer, Mrs P. Duguid, Max Fatchen, Helge Hergstrom, Joan Hewitt, Louis Kahan, Errol and Elaine Lobo, Jeremy Long, Creed Lovegrove, Bob Lord, Filomena Murrone, Lin Onus, Edwin Parker, the Paul family, Pushican, Jim Rea, Anslie Roberts, the Ricketts family, Mil and Mrs Roche, Brian Ross, Mrs E. Rumbold, Barbara Scott, Patricia and Maurice Seymour, Barbara Smith, David Smith, George Tippett, Doris Turner, Jim Westcott, the Wilding family, Les and Shirley Wilson, Ralph Wilson and Lance and Judy Wood.

The people of Central Australia, including Administrators and Council members of Ernabella, Hermannsburg, Kintore, Mt Liebig and Papunya Communities. Thanks to Alis' Burns, Elsa Corbet, Ted Hemsley, Benny Japangyardi, Yami Lester, Tony McDonald, Bryce Ponsford, Arnold Probin, Wenten Rubuntja, Johnny Scobie, Ron Trudinger and Gus Williams.

To Robert D. Croll and Jonathon Barnsley, for their separate encouragement, interest and editorial advice. I had to fight hard to keep the rough edges that remain.

To Pam and David Porter, of Scope Computers [Ferny Creek], for extraordinary after-sales service, help whenever it was required, support, encouragement and many laughs. To Bruce Bloemhoff of the Copy Spot [Croydon] for his ongoing support with all my copying.

To John Boucher for his help and guidance with the overall design and layout, and Bernard Hogan for his patience and typesetting expertise. To the staff of McPherson's Printing Group, especially Lazarus Gymnopoulos, who went to no end of effort to make the printing process as trouble-free as possible.

Most of all, posthumous thanks to Bill Ricketts for allowing me into his life and enduring with dignity my prying and my dragging his ever-forward-thinking mind backwards into the past.

Author's Note

I have tried to present the text in this book in such a way as to make it a little more "user friendly".

Generally speaking, my input is presented in normal type. In the normal type, words in italics are simply my emphasis. Quotation marks within the normal type generally identify colloquial or distasteful terms, eg. "doggers", but sometimes enclose very short, direct quotes, eg. "a couple of weeks".

Quoted passages or phrases are presented in bold italics, as is the case with this sentence. Such quotes will still be enclosed in quotation marks. Any words which are underlined in such quotes were, [a] either underlined or in italics as they appeared in the original written form, or, [b] strongly emphasised when given to me verbally.

Parentheses – ( ) – are only used where they were included in original quoted text. I have used square brackets – [ ] – for all of my simplifications, clarifications, amplifications and asides.

The three points of ellipsis – ... – exclusively represent omitted words from quoted text or transcript within this volume. Long pauses within transcripts are indicated by the use of a dash.

Any reader who finds typographic errors and/or definite and qualifiable historical inaccuracies in the text is invited to write to me via the publisher so that corrections can be made for future editions. Readers who feel that they have significant additional information or historically valuable photographs are also invited to contact me.

Peter Brady
Olinda

From beyond the frontiers of the sculptural
forms within this beautiful forest scene,
a supreme power can be evoked
a power within the human range, and by
its emergence it will be able to change
the course of everything and bring forth
the foundation of true educational teaching
Divine
A way of life indestructable to every other
aspect of life

I ask my friends to stand with me in

A Renewal of Life ABSOLUTE

William Ricketts

Portrait by courtesy of Louis Kahan
Original text by William Ricketts,
extracted from a 1987 statement given to the author.

Introduction

When I first came to know William [Bill] Ricketts intimately, early in 1986, he was eighty-seven years old and enjoying good health. In the pure, fertile environment of his forest home, he seemed to thrive on a modest, principally vegetarian diet and a little fine port or ginger wine. His all-consuming life's purpose gave him absolute focus. Reference is often made to a person's "spark of life", but within Bill Ricketts it was a lightening bolt. While he was small in stature and so thin as to appear frail, his eyes revealed a strength. Coloured a pale blue-grey, often more grey than blue, they could be warm and serene or electrifyingly intense. When he was consumed by a passionate rage and he closed in on you to emphasise a point, his eyes were piercing. Those were also the times when you couldn't help but notice that his breath was astonishingly sweet and fresh.

His favourite colour was green—like the forest, he said. The majority of his clothes were green, as were the sheets on his bed and the curtains in his home. The dark green he preferred contrasted sharply with the fresh, pink skin of his face.

He always wore a green corduroy beret, as he had done over the previous fifty years. His speech was animated by the fluid movement of long-fingered hands—hands which were strong yet nimble. There was often fresh clay embedded under his fingernails. Many of the knuckles in his fingers were nuggety, appearing arthritic, but he never complained of pain in them.

He lived alone within the grounds of his Sanctuary in one small room of a house built for him by the Victorian Government in 1962.[1] The room was originally the kitchen but then served as bedroom, studio and entertainment area. To say the room was cluttered would be kind. Boxes and piles of papers, small sculptures in various stages of completion, a disused record and cassette player, books, clothes and cooking utensils spilled from the limited bench space. A refrigerator, electric stove, single bed, more boxes of clothes and books and one chair occupied the equally limited floor space. On every day of the year an electric heater was used to drive away the forest damp: often the stove's hot-plates provided added warmth.

One doorway from his room led down a short passageway in which piles of wet clay were stacked, past the bathroom to the rear of the house. The other doorway opened into what was once his living room, but was then a display-room for smaller works which had not been set in the grounds.

During the hours when the Sanctuary was open to the public, the display room was visited by people whose voices carried through to Bill's inner sanctum, but he did not complain. He was warm and dry, which was a far cry from his original existence on the mountain over half a century before.

Although he had been creating everything from studio pottery to monumental clay sculptures

---

1 William Ricketts Sanctuary, Mt Dandenong Tourist Road, Mt Dandenong, Victoria.

for at least sixty years, he refused to be labelled an "artist" or "sculptor". He maintained that all of his work had been created *through* him and not *by* him. The real creator, he said, was the Divine, the Highest Consciousness, the Supreme Essence, or God, depending on the day. And Bill Ricketts refused to call his sculptural work "art", maintaining that any reference to "art" cheapened and detracted from the spiritual message he felt was embodied in his work.

So there was a man whose fame was largely based on the clay sculptures located in a Sanctuary which in times gone was variously called "The Potter's Sanctuary" and "The Mountain Gallery", whose work had been exhibited in galleries around the world for over half a century, but who would not tolerate being referred to as an artist, or his work art. Confused? Small wonder that interspersed with labels of praise like genius and visionary were such derogatory labels as mad and eccentric.

Another trait of Bill's which would start people wondering was his extreme and enduring respect for Life in all its manifestations. For example, the forests of Mt Dandenong support a thriving mosquito population in summer. On the rare warm days, the air can be thick with them. Yet never did I witness Bill, who used no repellents whatsoever, kill a mosquito—nor have I spoken to anybody who has. Just occasionally during the time I knew him did he *threaten* violence against them. The bush mice which sometimes shared the meagre comfort of his home were trapped alive and released alive into the bush nearby—and were probably back "home" before Bill.

He did not kill them because they were life-forms, just as he was. The view was extreme, but so was the devotion of a life to a cause.

For the same reason that Bill never married, he did not readily form committed friendships: he hadn't the time. The people he allowed into his life were those who could help or support his cause. Unless they devoted themselves wholly, which very few people could do for an extended period, they were left behind. Although he desperately wanted people who could offer the same degree of devotion as his own, he could not find them. Who would have been prepared to do as he had done and go for sixty years without a holiday of any sort? He had days off, but with the benefit of prolonged observation I suggest that his actual time off was measured only in minutes. Always his mind came back to his chosen cause.

His all-consuming passion is what set Bill apart. He cared not for money in the usual sense, although he was hell-bent on amassing a fortune, preferably a seven figure fortune. He thought that money was best fought with money, and with his fortune he would have taken on the governments and businesses which destroy the Earth and her life-forms. Yet Bill would raise funds through the sale of his sculptures only as an absolute last resort. That avenue, with the assistance of a resourceful agent, could quite easily have raised vast sums over the years—but that would have brought him down to the status of "artist". He saw himself as the non-violent fighter for the Earth as a whole.

Until a couple of years before his death, Bill dreamed with the millions of others who gambled against extraordinary odds in the hope of winning Lotto. His confidants often rebuked him for what they thought was his wastefulness, for he was somewhat more than a one-ticket-per-week man; but they did not acknowledge that Bill's gambling was completely altruistic. Instead of the tropical retreat, fast cars or fancy boats about which many other Lotto players dream, he envisaged a war chest with which to pay for full-page advertisements promoting ultimate conservation, money to inject into the environmental organisations already established—money which would give a greater power to his often repeated words. Some say it bordered on megalomania, but once again it fitted perfectly with his life of total commitment.

2 Although the terms "Aborigine" and "Aboriginal" are considered to be insulting and faceless generalities by many members of Australia's indigenous peoples, it is a fact that there is not one single non-English word with which the whole of Australia's indigenous population identifies. That leaves anyone sensitive to the matter in a quandary. Where I am referring to a particular language or regional group of people, and I know the correct term that is used by those

The most powerful images at the Sanctuary are of Australian Aborigines,[2] but Bill's involvement with indigenous Australians was a complex matter. I believe that his initial sympathies, way back in his early days, went to the environment as a whole. While searching for ways to engender a respect for the environment, he came to learn about Australian Aborigines and their spiritual relationship with the Earth. Bill firmly believed that indigenous Australians had truly mastered a way of life. He wrote:

"This life, based on the systems of totems, perfectly equates man with his environment."

Through their totemic beliefs, the land is not just a surface on which to live and survive. It is a spiritual relation. This results in a respect for the land which far exceeds that of the civilised newcomers. It was that sincere respect that Bill wanted to see adopted by non-Aboriginal Australians.

He recognised that there had been a major oversight on the part of "new" Australians in their totally dismissive attitude towards indigenous Australians. As well as his recognition of the spiritual wisdom to be gained from Aboriginal people, Bill learned of the inhuman treatment that they had suffered and continued to experience.

He set himself two tasks; creating a means to introduce "new" Australians to the concept of forming a spiritual, and therefore respectful, relationship with the Earth, and then bringing about a complete change in attitude towards Aborigines themselves. He wanted Aborigines to be respected in their own right. Bill did not expect "new" Australians to adopt a hunter-gather existence, but he hoped that the "new" society could temper their path of self-destruction through adopting aspects of the ancient wisdoms.

His Sanctuary has been a perfect catalyst for such change to occur through drawing visitors' attention to indigenous culture, and providing an environment in which concentrated thought may occur and from which visitors may draw inspiration.

If there is one general discordant note experienced by visitors to the Sanctuary, it is in the way that Bill included the image of what he called his "spiritual self" in many sculptural groups. This "spiritual self" was usually a handsome young man in his late twenties or early thirties, possessed of a good physique complete with initiation scars arching across his chest and a look of unassailable determination in his eyes. Apart from the initiation scars, which he did not bear, the "spiritual self" was not far removed from Bill's youthful appearance. It is not just that this "spiritual self" is present, but that it is often represented in a paternalistic or superior attitude. The pinnacle of these representations is a group consisting of four male Aboriginal Elders depicted with eyes upraised and arms outstretched towards the distinctly elevated and central "spiritual self". It is neither humble nor modest.

To understand the reasoning behind such self-portrayal we must consider the social attitudes relating to matters Aboriginal not only at the time of Bill's beginnings, but for virtually his whole life. For most of Bill's life Aborigines had no land rights, no religious rights and only token civil rights. They were a race of people being forcibly moulded into another civilisation's idea of what they should be, and that hot on the heels of a ruthless and in some cases genocidal treatment of what had been Aboriginal Australia. Bill Ricketts came from a time when it was not fashionable to support the "dying race"; from a time when even some academics referred to Aborigines by that most gross term, "niggers". He and any other like-minded people had to boldly stand up and confront those who, for whatever reasons, displayed a disregard for the human rights of Australia's

---

people, I shall use it. But when reference is made to Australia's original people as a whole, I must use the terms "Aborigine" or "Aboriginal". The use of the capital "A" is, regrettably, a poor show of respect to a race of people. There will be places in this book where the "A" is not capitalised, but they are direct quotes from less sensitive times.

Aborigines. Bill came from a time when the Aboriginal voice was not heard, because the decision-makers chose not to hear it. Nor was Bill's voice clearly heard, because he was never an effective orator: his passions were always too close to the surface. But his works were looked at, and in his works he conveyed his message.

Part of that message concerned leaving no doubt about on which side of the fence he was standing—hence the "spiritual self" portrayed shoulder to shoulder with images of Aborigines. Part of that message concerned his fighting for the betterment of the Aborigines' future—hence the "spiritual self" portrayed protectively cradling the images of a race's future, the children. And part of that message concerned his right to fight for and speak on behalf of the Central Australian Aborigines who gave him their permission to do so [although he fought for the rights of all Aborigines]—hence the works like the one with Bill as the elevated central character, flanked by the quartet of almost idolising Aborigines, which could appear at first glance to be the pinnacle of priggishness.

It sometimes came as quite a shock for visitors to the Sanctuary when they met Bill. Although there are some painful and brutal depictions in his sculptures, most of his work blends perfectly with the overall atmosphere of tranquillity prevailing within the Sanctuary. Yet Bill himself was never far from exploding in a passionate rage at what he perceived were the wrongs in Australia. And the spectacle of William Ricketts in a rage was awesome.

Although his words of condemnation rang true, they were often spoken with such vehemence and aggression that their substance could be lost in what appeared to be a flood of hate. He excused this form of action as totally justifiable, maintaining that he had a "righteous anger" at his very centre. Into his verbal torrents he threw just enough esoteric riddles and vagaries to leave many visitors quite dumbfounded. They departed wondering.

Bill was happy for that to occur, claiming that it helped maintain the mystery. As you will read throughout *Whitefella Dreaming*, he had nurtured the mystery to varying degrees for as long as people had been listening to him—well over half a century. We had long discussions about this. I wanted to demystify him, but Bill did not agree. This book should, according to him, startle, shock and rock readers. But couldn't it do that through the process of demystification, I would ask? Definitely not! That would weaken and cheapen and do a tremendous lot of harm to what he'd built up. He would have preferred that I left out the "rubbish", which he unfortunately considered to be the majority of his life story, and nurture the mystery.

Mystery: it was the word he used to sum up his life. When asked how his life came to travel the path it did, he'd tell you that he didn't know—it was not his doing. Asked to explain, he would tell you to look in the Bible for the quote, ***"God moves in a mysterious way, His wonders to perform"***,[3] and why God chose him, ***"a little man with nothing"***, was one of those mysteries. He would add that it was the same mystery which turns the smallest seed into a forest giant, or sends a delicate spear of orchid flowers from seemingly barren ground.

Press and pester him for days on end for details about what events brought him to where he was and you might have been lucky to get half a dozen vague sentences. Strap him down to chair and apply electric shocks, bright lights and bull-ants and he'd tell you that it wasn't important and so he'd forgotten. He would then tell you his latest plan while you swirled in a mire of exasperation. He said it was a mystery, so as far as he was concerned a mystery it would stay.

Undoubtedly, the events which brought Bill through to his final lot did include what could only be described as a series of fortuitous events. His theory of Divine intervention led him to fervently maintain that ***"no man has had anything to do with [the] Sanctuary, not even me"***. But if it was an unseen hand which had guided him throughout his life, that same hand had

---

3 This quote is attributed to the English poet, William Cowper [1731–1800], and while Bill agreed that it was not a Biblical quote when the fact was pointed out, he would, as little as five minutes later, tell someone else to "Look in the Bible…"

introduced many individuals into his life, without whom Bill's story could have been vastly different.

It was from Bill's acquaintances and helpers that most of this story came. They welcomed me into their homes, talked for hours on the telephone and wrote me letters. Event by event, the story of Bill's life came together. As new events came to me, I would take them to Bill for comment. Sometimes he was excited and thrilled as distant memories were rekindled. Sometimes he was dark and secretive, telling me that I'd come up with "rubbish" that was better left out. Occasionally he would tell me that it was a blatant untruth; but would modify it to "rubbish" when new evidence made an event irrefutable. And there were rare times when Bill would maintain that what I'd brought to him was incorrect, even after ample proof to the contrary had been supplied. It made for an interesting time of research, validation and writing up.

When I had finished the second draft, which changed little to become this volume, I sat down and read it to Bill. It was a slow process that took more than two months to complete. Sometimes he put his glasses on and followed the text as I read, but more often he contented himself to sit back and listen as my version of his life unfolded. It was, for me, a harrowing experience. There I was reading to the man who wished to remain a mystery my attempted demystification of him. Although I asked for his input—elaborations, comments and criticisms— Bill remained for the most part silent. In places he laughed, at times he cried, and he regularly shook his head when reminded of what he'd been through. Often at the end of a reading he marvelled at the extent of the research. Nowhere, though, did he pull me up and say that the text was inaccurate. If he noticed any inaccuracies, he chose to let them pass. Maybe that was his way of maintaining the mystery.

My hope was that when Bill was finally handed the completed book, and after he'd been able to absorb it in his own time, he would discuss it with me. But I was too slow.

You will not find in this volume any elaborate interpretations of Bill's sculptural creations or of his spirituality. The reasons for this are twofold. Firstly, I am not qualified to write authoritatively on the subjects. Secondly, and more importantly, Bill's art, his Sanctuary and his spirituality provide different stimulation to different people—sometimes vastly different. But stimulate it does. It is a personal and individual experience, the ultimate reward of which is self-interpretation. The last things Bill wanted were interpretative signs which spelled out hard and fast messages. He wanted people to think for themselves—to have a look within themselves for the answers which were already there.

This book was born out of a desire to learn more about a man whom I'd come to respect from afar. It was not an academic exercise. During the course of the research, my respect grew, for I came to know the human side of the man; his strengths *and* his weaknesses. More than anything else, I came to realise how great is the desire of many people to learn more about William Ricketts—this mystery of a man whom they have come to know and respect, and in many cases love, for his contribution to their lives.

1 | A Working Class Child
[1898–c. 1912]

The City of Melbourne was founded on land which John Batman had attempted to purchase or lease from the original Koorie custodians.[1]

On Saturday, June 6th, 1835, Batman entered in his journal that he had a treaty signed by eight Koorie Elders, whom he thought to be "chiefs", whereby he would gain access to approximately 600,000 acres of land in return for 20 pairs of blankets, 30 tomahawks, 100 knives, 50 pairs of scissors, 30 looking-glasses, 200 handkerchiefs, 100 pounds of flour and 6 shirts. In addition there would be a yearly rent of similar items. It was a meagre payment, but it was at least a payment; recognition of the fact that a large tract of land was to be occupied with the permission of the original inhabitants.

The British government did not see it in the same light. When Cook claimed possession of Australia, in the name of the British Crown, every inch of this land automatically became the sole possession of the Crown. Australia was considered as *terra nullius*—as a land belonging to nobody. The Aborigines did not occupy the land in the traditional European sense, which meant that, in British eyes, they did not have to be considered.

On this principle, Batman's treaty and purchase was invalidated. It did not, however, stop the settlement of lands surrounding Port Phillip Bay. It merely negated the need of any compensation for the local inhabitants.

Melbourne's initial growth was relatively slow, although the gold-rush boom of the 1850s saw a flood of emigrants heading for this southern land.

It was during that period when a carpenter, William Ricketts, and his wife, Mary Ann [née Clyne], made the three to four month voyage by sailing ship from Great Britain to Melbourne, arriving in 1857 when the city's population was a mere 71,000. The gold fields, by comparison, carried a population of approximately 163,000. Whether or not the Ricketts came in search of gold is unknown, but the birth at sea of their first child, a daughter named Christiana, could well have influenced their decision to settle in the Melbourne suburb of Richmond. They remained there for at least the rest of that century, during which time twelve children were born to them. Their seventh child was a son, Alfred, born in 1867.

Alfred Ricketts appears to have spent much of his first thirty-eight years in Richmond. He entered the trade of iron moulding early in life, working in various foundries to produce a wide range of cast products; from the ornately decorative to the simply practical.

The few people who remember Alfred describe a rather coarse fellow of the working class. He was not a tall man, but years of hard work left him solidly built and physically strong. Behind his thin moustache was a rugged, stern face which seldom creased with laughter, yet his eyes

---

1 The term "Koorie" was not being used by non-Aboriginal people at the time of the transaction. Dr Eve Fesl, Director of Monash University's Aboriginal Research Centre, advised me that it is the preferred term of indigenous people from the south-east of Australia; hence its use here.

flashed clear to reveal a lively man of confident outlook. He often drank to excess, smoked and chewed tobacco and gambled almost compulsively. All who remember him picture a gruff and dirty man, yet there is unconcealed respect when Alfred is referred to by grandchildren as being, *"as tough a man as ever there was"*. He was rarely out of work and no mention has been made of food shortages or the like, although reference was made to several midnight flits so as to ease the rent burden.

Of Susan Ricketts, who played such an important role in our William's life, we know very little. She was born in Pascoe Vale, Victoria, between 1867 and 1869 [depending on which reference source is viewed]; a daughter of farmer William Jones and his wife Mary [née Smith].[2] Susan was slight of build and is remembered as a woman of exceptional cleanliness and neatness. Her clothes, although simple, were always immaculate; often rounded off with a high-necked collar, a brooch at her throat and long gloves. She was a quietly proud woman of very few words and a timid, almost shy disposition. As will be seen, though, her capacity for devotion was immense.

Susan and Alfred were married in St. Marks Church, at the corner of George and Moor Streets, Fitzroy, on November 27th, 1889; aged 20 and 22 respectively. It remains a family riddle as to how this seemingly opposite pair became a married couple. No living relatives can recall any mention of there having been happy times at any stage, although Alfred was to publicly profess his love for Susan at various times throughout the ensuing turmoil.

The couple's first child, Edith Mary, was born in 1890 at Essendon; probably at the home of Susan's parents. Emily, their second child, lived only six months. There followed a son, Alfred Clarence, known within the family as "Son" or "Boy", and another daughter, Elsie.

The actual date of birth of their fifth and final child, William Edward, has been printed in many conflicting forms. Anyone sorting through the wealth of articles published about him during his years would have been left totally confused as to just what age he was at any given time. To compound the confusion, the varying dates published appear to have been supplied by William. They ranged between 1899 and 1906, with actual age quotations being out by as many as ten years—and always on the lesser side. When I eventually presented him with a copy of his Birth Certificate, which recorded that he was born at 23 Berry Street, Richmond, on December 11th, 1898, he just smiled.

Richmond was, for the most part, a solidly working class suburb, with only Richmond Hill being seen as attractive to the well-to-do. That the "low-lands" are remembered as a slum gives some indication of the environment into which Bill was born. It is now a fashionable suburb, the last of the inner-city to become so. But at the beginning of the twentieth century its meagre weather-board houses were overcrowded with large families who had a hard time surviving the years following the economic depression of the 1890s.

The Ricketts' household was no exception. Six people bound by close walls, shrouded in the acute tension of a husband and wife whose relationship apparently started on troubled waters and never reached harbour.

Maybe it was to escape the unpleasantness, or maybe it was a longing for the open space into which she was born, but every morning after Alfred left for his work in Payne's Foundry at East Melbourne, Susan Ricketts bundled up her brood and set off on the two kilometre walk to the Botanical Gardens. The treks began when Bill was still in a pram and continued for much of his early life. He said it was his mother giving him his first taste of nature, but it was more likely that she was attempting to lessen his taste of the slums. There were also infrequent visits to grandfather and grandmother Ricketts, but his memory of those was almost nonexistent.

Bill's earliest memories were of closeness. Not the closeness of a loving family, but the claustrophobic closeness of too much going on in too small an area. He remembered squatting

---

2 This information about Susan came from her Marriage Certificate. On her Death Certificate, however, it was recorded that she was born in Essendon, the daughter of William Jones and Frances Jones [née Le-Brattle].

down in the gutters of Bridge Road trying to cadge cigarette cards from people as they came out of shops—an art he must have developed well because he remembered his collection of the cards depicting football heroes as a large one.

Was it in those gutters that he learned what some consider to have been his greatest talent—how to extract from others exactly what he wanted? Or did those gutters instil in an impressionable mind a sense of empathy with the underdogs of society?

His most vivid memories of Richmond were the full gutters, the rats, the sour smells, the grime and the closeness.

During the rates year of 1904–1905 Alfred Ricketts pulled up whatever roots had taken hold during their ten years at Berry Street and headed north. Until that time Alfred had been regularly listed in the Sands and McDougall's postal directories, but there followed an absence of some six years. Bill said the family moved around the Northcote, Croxton and Thornbury areas, during which time he attended primary schools in both Thornbury and Preston South.

Alfred Ricketts reappeared in the 1910 edition of the directory, listed as living at 29 Normanby Avenue, Northcote, with the 1911 listing placing him at 10 Martin Street, Northcote. Both these addresses now fall within Thornbury. The 1913 edition listed Alfred at 14 Wild Street, Preston; now part of Reservoir.

Bill considered his schooling, which never progressed past primary, to have been a waste of time. The only subject to which he gave any worth was English, although he never quite grasped its intricacies. For the rest of his life he would rely heavily on others to edit his words so that they might be more readily understood. The bulk of his teachers' words fell on deaf ears. He became infuriated when asked to recall those days. He did not want to know who was born when, or on what day King so-and-so died, or that tea came from China. At exam time he resorted to cheating for his passes. The rest he forgot—apart from the fact that he hated it.

The same applied to the Sunday school which his mother made him attend. The chants about *"there is a happy land far, far away"* did nothing to inspire the youngster to the folds of Christianity.

The sports were the only activities which made his days of education bearable; cricket, Australian Rules football and swimming. His voice filled with unusual enthusiasm when he recalled the inter-school games. He maintained that he never captained a team and was only an average player, but it is easy to imagine the determination with which he played. The swimming classes were straight out of the pioneer's handbook. When weather permitted the teachers gathered their charges and trekked off to a large water-hole which formed part of the Darebin Creek. Bill positively beamed when he told of his introduction to the delights of aquatic pursuits.

It was by the Darebin that Bill developed the art of truancy. Sometimes in the company of other lads, but mostly by himself, Bill would replace his classroom drudgery with the wonders of nature.

Preston and Reservoir were then the city fringe. Down in the creek's nooks and folds a young lad could easily lose himself, especially one who'd known such oppressive closeness in the not too distant past. Bill claimed that those times spent alone gave him his greatest education.

For hours he would lie by the creek's edge, watching intently as the schools of small fish glided from one hole to the next. Then his attention would focus on the labours of a little reed warbler busily creating its fragile nest in the safety of slender water grasses. He became a serious student of nature, yet the youngster's use of his acquired knowledge came to constitute an old man's nightmare.

Using a basic long-pole, string and piece of bent wire, Bill pitted himself against the creek's fish and won. On the day he revealed this ghost of his past, his voice trembled. He said that he would rather treasure the sight of their flashing speed, but then he thrilled to the flashing fish dancing on the end of his line. He was standing by the stove in his room when I asked if he ever caught enough to take home for the family. His fresh face turned white as he clutched the stove's corner, almost fell to the floor, but managed the two small steps which allowed him to collapse ungracefully onto the bed.

It's very frightening when a nonagenarian does that in front of you. Fortunately his colour returned and his breathing steadied, and from his bed came what must be described as a confession of the heart. Yes, he caught enough fish to take home, and he would cook them himself, then he would eat them.

It was a dramatic reaction to the memory of having participated in a most popular pastime and having indulged in what nutritionists believe to be a beneficial part of a diet. Yet for Bill, who had been almost strictly vegetarian for at least his previous sixty years, it was too much. He became vegetarian not for health reasons, but out of respect for the lives which must be lost to sustain a carnivorous appetite. Don't forget that in the time I knew Bill, he quite literally wouldn't kill a fly. But it did not end there.

After lying quietly for hours and days watching the birds building their intricate nests, then waiting patiently for egg laying to occur, young Bill would creep back and rob the nests of their treasure. The cigarette cards had given way to a diverse collection of birds' eggs. He recalled, with pain, that no nest was safe—not even those protected by the laws of trespass.

A short distance from the Wild Street house were the water reservoirs which constituted part of Melbourne's water supply. That they were fenced and guarded did nothing to protect the birds which chose to nest there. Bill regularly conducted stealthy patrols through the reservoir's environs, carefully noting the various nests he discovered and selectively robbing them when the time was right. Nothing was safe; the parrots, the finches, the water birds and the birds of prey—anything he could find went into the collection. He visibly squirmed at the memory when he told me, blaming his parents for allowing him to indulge in what he would come to view as such brutal activities.

Not only did they permit young Bill the indulgence, they defended his right to do so.

There are two instances which Bill set aside as examples of what he termed, "father's fearless courage". One was a direct result of nest robbing.

Another favourite egg-collection site was the land surrounding the home of an ex-policeman. Bill remembered him as a huge man who was not used to having anyone cross him—least of all an upstart who constantly violated a protected garden to steal the wild birds' eggs. On the day he was caught red-handed, Bill easily evaded capture and made straight for home with the ex-policeman in pursuit. The man was wielding a branch, no doubt to reinforce his lesson on the laws of trespass which would be dealt out when the offender was caught. Bill ran into his house, but the ex-policeman was soon standing in the front yard shouting for a chance to administer justice. From behind a curtain Bill saw his father walk out of the front door and straight up to the much larger man. Without saying a word Alfred tore the branch out of the aggressor's hand, threw it down the street and told the ex-policeman to follow it. After a tense moment of standoff the ex-policeman left. Nothing was said to Bill about the incident; nor was punishment incurred.

Then there was the family dog, Brownie, an Irish Terrier of evil repute—in the eyes of an elderly Bill at least. Terriers are natural hunters; fast, aggressive and efficient, even more so when effectively trained. Quite often the Ricketts men would go off on a weekend hunting hares and rabbits, with Brownie going along to flush the game for Alfred's shotgun. Once again, Bill was right up there in the thick of it. He recalled a day when an injured rabbit took refuge within a stone fence. The trio had half the fence pulled down in record time to retrieve their prize, after which they promptly departed. Bill found it hard to believe how keen he was. Bill's greatest horror regarding Brownie was the memory of the coursing events held in a fully enclosed oval. Spectators would line the oval's perimeter to watch two dogs vying for a single rabbit or hare. Often bets were placed at competitive odds against which dog would make the kill. And there had to be a kill, for there was no escape for the quarry. Brownie was never a champion, but he had his days.

Bill bore no grudge against the dogs. It was instinct for them, further nurtured by training. But he came to loathe the supporters and spectators whose peculiar blood-lust kept such entertainment alive.

Life was not all killing for the Ricketts. One activity with which Bill used to help was the maintenance of his father's vegetable garden, from which the bulk of the family's requirements came. It was with a glowing smile that Bill recalled the quality of the produce.

The boy also became a competent handler of the family's horse, a piebald gelding named Prince. Once again, a tear came to Bill's eye when he remembered the thankless service Prince performed; but a cart-horse was then no more than a tool. Prince's main task was to haul the family's little jinker, although quite often he would be called on to haul huge loads of firewood from the distant stands of timber. Sometimes there would be an added bonus on the wood-getting trips, in the form of a bag of grain stolen from the reaped paddocks.

The best trips of all were over to Diamond Creek, visiting Susan's mother and father on their fruit orchard; a round trip of more than 40 km. The journeys were extended over at least a weekend, sometimes more, for it was by Prince-power that their goal was achieved. The sight of fruit trees with branches pulled to the ground by bumper crops was fresh in Bill's mind. Stone fruits, citrus and apples were all there for the picking at various times of the year, and the visitors feasted well when they could. They were happy family reunions, except for the case of Susan's mother, Mary. Bill became upset and reticent when asked to recall his grandmother. She apparently developed a sickness, possibly a mental illness, in her old age.

In Bill's words:

"They tormented her until she went out of her mind."

Apart from adding that she lived and died in the back room, he was silent. When I crassly asked if the family said she was crazy, he replied:

"Oh well, the poor woman was locked in a back room!"

The reason for her confinement could be one of many—Alzheimer's comes to mind—but it remained that she was not hospitalised and spent the latter part of her life out of touch with the rest of the world.

It was after one such journey to Diamond Creek that Bill had his first real taste of life in the fast lane. Prince, who was normally yarded in an enclosure close to the house, was given a brief spell in the paddocks upon completion of long hauls. Bill used to ride him out to the paddocks bare-backed, and Prince, as horses will, came to look forward to his brief bouts of freedom. Bill recalled that he had no sooner mounted the supposedly worn-out Prince than it bolted furiously towards the paddocks.

Bill could do nothing but hold on. Through gorse thickets, past clutching blackberry canes, around and under trees and boughs, Bill weaved and ducked and sweated—but he kept his seat. Finally the paddock gate was gained and Prince dropped his rump, skidding to a halt just inches away from the solid wooden rails—leaving Bill clinging halfway up the horse's neck. It was neither exciting nor exhilarating for him, in fact there was still a touch of panic in his voice when he related the tale almost eighty years after the event. But it led to his father formulating a plan.

As mentioned, Alfred Ricketts was a gambler. His greatest frustration was trying to pick the best of the thoroughbreds. Occasionally he would crack a winner, sometimes even lashing out and giving the kids a penny or two. Mostly, though, it was a bad tempered father who'd been pipped at the post. Bill recalled one time when his mother had somehow managed to put away £13—a considerable amount of money at the beginning of the twentieth century. Alfred rushed in one afternoon announcing that he'd been given a sure winner and demanded all of Susan's stash.

As Bill said: ***"She had to give it to him."*** The outcome was no surprise. Alfred came home dejected.

The sight of his youngest son disappearing into the distance atop a bolting horse, gamely keeping his seat and apparently fighting for control, sparked the thought of that same son riding winners on race days. What better way to beat the bookies?

Alfred set to work arranging an audition with Bobby Lewis, a successful trainer of thoroughbreds. The big day finally came and Alfred accompanied his boy to the stables, firing him up with enthusiasm and praise, telling him how famous a great jockey could become—and how wealthy. Bill was told how easy it would be:

"Just sit up on the horse and gammon you're riding the winner of a Melbourne Cup!"

Lewis would take it from there. The big moment came and the slight, wispy lad was given a leg-up onto the back of a fine, big thoroughbred. But what a difference to Prince—it was twice as high for a start! To be perched suddenly on a seemingly minute saddle so far from the ground, atop a rippling, eager racer, was too much. All thoughts of winners and race tracks were evaporated by the torch of self-preservation. As Bill sat rigid, clutching two handfuls of mane, his father's dreams of finally gaining an edge over the bookies evaporated with a shake of Lewis' head and the three words: ***"Take him home."***

It was a quiet trip home.

2 | Skills Acquired
[c. 1912–c. 1920]

The decision for Bill to leave school as soon as he could was made for him, not that there would have been any objections from the boy. Robert Valentine, the husband of Bill's eldest sister, Edith, worked as a salesman for Aronson and Company, a jewellery manufacturing and wholesaling business situated at 297–299 Little Collins Street in Melbourne's city centre. Arrangements were made for Bill to be accepted as an apprentice jeweller in the factory, and that was where he started his working life at fourteen years of age.

Initially he was, as he termed it, "a put-togetherer" of simple dress jewellery which was stamped out in great quantities. It was a big factory employing many people, but it provided no inspiration for the boy. He existed there, learning a trade, learning to put his hands to good use by assembling the intricate fittings, finally ending the day with a crowded trip on a steam train back to his home.

Little Collins Street provided some interest with its side-walk cafes, the odd musician playing for passers-by and the odd rat scampering around the rubbish where it accumulated. But there remained an emptiness in the adolescent; a vacuum that would become occupied by music.

Music was not uncommon in the extended Ricketts family. Bill's elder sister, Elsie, was taking piano lessons and showing a talent which would give her a short spell in a small orchestra. Many of his cousins were showing remarkable aptitude in the musical and general entertainment field, with some going on to become concert pianists and violinists. One cousin from the Rainford family became the conductor of the South African Philharmonic Orchestra. Bill's father played the tin whistle and on many evenings he could be found sitting in front of the open fire blowing a merry jig, pausing frequently to spit a stream of tobacco juice into the fire—sometimes missing and hitting Susan's dry morning-wood instead. Small wonder there were fights.

Young Bill came to love classical music with a passion which must have been obvious, for the brother of Edith's husband ended up giving Bill his first violin. It was never made clear whether the violin was Bill's choice of instrument or whether the gift made the decision for him. Whatever the case, he took to it with gusto.

With some of his wages, he chose to take formal violin lessons from an Australian teacher living in Fitzroy. For one hour per week he was taught a new language of music. The amount of time Bill put into practise at home had slipped from his memory, but a briefly-related anecdote suggests more than a passing interest.

The family home was a semi-detached affair, Bill said, which meant that it was not only one family who had to put up with the sometimes painful strains of a novice violinist. His immediate family coped with the intrusion, but the neighbours occasionally lost patience.

It was in a serious tone that Bill told me the following, with more than a touch of impatience at the memory of those unthoughtful neighbours of long ago:

"I'd be trying to get the best out of myself, picking difficult scales and arpeggios, or whole pieces, and playing them over and over again—sometimes until three or four in the morning. But they'd start bashing. Bash, bash, bash on the wall. Sometimes they wouldn't stop bashing until I'd stopped playing!"

He then held me with an incredulous gaze, waiting for a supportive comment. All I could think was how lucky he was to have a plucky father to deter any midnight raids by violin-smashing mobs.

After what Bill thought was a couple of years he progressed to a Russian teacher who worked regularly in the Princess Theatre Orchestra, providing musical accompaniment to the plays and other live theatre performed there. Those lessons cost 2s 6d.[1] Eventually he changed to a new tutor, an Italian named Tony Cursio who led the Paramount Theatre Orchestra in Bourke Street. Not only did he have his weekly lessons with Cursio, but he would often spend extra money to get into the theatre to watch his master at work. He recalled that he was deeply impressed and inspired by that orchestra's mastery of their music, which gave an even greater impetus to his practising.

A story has been passed down from those early days of Bill's musical ascendence which has it that one of his tutors said at the end of a lesson that Bill could not return for further instruction. When asked why, the tutor said: *"I cannot teach you any more—if anything you can now teach me."*

Two years after commencing his apprenticeship with Aronson's, much of the world was thrown into the turmoil of what would come to be known as World War One [WWI]. Then it was The Great War—"the war to end all wars". Its immediate effect on Bill was minimal. At sixteen years old he could not volunteer. When asked about it he said that the war had finished by the time he had come of age, which was not the case. He would have turned eighteen at the end of 1916. He chose not to participate, as did many others at the time, yet he gave no explanation of the circumstances surrounding that decision. He did remember the overly loud comments of strangers who queried why some young men didn't join the rest of the country's men in the conflict.

I got the impression that it was a time of confusion for Bill, a time when his sensitivities were being aroused, but when he was not sure enough of himself to follow his feelings with confidence. The side that told him that war was wrong won out, yet the side that wanted him to follow general opinion could not be ignored.

The only immediate effect the war had on Bill was that the workload at Aronson's increased when many of the employees signed up for service.

Life in the Ricketts' household continued to be marred by a seemingly endless conflict between Alfred and Susan. The conflict was stamped indelibly in Bill's memory, punctuated by his father's threats to knock Susan from one end of the room to the other. Eventually there came a point where a solution, or at least a compromise, had to be found.

With their three youngest children still at home and Alfred's undiminished love for his family, total separation was out of the question. But a partial separation could have been the answer. It resulted in Alfred sailing to South Africa. Bill recalled that his father secured foundry work before leaving, while some of Alfred's grandchildren recalled mention of his Australian employer organising a position for him within the South African mining industry.

With Alfred gone, the household settled down to a period of stability. The two boys were old enough to perform tasks such as wood gathering, gardening and general maintenance. Son, especially, was showing his colours as an inspired mechanic, building model steam engines from scrap in the back shed. Alfred's regular forwarding of money looked after his family's needs—in fact, all that seems to have been missing were the fights.

---

1 Two shillings and six pence.

Accompanying the money were letters telling of Alfred's adventures abroad. Though he continued working in his trade, tales of roaming a different land, where camp-fires had to be maintained throughout the night to keep lions at bay, helped add a touch of colour to the correspondence. There were also the occasional photographs. None of those photographs surfaced during the research, but Bill readily recalled one which depicted his father surrounded by a group of Zulu men.

Bill said that those tales and images never inspired him to travel, yet there was one instance where he almost succumbed to an apparent wanderlust.

At some point during his early days, Bill applied to join the Australian Navy. He claimed to have had a yearning for the sea as a youth, adopting a gruff tone when he told of the sailor's life he might have had. He forgot just when it was, saying only that he took his violin down to Port Melbourne, where a naval ship was berthed, to try out with a small Navy orchestra. He must have shown promise for he later underwent and passed a medical examination and was told that his fare would be paid to Sydney where he would join the training ship, *HMAS Tingira*. Bill withdrew the application, but he could not recall why.

Alfred and Susan's separation ended after "a couple of years" when Alfred returned to Australia. Bill said that the conflict resumed immediately, with a renewed vigour. The cause remains a mystery, but Susan would stand or sit passively while Alfred raged around her.

Bill's vivid recollections were a clear indication that not even the children's presence could forestall the clashes. He remembered sitting, cringing as the fights intensified—ever mindful of the shotgun which hung on the kitchen wall. Although he never said that the gun was used as a threat, it was the gun which inevitably figured starkly whenever he recalled those angry scenes. He had witnessed its destructive power on game over a distance and was acutely fearful of what the result would be if used point-blank on a human—on his mother.

The family left the Wild Street house and headed back towards the city. By 1918 Alfred was listed in the Sands and McDougall's as living at 111 Dickens Street, St Kilda, where a reunification of most of the family occurred. Edith and Robert Valentine and their two children boosted the occupancy of the house to eight people, six of whom were adults.

Although Bill shared a room with his brother, Son, he still managed to surround himself with the equipment of his profession and ambition. One area was set aside as a work-space for the crafting of jewellery, while another centred on a gramophone and a considerable collection of classical music recordings.

Phylis and Robert Valentine, Bill's niece and nephew, were infrequent visitors to their uncle's room, but both remembered the scene well. Sometimes Bill could be seen standing with his back to the gramophone, confidently accompanying recordings of the great orchestras of the world with his violin, striving for the degree of perfection which would enable him to be the star virtuoso of such orchestras. His practising was heard to continue for hours.

At other times he could be seen at his jewellery desk, carefully manipulating precious metals into objects of beauty. Although Bill maintained that he was a mere "put-together-man", the skills taught him by the elderly master-jeweller resulted in the creation of at least one marvellous piece.

Those who were children in the house can still vividly describe a miniature gold violin, just 4 cm long, yet perfect in every detail. From the symmetrically waisted body, the minute "f" holes in the belly, along the four thread-like gold strings to the scrolled head and tuning keys—it was exact. Bill said that he created only one such piece, which he gave to his tutor and musical mentor at the time, Tony Cursio. It is likely, though, that he created other pieces, for his niece and nephew remembered him spending long and busy hours at his work bench.

At some point along the way Bill achieved a standard of musicianship which allowed him to audition successfully for a position in a dance band. He enjoyed the work immensely, claiming great satisfaction from watching the crowds swirl and sway to the rhythms he helped produce. Although he was not playing the classical pieces he loved, the long periods of paid practice bolstered both his finances and ability.

Bill's energy and enthusiasm carried him through the busy period; the jewellery factory by day, music by night and the practising of both arts at home in his spare time. Yet whenever positions became vacant in the multitude of small orchestras which serviced the silent movie theatres and play houses, he would find extra time to audition for them.

Those auditions he remembered as cheerless affairs. Stern-faced folk would lead him to a room in the middle of which was a chair and empty music stand. After being seated a piece of music was placed in front of him. After a brief perusal he was required to play the entire piece. Bill recalled the auditions as invariably difficult, compelling him to muster every ounce of talent in an attempt to satisfy unforgiving observers.

He auditioned many times, but continuously failed to secure a position where his classical leanings could be fulfilled. It was the sudden illness of an orchestra member which caused Bill to be called up at short notice.

He ultimately played with many of the inner-city theatre orchestras, but had his start in either the Brighton or St Kilda theatre; two of the less salubrious venues of the time which endured frequent interruptions to the screenings. The more spectacular of these hiccups would begin with the house lights blazing into life mid-scene and the orchestra being cut off mid-note by police whistles heralding the arrival of an arresting force, come to capture a real life villain who'd sought cover in the darkened building.

At other times particularly malicious patrons would take it into their minds to upset the flow of music by pelting the orchestra members with projectiles. Bill well remembered the intense concentration required to perform a crucial piece, the violin solo accompanying a moment of dramatic suspense for instance, while at the same time dodging anything from paper balls and lollies to whole ice cream cones.

His appointment to the orchestras saw music take precedence in his life, although he continued his jewellery work, retaining his day-time position with Aronson's for quite some time.

Bill maintained that this period saw the ultimate collapse of his parent's marriage. Susan finally reacted to Alfred's bad habits and continual fighting by setting out on her own. She took work as a live-in assistant to a medical doctor. Possibly prompted by that upset, Bill also left the family to live for a time in a St Kilda boarding house.

Alfred continued to share a house with Edith and Robert Valentine's family, which numbered one extra with the birth of another son, Jim. Alfred's habits continued to create annoyance and ultimately resulted in a forcible eviction at the hands of his son-in-law, Robert. The story goes that Robert sought solace in a local pub, but returned with Dutch Courage rather than patience. Alfred's effects, all stored in the attic where he slept, were cast from the window into the street below, resulting in a stunned silence from all witnesses. Rather than cause a scene, Alfred followed—via the stairs.

Young Bob, the grandson, was Alfred's most devoted ally. Bob by-passed the gruff, smelly exterior to idolise the adventurer within. It was with Bob that Alfred shared his great desire to return to South Africa where he could see out his days. But Alfred never did. Why? Why would a self-reliant man endure a family who barely tolerated him? Why didn't he simply pack up and leave? His love for them was obviously great.

Alfred devoted much time to the sea, regularly fishing and swimming. He is remembered as a strong swimmer, often going kilometres at a time, sometimes with a grandson clinging to his back. His method of teaching others to swim was the time-honoured "push off the end of the jetty" method.

His fishing exploits are remembered with mixed feelings. Both Bill and Jim succumbed to sea sickness and fear when Alfred rowed them out into what can be the very dangerous Port Phillip Bay. Only Bob stuck with him, to be rewarded with many catches of fine table fish. Bob was also treated to the great excitement of experiencing boiling seas in a row boat, with only Alfred's brute strength and wits separating disaster from a safe anchorage.

On the subject of brute strength and wits, we can now reveal the other instance Bill referred to when recalling "father's fearless courage". This tale is not exclusively Bill's, for it recurs throughout the surviving relatives, although nobody is certain where it is set.

Alfred was employed at a mine in either Tasmania or South Africa; his method of transport at the time being a motor cycle. Alfred lost control of his cycle one day and went crashing over a cliff. In the process, along with the usual cuts, abrasions and bruising, he suffered a horrific abdominal tear through which various parts of his intestinal tract protruded. He was conscious throughout. Realising the severity of his predicament, he set to work at poking his protrusions back inside, held everything in place as best he could, climbed back to the road and walked several miles to help. Incredibly, but corroborated by all who recall the event, Alfred insisted on no anaesthetic whatsoever when finally he was treated by a doctor.

Of his days as a young bachelor out on his own, Bill revealed very little. St Kilda was to Melbourne what Kings Cross is to Sydney—a lively area of diverse people and activities. Whether or not he entered its social arena is unknown; although his hectic work schedule could not have left too much time for play. There has been mention made of lady friends [one of whom, it was said, was an already-married pianist for one of the orchestras in which Bill played]—but no conclusive facts have come to light.

When I asked if he ever went out with or pursued a lady friend, Bill replied:

"No, only make believe—you know. They bought presents to me—nice things—and I got to know them like that. But I was never attached to anyone specially chosen—you know."

He remembered the boarding house as cramped and noisy—nothing more. It is not surprising then that Bill decided to take an apartment of his own. It, too, was in St Kilda. He would eventually share it with his mother, presumably after she had ceased her employment.

It was around this time that Bill commenced his relationship with clay. I must say "around" because Bill refused to discuss the matter in depth. Indeed, when I was researching he repeatedly requested that I don't worry at all about his beginnings in clay because, he said, it was not important. Obviously, though, it was important.

Annie Osbourne [née Adam] provided the earliest, independent information about Bill as one involved with clay. She worked for the Australian Porcelain Company, a porcelain insulator factory in Banool Avenue, Yarraville [Melbourne], from August 1915, through to August 1924. She started when the business was owned by a German, Fiesch, and an Austrian, Ognar. The company was purchased by Archibald Ray Patterson Crow either during the years of WWI or shortly after. A. R. P. Crow's eldest son, Robert [Bob], was positioned as the manager. Another son, John, utilised his formal education in science to become the company chemist. One early innovation which the Crows made was to establish a small area for studio pottery within the factory.

By the time the Crows took over, Annie Adam was a knowledgeable and valuable employee. Annie told me that she met Bill there "a good while" before she left to be married in 1924; possibly even before 1920. The only explanation given to me for how Bill came to go to Crows' was supplied by Ron Olver, a warden at the William Ricketts Sanctuary from 1964 through to his retirement in the early 1980s.

Olver, claiming John Crow as the source of his information, said that Bill was introduced to the Crows by somebody from Aronson's; allegedly the result of Bill's having shown modelling skills at the jewellery work bench. I was unable to verify this. It was also suggested by children of the Crow brothers that Bill was actually retained at the factory as a studio potter; as they also say was the case with members of the noted Boyd family, including Merric.

From Annie's recollections, it would seem that Bill was given access to Crows' facilities and expertise. She did not retain a crystal clear picture of the works which Bill created and fired at the outset, remembering only that everything was definitely in miniature; animals and people [not necessarily Aborigines] with an Australian flavour was the best she could recall.

Annie was assigned to act as Bill's assistant, at Bob Crow's direction—not that she had to assist him greatly. Bill made no attempt at small-talk with her or any of the other employees, but simply went about his ceramic business. If he needed to know in which kiln a certain piece would be fired, Annie took him to the relevant person, introduced them, and left. If he needed clay [a specially ground porcelain mix blended from Scarsdale, Campbellfield and Axedale clays] or glazes, Annie would organise it. Sometimes he would disappear into the office to discuss matters with John and Bob Crow, but Annie was never invited to join those conversations.

Sometimes Bill would be absent for weeks or months at a time, then suddenly arrive without notice to continue where he'd left off.

By his own admission, Bill was introduced to the technique of "throwing" clay [using a potter's wheel] at Crows'. This fact came to light during one of his persistent and angry denials of the suggestion that his time at Crows' had anything to do with his creative progression. After being told of my conversation with Annie, he refused to confirm that he'd had an assistant, but asked if she'd said she was the one who showed him how to use a wheel. I replied that she hadn't. Unchecked, Bill went on to say that *"some woman"* had started to teach him how to make *"pretty pots"* [said scornfully], but that he wasn't interested in such "rubbish".

It remains a fact that Bill did create attractive jugs, vases and urns, some of which bear regular internal lines suggestive of their having been thrown on a potter's wheel.

It happened that on June 27, 1989, a man brought two such vessels to the Sanctuary. I was present when Bill examined the works, which he explained were the results of "practising" for the grander works now at the Sanctuary. I pointed out the regular lines progressing up the inside surface and asked if he might have made the piece on a wheel. Bill explained that he'd put those lines there deliberately, *"to make people think that I'd used a wheel"*—merely a sales ploy! I include this account to illustrate some of the inconsistencies encountered during the search for the story of Bill's beginnings in clay.

As to the personal reasons why he chose clay as a medium of expression, we can only guess. In the edition, February 1st, 1939, of the Adelaide *Advertiser*, possibly twenty years after his initial involvement, Bill was quoted as having said that he first began modelling clay as a recreation.[2] When I knew Bill, he claimed never to have used clay as a recreation, only as a means to aid in the fulfilment of his vision. Likewise, he was adamant that he never indulged in studio pottery.

Studio pottery, by which I refer to ceramic art produced by individuals or small groups exercising creative freedom [as opposed to mass production in factories], was still in its infancy in Australia in the early 1920s. The basic physical requirements such as a kiln and the technical skills necessary for successful firing precluded the medium from easy entry. Nor were there many facilities available in educational institutions to teach the science or the art.

Although not the literal first, Merric Boyd is considered by many to have been Australia's first studio potter of note, having established a studio in Murrumbeena c. 1910. He reportedly held the first solo exhibition of pottery in Australia in 1912 when he was twenty-four years of age. Interestingly, about one year after that time, Merric Boyd commenced working at the Australian Porcelain works at Yarraville—some of his work being purchased by A. R. P. Crow. Boyd lost several years to WWI, but managed to study pottery in England during 1918 as an indirect result of his translocation.

Peter Timms, in his book *Australian Pottery 1900–1950*, identified another spin-off from WWI:

---

2 The quote is reprinted in part in Chapter 6.

"The war created nationalism and the subsequent demand for Australian products which proclaimed their country of origin. Possums, wattles and gum nuts made their appearance as decorated motifs."

The 1920s saw this nationalistic demand being solidly catered for by studio potters, with probably Merric Boyd at the forefront. He was not alone, though, with artists such as Philippa James, Margaret Kerr, G. Evelyn Davies, Sybil Joske, Alan and Ernest Finlay, Tina Gowdie, Harold F. Swanson, Louisa Taylor and others presenting their wares in Melbourne. Exhibitions were not rarities, so Bill would have had ample opportunity to experience the works of established and emerging talents. With his own emerging awareness of the natural Australia, such work could have had a greater impact on him than on the casual observer.

So prevalent was this nationalistic fervour that Peter Timms subsequently wrote that:

"Throughout the 1920s, the use of Australian motifs was a moral duty and the art nouveau style something of a habit, especially for those craft-workers associated with the arts and crafts societies."

It is not known whether Bill was involved with the Arts and Crafts Society of Victoria, but almost certainly he would have visited the exhibitions they organised. Such a fertile period as the 1920s must have provided the perfect environment for Bill to focus his thoughts and incorporate them into the medium which was capturing an increasing share of his creative outpourings.

3 | Growing Awareness
[c. 1920–late 1920s]

Bill's presence at Crows' factory signifies the end of his time with Aronson's, but he did not sever his ties with jewellery. Milton Plumb, whom Bill had met as a co-worker at Aronson's, established his own small jewellery manufacturing business which concentrated on the creation of engagement rings. This business was operated from Plumb's house in Peel Street, Windsor. In working part-time for Plumb, Bill refined his skills to become a competent ring maker and stone setter, receiving a regular £5 per week for his effort. Add to that another £5 per week from his orchestra work, and we see that he was in a high wage bracket for the time.

Bill was by no means a total loner throughout this period. Whenever there was a family gathering or party, Bill would attend if he had no work commitments. Quite often the various musically inclined members would give impromptu performances, much to the delight of guests. Irene McGee, a first cousin of Bill's, was often present at those gatherings. Irene was an accomplished pianist, having played since she was four years old. She recalled nights when the street outside was lined with neighbours, drawn from their houses by the music made by herself and Bill.

When I mentioned Bill's assertions that his playing was not much better than a fowl scratching in a farmyard, Irene came back with a shocked: *"He played **beautifully**!"* When I suggested that, just maybe, family pride obscured her critical ear, she modestly qualified her statement:

> *"Excuse me for saying so, but I was supposed to be a gifted pianist. I'd won almost everything that could be won—cups, medals, a scholarship to go to England—so I know what I'm talking about when I say he could play well."*

Another example of Bill's sociability was given when he related the story of George Kulakov, a young Russian who'd escaped the 1917 Revolution in his homeland, fleeing through China and eventually securing a passage to Australia.

It was Bill's violin that brought the two in contact. A chance meeting somewhere, George's love of music and Bill's great respect for the Russian composers and Russian people in general, formed the basis of a lasting friendship. George was homeless when they first met, but Bill quickly arranged for George to share his and Susan's flat until alternative accommodation could be arranged. Eventually George secured work in a St Kilda engineering factory, among other Russian expatriates, but the two men apparently remained friends for many years.

Little else is known of Bill's personal life through the 1920s—and if Bill remembered, he did not share the memories with me. Yet it was during this time that he began to become sensitive to the environment and Aboriginal Australia. Maybe there was one single crisis event that turned him irreversibly towards his path. Possibly his years of seemingly innocent fishing, rabbit hunting and egg collecting rebounded. Or was the less than flattering reportage of the Aborigines' plight a catalyst that sparked his flame of empathy and concern? Unfortunately, we can only speculate.

The environment was then viewed quite differently than it is now. While there was not a total disregard, active supporters were few. The environment was thought to offer an inexhaustible supply of raw materials, from minerals to timber to open pasture.

Fire was then, and remained, one of Bill's greatest environmental nightmares. The way it was used by new settlers caused him overwhelming distress, but he never acknowledged that it was the Aborigines' principal land-management tool.

The preferred methods of land clearing at that time were either ring-barking or, where the land was suitably sloped, the half cut and domino effect. Victoria alone lost hundreds of thousands of acres of pristine forests in this way—millions of cubic metres of timber laid to waste and burned, and burned again until there remained no trace of the former glory. Sadly, much of that cleared land quickly became over-run with ragwort, bracken and blackberry to such an extent that it was rendered useless—and abandoned to the rabbits.

As great as his concern was for the forests, Bill's heart went out most to the wildlife of such areas. That which survived the initial felling had only the prospect of being consumed by fire.

Such acts as the declaring of an open season on koalas and possums in Queensland proved almost too much for Bill. His family tried to reconcile him to what were the plain facts of life in a developing Australia, to little effect. Under no circumstances could he see right in such actions.

At that time the Aborigines were seen as only a temporary problem. They had decreased in numbers so drastically that the commonly-held view was that they were a race heading for extinction. This belief was shared even by some of the most sympathetic observers.

Daisy Bates spent decades living with Aborigines around the Great Australian Bight at the beginning of the twentieth century. Enduring privations, she cared for the indigenous people as best she could. She had the misfortune of being present at the death of many who were the last members of their particular totemic or language groups. So certain was she, regarding the fate of the first Australians that she named one of her books, *The Passing of the Aborigines.*[1] That book featured an introduction by the author Arthur Mee, who wrote of **"these strange, backward, hopeless people…"**.

The attitude of the time is well reflected in the following excerpt from Mee's introduction:

> **"The race on the fringe of the continent has been there for about a hundred years, and stands for Civilization; the race in the interior has been there for no man knows how long, and stands for Barbarism. Between them a woman has lived in a little white tent for more than twenty years, watching over these people for the sake of the Flag, a woman alone, the solitary spectator of a vanishing race."**

It was estimated that Victorian Koories numbered between 11,000 and 15,000 in 1835, a figure which is now widely disputed. Equally disputed is the figure of about 750, given as the number of Koories living in the Port Phillip Bay and Westernport areas in the years immediately following Batman's attempted land purchase. Not disputed, however, is the fact that the Koorie population in these areas rapidly decreased in the years following European occupation.

With all good intentions, the Government in England suggested the formation of Protectorates, into which the Aborigines could be shepherded and Europeanised. There was a complete failure to address the huge culture shock rippling through the native populations. The Protectorate scheme's success is starkly illustrated by the reported number of Koories still in the Melbourne area in 1858—a mere thirty-three individuals.

While the major European settlement areas in Australia appeared to be quickly rid of the "native problem", the sparsely pioneered interior fought a long-running battle.

This conflict involved many facets of warfare, from the subtle to the barbaric. Even so simple

1 Oxford University Press, 1949 edition.

an act as denying Aborigines access to water holes, livestock deemed more needy than "blacks", brought about the disintegration of entire extended family groups. The newcomers also killed by "kindness". After forcing Aborigines away from traditional diets through stocking and cropping, many pastoralists gave "their blacks" rations of white flour, sugar, tea and tobacco. If the Aborigines dared supplement their diet with unauthorised beef or mutton, killed in place of traditional meats, the offenders could be discretely executed, openly murdered or, possibly worst of all, taken in chains for incarceration. If Aborigines dared kill a white, whole populations could be exterminated in retaliation.

It came that "half-caste" or "mixed-blood" children, providing that part of the mix was white, were taken from their mothers by white protectors on the grounds that even part-white children should not have to grow up with "blacks". These abducted children received, for the most part, a less than basic education and generally finished up becoming cheap labour in out of the way places.

Of course, there were the rapes, abductions and mutilations, but such actions were not reported to the general population—to protect sensitivities. Likewise, the recreational "nigger hunts" and stringing up of dead Aborigines in obvious places to discourage others from the area were not widely reported.

Listing such abhorrent actions could go on and on. They are documented, if readers care to look, but it would be a deviation to explore the horror to its full extent in this volume.

Anthropologists and ethnologists raced to secure what information was available before the Aborigines were gone. Churches established missions to save souls and it is a fact that while the majority of missions worked hard to replace Aboriginal culture and mythology with the European version, they proved to save "islands" of Aborigines throughout Australia where there could just as easily have been total displacement. There was, however, a dearth of people or organisations who actively sought to remedy the drastic decline in population on the broad scale, let alone bring about the circumstances which would enable the Aborigines to live their own culture and enter the European culture at their own pace, in ways of their own chosing and in their own right.

At some point during the 1920s, Bill's attention came to rest on the plight of the Aborigines. It did not appear to cause in him a torrent of rage—that would come later. He became merely aware; a conscious observer.

His family contented themselves with more practical matters. Bill's brother, Son, continued on his merry mechanical way, becoming more obsessed with steam power. Rumour has it that absolutely anything in his house that could be powered by steam, was. He even went as far as constructing a working scale model of a steam locomotive which became the centre-piece of a family business.

Close to where the Palais Theatre and Luna Park now stand in St Kilda, Alfred and Son constructed a miniature railway on which Son's loco could haul a number of carriages. Alfred, the principal financier of the enterprise, became the chief engine driver, while various members of the broader family, including Bill, helped out with ticket selling and collecting, crowd control and general ground maintenance. Old Alfred took to the venture with what sounds like gleeful enthusiasm; delighting in towing the loads of children and parents around the small circuit.

Alfred truly respected Son's fine work in constructing the loco and he delighted in the power it produced. No matter how large the human load, it would tow the weight with ease. Alfred became somewhat of a dare-devil, ever testing the track's capacity for speed. Of course, the day came when he found that limit, so revealed when the engine, carriages, passengers and driver all became derailed—fortunately with no reported injuries!

The track had a small spur line and engine shed in which the loco was housed nightly. The shed also housed Alfred for a long while. Rough and ready as it was, there were at least no sensitivities to be bruised by his habits. It was set up on a very practical basis. A small bunk, a box for a table, a little stove on which to cook—and work benches, tools, coal store, cleaning troughs, rags, grease, oil drums and all manner of other necessary items which belonged in a workshop-cum-home. It was a home which suited Alfred.

It was also the scene of yet another example of the man's raw strength. His grandsons, Jim and Robert, were watching him dismantle an engine part one day when the spanner bearing his full weight slipped—sending Alfred crashing after it. When he regained his feet, Alfred noted a deep gash which had been opened up on the palm of his hand, right through the fleshy part at the base of his thumb.

Young Jim was aghast. The large, open wound bled freely, the blood mixing with the grease, oil and dirt which is ever on the hands of a mechanic. Alfred settled his grandson with assurances that all was under control. He went to an open bucket of kerosine which was normally used for washing parts, but was that time used to wash the blood and muck away from the wound. A rough drying with a grease-rag followed. Alfred then went to his tool board and pulled out a sewing needle already threaded with black cotton—and proceeded to stitch up the bloody gash. Jim never saw the end of the procedure, for he was otherwise engaged in dashing outside for an out-of-stomach experience on the grass. But Robert became entranced by the careful and deliberate needlework carried out by his grandfather. In no time at all the wound was closed. Another quick dunk in the Kero tin, a clean grease-rag as a makeshift bandage, and Alfred was back to work. By the time Jim could look back inside, Alfred was again doing battle with the difficult nut.

The separation from his wife did not put an end to Alfred's emotional torment. Whenever Susan and he met there was usually an argument of some kind. On one occasion Alfred came to Bill and Susan's flat. The ensuing altercation degenerated, with Alfred ultimately raising his hand at his wife. He did not strike her, but in reeling from the threat Susan tripped and fell to the floor. Bill recalled:

> *"I went for him and made a swipe at my father—but I was stopped—something stopped—he went off and I after him."*

That particular brief recollection reveals the strength of character in the young Bill. Although he admitted that Alfred possessed a fearless courage, coupled with considerable physical strength, Bill went straight at his father in the defence of his mother. The recollection also illustrates the vague detail Bill offered as an insight to his early days. Such a major event as almost coming to blows with his father was merely mentioned in passing, with scant detail, then dropped. It was the same with his whole early life—snippets only.

By 1927 Bill was listed in Council records as living at 111 Peel Street, Windsor, just a suburb away from St Kilda. It may have been coincidence that the house was within a couple of doors of Milton Plumb and his jewellery studio. At any rate, Bill continued his part-time work for Plumb.

Undoubtedly, the driving force in Bill's life was still music. His vision was fame in the world's concert halls, an end to which he devoted much energy. He progressed through the orchestras steadily, securing more respected positions with each change. To keep abreast of his expectations and aspirations, he also progressed through his tutors, finally coming before the celebrated Polish master, Stanislaw Tarczynski.

According to Bill, Tarczynski was Australia's best violinist at the time, having had a long and distinguished career as both a musician and a composer. As a school boy Tarczynski had played for Czar Nicholas II on his Coronation visit to Warsaw. As an adult he was chosen by competition to perform before the King and Queen of Belgium during the Yssaye Concerts in Brussels. He emigrated to Australia in 1912 and by 1915 was leading the Melbourne Philharmonic Symphony Orchestra.

Tarczynski's career as a performing musician was severely curbed in 1915 by what would appear to have been what we now call repetition strain injury. As a result, Tarczynski devoted his time to conducting, composing and the tuition of Melbourne's most promising violinists.

It is possible that Bill's acceptance as a student of Tarczynski was the beginning of the end, regarding a career as a virtuoso violinist. Tarczynski was a demanding task master, finding his students' limits and pushing them always for extra. Bill recalled excruciating exercises that almost required a third hand to accomplish, and he recalled Tarczynski's stoney-faced silence and cold eyes when mistakes were made.

His failure to progress rapidly under Tarczynski's tutelage extinguished the dream which had carried him through, deflating all hopes he had of greatness in music. He continued to play in the orchestras, but he was not fuelled to strive ever higher in the art. Yet there was obviously a tremendous energy source within him probing for release. It is a matter for speculation whether or not he was conscious of seeking and choosing a different medium in which to excel to replace the one that had rejected him.

4 | Awakening
[late 1920s–c. 1934]

The Great Depression affected Bill little. It required repeated prompting to get him to so much as remember the period which saw world-wide hardship. Oddly enough, it was a revolutionary innovation which occurred during that time which pushed Bill a step closer to the course of his life's destiny.

Motion pictures with sound came to Australia just before the Depression struck in the early 1930s. Such was its popularity that the "talkies" actually prospered while most of the world's economies slumped. A natural consequence was that cinema orchestras became redundant. First to be hit were the large city orchestras, since the cinemas they supported were best placed for an immediate change-over to artificial sound. The best of the musicians tried for positions in the remaining orchestras of significance, with the rest doing battle for positions in the surviving orchestras. The huge demand for "talkies" meant that the battle was short-lived, for in a relatively brief time no cinema orchestras remained.

Bill had long maintained that the introduction of "talkies" was his turning point:

"I was thrown out on the streets like the rest of them. So I put Mother on my shoulder and came up [to Mt Dandenong] and became a different man."

That was how he described the major change in his life. The details of the period were unimportant to him, for he held fast to the belief that only *after* the move to Mt Dandenong did his new life begin. Once again, this was not the case.

With his dream of greatness in music gone, Bill did not attempt to gain a position within the surviving orchestras, but returned to the dance bands. It was regular work, combining with his wages from Milton Plumb to ensure the adequate support of his mother and himself. It allowed him to give more attention to his developing affinity with clay and further explore his unease at the plight of natural Australia.

It is quite likely that the burgeoning nationalistic fervour fuelled his passion ever higher, causing him to question the sincerity of Australia's non-indigenous people. On one hand they were idolising and championing Australia's native beauty, while on the other they were ripping the country and her indigenous people apart in the name of progress. It was an anomaly with which he could not come to terms.

Every summer when the hills around Melbourne belched the smoke of bush fires, Bill's rage increased. He was told that the Australian bush liked fire, that it cleared away the rubbish—but Bill could think only of the bush creatures meeting a hellish end. He moved closer to the clutch of obsession with every perceived and actual atrocity. Yet the rage was tempered when incorporated into the realm of his ceramics.

Bill admitted to having had minimal contact with only three ceramic artists of the time. They were Ola Cohn, Marguerite Mahood and Gustav Pillig. That there were others is made evident by his having crossed paths with the likes of Merric and Doris Boyd at the Australian Porcelain Insulator studio in at least the early 1930s. The striking similarities between Merric Boyd's and Bill's works of the time must raise the question of whether or not it was more than a mere crossing of paths.

To illustrate this similarity, I again quote Peter Timms:

> *"One of his favourite devices is a large modelled or painted motif (a bird, a leaf, the trunk of a tree) that sweeps around the pot from the foot to the rim, encircling the body in a broad spiral, which can only be read if the pot is picked up and turned. It is an elegantly simple method of forcing one's physical involvement with the object. Handles are often integrated into the body of a jug or vase in a similarly sculptural manner by turning them into branches that sweep down and around the form."*

The above is a description of Merric Boyd's work, but, as can be seen in some of the illustrations in this volume, it could just as easily be a quote taken from a description of Bill's early works.

Bill was adamant, and angrily so, that he never met Merric Boyd, had nothing to do with Boyd and certainly was not influenced in any way by Boyd's techniques—yet we can read a quote of Boyd's which describes almost the exact path of Bill's early years in clay.

The following was first printed in the Melbourne *Argus* newspaper, being part of a full-page article devoted to Boyd and his Open Country pottery at Murrumbeena. A fuller body of quotation can be found in Peter Timms' book.

Said Boyd:

> *"The use of our own flora and fauna is of the first importance... I would like to see small articles of pottery, such as bears [koalas], jackasses [kookaburras], kangaroos, emus, opossums, gum leaves, gum nuts, golden wattle blooms, and other articles of a typically Australian character, made easily available to tourists, particularly those from overseas. The articles would not only be a good advertisement for Australia, but they would also be a never ending source of interest as happy reminders of pleasant experiences."*

To my way of thinking, Merric Boyd's thoughts and works are too close to those around which Bill would build the first steps of his life as a public potter to be pure coincidence. The one difference I can perceive, and it is a major one, is motive.

Another excerpt from Boyd's quote is:

> *"The first impulse of the maker of hand-pottery ... is to obtain pleasure in making and decorating an article, and making that pleasure intelligible to others. Beside that is his ultimate aim to produce something beautiful which will give pleasure to all beholders."*

The term "art for art's sake" has been used in some quite derogatory ways, but it can also be looked upon as a description of the creation of something beautiful purely for the sake of bringing beauty into being. Background or underlying stimulation is often secondary. Bill, however, focused on the background and underlying motives, using his pottery's appeal to cunningly transmit a message. He could not fully use this facility immediately, because he first had to master the art so as to capture the public's attention.

Of Bill's self-confirmed associations with ceramicists, Gustav Pillig is perhaps the most interesting. From a technical point of view, Pillig could well have been to sculpture in Melbourne what Tarczynski was to the violin.

Born in 1877 in Gelsenkirchen, Germany, Pillig went on to study art and sculpture in Stockholm's Technical School [1900], Berlin's Royal Academy [1900–1903] and Dusseldorf's Royal Academy [1904–1907]. He emerged from those studies as a sculptor of great skill and quickly established a reputable name.

Nephew, Rudi Pillig, summed up his uncle's rise and fall quite succinctly:

"He was an established sculptor before he came to Australia. He did monumental work in Germany, in fact he was really set up for quite a good career there—except that he decided to shoot through with his model and come to Australia. He left his wife and two children [in Germany]. Gustav was a bit of a lad, or a bit of a black sheep—but he just shot through with his model.

But he had the backing of important people in Germany, the industrialists and others. He could have made a great name for himself as a sculptor there—but it wasn't meant to be. And of course, Australia was a different kettle of fish."

Gustav Pillig arrived in Australia in 1913. His fate during WWI is unknown, but it is unlikely that he avoided internment. At some point along the way he moved to Melbourne, with my earliest record of his residing there being found in the 1928 Sands and McDougall's directory, in which he advertised himself as a sculptor working from Dora Place, Toorak.

Pillig's success as a monumental sculptor in Germany could not be revived in Australia, where there simply was not the demand at the time. So he drifted into the lot of an extremely talented, struggling artist.

Pillig was a frequent exhibitor of his work. By 1931 he had established a studio and residence at 125 Little Collins Street, Melbourne, which he also used as an exhibition venue. It was at this studio that Bill claimed to have met Pillig, who was by then living alone. Again, Bill was reticent about the ensuing relationship. He insisted that no relationship existed beyond that of casual acquaintance—but this is not supported by the events of the time or by Bill's knowledge of Pillig's progress.

Bill's nieces and nephews who remember the 111 Peel Street studio also remember that their uncle concentrated on traditional portrait sculpture for quite some time. Joan Hewitt, a daughter of Elsie, vividly remembered the room set aside for clay work, for she had ample time to absorb the scene while posing for a life-sized bust.

It was a room made slightly musty by the piles of wet clay over which damp sheets of cloth were draped to prevent dehydration. Similarly, many incomplete busts mounted on revolving pedestals were draped with wet cloth. Although Joan did not get to see them all, there are a couple which she clearly remembers.

Her favourite was of the Austrian singer, Richard Tauber. *"At that time Richard Tauber was visiting Australia … and he went up to see Uncle Bill—was very interested—and Uncle Bill did a bust"*, Joan said, adding that it was a life-sized head and shoulders which ended up as *"a remarkable likeness"*. Joan recalled that quite a few people sat for Bill, including overseas tourists and folk from the music world.

It was not, however, the life-like portraits that captured the children's imagination, but the large Plasticine model of a house and garden. Bill had created the scene on a table top measuring some 1.3 m by 1 m. It was a highly detailed sculpture; gardens with trees and flowers, paths, rooms with furniture which could only be seen when a small electric light was activated. It was the undisputed favourite of all the children who visited 111 Peel Street—but Bill claimed no recollection of it whatsoever.

Joan continued the sittings for her portrait, but the long periods of inactivity took their toll. For a child of eleven or twelve years of age, the process of watching her image being recreated was not fun:

"I couldn't see the value of things like that. It was boring and all Uncle Bill would say was 'Sit still!' It was about half finished, but all I could think about was Grandma's apple pie at the end."

Joan's family moved farther away from Peel Street, providing the perfect excuse not to continue with the sittings. It was a most regretful Joan who told me of her opportunity lost.

These vivid recollections of classic portraiture being created contemporaneously with Bill visiting Pillig raises the possibility of a connection. That Bill was a regular visitor to Pillig's is made evident by the fact that he followed the creation of Pillig's work "Symphony Of Life"; a detailed and intricate depiction of a world turning sour. Many years later Bill would give one of his works the exact same name.

The two must also have shared thoughts and worries, for one day Pillig told Bill to meet him in Melbourne. Pillig led the way to the La Trobe Library and eventually to Spencer and Gillen's two-volume work, The *Arunta: A Study Of A Stone Age Man*, published in 1927.[1]

Bill described the event to me:

"He pulled the book off the shelf and opened it—and it was like the key to my life. He opened the door to my life.

By that German opening the book, I had to come to the point straight away. Who the hell am I? Am I going to live in this country and see these people being wiped out?"

It became one of his very rare acknowledgements of influence and inspiration, albeit one which still had to be coaxed. While acknowledging the book, Bill vehemently denied any connection with Pillig regarding the furthering of his abilities as a sculptor. But with equal vehemence, Bill initially denied that he ever dabbled in straight, classical portraiture.

I queried this conundrum on several occasions, the results of which were inevitably hostile discourses. During one such exchange Bill proclaimed in exasperation:

"I did <u>one</u> head and showed it to him! He thought I was a bit of a fool. I was a visitor to Pillig—he says 'Make me a head'. Oh, bloody mug!"

When Rudi Pillig was interviewed for this biography, he explained that he and his father were introduced to Bill by his Uncle Gustav in 1956. Gustav had told both his nephew and brother that he had taught Bill in times past, although Rudi was unable to elaborate on the extent of such tuition.

On another occasion I was discussing Bill with Alan Lowe, a potter who entered the scene in Melbourne in the mid 1930s and went on to earn a very respected reputation. I asked Lowe if he'd ever heard anything of Merric Boyd having a hand in Bill's development, to which he replied: *"No. The only one I know who taught Bill Ricketts was that bloke up in North Melbourne—ah—Pillig."* Lowe went on to recall a long discussion he'd once had with Pillig, during which Pillig had revealed that he'd tutored Bill in the practise of sculpture. Lowe also recalled recognising a strong similarity between Pillig's work and Bill's later work as Pillig showed him through photographs of his work.

Although he did not starve in Australia, Gustav was never able to rekindle the career he might have had in Europe. Again, Rudi's words offer a succinct appraisal:

"I think he was pretty disappointed with his life as an artist in Australia. I suppose that goes for artists all over the world. Only a handful really make it big, and the rest—

---

1 Arrernte is the current correct spelling of this indigenous language group, as supplied by Gavin Breen, Institute for Aboriginal Development [IAD], Alice Springs. When direct quotes are reprinted in this volume, the variations Arunta and Aranda may appear, so as to remain faithful to the original text.

they're also-rans. If he stuck to sculpture he probably would have been better, but he probably wouldn't have survived commercially."

Gustav turned to oil painting, pen drawing and etchings in order to survive, but sculpture was his love. He did survive. He even managed to establish a small name for himself as a painter. Yet merely surviving is not an artist's pursuit. Gustav Pillig kept his masterpiece, "Symphony Of Life", for many years. When he was eventually diagnosed as having terminal cancer, he destroyed everything, including his masterpiece, in a passionate rage of unfulfilled ambitions. Today Gustav Pillig is a virtual unknown.

We will never know the exact relationship which existed between Pillig and Bill. I personally doubt that Pillig's tuition would have been formal and structured. It is more likely that Pillig helped unlock Bill's quiescent abilities.

Bill purchased Spencer and Gillen's books soon after he was introduced to them, but he did not immediately swing over to interpreting Aboriginal life through his sculpture. Indeed, it would be many years before he left behind the domestic art which could more easily produce an income. Not that profit was the driving force.

John and Robert Crow continued to make available their facilities to Bill, offering their full support and encouragement. They recognised the young potter's potential and actively sought to assist his career. As Robert Crow's son, Bruce, recalled:

> *"I know Dad was trying to get Bill to do something on a commercial basis, to do something and let Dad put it in a plaster mould, and he'd sell it after that. [Robert Crow] thought it was so good. But Bill was only doing it for the pure love of it. He was just a natural sculptor and he wouldn't be in that at all. [Bill] would ... put up a few things to sell, but not much."*

Bill, too, recalled the Crows' desire to commercialise his work, and not in a forgiving manner:

> *"One famous man, one of the potters in England—a famous man who was doing all the models and ideas to be put through the factory—[Crows] wanted me to be that. Well they were mistaken. They tried to show me the twisting of the wheel and the clay, how it came up into a jug. I was going to be the big—whatever his name in England was—I don't know, I forget now—but [Bob Crow] was going to be the big top man..."*

Bill would come to view the commercialisation of his work in a different light, but it would be some years later and as a result of what was, in his eyes, justifiable need. The minor run in did not sour the relationship with the Crows, for Bill continued to have much of his work fired in their kilns, just as he continued to collect his raw clay from their stocks. He also continued to be a sporadic user of the Crows' studio facilities.

At some point in those early 1930s Bill decided to make his involvement complete by establishing his own kiln at the Peel Street house. This brought about, or was possibly brought about by, his contact with Marguerite Mahood and her husband, Tom. Bill supposed he met Mahood at one of her exhibitions, and learned that her works were being fired in a coke-burning muffle-kiln designed by her engineer husband.

Although some years the junior of Bill, Mrs Mahood was the superior craftsperson at the time of their meeting. Between 1929 and 1945 she wrote many articles for the magazine *Australian Home Beautiful*. Her writing revolved around pottery, both the practical aspects and what were then the current trends. This placed her as not only an eminently skilled doer, but also as an accurate observer.

Bill went to Marguerite and Tom Mahood's to buy a copy of the plans for their kiln. The following is an account of that contact, taken from my interview with Mrs Mahood in late 1988:

> *"He came to me. He was little, although maybe I thought he was little because Tom was big. A thin, wispy sort of man—fair, blonde, with rather sharp features. There was something appealing about him. I thought, well, I've always liked young people who are serious about what they are doing—I like to help if I possibly can.*
>
> *We didn't talk specifically about anything that I can remember. He brought some of his little things around. He'd only made small things then, but they still showed the imagination and feeling that went into his bigger things later on.*
>
> *He had a feeling for the Aborigines right from the beginning. His own ideas were all rather hazy and floating, but you could see that he did have a feeling for the Aborigines— which very few people had then.*
>
> *I grew up being told that they were a stone-age people who were simply dying out at the contact with civilisation—so you didn't have to think about them!*
>
> *He was earnest enough to pay 5gns for the specifications and plans for the kiln that Tom made. As muffle-kilns go, I suppose it was large—the muffle was about two and a half feet by three feet. But Bill Ricketts didn't really build that particular kiln! I didn't know how completely unpractical he was at that time. He made an awful looking thing that wasn't—he did try—but it wasn't according to the specifications, by any means.*
>
> *We probably gave him advice—it would be almost impossible not to, because he was right at the beginning of that phase of his career. But I doubt if he would have taken much notice of it.*
>
> *We went to his home to see the kiln. The general outfit was extremely bohemian. His mother was there, a retiring sort of person. I didn't get very much impression about her, except that she was elderly and thin and something like himself.*
>
> *Then he went off to greater things and different people helping him. But of course, Ricketts was inspired within himself. Most artists are not inspired—they only do it for the money, most of them. I wouldn't know who his associates were. I only knew him and I knew he had what it takes to be a genius—if someone else could organise it for him."*

Bill's degree of success with his first kiln cannot be calculated. He kept no records and any of the surviving works from that period could just as easily have been fired in the Crows' kilns under the care of experts. We do know that Bill was not shy in his use of and experimentation with glazes. This was shown by the diverse range revealed during my research.

The wares he produced could have been sold through any number of outlets within Melbourne. A principal outlet used by other artists, the Primrose Pottery Shop, was established in 1929 by Edith and Betty MacMillan.

It was situated in Little Collins Street, the same locale in which Gustav Pillig established his studio, and reportedly an area in which many similar businesses chose to operate in the early 1930s. Nor did Bill restrict his trade to Melbourne, for he went at least as far afield as Geelong to market his wares.

"Nan" Dobson [maiden name] told me that soon after leaving school in 1930 she took over a small private library, called The Book Nook, in Geelong. Nan quickly realised to her dismay that the library was "read out", creating the immediate need for diversification. Nan recalled: *"These little arty gift shops were starting up, so I decided to see if I could do something like that."*

Among other contacts, Nan met one of the Crow brothers, but recalled that she didn't particularly like their offerings because *"they were too commercialised"*. Undoubtedly, it was through the Crows that Nan met Bill:

"He used to arrive—just arrive. There he'd be standing outside my shop, possibly on a Friday night. He was so burning with love for the Aborigines—and his hate for the white man and what they were doing to the land and everything.

I can picture this one time, he'd come down on the train and he had a box of chocolates for me. I was really touched by that.

He wore this cut-away suit, which would have to have been his very best suit—not a bowler hat, but a very rigid hat—and these ox-blood shoes! All shined up! Not many people wore them—and they shone!"

How much business Nan conducted with Bill is forgotten, as is exactly what works were sold. Nan could only give a vague description of works which generally fit in with the work he was doing at that time. But she did recall that Bill continued making the trips down to Geelong until he made the move to Mt Dandenong.

Another point-of-sale established by Bill in this period was International Needlecraft in Melbourne's Block Arcade. Hilda J. King was operating the establishment somewhat along the lines of a gallery. As we will see, King was another key player in Bill's rise.

It has also been said that Bill tried at one time to establish his own point-of-sale in Chapel Street, Windsor, literally just around the corner from his Peel Street house.

Bill's niece, Joan Hewitt, recalled that the venture was short-lived, but remember it she could:

"Yes, right near Peel Street, near the railway station. He was only there a short time before he left ... it was when he started doing teapots like tree trunks."

Bill rejected totally the suggestion that he even attempted to establish his own outlet and I failed to find anything in the council rates records to support the claim.

It remains that Bill was not backward in coming forward to promote his work at that time. Somehow he came to hear of Robert Henderson Croll, an officer in the Victorian Department of Education. It was Croll's off-duty pursuits in which Bill was interested.

Born in 1869, Croll lived through a fascinating era of Australia's history, an era which his finely educated and probing mind utilised to the utmost. He had a great love for nature, leading him to indulge regularly the pastime of bush walking. This pursuit gave way to Croll's debut in writing; volumes entitled *The Open Road in Victoria* and *Along the Track* were the start of an eventual fifteen or sixteen publications. He also met and became friendly with many artists, writers and poets. The impressive list of his associates includes, to name but a few, Tom Roberts, Charles Condor, Hugh McCrae, Norman and Lionel Lindsay, C. J. Dennis, Charles Web Gilbert and J. G. Roberts.

As Croll's son, R. D. Croll, recalled:

"My parents' home was a fascinating sort of kaleidoscope of interesting people, mostly impecunious."

R. H. Croll was also keenly interested in the Australian Aborigines, which led a friend and colleague, Professor Stanley Porteous, then Professor of Psychology, Hawaii, to invite Croll to assist with a 1929 research expedition to the remote areas west of Alice Springs. An interesting facet of that expedition was the young Hermannsburg man who acted as the chief camel attendant, Albert Namatjira. After Croll retired in the 1930s he made many return trips to the Centre, one of which was in the company of Rex Batterby [the water-colourist] and Jack Gardener [the oil painter]—the result of the painters requesting guidance for the journey. Namatjira was again employed as cameleer, the flow-on of which is now a significant part of Australia's art history.

Obviously, R. H. Croll was the sort of person in whom Bill would have been greatly interested. As Bill later recalled:

"He was one of the fine men who solved many difficulties for artists and poets and the likes."

According to R. D. Croll, the first meeting between the two took place one Sunday morning, somewhere towards the middle of the 1930s.

It was the practice of the period to leave the window blinds drawn until such time that the household was ready to receive visitors. When Mrs Croll did draw the blinds "somewhat latish", she noticed a thin man pacing back and forth on the footpath opposite their Camberwell [Melbourne] home. The stranger carried in his hand a violin case and was seen to be staring directly at their home with each of his passings. Eventually the young man seemed to summon courage, for he opened the gate, knocked on the door and asked to see R. H. Croll by name.

During the meeting that followed Bill opened his violin case to reveal *"a number of his small, exquisite sculptures"*, and sought Croll's advice on how best to bring his work to the public's attention. R. D. Croll recalls that his father was *"very impressed"* by the work he saw and through his connections organised what was Bill's first recorded exhibition. It was held in the Mutual Store, opposite Melbourne's Flinders Street Railway Station.

The exhibition was reviewed by none other than Marguerite Mahood and published in the January 1st, 1935, edition of the *Australian Home Beautiful* under the title, "The Art of William Ricketts: A Poet in Clay". There is little doubt that the review was a result of "who you know", for R. H. Croll was a friend of *Home Beautiful's* editor and, as we have seen, Marguerite Mahood was already impressed by Bill's work. It does, however, appear to be a sincere document which offers a unique insight. Mrs Mahood wrote, in part:

"Never in the short, but vigorous, history of Australian handcraft pottery has there been a talent more imaginative and more individual than that of William Ricketts. Around all of his works clings a peculiar charm. The detail is full of tenderness and full of whimsicality … [The] underlying severity brings the frolicsome detail into subjection save where the artist … has allowed his love of intricacy to waft him away from all considerations of use into a state of delightful irresponsibility…

The modelling of tree forms is particularly good, the spring of the boughs, the natural tendency of the stems, is well observed …

Most of Ricketts' work depends on aboriginal ideas for its inspiration. It is based, not on the sentimentalised 'black brudder', or the comic 'piccaninny' of the superficial observer, but on the deep, dreamy, wistful, half-formulated mythology of a childlike and unspoiled race …

A very fine piece is … an amphora-vase of classical shape, with golden wattle modelled in delicate low relief on the shoulder. Below the wattle floats a nude figure, typifying the spirit of music, violin and bow in hand, snatched up in lyric ecstasy by the perfume of Spring … The difficulties of low relief modelling, which demands a sensitive and intelligent touch, have been well overcome.

But Mr Ricketts' art is not all serious. There is a tea-pot for instance, with a swaggy squatted on the lid, Matilda beside him, in an attitude that suggests his readiness for a refreshing cup of tea. In many pieces, such as 'Old Man Kangaroo', or 'The Breaking of the Drought', in which an aboriginal triumphantly rides a giant frog; in the frolicsome piece in which a sportive warrior plays hide-and-seek with a wallaby; in the impish humour of the bull-frog with the big base fiddle tuning up for his nightly concert in the swamp, the young potter shows an imagination which can play as well as dream.

Much of Ricketts' work is unglazed … The glazes this young artist has used so far have been the dreamy, suave greens of the native bush, the warm brown of gum-nuts, with occasionally a suggestion of amethyst or ruby …

Of a different type is the strange piece called 'Wild Life Trader of the Forests' …
A hideous octopus creature, whose coin-dripping tentacles reach out to strangle and crush
the helpless beasts of the bush, creeps relentlessly forward, while in its path bush-birds
huddle together, limp winged and paralysed …

The poetic feeling, the lyric sensitiveness that shows in the loving almost passionate
tenderness of much of Ricketts' modelling, is remarkable … It is a new departure in
Australian pottery, and one worthy of encouragement. The young artist is … no mere
dabbler or dilettante. From his studio at Windsor we may expect future work that may
some day be known beyond our own shores as a permanent embodiment in … clay of the
poetic and mournful memories of our vanishing native race."

What effect must it have had on Bill? *"Never … has there been a talent more imaginative and*
more individual …", *"… a new departure in Australian pottery …"*, and *"may some day be*
known beyond our shores …" It's not hard to imagine the smile of content as he sat reading the
two pages devoted to him all those years ago. But when I showed Bill that review half a century
later, he hated it. It described the artist and not the fighter. It elaborated on technique and not the
philosophy of his deep rooted motivation. Bill hated it so much that he almost demanded that it
be left out—but, of course, it had to be included.[2]

Mrs Mahood's observations and detailed descriptions reveal the level of development Bill had
achieved before his move to Mt Dandenong. By the very nature of the works exhibited, his
ultimate direction is seen to have been firmly rooted. Why he came to nurture the myth that his
life as one involved with clay began *after* his establishment on the mountain is a mystery—the
answer to which only Bill knew.

That Bill was well along the path of immersion into matters Aboriginal is obvious, so it came
as a surprise to read of his deviations in subject matter.

Mrs Mahood described works based on music and others with humorous undertones. Those
descriptions are unique in that they are the only mention of such subjects in Bill's work. Pieces
like the nude figure with violin and bow in hand *"snatched up in lyric ecstasy by the perfume of*
Spring", the warrior playing hide-and-seek with the wallaby, the bull-frog tuning his bass fiddle,
and the swaggy on the tea-pot—all are foreign to the subjects for which Bill has come to be
known. We must assume that before being overtaken by what he would come to call his
"Vision", Bill was an animated creator of a broad range of art, into which he injected the cheeky
humour and imagination which remained so evident in his later private life.

Just as the works mentioned give some insight to Bill's earlier dabblings, Mrs Mahood gives a
stark portrayal of his future in describing "The Wild Life Trader of the Forests". More than any
other, that work [and future works of similar concept] would come to represent Bill's profound
hatred and loathing for all who treated the bush, her people and her creatures with ignorance and
disrespect. That such a challenging piece should have been included in what was probably his first
solo exhibition indicates the strength of his conviction. Less courageous artists would certainly
have waited until they had achieved some recognition and respect before so vehemently
condemning those whose views were disparate to their own.

By the few accounts available, the Mutual Store exhibition was a success. Any personal
doubts about his possible future in the field of pottery would have been significantly allayed, if
Mrs Mahood's review is anything to go by. Bill had moral and material support from several key
associates. If he had been waiting for the right time to commit himself fully, then surely it had
come. Bill was satisfied with his motives and audience—he needed only the correct environment
in which to nurture his destiny.

---

2 When I read the manuscript to him, which then included the whole of Mrs Mahood's review, Bill did not so much as
raise an eyebrow.

5 | To the Mountain
[c. 1934–late 1930s]

The Dandenong Ranges had a fiery, volcanic birth. Time and weather softened the ruggedness of their beginnings, gradually cloaking the mountains with rich porous soils from which luxuriant flora could grow in perpetual cycles, for ever adding to the richness and diversity.

In times before European invasion, the indigenous Koories ventured into these ranges in the warmer months. Through gullies carpeted with mosses and small ferns, beneath dense groves of feathery tree ferns, they could follow the crystal clear creeks upwards to their source. Lyrebirds, whipbirds and scores of other feathered inhabitants filled the air with their calls. They would continue upwards through stands of what were then the tallest trees in the world, the mighty Mountain Ash. The whites would measure specimens of 128 m in height, and make reports of giants which soared 152 m from buttresses 25 m in circumference. Such facts were irrelevant to the Koorie travellers. Those massive life forms were simply part of their world; as they had always been and, for all they knew, as they would always be.

Ultimately they could stand on the summit of what is now called Mt Dandenong, just marginally higher than the sister peak, Corranwarrabul, but some 633 m above the waters which would be called Port Phillip Bay, 45 km distant. The gentle undulations of their country stretched into the blue haze, a view disturbed only by smoke from the widely scattered fires of other small groups of humanity.

By the 1840s Europeans were marking the Dandenongs with signs of progress. Holes appeared in the leafy canopies as the forest giants crashed to become the wharves, bridges and buildings of Melbourne. Tracks were cut ever deeper into the ranges to permit bullock and horse teams access to their heavy loads. Timber getting was the work of poor men, a commodity never lacking in Melbourne. The difficult terrain between the Dandenongs and Melbourne slowed the onslaught a little [in some cases Tasmanian timber could be landed more cheaply in Melbourne], as did the gold rushes, but falling trees were a sure sign of progress—and the colony was progressing.

It was not all rape and plunder in the Dandenongs. The area's beauty touched the hearts of many Melburnians, with Fern Tree Gully becoming a major tourist destination. The more adventurous made the stiff climb to One Tree Hill for a glimpse of the distant city, but most contented themselves with wandering among the lower fern glens.

The 1850s saw a rapid growth in permanent settlers about the ranges, but incursion into the hills themselves remained the lot of the "splitters", as the timber cutters were known. They saw no end to the resource and took only the prime cuts from the trees they felled, leaving the bulk to rot or burn. Melbourne's expansion increased the demand. It was to facilitate the transport of timber more than anything else that led to the railway being extended to Fern Tree Gully in 1889.

The most devastating blow dealt to the Dandenongs occurred during the 1890s when the then Minister for Lands, Sir John McIntyre, threw open some 2,833 hectares of land as part of the

Land Settlement Bill. It was a direct result of the severe economic depression of the time. The scheme was designed to relocate the unemployed and impoverished of Melbourne onto two and four hectare lots where, it was reasoned, they could survive and prosper. It did not seem to matter that much of the land was excessively steep and heavily timbered: *"...very beautiful to look and wonder at, but unfit for needy settlers"*, complained Robert Kerr, then President of the Fern Tree Gully council.

Despite protests, McIntyre pushed the scheme through *"on the principle that men on the land were better than gum trees"*.[1] To further reinforce that principle, one of the reported conditions of settlement was that every tree over 30 cm in diameter had to be felled as soon as possible.

While all settlers could accomplish the first stage of their new life, clearing the land, the very reason for the scheme's existence proved to be its point of downfall. The settlers were mostly penniless. They could barely manage to erect shelters, let alone stock their small farms with work animals and implements. Nor could their enthusiasm overcome the obstacle of their being ignorant of basic farming practises, an obstacle which left many families producing at below the level of subsistence. It proved not to be a lifestyle by which the needy could prosper.

Gradually they drifted away to more familiar poverty in the city, leaving behind a stark landscape dominated by ring-barked trees.

By 1905 the settlement blocks were being purchased by the more affluent of Melbourne, more often than not to be used as weekend retreats and holiday homes. So began the second transformation of the Dandenongs. This second wave of landowners brought with them visions of their European homelands and planted the mountains accordingly. Oaks, elms, beeches, birches, maples, sycamores, chestnuts, conifers and scores of other northern-hemisphere exotics took root and thrived in the rich soils and temperate climate. Fortunately the Mountain Ash had not had their day. They regenerated in competition with the carefully-nurtured exotics, resulting in today's rich, contrasting mosaic.

With the injection of affluence came an increased level of interest. Word spread of the magnificent views, the clear mountain air and the cool fern gullies, with the result that guest houses were established to cater for the increasing number of weekend visitors. These visitors mostly came by train to Croydon, from where horse-drawn carriages ferried them up the tracks into the mountains. The area was made more accessible after WWI, when returned servicemen were employed in the construction of a large section of a new road up to Mt Dandenong. That route exists today as the northern section of Mt Dandenong Tourist Road. With the completion of this vastly superior road, the first motor coaches were able to begin service.

One of the first to operate motor coaches up the mountain was Hubert Jeeves, who was born at Kalorama in 1895. He first took the reins of his father's horse-drawn carriages when fifteen years of age, progressing to his own stable of some fifty horses and ultimately motor coaches. Years later Jeeves told me that he'd heard William Ricketts tell listeners how it was in a motor coach driven by Jeeves that he'd first come up to Mount Dandenong as a tourist.

Bill recalled and family members confirm his having long dreamed of living in the Dandenongs. His first trips to the ranges, he said, were by rail to Lilydale, followed by what would have been a tortuous push bike ride up the rough and unsealed mountain road. Knowing of Bill's physical strength and determinedness, one could picture him accomplishing the feat.

On one of his trips Bill found an available block of land beside a lush fern gully through which a small stream flowed. The stream had its source outside the boundary further up the slope, where it flowed clear and fresh from the earth in the form of a spring. Many years later Bill wrote of his feeling: *"...that somehow I was related to the pure water gushing from the silent spring in the side of the mountain"*. Certainly from other eye-witness accounts, the block had little else going for it.

---

1 M. Jones, *Prolific in God's Gifts*, p. 118.

John Lundy-Clark, unofficial historian for that area of the mountains, recalled that a bush fire had burnt through the block in 1910, with another major blaze following through in 1932. The early destruction caused by logging, followed by the two fires, had left little timber of any size. Mostly it was rough scrub dominated by areas of dense bracken fern. Lundy-Clark speculated:

"The man's imagination must have caught the possibilities of the place, because the ordinary person would have thought, 'No, it's too rough'."

The actual details of his relocation and purchase are unclear. Lillydale rates records reveal that during the rates period of 1934-35, Bill became responsible for the rates on the four and a half acre block of land fronting the Tourist Road on Mt Dandenong's southern slope, but it was not until May 1941, that the title was transferred to his name. It was the practice of that time for a tenant to assume responsibility for the rates. Whether or not Bill rented the property for a time or whether he immediately commenced paying off the block in instalments is unknown.

Mention should be made of another version of Bill's move to Mt Dandenong, told to me by several people during the course of research, none of whom were first hand witnesses. They had it that Bill had become mentally disturbed or mentally ill to the point of his nearly being admitted as an inpatient to the Kew Psychiatric Hospital. It then had his mother buying the Mt Dandenong block, where she took Bill to keep him from harm's way. A subsequent therapeutic pastime was pottery, the medium in which his talent developed.

I found no substantiating evidence for that version. His name appears on no record at Kew. We know that Bill had been involved with clay for possibly fifteen years prior to his move up the mountain, and we will see that it would be some time after the move that his mother joined him there.

The "mentally disturbed" version does have a possible origin though. When I presented that version to Bill and in a round about way asked if he had any disturbances at the time or whether or not he'd visited Kew Hospital, he recalled that there was a doctor from Kew who had tried to encourage him to go *"down for a talk"*, but Bill was just too busy. It is possible that a well-meaning friend or relative was concerned with the radical ideas and extremely high passions evident in Bill at the time and sought to have the matter professionally assessed.

Returning to Bill's establishment on the mountain and his first priority, a shelter of some sort. There stands today a renovated version of what is generally accepted as Bill's original residence. It now serves as the Rangers' offices and work-shop. Within the walls of that building are sections of the original hut, but it is little known that the site was a second preference.

Bill initially chose to purchase a small house in Melbourne's inner-western suburbs at a cost, he said, of £50. The house was dismantled into its various parts and a haulier contracted to transport the load to Bill's block. The driver dropped the load at the bottom of the fern gully.

Bill had levelled a small pad well up the slope, on the edge of the gully, as the site for the new home. His brother-in-law, John Paul [Elsie's husband] assisted in the refabrication, but first the materials had to be moved to the site. A member of the local Gower family came to the rescue with a large-capacity hand winch, with which the individual sections were hauled around tree ferns and over fallen logs up the gully. The single room was erected and weather-proofed, scantily furnished and called home.

There followed a short, rather bizarre period which saw Bill begin his time on Mt Dandenong—his only companion being a pet Angora rabbit, named John.

By then Bill was some thirty-six years of age. It had been a long time since the boyhood solitude he'd enjoyed along the banks of the Darebin River. His nights had always been spent in company; be it his family, the theatres and dance halls or just the ever-present city noises. To be suddenly alone on a sparsely populated mountain-side was a major change. The still nights were new—and frightening:

"It's unbelievable. I had it built and I had a couple of nights sleeping in it by myself. I could have sworn that there was somebody walking around it—thump, thump, thump. It was so bad and so real that one night I opened the window and let fly my boots! I had a shot!"

I suggested that it may have been wallabies or wombats, once common on his block and throughout the ranges, but he would not entertain the thought for a second. *"I was haunted"*, he claimed, but he would not elaborate any further.

Then I thought of the spiritualists who firmly believe that Bill was a highly attuned individual who was quite capable of being aware of the presence of those in another realm. Was it possible that the sounds Bill heard were not natural? I asked him about it and tried to get him to share his thoughts, to no avail. His reticence was firm: *"If I said anything, they'd think I was mad."*

The reason Bill gave me for relocating the hut back down the slope was that the track to the shack would have been too steep and rough for his aging mother to negotiate.

At that time work was being carried out on the Mt Dandenong Hotel by a building crew headed by Oliver David. A member of the crew was the then sixteen-year-old Max Yunghanns, who gave me an account of his involvement in the construction of Bill's next dwelling, although the first thing to be constructed was a kiln. Peter Timms wrote that the first kiln on the block was constructed by Hatton Beck c. 1935. Beck, a Melbourne potter, was recognised as a glaze and kiln technologist. The kiln built may have been of Beck's design, but Yunghanns was adamant that he and Oliver David's younger brother built the first kiln on the site.

When members of the building crew were not required on the hotel, they would go to Bill's. Max Yunghanns described how the task progressed once the pad had been levelled:

> *"There was a great stone left on it but he wouldn't shift it—we had to work around it. We had great trouble with him, trying to shift the trees. He was very—well, if you looked side-ways at a tree he was straight there alongside of you in a way that showed disapproval at what you might be going to do. It would have looked like something out of Walt Disney, the way he wanted it.*
>
> *When people came he used to go hide in the bush, but it got so that he knew David and I. We made friends and he'd come down and keep an eye on us.*
>
> *David and I laid the foundations and then the carpenters took over. He got the pine logs from somewhere else. The home we built was small, with two bedrooms in it, but we had to build it around that great stone—he wouldn't shift it. Just like the floor, earthen— he wouldn't have anything on the floor. It was quite primitive."*

Exactly when Susan Ricketts moved to Mt Dandenong to live with her son is uncertain. Bill maintained that it was immediate, but the Prahran Council Rates Records show that Susan continued to be responsible for rates at the Peel Street house through the 1937 rates period, although she could have sublet. Family members recall Susan being most concerned about Bill living alone on the mountain and her apparently justifiable worries that he would neglect his own well-being in the process of realising his dreams. Max Yunghanns recalled that she was not up there while the house was being constructed.

Bill continued to devote much time to the more easily sold domestic ware, some of which were heavily and elaborately glazed, and none of which was in any way ordinary. On weekends he set up a table by the roadside on which his bush-inspired wares were displayed for sale, relying on the purchasers' honesty for payment. Above and behind the table, hanging from a tree branch, was a rough sign on which the words "The Potter's Sanctuary—Inspection Invited" were painted. An arrow pointed the way up a steep path to Bill's house.

Through the scrub Bill had cut narrow winding paths, along which his work was displayed.

To begin with the works were simply displayed on either trestles or the earth, as all pieces were for sale. By all accounts, his works sold well. To increase revenue, Bill constructed a wishing well, which proved to be yet another winner with the passing tourists.

One of Bill's morning and afternoon rituals was to stroll the perimeter of the block with his pet rabbit, John.

John happens to be one of Bill's darker secrets from the past, for John was a stolen bunny!— or one of Melbourne's first acts of animal liberation, depending on your point of view.

While he was living at 111 Peel Street, Bill often noticed the next-door-neighbour's rabbit bouncing around their back yard. He also noticed rat traps set and left in places which also threatened the rabbit, which Bill thought was grossly irresponsible. He waited until the neighbours were out and prised a paling from the fence. The rodent was coaxed through to a new life in a safer world and given the name, John.

Fifty years later, Bill still went sentimental at the thought of his bunny: *"John was my treasure. If I had the money to buy a cabbage, well Mother and I went without. It was like that."*

Now, this research did not extend to determining the vagaries of rabbits, so I was led to wonder at their expressions of affection and gratitude when Bill recalled those walks around his property. Apparently John would race ahead, bounding about in a madcap manner, then come suddenly racing back and make a flying leap past Bill. During this leap John would perform an aerobatic half-turn and "squirt" Bill across the thighs as he passed. To make matters worse, it was not an infrequent trick. Another foible of John's was an apparently irrepressible attraction to *any* human foot which, when legs were crossed, hung suggestively and provocatively [in the bunny's mind, at least]. It invariably flustered Bill, resulting in a quick and embarrassed disentanglement of bunny and foot, accompanied by a *"naughty boy"* admonishment.

One of the first people to get to know Bill on the mountain was Doris Turner. She and her husband moved up at roughly the same time as Bill, taking over the kiosk which sat on the very crown of Mt Dandenong. The area is now a bitumen car park crowned by a restaurant. Not too long after their move, the Turners purchased the Mt Dandenong general store and Post Office which was a short five minute stroll from Bill's place.

Doris quickly came to know the spattering of permanent residents. While the weekends saw an influx of the more affluent folk who owned the holiday houses and cottages, she remembered the locals as being for the most part elderly, recalling good-humouredly:

> *"And there were some very funny people—quite different from the people now. One friend of mine said it was the only place in the whole world where the inmates ran their own show!"*

Quite often in those early days, Doris would take an old hermit known as "Peter the Swede" an evening meal. He lived in a shack in the gully directly below Bill's block. Occasionally her progress was arrested by the sound of a solo violin emanating from Bill's hut and resonating through the still forest:

> *"He used to play quite a lot when he first went up there—I don't know why he ever stopped. He played for himself. Of course, he was very fond of music, but he was never happy with how he played. He always felt that he would have liked to have done better.*
>
> *But to walk along that road at night, of course there were no cars rushing past as there are now, and hear the music up there—it was beautiful. Mozart and Beethoven, mostly: some slow and sweet—and some of it <u>majestic</u>."*

It would appear that Bill tried to pay quite a deal of attention to the science of working with and firing clay during those early stages on the mountain. He continued to accept the support and advice of John and Robert Crow. They drove up on weekends, bringing clay that had been experimentally blended at their factory which, while unsuitable for their purposes, they knew would be well suited for the work Bill was doing. They even provided him with a clay press to facilitate his own blending and production of clay, although Bill's success with the press was neither recorded nor remembered. Undoubtedly there would have been long conversations on firing technique, although it would prove to be a science which he would never fully master. Another man to come onto the scene during these early times was Leo Junck, a Dutch ceramic engineer whom Bill described as **"the head man from Wunderlich Ltd in South Melbourne"**. We will see later that it was not only technical support that Junck would provide.

This technical support was not entirely wasted. Early reports of up to 100 per cent loss from a firing gave way to greater success rates, which meant more work available for the raising of funds.

While the invitation to inspect the Sanctuary resulted in many brief encounters and one-off customers, it also brought patrons of varying influence. On one Sunday afternoon not long after Susan had moved up to the house, a family named Solomon were out driving from their house in Sassafras when they saw the new sign advertising Potter's Sanctuary. They stopped to investigate and met Bill. Although young at the time, the now married Joy Cowen recalled:

> *"Even in those days he was going to make big pieces and he wanted the Government to come up and see what he had done. I don't know whether he thought about them ever taking it over, but he wanted help from the Government and he wanted to go to the land where these Aboriginal people were—but he didn't know whether he'd ever have the money to go. He didn't have then."*

Bill took the family inside to meet Susan. Mrs Cowen never forgot the sight:

> *"She was sitting there huddled up by the fire. It was the most primitive thing you've ever seen, but she was very, very sweet."*

Mrs Cowen's mother and aunt were of a similar age to Susan and a friendship of sorts was formed. It came about that the Solomons would regularly collect Bill and Susan on a Sunday afternoon and take them back to their Sassafras home for a meal. Any surplus food was given to Susan to take home, which was apparently greatly appreciated. The privations Susan endured were obvious, but Susan made it clear to the Solomons that she was leading the life of her choice. Mrs Cowen recalled:

> *"Mrs Ricketts was happy as long as she was looking after William and he was getting his work done. She grew old with the idea of knowing that this was what he wanted to do and she was there to help him—or look after him.*
>
> *William was always a dreamy sort, because he lived in the Dreaming himself. He used to talk about his people of the Dreaming, the Aborigines, and even then he was well up on the subject. He was always hoping that somebody, the Government or somebody, would come along with the money for him to go to them. His one idea was that he was going to help the Aborigines by doing this work and going to the places where they came from, but I never saw an Aborigine of any kind up there."*

There was at least one Aboriginal visitor to Potter's Sanctuary in those early days.

David Unaipon, a Ngarrindjeri man from South Australia's Point McLeay, was, during his lifetime, Australia's best-known Aborigine. Born in 1872, Unaipon came to be recognised as one who possessed a rare intelligence. His academic life was largely devoted to exploring the secrets of perpetual motion. In 1907 his successful conversion of curvilinear motion into straight-line movement streamlined the mechanical action of sheep-shears, for which he obtained a Commonwealth patent in 1909. He was acclaimed as an inventor, an authority on ballistics, an orator, lecturer and musician. He was a student of Greek and Christian mythology. He was also a recorder of his own race's myths, legends and folklore. This remarkable man was to be the first Australian Aborigine Bill would meet.

Doris Turner recalled that Unaipon had been staying in the Dandenongs and was more than likely taken to see the Sanctuary. Bill recounted little of the meeting, although he did say that Unaipon later wrote of the encounter:[2]

"But he said, 'It's all there'. He saw the work."

When I asked Bill if he had spoken to Unaipon about his people, he said:

"No, I don't think I was very charged at that time. But he saw in the work that it was all there. He knew that I must have been thinking deeply and was a little bit worried. So he put it that way. 'It's all there.' He just looked at me and gauged that I must have been a little bit upset, and perhaps a little bit anxious to do something to fill in the ugly gap."

Chances are that Bill would have been absolutely dumbfounded by his encounter with Unaipon. After all, Bill's knowledge came from text books about remote Aborigines whose culture was ancient and uninterrupted by European influence. His passion and empathy were fuelled by the timeless wisdom of a people whose race was generally accepted as teetering on the edge of the abyss of extinction. Yet before him would have stood a smartly dressed Australian Aboriginal gentleman who could speak as authoritatively about Greek and Christian mythology as he could about his own: a man familiar with modern sciences about which Bill would have been totally ignorant. I imagine that it would have been a quiet, humble and slightly confused Bill who met with David Unaipon.

Bill was impressed, though, because for many years to come he would publicly acknowledge Unaipon's writings on Aboriginal folklore and religious life as a source of his own inspiration and knowledge. Although Unaipon lived until 1967, it seems that their paths never crossed again.

Mr W. A. Waller and his wife Olga, who would become staunch supporters, also came into Bill's life shortly after the establishment of Potter's Sanctuary. Residents of Brighton [Melbourne], they regularly spent time at their weekender on Mt Dandenong. According to the Waller's daughter, Mrs Dixon, they first noticed life-sized sculptures of possums and koalas placed in the branches of saplings below Bill's property while walking one day. On reading the invitation to inspect, they followed the track up to the house. In the following extracts from what appeared to be an incomplete article manuscript, titled "Potter's Sanctuary—Mt Dandenong", Olga Waller [described by Mrs Dixon as a kindred spirit to Bill] related some of her discoveries:

"...A terrace garden in the making leads up to the Potter's house, and, arranged on low benches and trestles, and even on the ground itself are a hundred or more examples of his art.

On the one side are bowls, jugs and vases mostly in soft greens, blues and browns with leaf or blossom ornamentations. Many of these are replicas of one another and therefore not as expensive as those on the benches where stand his best creations.

It has been the artist's object in his finest pieces to attempt to translate the innate spirit of our land, and, in order to do this, he has gone back to the Australia of the Aborigines...

---

2 Unfortunately that piece, if it still exists, was not sighted during this research. I would welcome any reader's help in locating it.

A legend of the Arunta tribe about a great Kangaroo having the face of an old man has given rise to many delightful pieces. Here you see the 'Old Man-Kangaroo' crouched ready for the next spring, or turning a jovial bearded face for a last look before bounding off across the plain. Here again he stands erect and alert scenting danger; here a number of them in much smaller size as part of the pedestal of a pink bowl with tiny water-lilies, and yet another as the knob of the lid of a blue tea-pot of exquisite shape.

Tall vases for gum leaves are formed as part of tree trunks with aboriginal figures standing or crouching with some of the bush folk—snakes, Koalas, kangaroos and frilled lizards around their base. Another very charming idea has also been utilised several times by the artist, and that is, that the forest trees protect their own folk especially the koalas and possums from the onslaughts of the trappers and hunters and other evilly disposed persons. The limbs, branches and roots of a gnarled old gum tree have been fashioned in the clay, and somewhere as part of a knot on the trunk a wizened angry face appears—the spirit of the tree. One of the branches is upraised as an arm holding a waddy, and one is shown protectively around its little furry friend. The Potter has several variations of this same idea which must appeal to all bush-creature lovers who deplore the ravages of gun and snare upon our native fauna.

A very happily received piece is a group of native boys sitting in a circle and laughing at one of their members who is peeping downwards at a huge frilled lizard. Little ashtrays representing crude bark dishes with piccaninnies squatting chin in hand, should have many admirers. And so, one could go on describing these delicately made pieces of handicraft..."

Bill did not have to rely purely on passing trade at Potter's Sanctuary. An early promoter of his work was Leanore Drexler who had become, in 1929, the first female executive with the Railways of Victoria, attached to the Tourist Bureau section. At the mention of her name Bill enthusiastically recalled:

"Oh! She gave me a lot of encouragement. Mrs Drexler used to be the avenue for the overseas people. She was always with me, in spirit. She did everything she could to get people interested."

In that past age of leisurely world cruises on the great ocean liners, it was to Mrs Drexler, quite often with letters of introduction from embassies the world wide, that visiting dignitaries and the well-to-do were directed for the purpose of getting the most out of their visits to Victoria. On a shelf in her office was a piece of Bill's work, the bust of an Arrernte "magic man" which drew frequent interest and comment. On being told that the creator of such works was but an hour and a half away, they would readily allow Mrs Drexler to organise luxury car hire from City Motor Service. In chauffeur-driven limousines they bounced their way up to Mt Dandenong, ultimately taking Bill's works and message to stations of influence all over the globe.

The development of the Sanctuary continued, sometimes with the help of family members, more often with solitary dedication. Susan Ricketts suffered the privations in silence and with equal dedication, content to be looking after her son, happy as long as he was happy. She let him make the plans he chose without comment; plans which included such ideas as creating a wildlife sanctuary on the block. To this end Bill wrote to Irene McGee and her husband at Yarrawonga with a request for them to send down by train kangaroos and emus. The enormity of the task seemed not to concern Bill, but the McGees baulked at the request. The plan to import animals never came to fruition. Bill was left to try instead to ensure that the wildlife native to the block would have absolute sanctuary there.

He quickly developed a great affinity with the creatures which shared his bush block, going as far as to share his home with some of them. A small trap-door was built high up in one wall of the hut to provide access for possums. Every night he would save some fruit and bread to feed them. The possums, being quick to adapt and always ready to accept a free feed, became nightly visitors. Bill's favourites were, and remained, the ring-tails. They are smaller and more timid than their brushy-tailed relatives, but they sensed that there was no danger within the hut. Bill knew that their trust had been won when mothers came along for the nightly snack with young ones clinging tenaciously to their backs.

While all the birds were special to Bill, none captured his heart or imagination like the lyrebirds. The Dandenongs are home to the Superb Lyrebird, which are arguably the best mimicker of sounds in nature. An adult may have a repertoire of a dozen different bird calls, as well as any other sounds that might be heard in their territory. The males also have a dance, used to woo a mate once she has been lured by his songs, during which he folds his impressive tail feathers over his body and head and sets them quivering. While this tail-feather display is going on, he stamps his feet into the ground with high steps, moving with what seems to be a definite rhythm from side to side and back and forth. The quivering spectacle, and especially the feet movement, is not unlike some of the dances traditionally performed by Aborigines.

Bill used to feed the lyrebirds with grated cheese and if visitors wanted to take a gift that would really find favour, nothing could beat a block of cheese. The lyrebirds grew so accustomed to Bill that he could hand-feed them and watch their displays at his back door.

For reasons that he was unable to explain, Bill further embraced indigenous culture and adopted the lyrebird as his personal totemic animal.

6 | The Plan of a Visionary
[late 1930s–1944]

Bill's depictions of Aboriginal mythology, legend and folklore set him apart from his contemporaries by pricking the curiosity and imagination of those who viewed his work. Australia was then still a land with distances vast enough and transport inefficient enough to make the Centre and its indigenous people seem almost like another world. His were not words or poorly reproduced photographs which had the viewer working to get it into their minds, but delicate and well-executed three dimensional portrayals of a mysterious part of Australia which was as foreign as the surface of the moon to many who viewed them. The possibility of the portrayals not being completely accurate to the Aboriginal perception of events was of little importance. Bill's works brought his non-Aboriginal viewers closer than they had ever been. An added bonus was that his mythology-based work also kept the more conventional pieces firmly in the public eye.

His next recorded exhibition was opened on February 28th, 1938, at Margaret Maclean's Gallery in Melbourne's Collins Street. It was briefly reviewed in the *Argus* newspaper the following day by journalist and artist, Harold Herbert, who gave no indication of which pieces were exhibited. Nonetheless, it was another glowing review which could not help attracting interest, being studded with such statements as, *"The work is remarkable in every way"*, and, *"These pieces of bric-a-brac are the best expressions of Australia 'in pottery' that I have seen"*.

In April of that same year, Bill's work was exhibited at Anthony Hordern and Son's Fine Art Gallery in Sydney. It resulted in the beginning of a long and significant relationship with what was then the Sydney Museum of Applied Arts and Sciences [SMAAS], now known simply as the Powerhouse. The SMAAS became the first and remains the only public institution to show a serious interest in Bill's work when they purchased four pieces from that exhibition, providing the basis for what would eventually be built into the best and most comprehensive collection of Bill's works assembled anywhere, as far as I know.

Among the pieces purchased was a 1934 vase made prior to the move to Mt Dandenong.[1] On its base was a note on a paper sticker reading, *"My first modeling [sic] attempt. WR"*. The accuracy of that note is obviously doubtful. The other pieces were a 1937 lidded vase, the lid featuring miniature representations of four Aborigines and a white man said to be Baldwin Spencer, a 1938 kangaroo man and a 1938 vase featuring the legend of the kangaroo's creation. The latter was purchased for the sum of £10 10s.

The beginning of 1939 almost saw disaster strike Potter's Sanctuary. The brilliant summer suddenly turned into a nightmare. Wild fires filled the air around Melbourne with smoke and the Dandenongs were not spared. Bill recalled crouching with his mother in their shack while the fire blazed unchecked through the main gully below them. It continued right through to Olinda, but did not come back up the south-easterly facing slope to Bill's home. Bill forgot whether or not

---

1 The piece was inscribed "Melbourne" rather than "Potter's Sanctuary".

the fire was checked at the road, or simply did not come back up the hill. All he remembered was the terror of the moment.

Call it fate, providence or good luck, but since that fire over half a century ago, no bush fire has come within cooee of the Sanctuary.

An article about Bill in the February 1st, 1939, edition of Adelaide's *Advertiser* newspaper revealed how he wanted himself to be seen in the public eye at the time. In it Bill was quoted as saying:

> *"I first took up modelling clay as a recreation, but the urge to create a beautiful medium of artistic expression in ceramic art sprang for the first place from a deep love for my country Australia, and from all the living things, human and animal, native to it.*
>
> *This interest was intensified by my studies of the works of Sir Baldwin Spencer, describing his very human contact with the aborigines, and other writers who have dealt with aboriginal folklore and legends.*
>
> *Through these figures, I wish for the Australian peoples to know of the stories and folklore, but above all I want the people ... overseas ... to realise that ... Australia ... has behind it a history of years ...*
>
> *My greatest wish is to go to Central Australia and see the aborigines ... I'm trying to be one of the champions of the natural Australian environment and am striving to show that beauty is there. There is beauty and strength in the Aboriginal form and face ... "*

It is quite possible that the above article served also to introduce Bill to Theodore G. H. Strehlow, gatherer of the famous [or infamous, as it became for some of its history] Strehlow Collection of Central Australian sacred Aboriginal artefacts; one of the world's finest and most valuable private collections.

Born in 1908, the son of Carl Strehlow, a German Lutheran missionary at Hermannsburg in Central Australia, and his wife Frieda, Ted Strehlow grew up biculturally and trilingually with the mission's mainly Arrernte people. From the age of fourteen he studied in Adelaide, ultimately graduating from the Adelaide University with Honours in English Literature and Linguistics. In 1933 he returned to the Centre on a £100 grant and began what would become his life's work of recording and conserving principally Arrernte culture and tradition.

In December, 1939, Ted Strehlow visited Potter's Sanctuary with his friends, Mr and Mrs Harry Balfour of Toorak. Strehlow related the experience during an address he gave at the Sanctuary in 1973.[2] He said that he had developed, even in 1939, *"a strong distrust of white writers and artists who attempted to penetrate into the aboriginal world of the mind"*. He recalled that it was only at the insistence of Harry Balfour that he had gone to Bill's home, so firmly convinced was he that *"Ricketts could not have succeeded where other white men had failed"*. What Strehlow found appears to have come as a shock:

> *"... my eyes fell on a group of kangaroo totemic ancestors. In a flash I realised that here was a new world of true art—a world created by the mind of a man who was so closely attuned to the aboriginal thought processes and emotional attitudes that his clay-formed works seemed to breathe the same spirit ..."*

Where did it come from, that high level of Bill's understanding? Had the simple study of text books and a chance meeting with one Aborigine attuned Bill so closely as to amaze a man born and raised in an Aboriginal world? It's hard to believe that it could have. Had Bill simply stumbled

---

2 In a letter of April 16th, 1975, Strehlow gave Bill permission to release the text of that speech for publication on the one condition, "... that they acknowledge it correctly".

luckily upon that certain quality of expression in his work? This is equally hard to believe. It is one of the mysteries about Bill which will remain unexplored in this volume, because it beckons one into realms that cannot be approached logically.

Undoubtedly, Ted Strehlow would have kept in touch with Bill from that day on, but the details of the special relationship which developed are kept secret by Ted's second wife, Kathleen. Both Ted and his first wife, Bertha, are dead. Kathleen chose not to share any knowledge she has of Ted and Bertha's early days with Bill, or of her and Ted's later days. Some correspondence survives, but it becomes relevant at a later stage in the biography.

It was about this time that Bill became uneasy with the name that he'd given his mountain home. There is some speculation that the "Potter's Sanctuary" title aligned him too closely with the lot of being a mere potter—a creator of the mundane. It was not yet the time for disassociating himself from the concept that he was participating in a field of art though, for he renamed the site "The Mountain Gallery". Similarly, Bill called himself not a modeller or potter, but a sculptor of clay.

The notion of journeying to Central Australia to gain first hand experience of the Aborigines he was now so close to in spirit lay strong upon Bill's mind. Two things would have kept him back—his mother and the method of how to do it. His mother was aging and such was the relationship between them that Bill would have found it very difficult to leave her in the care of others should he go away.

Regarding the how to do it, we rely on the memory of R. H. Croll's son. R. H. Croll had already participated in successful expeditions to the Centre, and it was only natural that Bill should turn to him with his plans for advice. But it seems that Bill, who at that stage could not drive a motor vehicle, was in for an adventure. He wanted to undertake the journey in the manner of the great explorers and adventurers; by bullock wagon, horse or camel. R. D. Croll recalled:

> *"Father dissuaded him from going up in the manner by which he desired, and he had a difficult job persuading Bill Ricketts to go by safer means. He's a very difficult chap to dissuade from his ideas, but fortunately for Ricketts anyway, father was apparently successful.*
>
> *Father used to come back almost in despair, saying 'I hope I can save the silly fool's life!', because Ricketts is about as practical as—well, he's not practical, and the idea of him going up and battling as a bushman just absolutely appalled my father because he knew he wouldn't have had a hope."*

While the desire to reach the interior by more romantic means than a motor vehicle was surely influenced by the practical fact that Bill could not drive, it is easy to imagine more subtle matters of the mind coming into play. Bill was pioneering a bridging of the gulf between races via the medium of sculpture, and being favourably recognised for his efforts. He may have thought that the impact of his work would have been magnified had he taken the pioneering image to its limit of man battling the elements in order to progress his mission. Or he may have thought that the journey should be completed in the manner of the man for whom he then saved his greatest respect, Sir Baldwin Spencer.

This respect for Spencer must have been immense, extending to the point where a catalogue written by Olga Waller for a 1941 exhibition [and presumably sanctioned by Bill] included the statement: **"Ricketts has a deep and loving veneration and hero-worship for Sir Baldwin Spencer, for his sympathy and understanding of the Aboriginal mind and life."** Bill honoured Spencer, who was by then deceased, by making him the only recognisable non-Aboriginal, other than Bill himself, to be included in his work. Spencer was always depicted with Aborigines who were either explaining their culture, or guiding him through the features of their land.

The culmination of this idolisation seems to have occurred in 1940 when it was reported in

Melbourne's *Sun* newspaper that Bill was working on a two and a half metre group which was to be a memorial to Spencer. No subsequent reference to that work has been found, so it is assumed that, like many other major pieces, it did not survive a firing.

In mentioning so large a sculptural group it is time to bring into the story the Australian Tessellated Tile Company Pty Ltd [ATTC] of Mitcham [Melbourne]. The company was operated by brothers Edgar and Donald Walker at the time of Bill's first association. ATTC produced a range of kiln fired clay products and had kilns which were capable of taking the large-sized works which Bill wanted to produce. Edgar's son, Geoff, now operates Walker Ceramics, in Croydon [Melbourne], and continued the support commenced by his father and uncle by supplying clay and doing the odd bit of firing for Bill. Geoff remembered seeing as a young boy the shattered remains of Bill's large-scale works, of the size that now feature in the Sanctuary, at the Mitcham factory. No doubt the transition from creating and firing small works to the monumental-sized pieces was a painful one for Bill.

Bill was again given national exposure in February, 1940, when *Pix* magazine devoted a full page to him under the heading of "Aboriginal Legends Told In Potter's Clay". The mainly pictorial article featured four photographs with captions and one paragraph of text in which Bill is quoted as saying: *"I am hoping to play my humble part in paving the way to a new world, where all people, white and coloured, will advance side by side with the light of understanding in their eyes."*

In May 1940, an exhibition featuring Bill's work was organised by Miss Hilda J. King, and shown at International Needlecraft in Melbourne's Block Arcade. It was a fund-raising event for an organisation called the Aboriginal Uplift Society, whose stated aim was *"to help the native to help himself"*,[3] although it appears that this help was directed towards assisting Aborigines to become urbanised. As well as Bill's sculpture, there were examples of Aboriginal implements, basket-work, weaving and other handicraft displayed. Just over a year later, in August 1941, another educational show was put together by the Australian Museum in Sydney. Held in the David Jones Auditorium, the exhibition featured static displays of Aboriginal art, commercial applications of Aboriginal motifs and art which had been inspired by Aboriginal daily life, religion and mythology. The last category included ten privately and publicly-owned works by Bill. The exhibition was also a stage for seven lectures by such experts in indigenous culture as F. D. McCarthy, A. P. Elkin, and Margaret Preston.

Olga Waller's catalogue for the February 18th to March 10th, 1941 exhibition opened by R. H. Croll at the Velasquez Galleries in Bourke Street, Melbourne, provides a good overview of what Bill was putting before his public. Mrs Waller began by laying Bill's cards face up, leaving no doubt as to where his sympathies lay:

> *"The trapping of ... wild things ... to bedizen women with furs, the wanton shooting of birds, the needless felling of ... trees and the hideous ruin of both plant and animal life through bush-fires ... fill him with a raging sorrow and a flaming anger that he cannot put into words, but must express in some way. That way is by sculpturing ... the legends of the ancient Australians, whose folk-lore shows clearly that ... they did feel the divine behind the common things of life, and therefore they felt the comradeship between their human life and the plant and animal life around them. Thus Ricketts, by his 'legends in clay', is making the black man the missionary to the white man, to teach again the brotherhood of all living things."*

Mrs Waller gave brief explanations of the twenty-one major works featured at the exhibition, although it would seem that a number of smaller pieces were available as well.

---

3 As stated in a review of the exhibition by W. Whitford Hazel which appeared in the *Sun News-Pictorial*, May 21, 1940.

The first work mentioned was titled, "A Call". Olga Waller did not describe it, saying only that it was *"both a self-portrait and a self-revelation of the way in which he regards his work"*. While I have not seen this piece, I imagine that it would be based on the same lines as the pieces entitled "My Country", which are discussed later.

David Unaipon's writing about his *"ancient father's"* version of the creation of all things was then quoted, which set the stage and provided a starting point for Waller's descriptions:

> *"At the beginning of creation, Man was present in Spirit, and with spirit vision beheld the wonderful transformation of Life coming out of the slimy water, overshadowed with dense atmosphere and heat. The first of the Spirit Life to select bodies of flesh and blood were the lower orders and kingdom of the earthly spirit, which consisted of such forms and shapes as those demonstrated in the varieties and diversities of fish, reptiles ... and insect life—creatures evolved by the power of their intelligence and capacity, according to their own fancy—each species considering itself superior to others. As observed, some were walking, crawling, hopping, wiggling and flitting on the surface of the earth, and some were swimming and paddling and floating in the water, and making a wonderful array of body shapes and forms ... When the appointed period arrived, Spirit Man made the great decision and adventure to be clothed with earthly body of flesh and blood. His spirit consciousness experienced a great change, for he was overshadowed by another self—the subjective consciousness, which entirely belongs to the earth, and not to the Sacred Realm of the Spirit, the Father of all Mankind—Eternal Home. He began to realise that the spirit self was controlled by an earthly subjective consciousness, which bound him to earth's environment, with all its blessings, disappointments, discomfort, and its pain and sorrow. Being a stranger to a strange land, he found it difficult to adapt himself to Earth's environs. His spirit began to fret and pine for its Heavenly Home. The living creatures of the earth saw his plight, and were moved with pity and with sympathy. They gathered around him, and by their knowledge and instinct, taught man how to seek shelter in a tree top or within a cave, and warned him of approaching danger of storm and hail and rain.*
>
> *And thus did Man's subjective consciousness grow in wisdom and in knowledge, from instruction of earthly creatures—the kangaroo, emu, goanna, and the insect life—the beetle, the spider and the ant. Thus all the tribes of Aborigines of Australia have, from time immemorial, selected living creatures as companions and guides. This is Totemism, one of the most ancient customs of primitive man—companionship of earthly creatures— each tribe having its own particular animal totem—thus we have the tribes of the kangaroo men, the emu men and the lizard men, and so on."*

The other major works were:

No. 2 "The First Man", which came straight from Unaipon's story and featured the fretting and pining first man being comforted by the earthly creatures.

No. 3 "The Upsurge of Life", represented humanity's struggle towards the light from the mass of newly created life.

No. 4 "The Kangaroo Men", portraying men of the Kangaroo Totem carrying their tywerrenge stone.[4] [Although not specified in the catalogue, some or all of the men portrayed would have been depicted in the half-human-half-kangaroo form.]

---

4 "Tywerrenge" is the current correct Arrernte spelling for the sacred stone or wooden objects, often elongated-oval in shape, into which intricate lines are carved as representations of a Dreaming story. They can be of varying significance and power, from personal tywerrenges handed from father to son, through to tywerrenges holding the story of an entire totemic group or clan. Bill's repeated use the oval shape and simple representations of tywerrenges in his creations was an attempt to incorporate an element of ancient sacredness, which he believed added to the overall power and spirituality of his message. Variant spelling includes "churinga" and "tjurunga". Spelling of "tywerrenge" supplied by Gavin Breen, IAD, Alice Springs.

No. 5   "The Friend of the Arunta", portrayed Baldwin Spencer being told of a tywerrenge's story and powers by it custodians.

No. 6   "Sir Baldwin Spencer at Eyre's Rock",[5] featured Spencer and two Aboriginal men.

No. 7/8/9 Depicted variations of the legend of the euros' [a kangaroo-like animal] creation, whereby in a time of need two great personalities from the Dreaming blew along their long beards, from the end of which jumped the first euros.

No. 10 "The Legend of the Evening Star", depicted the young maiden who, as the evening star, journeys across the sky, to sink into the stones on the horizon each evening.

No. 11 "The Origin of Heavitree Gap", showed how Alice Springs' southern gateway through the Macdonnell Ranges was formed in the Dreaming by Intwailuka.

No. 12 "The Lizard Inkata", portrayed a guide of the people of the lizard totem.

No. 13/14 Depictions of individuals at their Nanja; a personally sacred and safe place within an individual's country.

No. 15/16 Variations of the theme that has the spirit leave the human body at death, usually in the form of a small bird, to hurry back to its Nanja. These spirits can be reincarnated at the right time and can be seen by specially gifted individuals.

No. 17 "A Symphony of Legends", was a fountain piece featuring two large pitchis and adorned with many of the legends already mentioned.[6]

No. 18 "Three Initiates at the Wollunqua Fountain", portrayed three initiated men at a fountain around which is coiled the greatest mythical serpent, said to be 150 miles long, which travelled in subterranean tunnels, leaving behind spirit children. This serpent is widely known as the Rainbow Serpent.

No. 19 A fun piece featuring a group of boys telling each other stories in the company of a giant frill-necked lizard.

No. 20 "The Spirit of the Great Tree", in which Bill developed his own mythology, giving a forest tree scarred by wild-fire a spirit of its own which sought to protect the bush animals from the carelessness of the white man's burning.

No. 21 "Mother and Son", a portrait of Bill and Susan Ricketts.

As can be seen, Bill's exhibitions were not mere displays of art, but, for the most part, journeys into a mysterious unknown.

The undated manuscript of a short essay entitled "William Ricketts—His Ideals and His Art",[7] written by Hilda King at around this time, reveals the extent to which Bill was publicly revealing his spirituality, which had previously only been hinted at and not taken up in the press. Miss King, a Quaker, seems to have been the first to concentrate on Bill's philosophy and spirituality, rather than the usual appraisals and descriptions of his work. For this reason it is significant and reprinted here in part:

> *"At the opening of an Exhibition of Aboriginal 'Legends in Clay', now being held at the Melbourne Technical College, Mr Ricketts ... spoke of his great desire to have us see and understand his idealism, and his faith that 'Ye all shall be one' ... His description of 'art as a continuous prayer', and his belief that 'art is only giving back to God what already belongs to God,' make us realize how inspired and spiritual is his sculpture.*

---

5 "Eyre's" was the spelling given in the catalogue, as opposed to Ayres. The rock is now known by its original name, Uluru.

6 The "pitchi" is the shallow, oblong bowl carved from wood. It is also known as a "coolamon" or "wirra".

7 The manuscript suggests that Bill has been on the mountain for eight and a half years, which would date it at approximately 1941 or 1942.

When the sculptor spoke of those visitors to his sanctuary in the mountains, who failed to find their conception of God 'in the lovely saplings all around me reaching up to the light', one felt that here is a man who has identified himself with nature in such a way, that surely he is part of the Eternal plan for the Universe. His philosophy is more than pantheism, for he combines his love for God in nature, with a passionate love for the divine in all men. For eight and a half years, Mr Ricketts has grown with those saplings, until his hate for the white man ... 'has been purged out of me by beauty', and now he feels transformed ...

He spoke of ... how the greatest in art and music has been drawn from the folk-lore of different countries. 'Grieg of Norway, Sibelius of Finland, Richard Wagner and his Siegfried legend, all these men drew their glowious[8] music from the legends of their beloved soil. Smetana, the Czech, in his symphonic poem, gives out in his lovely music the tiny spring bubbling from the side of the mountain, then joined by other springs, flowing out to become the Moldow River, which not only waters the soil of Czecho-Slovakia, but flows over the Czech frontier and in to the world beyond.'

'I therefore link my thoughts ... with these great composers, and in the sanctuary about which I dream, and for which I plan for Australia, I will regard my art as a tiny spring, which will grow in magnitude and do something to help give back to the Australian Aboriginals that which they have lost. Give them back their self-respect and a bigger chance to live the life God meant them to live alongside the white man.' "

An important hint of things to come was given—his *"plan for Australia"*.

WWII was well under way, but unlike WWI which passed him by, Bill would this time have the threat of horrors undreamed come knocking on his door. At some point near the beginning of 1942, Bill was notified of his call-up into the Australian Infantry Forces.

How he reacted is not clear, but the issue did not seem to worry him too much. The first mention of it I found was contained in a letter to R. H. Croll, dated April 24th, 1942. The two page letter went into some detail about past and current financial struggles, his thoughts on when to go to Ernabella in the Musgrave Ranges and what work he would like to take. In one short line he wrote, almost in passing, *"I have put the military people off for a few weeks"*. The next reference comes from a letter dated six months later, in October 1942, by which time things must have been getting a little warm for Bill. It came in the form of a letter of reply sent to W. A. Waller [Olga's husband] by F. R. Sinclair, of the Department of the Army. It reads:

"I am in receipt of your letter of the 25th October, 1942, regarding William Ricketts, a sculptor in clay at Dandenong, and have had action taken to investigate his case.

Unfortunately, this case is typical of thousands that are coming constantly under notice where the man who is called up is firmly of the belief that the work he is doing, or the principles of his life are such that military service for the nation should not be undertaken under any circumstances.

I regret that, keeping firmly in mind the knowledge that at a time like the present when our nation is at war with a deadly enemy and in danger of being overwhelmed, my own feeling is that every man, no matter what his walk of life may be, should be prepared to place his services at the disposal of the nation, and if necessary, throw himself into the breach as they are doing at present in Stalingrad.

Probably 20% of our people adopt, for some reason or another, the same attitude as Ricketts, but I shall do what I can in regard to this case, and see that it is given every consideration."

---

8 Glowious is spelled faithful to the manuscript.

Although I did not sight Mr Waller's original letter, a hand-written copy of his reply to Sinclair, dated November 1st, 1942, gives some indication as to the original's contents, as well as hinting that special influence was at work. It reads:

> *"I thought I might have seen you at Church today to thank you for what you have promised to do in regard to Ricketts' case. I appreciate your undertaking all the more considering your personal attitude to the case. I understand your point of view completely. It is natural for anyone who does not know Ricketts intimately to put him with the thousands who, for various personal reasons, try to avoid their duty to Australia; but Ricketts, so far from being of use in any military capacity, is likely to become a charge of the state if he is coerced; for, as I think I said in my previous letter, I fear that he will be mentally deranged if he is taken from his 'mission' as an interpreter in Clay of the Aborigines and their folklore with its revelation of their spiritual background."*

It would appear that Mr Waller forwarded Bill a letter of support and advice at a similar time to his first letter to Sinclair. Bill's reply to that letter, dated October 30th, 1942, gives a good indication of how he mobilised himself to protect his own freedom so that he could continue to fight his own battle:

> *"I received your welcome letter, & I shall do all I can to help the position. I am most thankful in the effort you are making regarding the call up. Just before I received your letter I sent a letter to the Clerk of Courts Ringwood asking for exemption.*
>
> *The man power man at Ringwood told me to do so straight away.*
>
> *They said I had nothing to fear about. Mr. A. Williams of the Tourist Bureau Mlb ask the man power people to do what good they could and they have kept their hands off here. Mr. Williams has a very important position there. I am sending money for catalogues. Two pieces sold and many small ones.*
>
> *One fine bush loving girl from Sydney wants to send 5gns towards the full amount for something I could send her. So I have finished something for her for 5gns. Two others from Sydney have sent money for small pieces. They saw something in someones place.*
>
> *I look and hope to have my position cleared then I shall try and take away a set of conditions holding me up. My reason for exemption is hardship. My mother needs attention and has nowhere to go. The military have power and if they also have wisdom then they may want to do the right thing.*
>
> *Again my thanks for all the kind help towards making the opening day a success ..."* [9]

Another letter sent by Bill to Mr Waller, loosely dated November, furthers the call-up issue and provides more to look at on the periphery:

> *"I just received a letter from Dr. Short of Lilydale. I asked him for it.*
>
> *He attended my Mother and his letter says my Mother is in failing health and needs constant care and attention. I shall present to Ringwood court on 25th Nov. I have decided to sell this property and try to see what is to be had in Victoria. I have to give my Mother something better than bare boards and boxes to live with. Also I need studio and kiln and a little furniture for house. I have put something in Saturday's Argus, it will be just near the leading column. I have asked people of Victoria for their help in my getting*

---

9 The grammatical mistakes in Bill's writings are many and varied. So as to maintain the authenticity, I have not edited the transcripts of his letters or quoted statements; apart from joining some paragraphs for reasons of space efficiency. Nor have I inserted the academically required "sic" after his mistakes.

a large mountain property. I must do this to take away a set of conditions that has been with me all along.

I have given much thought to my plans. As I see things now I think I must not leave my own white skin folk to work all the time among our dark skin folk. If I leave my own people then I would deprive them of something they have taken to heart. So I think my plans will be both here and sometimes among our native folk.

I want something like 5 to 10 years thought and work, and then a mountain spectacle would begin to appear.

Mr. Leo Junck of Wunderlich Ltd Sth. Melbourne is a splendid man who has done a very great deal for me here. He is a good man of means and said to me last night when he called here that a committee should be formed and he would join it. He would do much.

Mr. Croll I am sure would do much also. As my vision is nothing short of a contribution to that beautiful and true expression of life among two peoples now living alongside one another in this country, I want to ask you what you thought.

Mr. Junck will buy this property without works of art. If you think a committee should be formed I would have 400 pounds towards this Australian mountain spectacle devoted to our native race and Australia. Mr. Junck said now would be a good time. He said men have money they can not spend on property etc and therefore he thinks if a few men got together and contacts with other men would bring results. Mr. Elizah of Education Dept has 800 acres running down from Bourkes lookout here. Tom Bourke's old place. Mr. Croll asked him for me but he said he did not want visitors on it to spoil it. I would not do the wrong thing. The place would be more like a doctor's place if I had it."

Bill went as far as reporting to the Army camp at Ringwood for his medical examination, which he says he passed, with it being only *"a week or so"* away from actually stepping into the khakis before he was exempted from any military service. Whether it was as a result of Mr Waller and the other supporters who rallied to his defence or Bill's actions is not known.

When I asked him about it, Bill had distilled the incident to its basics:

"My dream could have been buggered up if I had of gone—I could have met with an accident, anything could have happened. So I just went sailing along here, preparing my way for what was to come."

The *"two pieces sold and many small ones"* mentioned in the October 30th, 1942, letter refers to the first "official" opening of the Mountain Gallery, conducted at some time during that same month, with the honour of opening going to R. H. Croll. The *Argus* mentioned the exhibition two days before it was due to end in spite of the fact that the Sanctuary was a permanent exhibition, but said nothing of the opening. They did, however, report that attendances had been surprisingly good, considering the wartime restrictions on travel—so good in fact that Bill had hinted that he may move the whole Sanctuary to a better location, *"if one can be procured"*. Bill's statement in the next letter that he intended to sell relates directly to his wanting to take away the set of conditions mentioned in the first.

Bill had forgotten completely what those conditions were when I asked him about it. The Land Title shows that there were two caveats taken out on the land after his assumption of rates responsibility; the first lodged on June 26th, 1935, which lapsed on July 22nd, 1941, and the second lodged on May 17th, 1937, which was withdrawn on April 30th, 1938. The caveat documents are no longer in the Titles Office and are presumed destroyed.

In a letter to R. H. Croll dated April 24th, 1942, a vague hint was given to a potential cause of the unfavourable "set of conditions":

"... I spent my last money at the time as a deposit on this land & I owed money everywhere. At that very time business men came at me wanting to do this & that (set me up). At the beginning I realised that I had very precious material in my hands. This very material I have given my life to. That precious seed of Australia was planted in the soil of my mind, & is growing with grace & strong arms.

I had to tell those business men, that I had only one path to take, & I took it (Thank God). I let everything go, & just before my last exhibition I got into trouble over my last payment on my land, & many times before that. At the point of being thrown out, a man 27 miles from here stopped the rot.

However I still owe £275 on my land here ..."

Were the caveats results of previous debts? It is more likely that the first caveat was taken out by the previous owner, Campbell, to protect his asset until such time that it was paid off, especially when the lapsing date is considered. The second and shorter caveat, I'd imagine, would have been unlikely to cause Bill bother three years after its withdrawal. The "man 27 miles from here" was Leo Junck, who loaned Bill the £275 which effectively refinanced the land loan, but gave him a sympathetic creditor. This resulted in Bill finally having the title transferred to his name on May 5th, 1941. Since Junck was offering to buy the block from Bill, and receiving Bill's praise, it could hardly be to Junck that the "conditions" referred.

The advertisement which Bill placed in the *Argus* newspaper in an attempt to find another property on which to create his mountain spectacle read:

PEOPLE OF VICTORIA—I Need Your Help

I require MOUNTAIN PROPERTY, with Natural Forest and Running Water, on which to create a Permanent Clay Sculpture Art Gallery devoted to the Australian Aborigine and all Australians.

MY LIFE GIFT TO AUSTRALIA

Write with full particulars to

WM. RICKETTS, THE SANCTUARY, Mt. Dandenong

That this plea was unsuccessful is evidenced by the present location of the Sanctuary, but to my knowledge he did not continue to run the advertisements.

Wanting to *"give my Mother something better than bare boards and boxes to live with"*, and needing a *"studio and kiln and a little furniture"* make it clear that Bill was not simply forgoing any luxury for the sake of his chosen mission. He didn't necessarily want the privations that came with total devotion to a cause, and still didn't later in his life. Anyone who had Bill to their house will confirm that he desired a warm space to stretch out in, a table at which he could seat himself and visitors, or a spacious kitchen. Yet, as will be seen, when the Government takeover came around and he was supplied those "luxuries", he quickly converted any spare space into working and display areas. Bill's privations had always been self-imposed, although maybe imposed unconsciously. That his mother endured the same is a clear measure of her devotion to her son.

Bill's statements that, *"... I think I must not leave my own white skin folk to work all the time among our dark skin folk"*, and *"If I leave my own people then I would deprive them of something they have taken to heart"*, go towards answering an often-asked question. If he had such great respect for the Aboriginal race and a general loathing for the whites, why didn't he seek to live with the Aborigines permanently? Quite simply, he was working towards changing the attitudes of non-Aboriginals, and what better base could there be than on the doorstep of a major capital city where he had access not only to a large population, but an active press?

Bill was now giving much thought to his plan for Australia. The degree of public support he was receiving allowed him the luxury of confidently formulating a grand plan. In December 1943, he wrote to R. H. Croll:

> *"... My plan will now be National.*
> *An American officer called looked at the work took a lot of small pieces & said You are the Sibelius of Australia. That great man of Finland used the folk lore legend of his native land sometimes. And because his music was truly National the Government gave him a grant to carry out just what he wanted to do. I do not & will not ask the Government for any money. I will do the giving. I will now write out my plans."*

He went on to outline his plans to seek input from Dr Charles Duguid [who was doing much to improve the lot of Aborigines, and was instrumental in establishing Ernabella[10]] and Charles P. Mountford [ethnologist], both of South Australia. He would sound out Sydney *"where a great deal of my work goes"* for support. He would encourage the press to support the plan and asked Croll to see if he could interest Harold Herbert in visiting the Sanctuary: *"... not for myself, but [for] the whole plan"*. He also asked Croll for help.

In February, 1944, Herbert had a small article published in the *Australian*. It was a little vague and while acknowledging that *"Reckitts"* [*sic*] was *"fired by an enthusiasm ... that knows no bounds"*, he only gave Bill's work an *"interesting to a degree"* rating. Of the plan: *"It is decidedly the plan of a visionary, and the idea is generally good—a great reserve for the native race. To achieve this, however, and certain educational reforms, the hand of the white man must come into it. And he is against that."*

The plan was finally released in the form of an Open Letter, dated April 20th, 1944. It is a lengthy document, over 2,600 words long, which does not need to be fully reprinted for the foresight exhibited by Bill to be understood.

The letter started with a brief explanation of his work and purpose, and of the favourable response he was receiving. He told how humbly proud and thankful he was to receive a letter from Dr Duguid, in which was written: *"Your work is going to do a tremendous lot to bring the white overlords to their responsibilities which, so far, they have largely evaded."* He quoted an American, Dr E. Stanley Jones, who wrote after visiting Australia some years before WWII: *"I have reluctantly come to the conclusion that the aboriginal is not dying off but he is being killed off ... Each nation has a blind spot, and this is Australia's blind spot ... The basis is ignorance, prejudice and unwillingness to face facts."* He quoted from an ABC radio broadcast given by Dr Duguid, in which the pastoralists' land grab and the subsequent poor working conditions of station Aborigines was outlined, as was the good work going on at the Ernabella mission. Then Bill went on to outline his plan:

> *"Briefly put, my plan is that with the help of others—both white and native folk—I may, before it is forever too late, found a great cultural centre for our native folk. It is a plan that is national in its scope, for its ultimate aim is a fuller understanding between ourselves and the native folk, and also when it is a working reality, it will be there for all the world to see that, at long last, we white Australians have recognized the dignity and worth of the aboriginal people, and honour the beauty of their ancient folk lore and their folk arts.*
>
> *We who have robbed them of so much will now try to make them a little restitution.*
>
> *It will, naturally, be necessary to set aside (either by Government grant or by the gift of some understanding person) a tract of land as a great sanctuary somewhere in Australia where in later times, when fully developed, it will not be entirely inaccessible from our*

---

10 Ernabella's establishment is discussed in Chapter 7.

great centres of population where future generations will also need to learn to honour our native folk.

I would desire mountain, plain and river country, partly set (if still possible) amid virgin forest—a piece of the 'real Australia' as our native folk knew it before the white man came. This great reserve must be kept inviolate through all future generations—its trees, its native flora and fauna are not to be despoiled by any man."

Into that tract of land would go Bill, and he would spend an estimated five years preparing life-size sculptures depicting the ancient tales from folklore and setting those works into the natural rock features present.

"Thus, by these, my works in that sanctuary, I want to show not only to all the world, but most especially to our native folk how much I honour them, and pay a tribute to the beauty of their folk lore. I want them to feel that when they come there, here is one who has prepared a welcome for them in a great art spectacle of their own people's ancient beliefs and customs."

During the initial build-up, Bill proposed, word would be spread among Australia's "full-blood" Aboriginal population, telling them of the centre's establishment and inviting them to come as families to participate in the building. When it was finished, the "detribalised" and dispossessed Aborigines would be invited to attend and relearn what had been denied them through the robbing of their cultural heritage.

"... Artists among them will, I hope, want to come in from anywhere in Australia and teach those amongst them wishing to develop their ancient skills in aboriginal designs in drawing, woodwork and carving and stonework, and, above all, in expressing themselves in music and dancing—a new form of ballet. I myself could teach the younger children and older folk how to express themselves in clay. All these arts and crafts would be developed along true aboriginal lines, and one can envisage in the distant future our native folk giving to the world their own special contribution of beauty in music, art, ballet and also in literature.

Works of art by these native craftsmen could be sold and so help to support them, and I myself would help with this by the sale of my own works."

Bill proposed an extensive library of collections of legends, folklore and subjects relevant to Aborigines from all over Australia, as well as a concerted effort to develop written forms of Aboriginal languages to aid with education. Bill envisaged a leisurely introduction of agrarian skills to assist with the transition that must dramatically reduce the dependence of a hunter-gatherer existence. Ultimately those coming to the centre would be taught building skills, from which Bill foresaw a distinctly Aboriginal style of architecture being developed.

"... Native folk will be coming and going I hope from all parts of Australia, and others living there permanently. All native children living or born in south-eastern Australia and elsewhere can come in at their wish to breathe in the language of the art and music of their native race.

Thus the children of the eastern part of Australia will learn to know their brothers and sisters from the Musgrave Ranges and elsewhere, and a new feeling of national unity will begin to make itself felt amongst them ...

It must of course be clearly understood that no white man can come into this reserve without proper procedure, or even be allowed to live there unless they are acting temporarily as teachers, anthropologists, or advisers to the native people.

White people and, above all, white children may visit under the conduct of native guides, so that they learn and understand at first hand about the folk-lore of the Australian native race. This sanctuary and all therein shall be the property of the native folk ..."

It was a truly grand and visionary concept which could have done much to stem the decimation of Aboriginal culture which had proceeded virtually unchecked since the first white foot stepped onto Australian soil. Admittedly, much had already been lost beyond saving, but the start would have at least been made. The potential ramifications of such a program having been instigated in 1944 are well beyond my comprehension. How many languages alone could have been saved from extinction—not to mention arts, folklore and legends, or knowledge of survival techniques, bush foods and medicines? Such a centre could have been the repository for knowledge that the old people were looking for. More importantly, it would have given such ancient knowledge a greater sense of worth and made it desirable knowledge to have. The younger generations of Aborigines would have had reason to learn, because it would have been seen to be worth learning. What the evolution of artistic endeavour would have produced can only be guessed at, but if the growth of Aboriginal commercial art during the past fifteen years is any sort of guide, the results could well have been extraordinary.

Unfortunately, Bill's timing could not have been worse. WWII was the overwhelming captivator of public attention, to the exclusion of almost everything else. Australia, like the other WWII Allies, was devoted to winning a battle greater than that which Bill fought. Besides which, Australia already had, as far as it was concerned, a solution to the Aboriginal "problem".

Those were the dark days of the assimilation policy, when curiosity value was the only worth assigned to anything traditionally Aboriginal. The Aborigines' "primitive" and "uncivilised" lifestyle was to be replaced as they were brought into the folds of the white community. After all, how could a "black" who wasn't worthy of the responsibility of citizenship, as far as the country's decision-makers were concerned, be capable of determining their own future? Contemplation of Aboriginal Land Rights would have been unthinkable for most in 1944, especially with white Australians so recently fearful that they would be negotiating their own land rights with the Japanese invasion forces.

There were, of course, matters for which Bill did not have immediate answers. The costs associated with establishment and administration, and transporting penniless Aborigines to and from centres within various regions of Australia would have been astronomical, for Bill ultimately envisaged such centres dotted all over the country. How potential cultural clashes between different groups would have been avoided was also left unaddressed. Such matters could have been solved by brain trusts put together to realise the project—but the nation's thinkers were otherwise occupied.

Bill had done his job—he provided the vision. But it quickly became apparent that if it was to become a reality, Bill would also have to provide the means.

1 *My earliest photo of Bill. Written on the rear of the original, in Bill's hand, was: "To Auntie Nell, With Love from Will Ricketts. St Kilda 2.5.18". Bill would have been 19. Photographer unknown.*

2 *Susan Ricketts, Bill's mother. Date and photographer unknown.*

3 *Alfred Ricketts, Bill's father, with the miniature steam train at St Kilda. c. 1920, photographer unknown.*

4 *The kiln identified by Bill as the first at Potter's Sanctuary, taken shortly after his move to the mountain. c. 1935. Courtesy of the* Age *newspaper.*

5 *Bill at Potter's Sanctuary c. 1935, holding a vase titled, Nanja, which was purchased by the SMAAS in 1938. Ins: "Wm Ricketts 1934 Melbourne". The piece bore a paper sticker on which was written, "My first modeling [sic] attempt. WR"; obviously inaccurate. 343 mm high.*

6 *Small dish with female figure. Ins:
"William Ricketts Melbourne 1934".
90 mm high, PC.*

7 *Tree man. Ins: "Wm Ricketts 1934".
185 mm high, PC.*

8 *Tree spirit vase. Ins: "Wm Ricketts Potter's Sanctuary
Mt Dandenong 1936". 192 mm high, PC.*

9 *Separate koalas. The piece on the right is unsigned, but
almost identical to that on the left which is inscribed: "Wm
Ricketts Potters Sanctuary Mt Dandenong 1936". Left,
97 mm high; right, 94 mm high, PC.*

11 *Lizard. Inscription obscured. 43 mm high, unglazed, PC.*

10 *Reproduced from a post-card titled: "Self-study of the Potter with his pet rabbit at his feet. Photograph … Mendelssohn Studios." Size unknown, c. 1930s.*

12 *Pepper shaker decorated with gum leaves and gum nuts. Ins: "Wm Ricketts 1934". 86 mm high, PC.*

13 *Vase, rare for its colouring. Ins: "Wm Ricketts Melbourne 1934". 173 mm high, PC.*

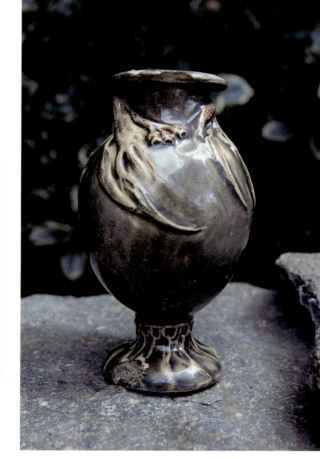

14 & 15 *Arrernte men explaining the mysteries of a large tywerrenge to Baldwin Spencer. Ins: "Wm Ricketts". c. 1940. 600 mm long, PC.*

16 *Explorer [unidentified] being guided through traditional country. Ins: "William Ricketts 1934". 258 mm high, unglazed, PC.*

17 *Reproduced from a post-card titled: "The Potter at work in Potter's Sanctuary. Photograph ... Mendelssohn Studios." c. 1930s.*

18 *Ancestral kangaroo-man. Ins: "Wm Ricketts Potters Sanctuary Mt Dandenong 1938". 184 mm high, PC.*

19 *Ancestral kangaroo-men. The tallest being holds the totemic group's sacred tywerrenge. Date, size and photographer unknown.*

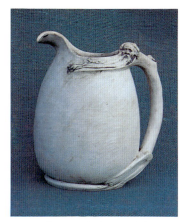

20 *Jug featuring the legend of the euros' creation. Ins: "Wm Ricketts Potters Sanctuary Mt Dandenong 1936". 224 mm high, PC.*

21 *Jug or vase, unusual for the tree fern decoration. Ins: "PS MD". 228 mm high, PC.*

22 *Jug featuring a spearman in a delicate bas-relief. Ins: "Wm Ricketts Potters Sanctuary Mt Dandenong 1937". 170 mm high, PC.*

23 *Jug with rare colouring. The top is pitchi shaped. Inscription obscured. 120 mm high, PC.*

24 & 25. *"Pitchi" bowls are not uncommon and vary greatly in their size and delicacy of construction. Top ins: "Wm Ricketts Potters Sanctuary Mt Dandenong 1937". 390 mm long, PC. Lower ins: "Wm Ricketts Potters Sanctuary Mt Dandenong Jan 4th 1938". 486 mm long, PC.*

26 *Child sitting beside a stump. Ins: "Wm Ricketts Melbourne 1936". 70 mm high, PC.*

27 *Lidded vase, titled Churinga Talk. The lid, which fits inside the pitchi shape, has a small version of Spencer receiving instruction from Arrernte men. Unfortunately, Spencer and one Arrernte have lost their heads! Ins: "Wm Ricketts Potter's Sanctuary Mt Dandenong 1937". 290 mm high. Courtesy of the Trustees of the Museum of Applied Arts and Sciences, Sydney. Photo by author.*

28 *Kookaburras often featured in Bill's early work. Ins: "Wm Ricketts Potter's Sanctuary Mt Dandenong 1936". 88 mm high, PC.*

29 *Susan and Bill outside their original hut at Potter's Sanctuary. c. 1940s.*

30 *This swagman is a diversion from Bill's usual themes. The character's "swag" is hidden from view on the far side. Ins: "Wm Ricketts 193 [2 or 3]". Actual figure 110 mm high, PC.*

7 | Taking the Plan to the People
[1944–1949]

"Smack in the middle of this golden age of mediocrity after a flatulent artistic period during which every budding Rembrandt has done little more than exploit a drearily familiar Europeanism a little worse than the one before comes William Ricketts to the Velasquez Gallery to revive hope in Australia's artistic future with a brilliantly individual medium.

This little man, with a fantastic sweep of imagination, has interpreted in clay aborigine legends which are older than time, and each piece captures in a thoroughly virile way the genuine spirit of Australia. Although it may seem startling on first thought, it's perfectly logical that the reputedly decadent aboriginal should have inspired the most virile Australian art of our time. We've always been chary about applying the label genius, but there it is starkly displayed at the Velasquez Gallery right now ..."

So ran the inimitable review by the Melbourne *Truth* newspaper, more noted in recent times for its flourishes of sensationalism and exposed female flesh. The occasion was Bill's major exhibition at the Velasquez Gallery, jointly opened by R. H. Croll and Mrs Helen B. Wessells of the United States Information Library, on April 26th, 1944, only a matter of days after the Open Letter's release. Even news of the war did not completely overshadow the wide and favourable coverage the exhibition received.

In the *Age*, J. S. MacDonald wrote:

"His enthusiasm fills his life and he teems with matter to express it ... The fertility of his invention in all these sculptures is astonishing, and one wonders how the supply can be kept up, but this fear no doubt is groundless. No one is putting up a finer fight against the destruction of our noble trees, beautiful and unique animals and birds, soil erosion, the uglifying of our landscape and the extinction of the first occupants of this weird and lonely land than William Ricketts."

The *Herald* finished its review with:

"It is a pity that, because of a lack of technical apparatus for treating his work, the sculptures are more fragile than need be. One hopes that this can be overcome.

Here is a show that is truly different and that deserves to be treated with respect. It has genius about it."

Conspicuous by its absence was any real comment about Bill's Open Letter and his plan. Just three days after its first review of the exhibition, the *Herald* ran another three paragraph snippet entitled, "Man of Vision". After barely outlining the plan, the journalist rated it this way:

> *"Is such a project practical? I cannot say. At the least, however, it merits consideration, coming as it does from the heart of a man who, although visionary, is a very sincere and highly talented son of Australia."*

Bill sent a copy of the Open Letter to the Director of the SMAAS, Mr A. R. Penfold, who in turn forwarded a copy to Professor E. P. Elkin. Elkin was a recognised and published authority on matters Aboriginal. A major contribution of his, first published in 1938, was *The Australian Aborigines: How to understand them.* In 1944 he published *Citizenship for the Aborigines,* in which he offered his approach to achieving such a goal.

In his reply to Penfold, Elkin agreed that Bill's plan was a most desirable one, but recommended that Bill broaden his knowledge by studying the research of people other than just Spencer. Elkin also doubted that "full-blood" Aborigines, who Bill proposed as the teachers in the Cultural Centre, would want to leave their tribal home-lands to participate in the enterprise. Wrote Elkin:

> *"His idea that the natives from the Musgrave Ranges might come to his reserve is looking a long way ahead; moreover, it is trying to keep the tide back to talk of preserving the Aborigines in their original hunting stage, or reviving something like it elsewhere. Our duty and policy is to help these people develop the settled life and to play their part in Australian national life ..."*

When Penfold forwarded Elkin's reply, Bill was not disappointed by the comments. In fact he thought it was quite good. In replying to Penfold, Bill clarified his intended method of approach:

> *"I feel I will go at it as a little child rather than a hard headed anthropologist (yet not quite without science and anthropology) ..."*

Penfold, in the meantime, had been doing some homework and, along with the museum committee, decided to purchase "My Country" to add to their collection. In the July 4th, 1944, letter containing the offer and requesting a price, Penfold described it as *"an outstanding piece of sculpture".* It is almost a certainty that the SMAAS people appraised "My Country" from photographs only, for the ensuing saga could never have eventuated had they inspected the piece first hand. Bill replied that he would not put any price on the work—they could take it!—and then make a donation to his plan as described in the Open Letter. Bill wrote to Croll on July 25th, telling him that the SMAAS Advisory Committee would decide on an offer at their next meeting. His respect for Croll's judgement, along with his lack of faith in finding the support he sought in Australia can be gleaned from the following, taken from that letter:

> *"I do hope you will think my action right. I tell you my plans only & for the time will tell no one else.*
> *I did not think I would but I am working on large works for America. They will go straight to Sydney then to America after Sydney sees them. My work should not in a way leave this country. I do not think artists here or in Sydney will help my plan. So I will speak to America in a very profound way.*
> *I am just about to start on the other My Country. This & the sandhill & others are for America. This new My Country twice as large and a great deal more powerful.*

These new works will show to a much more marked degree what the Herald writer wrote in THE MAN OF VISION shown on my press remarks.

The family who run the Mitcham tile works are placing a special kiln to fire my works at my disposal. So these works will be alive when they come through the fire."

This was the first mention of Bill's going outside of Australia to seek support for his plans. America was probably chosen as a result of the interest shown in his work by the large numbers of US service personnel who visited the Sanctuary and purchased works during WWII, many of whom told him how big a hit the works would be when they arrived back home.

In late November, Bill wrote to Penfold with news that "My Country" was ready to send, although he would have to wait until more coal came to refire the piece. Bill's kiln on the mountain was not large enough to take "My Country", so was the Mitcham tile works waiting for coal? In the letter, Bill stressed that it was the original piece. That may or may not have been the case. When Bill created a work he liked, he very often recreated the concept many times over in an attempt to improve upon the last—as can be read in the July 25th letter to Croll. On January 5th, 1945, "My Country" and a much smaller piece inscribed with the words "Mind Thought Beauty Wrought" left the Sanctuary in packing cases bound for Sydney. They arrived on February 19th, intact according to the acknowledgement forwarded to Bill.

By this time, the beginning of 1945, Bill had rethought his plan of attack for fostering support for his Open Letter vision. Rather than journey to America with his newly created large works, he would give Australia another chance to honour what he saw as its obligations to the dispossessed Aborigines. The new plan would see him take a load of works on a tour, challenging each State with the question of which tract of land they would put aside to be used as a Cultural Centre. All this was explained in a letter to Croll dated February 24th, 1945.

Bill went on to say:

"I have prepared many large works and they will all go to the kiln at Mitcham to be well hardened. They will go there next Thursday so I will be ready in a months time.

First I will show them in Melbourne for the last time. I will not come back. Would you help me. I want to show them in the lower town hall one third of that space would do. Perhaps something else would take the rest of the space with me. I would want it for a month from about the first week in April. If it is done this way it will be a great success. I have the money to pay for the hall & would give something to the red cross if desired.

My open letter is my drive, now or never.

I have £1,000 towards that plan also I will make another £1,000 from the small pieces heads and plaques about 1,500 of them. I have done these small heads to sell while my works are on show.

I can make as much money as I want at any time when I need it. My works are going to every country oversea. Some one called here the other day. She wants from me a fountain for a dream garden in New Zealand.

Apart from the £1,000 I have towards my open letter I have enough money to buy land & have a house built for my Mother to live in. All this money shows progress because every penny has come from my works. Those works were asked for ..."

Obviously, as far as Bill was concerned, things were going extraordinarily well and he was ready to take on Australia single-handed, if need be. In less than three years he had gone from being deeply in debt to having £1,000 cash in hand, as well as enough money to buy land and have a house built. And he could make as much as he wanted whenever he wanted! A fortunate man—or a naïve man?

By late April, Bill must have grown impatient waiting for the SMAAS to decide what they would offer as a donation in exchange for "My Country". He wrote to the SMAAS stating that he wanted 450gns for "My Country" and 30gns for the smaller work.[1]

The exhibition Bill wanted at the Town Hall never eventuated, and neither did his tour around Australia. What did eventuate was a major problem with the work "My Country". Although it was not mentioned in the letter notifying Bill of the work's arrival, the SMAAS sub-committee came to find firing cracks throughout the piece and claimed that there had not been a fusion of the clay during the firing process. Over a period of four months, while the world was finishing WWII, letters went back and forth, with the SMAAS not wanting to take responsibility for the work's safe return to Victoria, so fearful were they that it could collapse at any time. They did accept the smaller work for 30gns.

On August 12th, 1945, two days before Japan capitulated to end the war, Bill wrote to the SMAAS with news that a new "My Country" had been created and had come through the firing *"hard like marble"*. He offered them this new work in place of the cracked one, claiming that: *"It is a splendid example of my work and I believe it says all I want to say."* Bill again offered the replacement "My Country" on September 25th, and on October 23rd Bill wanted the SMAAS to accept the cracked piece free of charge, and purchase the replacement.

The saga continued right through until December 1948, with yet another letter from Bill in which he apologised for the cracks and speculated that it must have been the carrier. Bill could not clarify the final outcome, and the SMAAS records I sighted did not positively clarify the purchase. The Powerhouse does, however, have a "My Country" piece in its collection, which appears from both the photograph and advice from the curator to be quite sound.[2]

Back to 1945, by which time Bill had established contact with another Adelaide-based ethnologist respected for his work with Australian Aborigines, Charles P. Mountford. The extent of this relationship and how it began was long forgotten by Bill, but it went at least a little further than correspondence between the two.

On September 17th, 1945, Bill wrote to Mountford with news that he had just received "the packet". This was a packet of Mountford's photographs of Aborigines, which Bill used to give more individuality to the characters portrayed in his work.

A look at Bill's work over the full span of his career shows a dramatic change in the detail of the Aboriginal people he portrayed in clay. Initially they were depicted as almost faceless in character, because he was portraying people he did not know. In the early days he was working with a broad concept—the Aboriginal people of Australia. As he became more involved, he realised that his broad concept failed to recognise the individuality within the race. As a result he obtained accurate photographs of individuals, which he translated into the characters in his depictions. The next step, one that he had been wishing to take for years, was to know the living personality with its myriad subtle shades that can only be experienced when meeting face to face. To this end Bill made further moves to visit Ernabella.

Dr Charles Duguid was directly responsible for Ernabella's existence as an Aboriginal mission. In the early 1930s he had seen at first hand what degradation was being suffered by the Central Australian Aboriginal populations who crashed into contact with whites. Yet, by journeying far into the Centralian outback, he was still able to meet a people who retained, to a large degree, their health, pride and dignity. He quickly realised the importance of tribal

---

1 The guinea [gn] was worth 21 shillings, 1 shilling more than the pound [£]. It dates back to the British gold coin taken out of circulation in 1813, but continued as a slightly elitist unit of currency charged for professional services, quality livestock, art and the like. As there was no longer a guinea note or coin, the guinea value was converted to pounds and shillings for actual payment.

2 As a result of one of those ill-timed moments of confusion that besets research every now and then, I did not get to personally view and photograph this "My Country". The photograph appearing on page 107 was kindly supplied by the Powerhouse some time after my visit there in late 1987.

homelands to Aborigines and noted with dismay that the official and social practices towards Aborigines were not only failing, but were in many cases blatantly destructive. He also recognised that the more bad contact with white civilisation had been experienced, the harder it was to rectify the residual problems. Duguid journeyed to the Musgrave Ranges in mid-1935 and after meeting with people of the Pitjantjatjara became *"determined that they should be given the chance to survive in their own country"*.

Back in Adelaide after that journey, he and his wife considered what should be the principles fundamental to the establishment of a mission, deciding that at best it should act as a buffer between the Aborigines and the encroaching white man. They then put the conception of freedom as the most basic principle. In his 1972 book, *Doctor and the Aborigines*, Duguid continued with the principles:

> *"There was to be no compulsion nor imposition of our way of life on the Aborigines, nor deliberate interference with tribal custom. We believed that medical help should be offered at the outset, that only people trained in a particular skill should be on the mission staff and that they must learn the tribal language. As the economy of the mission developed, responsibility should be passed on to the Aborigines as soon as possible.*
> *With the setting up of a school the acceptance of the native tongue would be vital and all teaching for the first years should be in Pitjantjatjara tongue ..."* [3]

The plans were presented to the South Australian Government, which accepted them in principle and authorised Duguid to proceed with the proposal on the condition that he could have it run by a responsible church. The Government would subscribe £1,000 if Duguid could come up with a similar sum. Being closely aligned to the Presbyterian Church, Duguid thought that they should take up the task and set about convincing them of the same. He succeeded in gaining their official support in 1936, with the mission being founded in 1937 and within ten years Ernabella was transformed *"from a rendezvous for Aboriginal-exploiting 'doggers' into a thriving Aboriginal community"*, operating as Duguid had originally proposed.

Bill had corresponded with Rev. J. R. B. Love at Ernabella and in his September 1945, letter to Mountford wrote that Rev. Love had offered to try and make any visit he made a happy one. *"Well I will go there"*, wrote Bill, *"and on my way will exhibit all in Adelaide"*. Mountford was soon to do a lecture tour in the United States, and Bill did not chance a missed opportunity:

> *"I would like the military to lend me one of their trucks to make my tour. I want to hold my money for my big plan. I will ask the military here.*
> *If any Americans would help me this way, I would send a large piece of my work over. They here may refuse me anything in this country. So if you show my photos; and the need of a truck to the Americans, they may do what this country should do ..."*

Things did not move quickly, though, and it was 1947 before Bill was getting close to being ready to leave for Adelaide.

He had an exhibition at the Velasquez Gallery before he left and received an unexpected bonus on the day of the opening. He was given a copy of the December 28, 1946, edition of the *Illustrated London News*, which featured two pages devoted to his work. The feature was titled: "Clay Sculptures Which Summarise The Blackfellow's Legends And Culture: An Australian Artist's Thoughts About The Aborigines". It was a pictorial only, with the photographs of ten works and captions which were little more than rehashed catalogue excerpts. But it did provide

---

3 C. Duguid, *Doctor and the Aborigines*, Rigby, 1972.

an overview of the larger works being created by Bill at the time and it was significant in that it was, to my knowledge, his first exposure in the international press.

By most accounts the exhibition went well. Bill was able to raise £360 through the sale of small pieces and had to resist offers to buy his large works so that the exhibition would remain intact for his Adelaide tour. The show was this time opened by respected sculptor and ally, Ola Cohn, whose most lasting contribution to Melbourne is the famed Fairy Tree in the Fitzroy Gardens.

The exhibition featured a couple of newly expressed themes, including two pieces simply entitled, "Inscribed work". The exhibition catalogue, still being written by Olga Waller, contained a transcript of one of those inscribed pieces, which read:

> *"Life is love all enfolding for being part of nature, we are brothers to the birds and trees. Will you then join with us in the sacredness of beauty.*
>
> *Because at our highest, we are part of the beauty of the world, we know we are part of its creator and designer, and so, in the expression of our minds, and hearts, and hands, we give back to God what emanates from God.*
>
> *Each one of us is a transformer of divine power, and when love finds form in sculpture and music, we are richly blessed because through such we can reach God. The only way to retain love for oneself is to give it abundantly to others. So I, your brother, William Ricketts, hope you will share and enjoy all these things with me.*
>
> *Let this be our prayer —*
>
> *May we consecrate the Australian bush, and speak both for and of it as poems of God. May the power of abundant living be so great in us and our God given imaginations so quickened, that having read this message we become crusaders in the supreme quest of true beauty.*
>
> *Man is nature's masterpiece. Therefore claim your inheritance by giving her the co-operation you owe."*

This particular "Inscribed work" was ultimately installed in the Sanctuary and, although the heads of the flanking Aboriginal figures were broken off, it survived almost intact until the late 1980s. The Rangers came in one morning to find it laying smashed on the path below where it had sat in an earth bank for decades. It did not appear to be the victim of foul play, but bad luck. It had never been pinned back into the bank, and so needed only an unfortunate bit of erosion or slight pressure to unseat it.

The show was favourably reviewed in the *Argus*, however the *Age* reviewer was left with some doubts:

> *"The sculptor's style in many of his works is smooth and attractive, although the legendary subject matter rarely lends itself to such qualities. In a number of works, however, the sculptor spoils his artistry by striving too hard to put the aborigine's case— that of a persecuted race. On one statue he goes as far as to attach a model rocket bomb to the hands of a monster.[4] Much of the work is attractive and—a rare thing nowadays— beautiful. The general effect, however, is spoilt by the sculptor's convictions rather than by his artistry …"*

This was the first review to express what could be termed as negative criticism, but I doubt that it would have had any negative effect on Bill. Probably quite the opposite. It would have expressed to him a positive indication that his fervour was blazing brightly for all to see. Bill knew

---

4 This would probably have been a protest against the Woomera Rocket Range.

that he could never strive too hard to show that the Aborigines were a persecuted race, for he would strive until their burden of persecution was lifted.

In late April, Charles Mountford received a letter from Jessie A. Wunderly, forewarning of Bill's impending arrival in Adelaide and requesting that Mountford do what he could to assist, explaining:

> *"He is a white hot fanatic, but a nice young man all the same. He has a dream idea, and with help and interest and encouragement he might achieve where more practical folks have failed …"*

Shortly after, Mountford received a letter from Bill. He wrote that he would be leaving for Adelaide on May 7th and planned to arrive sometime on May 9th.

Bill had purchased for £510 a 6.4 metre long covered trailer for transporting his works, at one end of which was a small cabin set up for accommodation. *"I will be alright in the important matter of rest"*, he wrote to Mountford. The only definite hint as to how the trailer was moved comes from a 1951 *Women's Weekly* article which reported that: *"Previously he had travelled by trailer, relying … on trucks and cars to give him lifts."* It would seem a haphazard way of getting around, but it is supported by a conspicuous absence of memory of a towing vehicle. I contacted four first-hand witnesses to this South Australian journey, but only one thought he remembered how the trailer was moved around. Mr M. Dalwitz, of Nuriootpa, thought that Bill contracted the towing to hauliers.

As well as the large works for exhibition, Bill wrote that he was taking 6 gross of small works to sell and thereby pay his way about.[5] Bill requested that Mountford open his exhibition, but added that if that were not possible he would ask Dr Duguid. One blow to the plans was brought about by the death of Rev. Love, who, having by then left Ernabella, had offered to "support" Bill while he was in Adelaide.

One week before he departed, Bill wrote to Croll outlining the forthcoming journey:

> *"I will make one step at a time & so I look forward to success in Adelaide. Then I hope to make enough to move up north & out west.[6] My show in Melb went well. I … could have sold two or three of the large works. I may do this in Adelaide …*
> *I hope I may have good news to write back to you sometime and somewhere."*

Susan Ricketts was taken down to Melbourne to stay with one of her daughters and a nephew, Jim Valentine, came up to keep an eye on the Mountain Gallery for the duration of Bill's journey.

Bill arrived safely in Adelaide and set up camp on the five acre property of Dr and Mrs Duguid. Mrs Duguid was in hospital at the time and she remembers clearly being visited by a polite young Bill, who came bearing the gift of a small bunch of violets. Organising a venue in which to exhibit was his first priority, but he searched without success. It was not until he made contact with Ted Strehlow that his luck changed. Strehlow introduced Bill to the proprietors of Laubman and Pank Appliances and Photographic, who had established in Gawler Place, Adelaide, the Curzon Theatrette for the purpose of showing films. It was small and, as Bill described it in a letter back to Croll: *"very new & ever so lovely … Adelaide is a lovely city & the people are friendly."*

The theatrette was converted and on May 20th, Dr Duguid opened Bill's first South Australian exhibition, which was to run for two weeks. The *Advertiser* gave the show a prime

---

5 1 gross = 144; 6 gross = 864
6 "Up north and out west" was Bill's long way of saying Ernabella, which is northwest of Adelaide.

page five review the next day, complete with a photograph showing Bill and Dr Duguid standing next to the latest "My Country".

Immediately next to this review was an article which highlighted the outstanding degree of positive community spirit present in the Barossa Valley community of Nuriootpa. Among other things, it mentioned in the article that large sums of money were being generated for community work: £7,000 and £8,000 easily caught the eye.

At that stage in 1947 the old Exhibition Building in North Terrace, Adelaide, was undergoing a reconversion back to being the School of Art, after having been used by the military during WWII. The Education Department made space available on the ground floor of the building for Bill to hold a second exhibition. This exhibition was reportedly seen by thousands of school children who came to know of it, more than likely, through the efforts of one Mary Packer Harris. Miss Harris was a Quaker and the Art Mistress of the South Australian School of Art. According to her autobiography, she first met Bill when she took a group of her students to see his show.[7] She wrote:

"Ricketts himself was a shy man and shrank back when I asked him to speak to the students about his work, which in its peculiar symbolism and mysticism, reminded me of Blake ... He at once denied any kind of influence in his work interpreting the Australian Bush and Beliefs of the Aborigines. He consented to let me talk to the students, and I think may have listened from a hidden place. For thereafter I heard from him in a letter of friendship."

So popular was the exhibition with the children that the Combined Schools wrote to the National Gallery of South Australia urging its Board to purchase one or two works for permanent display. Bill related the outcome in an undated letter to Croll:

"Same old answer. NO Impossible people in galleries & the like. However the children may do it another way. I consider my visit a success on account of the children ...
The ugly wide gap between the child and the older hardened people will be made narrow as far as I am concerned. I will be as a child work for the children and so build a better & more kindly world.
Friday I move on. My show opens in Nuriootpa next Monday ... Ted Strehlow will come up and give an illustrated lecture also films will be shown. I will be in the Lutheran Hall.
It is 47 miles north of Adelaide in the Barossa Valley where rivers of wine flow ..."

Louder voices called after him, though. At least two letters were sent to the Editor of the Adelaide *News* newspaper arguing that the National Gallery of South Australia should be buying some of Bill's work. A. S. Hoffmeister, in his letter to the Editor, wrote:

"... these sculptures have a strong appeal to youth. They should find a place in the National Gallery ... Such works would bring a thrill to every passer-by—they belong to no other land but Australia. As a lesson in finer national feeling, they are unsurpassed."

---

7 *In One Splendour Spun: Autobiography of a Quaker Artist*, Mary P. Harris. Published by the author, 1971. Mary would also write a biography of Bill, *The Holy Mountain of a Crusader in Clay*, which remains unpublished. In quoting Mary Harris I must point out that I have found numerous errors regarding her recording of dates, for instance, her giving 1952 as the period in which she first met Bill. Her attention to other detail, though, has made it possible to use her material in conjunction with events accurately dated by other sources.

Bill arrived in Nuriootpa, set up his camp in the shade of spreading gums on the banks of the Para River and quickly settled in. Arthur Reusch, a community leader, explained to him the concept of what they were trying to achieve.

At the time, Nuriootpa was in the spotlight both nationally and, to a small degree, internationally, as a result of what was termed its "Noble Experiment" in actually realising the full potential of truly democratic, community endeavour. It was hailed by Dr Lloyd Rees, Director of Public Relations for the Department of Post-war Reconstruction, as *"the most important advance of all community experiments in Australia"*. By working together as a community, the townsfolk of Nuriootpa had, among other things, built a new kindergarten, raised £2,000 to construct an Olympic swimming pool and, for £7,000, built themselves what was described as *"one of the finest country sports ovals in the State"*. Projects for the future included a new sports field house, a public housing scheme, a children's club, a soldiers' club room and, prominent on the list at the time of Bill's visit, a living War Memorial.

Bill's exhibition in the local church hall was received well, but it was his Open Letter plan that really found the heart of the community. The exact sequence of events is lost, but Bill possibly took the initiative by composing an open letter to the community, dated July 29th, 1947, in which he proposed a *"living and growing"* memorial. It began simply, *"Dear Friends"*:

> *"This morning I sat in the grass on the island joining the Child Centre. I thought just what I would do to make this lovely part a child's dream. In my works and myself I have tried to show that the child is the father to the man."*

Bill proceeded to describe an area planted with a profusion of Australian native plants, through which winding paths would take a visitor on a journey of wonderful discovery. On the islands he envisaged the creation of rocky habitats for a colony of yellow-footed rock wallabies. Discretely placed on these rocks would be one or two of his sculptures: *"to express the spirit of Australia as the aborigine knew it"*. More of his work could be placed along the paths where they followed the creek bank. Bill continued:

> *"Nature is the best guide of which we know and its simple pleasures the best religion. Nature strives for the right adjustment so she needs you in her business. Everywhere man has been trying to throw out the Australian bush, cage its birds, burning out, etc. He is paying for the misuse of nature in many ways.*
> *Culture is the cream of conduct.*
> *So here I would build up a powerful love of Australia.*
> *Thus the child having this love as an inward emotion must express it into works or human effort. And without the glory of nature the artist or composer or poet is quite helpless. This great love of country or ideal life is only the normal or natural life as we may yet know it."*

The Nuriootpa War Memorial Community Centre Inc. committee concentrated the general feeling of goodwill towards Bill and told him that they would indeed launch an appeal to raise funds for the purchase of some of his works, and thereby help Bill realise his goal of the Open Letter plan. In response to this news, Bill composed another letter on August 14th. He gave his address as, *"Caravan Among the Branches of the Eucalyptus Tree, Nuriootpa"*, and wrote:

> *"Your decision to create a fund to purchase my indigenous works of art of the Australian bush means only one thing to me. Your faith and trust in me and my mission is complete.*
> *God being with me I would only want people who read my open letter to cast fear and doubt away. Some will say the Aboriginal is dying out. Some will say impossible.*

All things are possible with God, and my creator is using the (so-called) lowest people on the earth to develop the highest in me ...

All that I ask for myself is that I shall be a good transformer of divine power and happy I am to know that I have been chosen to liberate some measure of love and joy into this holy mission.

The time has now been reached for me to ask the people of Australia and overseas, for their support to acquire a portion of the Flinders range, South Australia, also part of South East Australia for just what my open letter says ..."

The preceding two letters from Bill, a full transcript of the Open Letter and other related letters and articles were incorporated to make a special Spring issue of the town's newsletter, aptly titled "Community", for distribution. Included was a letter from the committee chairman, Mr Arthur Reusch, which requested support not only by way of funds, but in letters as well. Reusch continued:

"We would particularly like to stress that this is not an appeal for funds just for Nuriootpa but for a venture and a crusade which is of national and world wide importance ..."

The Memorial committee had received correspondence from Dr Duguid, Ted Strehlow, R. H. Croll and another Ricketts' supporter from Melbourne named Moir,[8] all supporting the concept of incorporating Bill's works in their Memorial and reinforcing the worth of his Open Letter plan.

The works the committee intended to buy were, "The Sandhills are Good", "The Spirit of the Great Tree", "The Origin of Two Euros", and "Intwailuka". It was proposed that the community would raise *"£1,000 or more"* as payment, although it was clearly understood that the money would go towards Bill's plan.

Bill did not sit idle waiting for the outcome of the newsletter's appeal for funds. His first project was to install "The Origin of Two Euros" beneath a spreading river gum on the bank of the Para River, in the area designated to be the Memorial. A small amount of earthwork was required and the finished result was pleasing. Bill was photographed explaining the work and its legendary background to a group of local children for an Adelaide *Sunday Mail* article by Max Fatchen, published on September 27th, 1947. The article told that Bill would be returning home to Mt Dandenong in a week, where he would construct a scale model of his proposed plan for the Memorial, which he would send to Nuriootpa for approval. He then planned, Fatchen wrote, to travel up to the Centre. In the meantime, the three other works would be left in Nuriootpa, awaiting installation.

Bill returned home, but whether or not he continued with his modelling of the proposed Memorial plan is not known. The work he'd installed was vandalised by, reportedly, a bus load of visiting football players who used it for target practice with empty beer bottles.[9] The other works suffered a similar fate, although their locations at the time of their destruction was not recorded. Bill was notified of the vandalism, but wanted nothing to do with restoring the works. The surviving remnants were gathered and put in the cellar of Coulthard House, the local museum, while a plan could be formulated. The piece, "Spirit of the Great Tree", was restored as best as the locals could and placed in the grounds of the kindergarten; but even there it was no match for the inquisitive children. It was restored again.

---

8 J. K. Moir, founder of the Bread and Cheese Club and a firm patron of Australian Arts and Letters.
9 Mary Harris wrote this account in both her autobiography and unpublished biography on Bill, and Bill recalled the same, but it does smack a little of type-casting. The culprits were never caught or identified.

Mary Harris was aghast when news of the vandalism reached her. She immediately wrote to Bill asking if she could collect the works and bring them down to her Adelaide house, which she called "Bundilla", for safe-keeping. When she received permission from Bill to do so, Mary organised for a friend, Mr Hergstrom, to drive her to Nuriootpa to gather the remains. On arriving and making known the purpose of her visit, she was informed that the community fund had already reached £200 and could therefore not allow any of the pieces to be removed.[10] She left with empty hands.

The only piece which retains any semblance of its former looks is the "Spirit of the Great Tree", which now lives out of the general public's eye in a quiet corner of Nuriootpa, relatively safe in the midst of gentle people. Since I saw it, the piece has been incorporated in a water setting, giving it a further buffer. The only other remnant of the four large works was part of the main face from "Sandhills are Good", which occupied a space in the back yard of a private house. Whether or not Bill received any of the money raised is not known, but I doubt that the fund would have progressed much after the works were vandalised. This episode proved to be the first indication that Bill's works could not be left unprotected for public display. Unfortunately, it would not be the last.

For reasons unknown, Bill again failed to set off for Ernabella at the end of '47 or in the beginning of '48, which was the time he had told everyone he was going. The beginning of 1948 did see a turn of events, though, for it is recorded on the land title that his block was mortgaged to the Commonwealth Bank on March 16th of that year. The man who claimed just three years earlier that he could make as much money as he wanted whenever he wanted was borrowing. Frustratingly, the circumstances surrounding the loan are unclear, and no detailed records remain. Bill told me that the loan was to fund his journey to Central Australia. The mortgage was not withdrawn until June, 1951.

The year 1948 also saw the respected landscape gardener/designer, Edna Walling, take interest in and make comment on Bill's work in her book, *A Gardener's Log*:[11]

> *"I have confirmed, once and for all, my feeling that sculpture and pottery go hand in hand with landscape gardening. For a brief hour we have looked upon the works of William Ricketts ... in his unusual studio, one that is more out of doors than in, and one that is quite perfect. There is not a jarring note in the place, where one may see the work of a great artist in clay. What struck me forcibly was not only the exquisite delicacy of the clay figures themselves ... but the buoyant grace in the design of the bases of the figures, and the extraordinarily gifted manner in which these masterpieces are fitted onto boulders, into niches, and by the side of pools ..."*

USA author and lecturer, Helen Keller, visited Australia in 1948. At the completion of her Melbourne stay, during which time she gave lectures at the Institute for the Blind, but was not taken to the Sanctuary or introduced to Bill, Keller was presented with a parting gift; a small sculptured Aboriginal man, created by Bill, which she would treasure as a "beautiful talisman to guard me at home". On May 23rd, from her room in the Hotel Australia in Sydney, Keller composed a letter of thanks, in which she expressed what she "saw" through her hands and mind:

> *"As I passed my hand over the bas relief I was thrilled, sad and delighted by turns. The thrill came from the expression of the old man, through whose long hair and flowing beard the winds from mountains and deserts were blowing their message and strength and liberty. Sorrow filled me as I thought of the brave plant of Aboriginal life which has clung to this continent with such tenacious roots during unhistorical ages and which now is so*

---

10 £200 was the figure quoted in her autobiography.
11 Edna Walling, *A Gardener's Log*, quoted from 1985 edition.

close to extinction. I blessed Mr Ricketts for his humane efforts to save some unique blossoms and fruit of that unique growth in a lonely land, and to impress upon other races the Eternal oneness of mankind …

Truly shall I be proud to have among my possessions that memento of my visit to Melbourne."

Plans were taking shape for Bill's first booklet, for which he was seeking written input from his various supporters. To Ted Strehlow he wrote requesting a few paragraphs *"which would turn around the idea that 'the soul of a race is enshrined in its legends' "*. Strehlow was not at all sure just what Bill wanted from him; be it an introduction or foreword or simply a few lines for inclusion as a quote somewhere. Early in February 1949, Strehlow sent over five paragraphs from his work *An Australian Viewpoint*, along with a short 130 word summary in which he had *"merely tried to point out one aspect in which you and the natives seem to me to be thinking along identical lines"*. While the plans were certainly underway, that particular book would take many years to see the light of day. There were more pressing plans at hand.

Early in 1949 Bill arranged to have another exhibition at his home, the Mountain Gallery. In a letter to Ola Cohn, written three weeks before she opened this latest display, Bill explained that he would show *"this large work"* before taking it up to the *"native people"*. He did not describe the work, so there is no way of knowing what his first clay expression to the Aborigines was. His two main concerns, as expressed in the letter, were that his aging mother, at some 80 years old, would have to again go back to one of her daughters in Melbourne, and his fear that his home and works would be left unprotected during his absence. He admitted that he just did not know what to do.

The show was opened on March 6th and news of it went around the country via an article written by one who chose to be known as F.F. which appeared in the April 7th edition of the *Australasian Post* magazine. The inaccuracies of fact in the article, possibly the result of Bill supplying inaccurate information, suggest that Bill was well on the way to showing disregard for the events of his past. It was reported that he had only been on the mountain for eleven years, dropping three or four years somewhere. It also had Bill as being 43 years old, with another loss of some nine years. More significantly though, there was a strong implication that Bill had *"set himself to learn the art of modelling clay" after* the move and after he had built his house. It could have been a misunderstanding of facts, but it could also have been the commencement of the history that Bill, for whatever reasons, wanted known. While *Post* told that Bill's latest work was called "The Symphony Of Life", they did not provide an illustration of the piece.

Ola Cohn, in opening the exhibition, gave guests the benefit of her understanding:

"In the atmosphere and beautiful surroundings of nature's gallery we can get the depth and significance of William Ricketts' work, because it is meant for a natural setting. It is meant to be placed as he has placed it, among the trees and rocks of his mountain home. On the spot where we stand, William Ricketts plies his tools and feels his subjects so deeply and intensely that he is able to make his figures vibrate with life."

Ola also showed her foresight with what *Post* described as a ventured prophecy:

"Men such as William Ricketts suffer through lack of help and understanding. They suffer because they are trying to say something that has not been said before, and that gives expression to a new thought. It is the new thought that counts. I feel that Mr Ricketts has that new thought, and that new expression, and that his work will go on. Even if it is not recognised in his time, I'm sure it will be later."

The *Post* article made no mention whatsoever of Bill's plans to travel inland. Maybe F.F. had done some research and seen that Bill had been forecasting an imminent journey to meet the Aborigines of Central Australia for as many years as he'd been reported in the press, deciding not to make the same mistake by reporting it again. This time, though, plans were taking shape.

8 | Ernabella Journey
[1949–1951]

Bill must have discussed travelling in Central Australia with many knowledgeable people over the years. Croll, Strehlow, Duguid, Mountford and others would have warned him of the heat, discomfort and danger of the Centralian summer. It is almost incredible then that Bill chose to make his first journey a summer one. On July 20th, 1949, Bill wrote in a letter to Ola Cohn that he would be leaving for the Musgrave Ranges during the next month. He was confident that his long awaited meeting with members of the race which had captivated his life would go smoothly:

"I know we will get on well together ... Up until now my process here has been to just prepare myself in every way for the real indigenous and beautiful works just ahead."

Susan packed in preparation for another stay with her daughter, but one task she set herself before leaving was to cook Bill a supply of puddings and cakes which could withstand the travel. He might have been going a thousand miles outback, but there was no reason why he shouldn't take some of mother's home cooking along.

Bill again loaded a trailer with the works which he was sure would convey his message across the barriers of language and race.[1] He arranged for the trailer to be railed to Finke; a siding on the Ghan line some 275 km south of Alice Springs, consisting of a pub, a store, a Post Office, a Police station, stock yards and a camp for the railway maintenance gangs. Bill also notified Ron Trudinger, Superintendent of Ernabella, of his arrival date at Finke.

John Bennett, stock manager, mechanic and jack of all trades at Ernabella, was given the job of driving the mission's truck into Finke to collect Bill. The journey, in excess of 300 km on rough unmade tracks, took at least one full day, but often required a night's camping somewhere along the track. John was there in time to meet the steam train and found Bill without trouble. With the help of railway staff, the trailer was loaded onto the truck and Bill set about making sure the contents were secure for the journey ahead. John knew only what little Ron Trudinger had told him about Bill—a sculptor coming to model the Aborigines. But as Bill checked the load, John realised he was in the company of a most talented individual. He could not recall the individual pieces when I spoke to him, only that all works were *"first class"* and obviously the work of a man who *"definitely knew his job"*.

John was not given time to admire the works too much, though, because Bill was most impatient to depart for Ernabella. The journey from Finke to Ernabella passes through beautiful country, but it's hard to imagine Bill's mind being on anything other than the soon-to-occur meeting with "his" people.

---

1 Because we see that the trailer was loaded on top of a truck, it appears unlikely that Bill took his 6.4 metre long trailer, but rather a smaller one either loaned or newly purchased for the trip.

The truck could not arrive at Ernabella unannounced; just the noise of its approach would ensure a welcoming committee. It came to a halt in a cloud of red dust out of which emerged Bill. He took a couple of steps towards the small crowd of Anangu who had gathered,[2] spread out his arms, and in his clearest, most sincere voice greeted them with, *"Hello Brothers! Hello Brothers!"* Ruth Dawkins was the nurse there at the time and witnessed the scene. She recalled with a laugh the Anangu's reaction: *"They jumped back in terror!"*

Bill paid scant attention to the staff while his trailer was being unloaded, telling them only that he would camp with the Anangu. He was advised against it, if only for the fact that he wouldn't be able to communicate effectively—but Bill was not to be deterred. It was then that the staff began to wonder if Bill had come up mentally unprepared for his stay. While Bill was totally confident that he and the Anangu would click straight off, the experienced locals worried that the reality might be different. Bill gathered up his goods and chattels and set off to where the Anangu had their wiltjas set up near a dry creek bed.[3]

The Anangu love their dogs, but in a different way to the majority of non-Aborigines. They're left to breed at will and scavenge for most of their food. This leads to the survival only of the most cunning. On Bill's first night camped by the creek, the camp dogs gave the whitefella a lesson in the importance of secure food storage. Bill woke the next morning to find that the cakes and puddings which Susan had gone to such trouble to prepare for him were gone. Over the course of a week, nearly all of Bill's food supplies were ransacked, proving beyond doubt that great sculptors are not necessarily the fastest learners.

Ron Trudinger, a fluent speaker of Pitjantjatjara, told me that he had attempted without success to forewarn the Anangu of what Bill would be doing. He could not adequately explain sculpture because there was no word for it. The Anangu had never seen or heard of sculpture. They had no concept of it, no point of reference with which to compare Bill's works. That Bill had attempted to cross the cultural bridge by interpreting legendary mythology in his work was of little help, because it was not Anangu mythology.

Ron Trudinger explained:

> *"He thought that he had a real understanding of their mythology and that he was expressing it in his sculpturing. However, that was not reciprocated by the Aborigines. If he thought that he was giving an example of their Dreaming message, and he showed it to them, then they wouldn't identify with it at all.*
>
> *Now you must understand that their Dreaming, their whole concept of the Dream World and where man came from and all that sort of thing is very deep and profound to them and very hard for a mere white man to understand. He thought he was interpreting that, but he wasn't really. Not at Ernabella anyhow.*
>
> *While he was a clever sculptor, I don't think that his work, as far as the Aborigines were concerned, represented their thinking. It sounds terribly negative, but that was the truth …*
>
> *I've been [at Ernabella] off and on now for the last fifty years, and you've got to be very careful when you say 'this is what they say' and 'this is what they think' and 'this is the way their Dreamtime stories go'. That is not very easy for a white man to elucidate from them."*

When Bill showed the Anangu the works he'd brought up, their reaction was, according to Trudinger, polite indifference.

---

2 "Anangu", according to Ron Trudinger, is the word used by Pitjantjatjara-speaking Aborigines to describe themselves.
3 "Wiltja" is the Pitjantjatjara word for a simple shelter made by boughs overlaid with a thatch of brush and grass. They offer protection against sun and wind but are not waterproof.

Bill encountered another problem when he set about modelling the people. For religious reasons, the Anangu did not want reminders of individuals after death had occurred. Even the name of a recently deceased person could not be mentioned and, most certainly, the image of that person should not remain. This applied to photographs, about which they had learned. Bill's three dimensional replicas in white clay presented a new threat. He was faced with a major quandary:

"They didn't want to be seen after death. How difficult it was. All I wanted was, in the end, to fashion a beautiful weapon that no one could pick at—'Oh, you should have done it this way or that way!'—something that no one could pick at.

The first Pitjantjatjara man I asked, oh, he just looked at me then he off for his life and he peeped out behind a rock. That meant, 'No, but I want to see what you're doing'."

The Anangu did recognise the talent which Bill possessed, and many remember that cleverness today, but for the most part in late 1949 they did not want to be the subject of that talent. Bill's camp near the creek was not an isolation area, though. He had many visitors, and the old men who came were apt to express an interest in the spare clothes that Bill had. Piece by piece, Bill gave away his clothes until all he had left were the thick corduroy trousers and heavy jumper which he wore. With day-time temperatures regularly reaching 40°C and often climbing much higher, Bill's attire was anything but suitable.

After about a week Bill had lost most of his food, given away most of his clothes and, one assumes, would have become aware of the problems he faced regarding modelling the Anangu. You could say that he would have been quite settled into the camp, but there was apparently one obstacle he could not cope with. *"I had to get out of the flies"*, was another of the few comments he made to me regarding his Ernabella sojourn. He asked John Bennett if he could share some space in the bachelors' house and was welcomed in.

Quite unaware of what was happening, Bill then began to lose favour with the staff. Apart from his distant manner which all the ex-staff members with whom I spoke remembered to some degree, Bill made a couple of unfortunate blunders. The first was when he created a studio of sorts on the verandah of the bachelors' house by nailing up blankets to keep out the drying winds which sapped the moisture from his wet clay. Bill happened to use some of the best blankets to be had on the entire mission, which was not quite appreciated. The second misdemeanour was potentially much more serious.

Coming from the Dandenongs, Bill had no concept of the value of water in the dry lands. This was not and is not an ignorance limited to Bill alone. The great majority of Australians believe that taps are full of water for as long as you want to leave them turned on. Bill, always an impeccably clean man, took to having the odd shower under the tank stand, wasting the mission's most precious commodity on a luxury. Unfortunately, it seems that nobody jumped on him and explained just how precious their water was. Instead, a silent resentment was fostered.

Ron Trudinger was left scratching his head one day over Bill's attitudes towards Life:

"He had some funny ideas, for example he—a lot more people have it nowadays— but he wouldn't kill a fly. I said to him once, 'If a snake turned up', which was quite likely at that time, particularly, 'If you were sitting on a log or something and a snake turned up—you wouldn't push it away or touch it or kill it?' 'Ooo no', he said. He'd let the snake kill him! Well, that's what he said. So we all thought he was a bit odd that way."

Bill did not help matters any at meal time. Ruth Dawkins cooked for a while and recalls the scene of the six or so of the staff gathered in the manse for their evening meals:

"There'd be dead silence, when suddenly he'd start ranting, really, on white people and how he belonged to the Aborigines. The Red Indians, he seemed to be caught up with them also. But he'd rant and rant. We just didn't say a word. We kept eating and just kept quiet. [She laughed at the memory] *And this went on every night—same story!"*

One of the first people to actually sit for Bill was a young girl in her late teens named Tinimai. She had chosen to spend a lot more of her time in the mission with the staff than was usual, helping out in the houses and the school. She did not seem to share the same concerns about her image surviving after her death—or maybe her youthfulness put such a thought so far in the future that she discounted it. On the first day that she was going up to Bill's "studio" she was in the company of Ruth Dawkins and another Anangu girl. Ruth recalls that as they were walking up the other girl said in Pitjantjatjara to Tinimai, in a quietly excited manner, *"He might give you a shilling."* Tinimai replied, *"No, no, no—he's mad. Have pity on him."* Ruth did not question the girls on the matter and simply let it pass.

I asked Ron Trudinger about that comment and what he thought it meant:

"That expresses [the general opinion] in a nutshell. They thought he was kawa kawa, that means looney. It just shows how little they knew about his work, his background and what he was doing. If he'd walked around on his hands, it would have been the same. It was just outside their sphere of experience."

When the trio reached the bachelors' house Bill directed them to his studio, where he had Tinimai sit naked from the waist up. Ruth remembers her there, *"beautifully poised"* and relaxed, happy to help this strange man do what was, for reasons unknown to her, so important to him. Bill commenced work in silence, modelling her *"with his clay and his spit"*, as Ruth recalled. The afternoon dragged on and still not a word was spoken, but all the while a likeness of Tinimai was emerging from the mass of white clay. While she had some reservations about Bill himself, Ruth was captivated by his work. She thought the pieces that he'd brought up were absolutely fascinating and beautiful. Her mind wandered through the afternoon and at one time, before she realised what she was doing, she innocently asked: *"Mr Ricketts, do you ever sell your work?"* Bill stopped working, glared at her and then: *"He almost went hysterical—he shrieked 'My work? My work!' and then he went on with his work. We spent the entire afternoon there and he never said a word."*

What happened to the finished work of Tinimai is a mystery. Ruth can't remember having seen it completed and Bill never, to my knowledge, included her likeness in a work after his return to the south. One explanation is that the unfired work did not survive the arduous return journey. Interestingly, not one of the ex-staff to whom I spoke could remember ever seeing a completed work which Bill had done at Ernabella. Did he put them straight into his trailer and under cover so as not to offend those Anangu who were worried about the existence of the likenesses? Nobody can remember.

Bill did other models, almost exclusively of children, some of whose names and/or ages were recorded at the time. There were the girls: thirteen year old Iwana; and Intjitjin and Tjikalyi, both seven year olds. Then there were the boys: twelve year old Tjurki [now Douglas] and Tjapiya; nine year old Purampi; Wirkima, Langkai Tjukur, Kwian-kwian [now Wally] and Tjiyangu, all eight years old; seven year old Tjukintja [now Bruce]; and Pinku, whose age was not recorded. These children were all attending the school at Ernabella at the time Bill modelled them. Some of them have gone on to become leading community members, with two of them, Tjikalyi and Tjapiya, now married with a family.

It is assumed that those children modelled by Bill did not have any concerns about being reproduced in clay, although I imagine that many were too young to care. There were some children who were not comfortable, though. One woman who is now in her fifties told Ron

Trudinger that she was frightened not of Bill's works, but of Bill himself, because of his ability to reproduce faces. She did not sit for Bill, but her emotion was strong enough for her to remember that fear some forty-three years later.

There was one mature man who paid quite a deal of attention to Bill and who seemed genuinely interested about what Bill was doing. He was known as Jacki [I was not able to find out his real name], a traditional Anangu aged between forty and fifty years. His intellect was above average and he had been of great help to Ron Trudinger with translation work and other linguistic studies. Most probably as an expression of friendship, Bill gave Jacki one of the smaller works he'd taken up. It was a piece called "Moon Man" and featured a large round face with eyes and mouth, with both legs and arms coming from the "moon" head. Jacki was pleased with the gift, but when he showed it to Ruth Dawkins he said, good-naturedly: *"This is mad—it has no stomach!"*

I asked Ron Trudinger if he ever saw Jacki's "Moon Man"? Although he had not, he offered his thoughts:

> *"[Jacki] would have accepted it and considered it interesting, but I doubt that it would have had very much significance. I'm sure that he wouldn't have thrown it away, but they were not people who kept artifacts like that. They were totally nomadic and probably within a week it would have been left somewhere—a month at the most."*

The summer was well and truly upon Ernabella, and Bill with his winter clothes was seen to wander around sometimes quite aimlessly: *"In his own little world"*, as Ruth Dawkins recalled. His drifting around the place, not saying hello or even waving a hand, led Ruth to secretly call him the *"Spirit"*.

Christmas came and Bill was still at Ernabella. On Christmas eve he was treated to an event which disturbed him more than a little. Ron Trudinger had assembled a small children's choir and they went from house to house at dusk singing Christmas carols in English. Almost 1,000 miles from the nearest capital, in the heartland of Australia and in the homeland of the Anangu, Bill listened to the beautiful voices of beautiful children—but the words were all wrong. His one criticism of Ernabella:

> *"They were guarded. They wanted [the Anangu] to keep their ways—but the church bell would still ring."*

On Christmas morning the truck left Ernabella at 6.00 a.m. bound for "Kenmore Park", a nearby cattle station from which the mission would get their feast. No Christmas turkey up there—they were off to get their Christmas bullock! When the truck returned the beast was butchered and the meat distributed throughout the camp. Bill did not recall how he spent the day.

Bill stayed another month before being driven into Finke in late January or early February. Before he left, though, he gave to the Anangu some of the large works he'd taken up with him. They accepted the works, but the works were seen to be badly damaged soon after Bill had left. None of the ex-staff with whom I spoke witnessed the destruction, but four out of five mentioned it without prompting. The fifth, Ron Trudinger, said in response to my enquiring that he would not have been surprised if it had happened. It could have been accidental breakage, but it could also have been because the works had within them the likenesses of other Aborigines and Bill. Were they clearing their land of potential threats, or helping out those whose likenesses appeared in the works by ensuring that there was nothing of them surviving them in death? Or did someone not want the image of Bill, which was included in the works he left, to be around the camp with its permanent threat of stealing likenesses. They are questions without answers, but they arouse the curiosity.

From the accounts related here we see that Bill's Ernabella experience was not particularly triumphant. But we will see that on Bill's subsequent journeys to the regions around Alice Springs, he was accepted, trusted and almost lauded by the Aborigines he interacted with; a vastly different response.

With all due respect to the 1949 Ernabella staff, the lack of understanding on the Anangu's part may have resulted from a lack of understanding about Bill on the staff's part. They would have introduced Bill and discussed him according to their interpretation of who he was. The future good relationships would have been grounded on Bill's initial introduction by non-Aboriginal staff into the communities. There is, of course, the possibility that Bill's subsequent good relationships may also have been influenced by his modifying his actions in response to his experiences on the Ernabella journey.

There was one more mystery from the Ernabella adventure involving cultural degradation. A photo would appear in the January 20th, 1951 edition of the *Australian Women's Weekly* featuring a majestic life-sized sculpture of an Anangu man who Bill had seen at Ernabella. In the very bottom of that photograph can be seen a wooden tywerrenge, one of four tywerrenges [three wooden and one stone] that would be in Bill's possession.

Bill and I sat looking at one of the wooden tywerrenges one day. My imagination made my hands seem to feel a power in the engraved wood, but I did not mention it. Bill was examining the intricate lines and patterns, the meanings of which had been passed down for generations but are now unknown. With his typical vagueness, leaving out dates and places and names, Bill told me his story of coming to have those most sacred of objects:

> *"Some man up there was a gambler, he turned into a gambler, he went out and stole them. I paid £3. He'd go off and gamble that and perhaps win money off the other fellas, which was a terrible thing to do. I gave Ted Strehlow one to put into his collection, a beauty—same fella.*[4] *Some poor old man has done that, see, there's not a mark out on them. If I tried to do that I'd have all criss-crossed lines—yet he had only a kangaroo bone. I don't know what to do. Sacred. Hard to know. They were hidden away out in the bush. The old man [who guarded them] passed out of life, and [the gambler] knew where it was, so he got the money to gamble with. If I hadn't got them they'd be in America by now. So I had to save something. I'd like to give them back if I could. They belong to the people, but how do you give them back? I might give them to the wrong one, and he'd go and buy a pot of beer with them. They're historical tablets. It's hard to know."*

Indeed it is hard to know.

Bill went home and began to turn his visions of Ernabella into works which now had a real people at their conceptual heart.

In May 1950, Bill was visited at the Mountain Gallery by the SMAAS Director, A. R. Penfold and his wife, where they saw the fruits of the Ernabella journey. Penfold was clearly impressed by what he had seen during his visit, so much so that immediately on arriving back to Sydney, he wrote to Bill:

> *"As you are well aware I am most enthusiastic about your creations, but the magnificent series which you showed me on Monday last is a revelation in modelling. It is the best modelling I have ever seen. I congratulate you on your achievements ... You intimated to me that under no circumstances would you dispose of any of your works after firing ... Notwithstanding your decision, I should very much [like to] acquire from you ...*

---

4 Strehlow was given the stone tywerrenge.

one of the aboriginal children. I do not [think] your collection in this Museum would be complete [without] one ..."

This is fine proof that Bill had indeed achieved at least a remarkable sculpting success in that remote corner of South Australia.

Bill replied in the negative. The original heads would remain at the Mountain Gallery,[5] although he offered to make a full set of thirty by thirty centimetre copied masks of the originals, twelve in all, which Penfold promptly accepted. Bill warned that it may take some months to complete the works, as he was building a new, larger kiln. This way he hoped to liberate himself from all dependence upon the ATTC at Mitcham for the firing of his big works. Penfold, possibly sensing an imminent creative surge, also expressed a readiness to acquire for the SMAAS any works with legendary themes.

Penfold's patience lasted only eight months, by which time he wrote to Bill with a polite enquiry regarding how the promised works were coming along. Bill responded immediately:

"Just as I got your letter this morning I was just about to put your works into the kiln ..."

As promised, Bill soon wrote to Penfold with news that a box was on its way by rail to Sydney. He'd changed his mind about the masks and had instead incorporated the faces into one large work—which he was sure Penfold would like. Bill wrote that he was happy with the work, having been able to hold a maximum temperature of 1,100°F to ensure fusion of the clay, as well as having at last mastered the colour he'd been after for years. Bill enquired about the work "My Country", wondering if they still had it:

"As weak as it is you have the original of the same work that I have just finished (one ton in weight)."

Bill had also finished and fired what remains for me one of the most impressive pieces of sculpture in the Sanctuary—the life-size Anangu man still located on the large rock in the alcove of the original residence, now the Rangers' hut. He drew Penfold's attention to *"a good article on my work"* in the January 20th, 1951, edition of the *Australian Women's Weekly*, in which a photograph of the old man Anangu work appeared.

It was a good article which contained good quotes, written by Elizabeth Hanson. Bill again took the opportunity to continue the propagation of the myth of his beginnings, with Hanson writing that he did not turn to sculpture until he was thirty-five years of age, after he'd moved to the mountain and built himself a log cabin.

Hanson wrote of a subdued Bill: *"sensitive and publicity-shy"*, who, *"when inquisitive visitors are about ... takes shelter behind drawn blinds"*—a man who was up all night feeding coke to his kiln and spent his days working in a *"strictly private"* studio in the rear of his hut. Of marriage, Hanson quoted him as saying: *"I can't afford to waste time. Marriage would set my work back five years, and my work is all that matters."*

Of greatest interest to me were a few short quotes from Susan Ricketts which remain, as far as I know, her only recorded words. Although always there, providing her selfless, unconditional support that could well have been the pivotal factor in freeing Bill's time and mind so that he could devote himself fully to his work, Susan's own reticence and the fact that she was *only* the artist's old mother meant that she was never given her due credit. Elizabeth Hanson gave us a fleeting glimpse:

---

5 "Original heads" is a macabre way of phrasing it, but that's how they've been referred to ever since I became involved with Bill. It sets them apart from all else, and is literally descriptive.

"Because Mrs Ricketts believed in her son, the only artistic one of her four children, she forsook her little house in … Richmond and 'went bush' with him.[6]

'Somebody had to see that he was fed and looked after'. she explained. 'I like it here, although I miss the trams and the shops. Still, I have the birds and my wireless for company. It's a lonely life, but I think Bill is right in having taken the step he did.'"

And under a rare photo of Bill and Susan, a comment which reflects just how much she cared for her son:

"He would forget to eat if I didn't remind him."

Bill also gave an account of his meeting the Anangu at Ernabella:

"They are wonderful—happy, full of laughter and kindness. They accepted me into the tribe, and I was admitted to sacred tribal corroborees and able to watch the wonderful spectacle of many dark-skinned people, painted with the ritual markings of ochre and pipeclay, chanting and dancing far into the night. The scene was lit with small camp-fires and whole burning bushes of spinifex which dotted the hillside."

I asked Ron Trudinger whether or not he thought Bill would have been admitted to sacred affairs, to which he replied:

"He would have been invited, as most visitors were—the rare visitors we had. He probably wouldn't have seen the sacred inner sanctum type ceremonies, but they have a lot that are more public. By the same token, if he implied in that [statement] that he'd been, as it were, initiated into some special relationship in the tribe, that would be wrong. They would have done it just out of generosity—the same as we would take a person out to a show. No more significance than that."

Bill also told Hanson that he was off again to the Centre in the April of that year, travelling alone, this time in a vehicle borrowed from a friend.

The latest work for the SMAAS had a mixed reception. The first thing that staff saw when they opened the packing crate were fresh fractures over the top of the work. They put it down to inadequate packing on Bill's part; the crate was too neat and there was not nearly enough straw packing. But on seeing the rest of the piece, sorrow turned to joy, with Penfold offering congratulations *"upon its excellence"*. It was immediately placed on display in the Museum.

Just one month later, though, Bill wrote to Penfold:

"I thought it best to let you know that I have executed another work larger than yours. It has the same number of children and the same ones with a fairly large figure of a Musgrave man holding his child right to his side. The man & his child are placed on top of the base of children.

The colour is beautiful & the man & child is a beautiful light bronze. I have been here 13 years & only now I have been able to see results, that is a good measure …

I strongly suggest to you to consider this work before I send it to America. I will ask 300gns in America if you do not consider it. At that figure of 300gns it repays me very little in money …"

---

6 We know that Susan Ricketts moved from the Peel Street, Windsor, house—not from Richmond.

Penfold jumped at the offer, writing back almost immediately with a request for the new work's dimensions so that he could have an adequate crate constructed. He would forward the crate down free of charge and pay for the return freight. Quite obviously, while he trusted Bill's self critique of the new work, he did not want to trust his packing again. Whether or not Bill complied is not known, but the work was sent up a week and a half after Penfold's letter—and it arrived with fresh cracks caused by poor handling.

In his letter forewarning Penfold of the work's arrival and in which he gave the names of the children featured, Bill gave his thoughts on the piece, which was something he would never do publicly. Yet in the letters to Penfold, he relaxed his guard and spoke a little more freely on how *he* felt about his works and the progression or maturation of his style, which I imagine must have been a welcome release for him. Although publicly distancing himself from the art world, he was still an artistic creator who experienced normal feelings about his work. Yet he was setting himself up to have to repress those feelings. Even in the late stage that I knew him, Bill would sometimes, in absolute privacy, examine his new work critically, and in whispers. In his letter, he also made an admission:

> *"I have enclosed the names of the children. The name of the man with the child must not be told, because he did not want me to model him. He was a very lovely man and he used to come in to see me each day, and each day he came I did his head as soon as he left me. He had a fine sense of humor and I did something to a figure then showed it to him and he laughed until water run out of his eyes.*
>
> *The children as they appear to emerge from the rock is the one and only theme in all my work & it is the highest message for all life and that is All life is one and that we are part of all that is even every grain of sand.*
>
> *So then the children's heads & the child figure TJIKALYI are all meant to be small in proportion to the man. The work is fired to 1060° of heat and is not hard looking and I think you will agree that the colour in the children is much better than the other piece and you will notice that they are modelled into the rock in a much better style. Also the man & the child has the exact colour I have been trying to get for years ...*
>
> *I trust you will be pleased and when I take my works over sea it will prove before the world the value of the message enshrined in my work. Your faith in me & my adventure will also be proved. My plans are such that I cannot see how any other gallery can get any thing of my work. Should you want something in the future, I shall be very glad to do what you wish."*

The man who did not want to be modelled is not, as I thought, Jacki. This has been confirmed by Ron Trudinger. Oddly, when Trudinger passed around the Ernabella community a photograph depicting the work and clearly showing the man, nobody could remember who he was. It's hard to believe that he is a product of Bill's imagination, because he is just too real. But if, as Bill claimed, the man was a regular visitor to Bill at Ernabella, you'd think that he would have been recognised by those who were there at the time.

On receiving the work, Penfold wrote that he was delighted with what he thought was *"probably [Bill's] best work to date"*. Bill had said that he would consider 300gns or thereabouts, so the SMAAS Trustees gave him the "thereabouts" sum of £300.

Bill repeatedly postponed his next journey to the Centre; by a month, two months and to the next year. But he kept busy. His major project, monolithic by clay sculpture standards at least, kept growing—ultimately reaching a height of some 3.6 m. It was, I believe, the first of his most often repeated theme; the black man and the white man [who was always Bill, for reasons that I have explained] coming together in unity. This particular work would be on the go for years. Bill mentioned it to Penfold in one letter, which caused immediate concern among the SMAAS staff knowledgeable in the science of firing clay. Penfold passed on advice regarding how best to treat such a large work, but Bill assured them that there was no need to worry. He had constructed it to a uniform thickness of thirty-two and thirty-seven millimetres and would cut the work into six pieces for firing in an oil-burning kiln which:

"could be built straight away but a long wait to get about 2,000 fire bricks is the snag ... then I will burn these works at the slowest possible rate say about six days to bring the heat up to 1000° or perhaps about 1020°. I expect some cracks but with steady firing not much should happen."

Ultimately though, the work dropped out of existence, to be heard of no more. Bill told me that it was an over-ambitious project in which he tried to far exceed his capabilities—itself a rare admission of defeat.

The Department of the Interior showed interest in Bill and his Mountain Gallery in 1951 by making a short feature film. It ran for only five minutes or so, giving a scant overview of what Bill was up to. It showed him "at work" on his new large piece, which is to say it showed Bill carefully attending to a finished section of the piece. No movie would ever be made of Bill actually creating a new piece, although several would have him hovering around a completed but unfired piece on which he pretended to work. While the makers of the film informed Bill that it would be shown throughout Australia and then sent overseas, the actual extent of its distribution is not known.

In between trying to organise the fire bricks for his new kiln and his general sculpting, Bill found time to accept a small commission from Penfold, who asked for two more Anangu children's portraits; one for himself and one for a staff member who was also impressed by Bill's output. Just which children Bill did for them was not recorded. He had them finished on November 20th, 1951, notifying Penfold by letter that he had sent them to Sydney on that day's passenger train. Penfold received them two days later and was again delighted, writing a letter of thanks on the same day which he ended with the words: *"I could not wish for anything better."*

At some time on November 21st, 1951, a Wednesday, Bill came in to his hut and found his 84-year-old mother asleep on her chair, a bowl of shelled peas on her lap. She often drifted off to sleep, so he did not wake her. When next he looked in, Susan was still asleep, in fact she had not moved a muscle. When his fears became aroused was not recalled. Did he sit up with her all night, stoking their small stove in an attempt to drive away the chill which no fire could overcome? Did he try to gently wake her when it was obviously time that she should be in her bed? Did he realise what had happened? If he did, he did not accept it. The next day he walked over to his next-door-neighbours and asked if they could come over to look in on his mother. He told them that she was asleep and wouldn't wake. The neighbours accompanied him back to the hut, and immediately realised that Susan was dead. They told Bill, but he wouldn't believe it—he insisted that she was asleep! Nor would he let his mother be touched. While Bill sat with Susan's body in stunned disbelief, the neighbours contacted Dr Burns in Croydon and asked him to attend.

Dr Burns recorded on the Death Certificate that Susan had died of a cerebral haemorrhage, which he noted had been present for one day, and arteriosclerosis, from which, he noted, she had been suffering for many years. The funeral service was held the next day.

The body of Susan Ricketts was cremated at the Springvale Crematorium, attended by a small crowd of relatives and friends. They tried to comfort Bill, but the shock was deep. He was quiet and drifted through the service in a haze.

There was one old man in the crowd who could barely walk, so crippled was he with arthritis. He had come to the crematorium by train and by bicycle, which he could ride as well as any youngster. Only when he had to walk did his legs struggle to carry him. The pain and discomfort he bore stoically. The other mourners were shocked to see him, with very few even talking to him—for he was a virtual outcast. Bill did not welcome or talk to the old man. But old Alfred Ricketts was not to be deterred—he had come to pay his last respects at the funeral of his wife. The service was simple and after it was completed Alfred stood looking emotionally drained. The one lament he made which is recalled was: ***"She's still the only woman I'll ever love."***

Bill never saw his father again. Alfred lived until 1959, and reportedly rode his bicycle until the last. He died in the September of that year, while Bill was again away in the Centre.

Some of the mourners met back at the Mountain Gallery. It would have been a very quiet affair. What words could console the loss of such a devoted mother? Bill was not set up to cater for any number of people, not that he would have been capable. One by one they left him, until finally he was alone. Completely alone in the empty hut in which Susan had turned cold.

9 | Life Without Mother
[1951–1954]

Bill was devastated by his mother's death. He stayed on at the Mountain Gallery and although the progress of his vision and creative output didn't completely stall, the wind was certainly taken out of his sails. Bill created a small clay urn for Susan's ashes, which he set into an earth bank only a matter of metres from the front door of his cabin. As far as he was concerned Susan still shared his home, in spirit.

On March 17th, 1952, almost four months after Susan's death, Penfold wrote from Sydney to offer his congratulations on the quality of the film which the Department of the Interior had made. Penfold had seen it at the Century picture theatre and thought it excellent. Bill did not reply. A fortnight later Penfold found out why. At the Annual Meeting of the Royal Society of New South Wales, Penfold by chance sat next to a mutual acquaintance of Bill's, Mr A. E. Stephen. Stephen showed Penfold a letter from Bill in which news of Susan's death was revealed. The next day Penfold sent a letter on behalf of the SMAAS staff expressing their deepest sympathies. One week later he received Bill's reply, written in a much heavier hand than usual:

> *"I want to thank you & staff very kindly for the sympathy in respect of my dea Mother.[1] I miss her so much. She grew so tired that she just fell asleep in front of me ..."*

No records survive to show that Bill was making big works through his extended period of mourning, although he was producing a few smaller pieces. That he was quite reclusive during this period is revealed by the fact that none of his usual acquaintances saw him or can shed light on exactly what he was up to. Apart from making short visits to the corner store for supplies, he seems to have stayed hidden away.

His peace was being more than usually disturbed on weekends by activity on the block directly across the road from the Mountain Gallery. A man and woman were appearing every Saturday and Sunday, engaging themselves in clearing and levelling the land. Bill secretly watched them work from the cover of the bush on his block, wondering what they were up to. They sometimes saw Bill at his spying, but took little notice. They remembered him as seeming like a *"frightened little mouse"*.

The couple eventually introduced themselves as Dorothy and Lou Atkinson, telling Bill that they were building a home and a plant nursery. The idea of a nursery pleased Bill. The Atkinsons would be nurturing life and not destroying it. He decided to accept them as neighbours.

The building process took a couple of years to complete and when it was finished Dorothy set about naming the property. She turned to a book of Aboriginal words for inspiration, and came upon the word "Churinga". She liked it and when next she saw Bill asked him what he thought? *"Oh, I'd have to think about that"*, Bill said. Dorothy didn't realise that Bill thought of

---

1 In the original, only the letters "dea" were written. I suggest it be read as "dear".

his own place as tywerrenge-like. After a short period of silence, he consented: *"Yes, you can—because you love this place. You built it, you love it, and tywerrenge is all that—no beginning and no ending—concentric circles—they go on forever."* With that little speech, the Atkinsons were welcomed onto the mountain by he who would control the mountain's affairs—given half the chance.

It was in those early 1950s that Bill re-established his link with live classical music, as a result of his long association with Micha Kogan.

The pair first met in the Palais Theatre in St Kilda, when both were resident violinists of the theatre's orchestra. Kogan had come to Australia via a most roundabout route, having escaped from Russia to become an Albanian citizen. Then he moved through Britain, Palestine, Vienna and finally to Australia.

Ms Elizabeth Clark, a long standing friend of Kogan's when he was alive, explained his path from there:

> *"He then came down to Melbourne. In order to get work at the very beginning he joined this Palais Pictures Orchestra, in the Palais Theatre on the Esplanade at St Kilda. Their duty was to play at dances—not the general Saturday dances but the ballroom-type dances where the people really dressed up. They also accompanied screenings of films there. He met Bill Ricketts very early in the piece, at the theatre, and he said to me that he was a very able 'fiddler', as he referred to it.*
>
> *Micha went on to audition for the Melbourne Symphony Orchestra, which was then the Victorian Symphony Orchestra and was one of the founding members.*
>
> *Any visiting musicians and artists who came out over the years were taken up to Ricketts' place, and they just loved it. Micha used to go out of his way, when he was in the orchestra, to act as interpreter and take these visiting artists for a tour and always the Sanctuary was on the list of places to go.*
>
> *Their relationship was extremely close, to the point where they'd be hugging each other when they met and acting like they'd been apart for years."*

During WWII, Kogan formed a quartet and travelled to the various military camps within easy access to give free concerts as morale-boosting exercises. The quartet also held fund-raising concerts for the benefit of such organisations as the Red Cross. In the early 1950s, by which time he was playing the viola exclusively, Kogan began an event he called the Soirée Musicales. Ms Clark explained:

> *"The first concerts were held in private homes in Toorak, mainly places with ballrooms and large seating capacity. He eventually was able to hold regular concerts in some of the most important homes in Melbourne, and people were very pleased to have him there so that he could present these chamber music concerts. The crowds grew to such an extent that they could no longer be housed there, so he ended up having to go into the Victoria Hotel, which was the Victoria Coffee Palace; meeting on a mezzanine floor. People would dress in tails for the men and long dresses for the women, and his reputation grew to such an extent that he had to move to Coppin Hall, Richmond. He eventually moved to the Caulfield Arts Centre.*
>
> *Being in the MSO ... he was perfectly placed to meet every visiting musician. So he'd just write to them before they came out, get to know them while he played with them, and then sign them up to do chamber nights. Some of them, virtuoso musicians, had gone beyond chamber music, but many of them, the world's leading artists, would happily agree to play without payment. But he did give them a gift, something to take home as a memento of their visit to Australia."*

That was where Bill came in. In an arrangement that lasted many years, Kogan gave Bill tickets to every Soirée Musicale organised, to which Bill would take a small piece of his sculpture. At the end of the evening, Kogan, with great formality, presented the visiting musician with their unique memento, after which they were introduced to the creator of their gift. As a result some of the world's best and most influential musicians left Australia with a piece of Bill's work packed in their bag and some of Bill's philosophy providing food for thought.

Bill's regular companion to the Soirée Musicales was Doris Turner. Her most vivid recollection of these nights, apart from the fact that they were invariably wonderful entertainment, concerned Bill taking his concept of being part of the bush one step further by wearing eucalyptus oil as a scent.

Doris recalled the reaction Bill used to cause when mingling with the Soirée Musicale patrons. It seems that he was not discrete in his application of the oil. *"He smelled like he just poured it on!"*, she laughed: *"And of course, it's such a strong oil—people just couldn't stand close to him. So we were never really a part of the crowd."*

The SMAAS had contacted Bill with a request for a work featuring gum leaves, which would be the Museum's permanent memorial to the centennial celebrations of the Eucalyptus Oil Industry, which commenced in 1852. On reading that the SMAAS had an interest in eucalyptus oil, Bill wrote to Penfold in September 1952, requesting plans for a distilling unit so that he could attempt to extract his own sassafras oil.

Penfold passed the request on to the SMAAS's Chief Chemist, who obliged Bill with the relevant plans and instructions. It is highly unlikely that Bill succeeded in constructing an effective extractor, if indeed he made any attempt to proceed with his plans once he saw how complicated the apparatus was.

Included in that September letter was a request that Penfold return the first group of Ernabella children which Bill had sent up. Bill explained: *"So many American people are brought here and I never seem to have anything for them."* Penfold had forgotten about the piece, but replied with a plea that a price be put on the piece so that it could be purchased and allowed to stay on display at the SMAAS. Penfold also offered a full set of photographs of the SMAAS's Ricketts' collection, which he suggested *"would enable ... visitors to observe at a glance the versatility of your genius over the past twenty years"*. Bill acquiesced: *"Your wishes are as you know my pleasures ..."* After explaining that he had great costs ahead of him—the new oil burning kiln and a journey to Central Australia the following March—he wrote:

> *"I can only pay for these from sale of some works. If you wish you can as you say pay for that group. I leave it to you, say a third of the last group or a quarter or a third. I do not mind so long as it helps my project."*

Penfold arranged a payment of £100 for the work and by late September had forwarded a full set of photographs, which Bill speculated that he would use in a *"special part"* of his still-planned illustrated book. In December 1952, Bill wrote back to Penfold obviously pleased with the photographs and glad that there was a record of what he described as his earliest work. He dropped a bit of a bombshell on Penfold with his last line, though, when he wrote: *"I hope to visit you one day before I go oversea."*

Penfold made the mistake of taking Bill at his word and, with his usual diplomacy, replied requesting ample notice of any departure overseas, so a chat could be arranged about the future of the works at Mountain Gallery. He urged Bill to be sure to take adequate steps to protect the works or leave them in the care of somebody, and then made the offer to look after them himself. Bill rocketed back his reply, which landed on Penfold's desk three days before Christmas:

> *"I feel that something should be done straight away about this gallery and Sanctuary of 4½ acres of land.*

I am now working towards my great plan (A Holy Mountain) and all the large works I am now about shall go into that mountain. I do not know yet where that mountain is, but, will when the time comes for me to say.

Until that final plan is to hand can we make some sort of cover over my whole endeavour. That the gallery situated at Mt. Dandenong with all the works all the large works I am now on, also, all the native studies in clay I did in the interior house & studio also an oil fired kiln now being built at a cost of £800 shall be held on trust by you and your committee.

The 4½ acres of land belongs to the birds and so must never be touched. I wonder what you think? ..."

Penfold did not reply until the second week in January, 1953. He tried to explain that while Bill's plan was a good one, the practicalities of vesting Mountain Gallery and the works located therein to the SMAAS made it a difficult exercise. He suggested a resident caretaker, but doubted if anyone could be persuaded to maintain such a person for an unknown length of time. The best Penfold could come up with was to repeat his offer to accept full responsibility for any works which were sent up to the SMAAS for safekeeping. He urged Bill to consider the matter carefully.

Bill's reply gave Penfold no joy, for it told of an impending Central Australian journey which he proposed to commence in April. *"Something should be done"*, urged Bill: *"I would value your thoughts a little further."*

Penfold bought some time by telling Bill that he and his Deputy Director would be visiting Melbourne in late March for a conference. He suggested a meeting to discuss Bill's problem and took the opportunity to remind Bill about the official request for a work featuring gum leaves, to which Bill had not responded. Bill replied quickly with news that he had the work ready and would show it to Penfold when he came down. Unfortunately Bill had a memory lapse and added, *"It is the only one I have done on the gum leaf"*; obviously forgetting the many pieces he had made in his domestic-ware days which relied heavily on the eucalyptus leaf for design. Bill again reiterated his intention to leave for the Centre in mid-April.

Penfold's conference was postponed. He asked Bill to reserve the gum leaf work, but wrote that they would not be able to meet until after Bill's trip north. Penfold did not further the matter of the Mountain Gallery's security.

In May, however, Penfold received another letter from the Mountain Gallery [the last sentence telling that the trip to the Centre was "a little delayed"], written in what seemed an almost frantic hand. It concerned the Department of the Interior's film, which Bill feared had been cut. Two groups of visitors had told him that they had seen the film, but nowhere had they seen the "White Brute" piece, Bill's sculptural condemnation of white Australia. *"That figure has a world wide meaning, not just Australia"*, Bill protested: *"The film was as I was told ... to go oversea."* Penfold confirmed Bill's fears, but repeated his earlier praise of the film, supporting his views with news that the SMAAS had purchased a copy for regular screenings in their own theatrette.

In June 1953, Penfold was approached by unidentified *"representatives of the Australian Government"* who sought his advice on whether or not Australia should be represented in the Kiln Club of Washington's Fourth Annual Exhibition of Ceramic Art, to be held at the Smithsonian Institute during the coming September. Penfold replied that he was in favour of participation, adding that he would approach Bill, the only ceramic artist he would recommend, on their behalf. In his letter to Bill, Penfold urged a special effort to have one or two outstanding pieces ready by August 24th, so that Bill alone would be the Australian Government's representative in the USA.

Bill replied that although he was enthusiastic about the proposal, he was having major problems with the new kiln: *"Some guesswork took place and I cannot get the heat."* Penfold again urged him to make an effort to have at least one work to submit, it being such an important opportunity. If all else failed, Penfold wrote, he would send one of the Anangu children's busts over on Bill's behalf. He also informed Bill that he had chosen a photograph of the work, "My Country", to feature exclusively on the SMAAS's 1953 Christmas card, which had a world wide circulation and was sure to provide valuable publicity for Bill's work.

Bill had an unfired work in his studio which he claimed had been made for the French Consul, but having lost touch with him, decided that the piece would do as his entry to the exhibition. While the problems with the new kiln were being sorted out, Bill put together a small kiln in which he hoped to fire the piece. It was the life-size head of an Anangu girl, with smaller faces moulded into the base; very much a standard theme for Bill, but still potentially outstanding depending on the amount of time he had devoted to detail.

Unfortunately, the small kiln also failed, resulting in the piece cracking irreparably. Bill wrote despairingly to Penfold telling of the mishap, explaining that although the large kiln was again ready for a trial, it would be at least two and a half weeks before a work would be ready. Bill gave up the idea, only to have Penfold write back saying that three weeks would be cutting it fine, but he was prepared to wait for a *"really good piece"*, adding that he was sure the piece would be worth waiting for.

It was not meant to be. Two and a half weeks later Penfold received news that the large kiln had again failed and Bill had, in utter despair, given up on the idea of oil and asked the suppliers to convert the kiln to burn solid fuel. Bill's only good news was that a substantial article about his endeavour had been printed in the August 3rd edition of the *Woman's Day and Home* magazine.

Julie Walton took Bill at his word and entitled her article as Bill saw himself; not an artist or sculptor, but a "Crusader in Clay". Bill gave his usual story; almost nine years younger this time, and not even the sheet of tin to shelter under when he first moved up—he slept on the ground in the rain with only a blanket. And he was entirely self-taught, having never *"studied the work of any other sculptor nor anyone's literature"*. The main illustration showed Bill "working" on the 3.6 metre group, which he said was only one of many large works which would go into his proposed Holy Mountain as part of a great spectacle of life; a mountain facing the Pacific ocean for all the world to see.

Despite the inaccuracies of his dreaming, Bill's quoted words were thought-provoking, as shown below in his reported response to Julie Walton's questioning him about the big work:

> *"It is a legacy handed on to me from my people, the Australian aborigine. I seek the highest meaning to life itself. Enshrined in this work is the ever present act of creation—the oneness of life. The native children are the symbols of creation.*
>
> *The white man [in the sculpture] is in a measure my spiritual nature which I liberate into my works. I did not come to this mountain just to make art. I am prepared to fight and shall die in that fight—my crusade.*
>
> *The white fellow has a fixed idea in his head that creation or the Australian bush is there just for him alone. He does not want to think that my beautiful lyre bird who looks into my eyes wondering, and beautiful Rufous fantail are just as much children of God as any human being.*
>
> *I know myself as a normal man knowing life and creation as a trust. With my mind, heart and hands I give back to God what emanates from God."*

By the end of October, Bill had set yet another departure date for his outback trip. He claimed in a letter to Penfold that in late February 1954, he would travel north *"to Arnhem Land and elsewhere"*. He again raised the question of whether or not the SMAAS Committee would provide a safe-guard for the Mountain Gallery during his absence: *"It should be made safe in the keeping of your committee. As it is it could be badly handled should anyone decide to take my life at any time."*

31 *"He would forget to eat if I didn't remind him."* This is the last known photograph of Susan Ricketts, published in the Australian Women's Weekly *on January 20th, 1951. Reproduced courtesy of the* Australian Women's Weekly.

32 *An "Inscribed Work", the text of which is reproduced on page 78. WRS [in pieces]. 750 mm high. Photograph courtesy of W. Grevis-James.*

33 *A Moon-Man, similar to, the piece, given to "Jacki" at Ernabella in 1949. Photograph only, size unknown. Photograph courtesy of W. Grevis-James.*

34 *Dr Charles Duguid opens the Laubman and Pank Exhibition [Adelaide, 1947] in front of the* second My Country *piece. Courtesy of the* Advertiser.

35 *Nuriootpa, 1947, Bill explains to local children the legend of the euros. Bill installed the piece as part of his proposed "living war memorial". Courtesy of the* Advertiser.

36 *Nuriootpa, 1947, Bill "working" on an already fired piece. The work is now in the WRS collection. Courtesy of the* Advertiser.

37 & 38 The Sandhills are Good *was donated to the people of Nuriootpa in return for their proposed financial support, but suffered tragic vandalism. Below left shows all that remains. Remains, 350 mm high.*

39 *Child's face emanating from branch. Bill reportedly called them, "pot boilers", sold simply to survive. Purchased c. 1941. Ins: "Mountain Gallery". 350 mm high, PC.*

40 *Bill and the artist, Ola Cohn. Date unknown, details of sculpture unknown. Photograph courtesy of the Age.*

41 & 42 *At right, Bill and a tree spirit piece, also donated to Nuriootpa in 1947. The only piece to survive largely intact. At left, detail of the "spirit's" face, contorted and enraged by senseless bushfire. 1650 mm high.*

43 *A more traditional miniature portrait. Unsigned, but given to the owner by Bill in the early 1930s. 68 mm high, PC.*

44 *The* My Country *piece now in the SMAAS's collection, claimed by Bill to have been the "original". 740 mm high. Photograph courtesy of the Trustees of the Museum of Applied Arts and Sciences, Sydney.*

45 *The* My Country *located at the WRS. Beneath the original photo Bill had written, "… how my joy and wonder is multiplied when I liberate these precious thoughts …". Photographer unknown. 1200 mm high.*

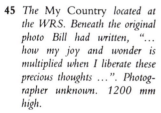

47 *Toby jug. Ins: "Wm Ricketts 1934". 130 mm high. Courtesy of the Art Gallery of South Australia, Adelaide. Photo by author.*

46 *Toby jug. Ins: "Wm Ricketts Melbourne 1934". 168 mm high, PC.*

48 *Twin-spouted tea-pot. Ins: "Wishing you good Christmas cheer 1940 Wm Ricketts". 195 mm high, PC.*

49 *Toby jug. Ins: "Wm Ricketts 1934". 74 mm high, PC.*

50 *Twin-spouted tea-pot. Ins: "Potters Sanctuary Mt Dandenong". 198 mm high, PC.*

51 *Jug. Ins: "Wm Ricketts Potters Sanctuary Mt Dandenong 1937". 150 mm high, PC.*

52 *Twin-spouted coffee pot. Ins: "Wm Ricketts Potter's Sanctuary Mt Dandenong March 30th 1937". 225 mm high. Reproduced by courtesy of the Art Gallery of South Australia, Adelaide. Photo by author.*

53 *Toby jug. Ins: "Wm Ricketts 1934". 105 mm high. Reproduced by courtesy of the Art Gallery of South Australia, Adelaide. Photo by author.*

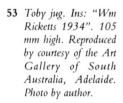

54 *Depicting a myth that ancestral beings extracted the original humans from a conglomerate of life. Size unknown, c. mid 1940s. Photograph by Steven Henty, courtesy of the Mountford-Sheard Collection, State Library of South Australia.*

56 Lizard Inkata, *reproduced from a photograph by W Grevis-James. Size & date unknown.*

55 *Child sitting. Unsigned, 47 mm high, PC.*

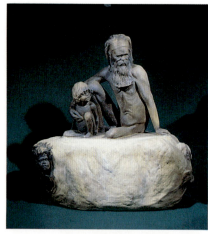

57 *The second work Bill sent to the SMAAS after his return from Ernabella. The young girl is Tjikalyi, but Bill did not reveal the name of the man. Bill wrote that the face on the far left is also Tjikalyi's. See also photo 59.*

58 *Tjikalyi was a firm favourite of Bill's. She was depicted often in works large and small. This piece unsigned, 255 mm high, PC.*

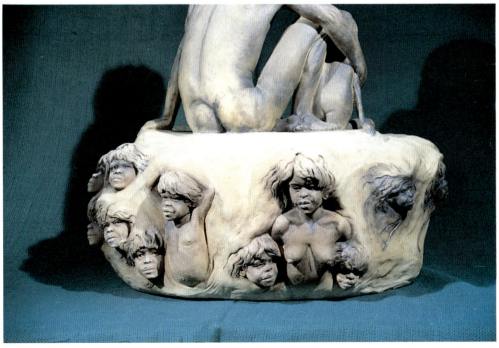

59 *Depicted on the rear of the work, L to R, are Wirkima, Langkai Tjukur, Pinku, Tjiyangu, Tjapiya, Intjitjin, an unnamed boy, Iwana, Purampi, Kwian-kwian, Tjukintja and Tjurki. 690 mm high. Courtesy of the Trustees of the Museum of Applied Arts and Sciences, Sydney. Photos by author.*

60 *An early attempt at large-scale work, reported to have been "12 ft high", which did not survive. Photograph reproduced from the* Woman's Day and Home *magazine, August 3rd, 1953.*

61 Numbakulla, the Creator Spirit, Calls the Spirit World into Life. *All but two of the lower men's heads are now missing. WRS. 1000 mm high. Photograph by Steven Henty, courtesy of the Mountford-Sheard Collection, State Library of South Australia.*

Bill had reached the point in his dreaming where he saw himself as such a threat to theestablishment and all who opposed his views that he perceived himself to be a potential victim of assassination. Whenever he said that he was prepared to die in his fight, he was picturing a death by the assassin's knife or bullet—just as Mahatma Gandhi had been gunned down in 1948. He entertained this delusion for the rest of his life.

Bill also asked Penfold for a "couple of dozen" of the SMAAS Christmas cards, so that he might send them off himself. He was a little worried about how people would react to "My Country", going as far as to suggest that Penfold might word the cards to inform recipients that: *"This work is among my earliest works & therefore is not mature."*

Penfold disregarded Bill's suggestion and refused his request for cards, their being worded in such a way that they were of use only to SMAAS Committee members and staff. But he promised to send a sample down when they came back from the printers. On the matter of safe-guarding the Gallery, Penfold could only reiterate his concern over the practicalities of having the SMAAS provide any protection while the works remained in situ. *"Do you have a friend who could reside on the property during your absence?"*, Penfold queried, handing the problem back to Bill.

When the SMAAS Christmas card arrived, Bill must surely have been quietly impressed. The cover print showed "My Country" to advantage. On the inside cover were words of pure praise, although the author was not acknowledged:

> *"The Museum of Applied Arts and Sciences, Sydney, is very fortunate in numbering among its Collections several outstanding ceramic sculptures by William Ricketts, of Mount Dandenong, Victoria.*
>
> *'MY COUNTRY', the frontispiece of this Greeting Card, is an inspiring study.*
>
> *William Ricketts is a genius with an ability to express in clay a deep spiritual significance of Aboriginal lore and life. This sculptor's great love of the Australian Aborigine, and his deep knowledge of their folk-lore, have been expressed in many delightful studies in clay. His object is to foster a better understanding of the Australian Aborigine."*

As chance would have it, Hilda King had made up her own Christmas cards for 1953 and what should they feature on the cover but a picture of "My Country". When Bill drew the coincidence to her attention, she felt it only proper to write to Penfold and forewarn him of the similarities of their thinking. After explaining that she had known Bill ever since he had been on Mt Dandenong, and explaining the coincidence, she offered some of her thoughts:

> *"I have a studio at my home where I have many of one Melbourne artist's pictures for sale, craft-work, and always some of Bill Ricketts' work.*
>
> *About 1940 or 41 I had an exhibition of his work in a room I had in the city. He was then doing his best work, but he is now quite incapable of doing the fine small figures he did and in his effort to make his 'message', as he calls it, known, he is working on larger and larger masses of clay which I feel sure will never be burnt.*
>
> *He is, as W. Chinnery of the Northern Territory once said after visiting [Mt] Dandenong,[2] 'definitely a genius but a pathological problem' ... Nevertheless, he has done a great deal—more than he will ever realise—to arouse people to the first Australians ..."*

Hilda King finished by asking Penfold if his cards were for sale, because she would like to buy some if at all possible.

Penfold received the letter on December 17th, the eve of his departure for Europe, and, to put it mildly, he was not impressed. At first glance, the photograph on King's card looked exactly

---

2 E. W. P. Chinnery, Director of Native Affairs [Darwin] c. early 1940s. See *The Go-Betweens*; Long, 1992.

like a copy of the photograph Penfold had sent down to Bill months before. In his haste he assumed that Bill had passed the photo on to King, which she then used for her card. In his haste Penfold sent off a strongly worded letter to King which left no doubt as to his displeasure:

> *"In the first instance Mr Ricketts had no authority to give you permission to reproduce a photograph of one of these pieces, which are the property of the Trustees and displayed in this Museum. Under the Museum Act No. 31, 1945, the Trustees have the power to prosecute any person who reproduces an exhibit in this Museum without their permission.*
>
> *It is a matter for regret that you did not see fit to approach me for permission in the first instance, because the exhibit in question is not the property of Mr Ricketts, but the Trustees of this Museum. Moreover, Mr Ricketts knew a long while ago that it was the intention of the Trustees to use this subject as a greeting card. I am sorry that I cannot look upon your action as a coincidence."*

Penfold then sent off a letter of similar indignation to Bill, blatantly accusing him of giving King the photograph when he had no right to do so:

> *"... the Trustees and I are now placed in a very embarrassing position. It has also raised a doubt in the minds of the Trustees about the wisdom of having provided you with a set [of photographs] of your exhibits in this Museum."*

Penfold then left his office, went home and made ready to leave for Europe, having no idea that he had just, in effect, done a tap-dance on a bee hive—a parting Christmas gift for the Acting Director, F. R. Morrison.

Hilda King's letter landed on Morrison's desk two days before Christmas. Unfortunately, the letter survives only in part, but its second paragraph sets the tone:

> *"As my reproduction was taken from a photograph given to me by Mr Ricketts in 1943, and before this exhibit was acquired by you or sent to your Museum, I do not think I come under the Museum Act No. 31, which you mention?"*

I imagine that Morrison sank a little in his chair. Then he opened a letter from Bill:

> *"I am sorry that you did not write to me first because what you said of me in your letter is not true. The photo's you sent me I guard and no one but me has seen them, so how could Miss King use them as you said.*
>
> *... she is a quaker and a very good woman and I feel sure she will be very upset when she knows.*
>
> *I work very hard for my plan and your letter has only caused me to be upset ... and to think I should be so vain as to do what you said in your letter makes me angry."*

I fancy Morrison sighed as he wondered at the speed with which news could travel—for he next received a letter from none other than Mary Packer Harris, in Adelaide:

> *"I am grieved to hear of the mis-understanding that has arisen since Miss Hilda King ... reproduced a fine sculpture of Bill Ricketts, interpreting his work & ideals through the medium of a sensitive poem.*
>
> *When Hilda King realised that a question of copyright might be involved she immediately notified you in the most courteous manner. In your reply you cast an aspersion on the character & intention of a most notable woman.*

Hilda King is a member of the Society of Friends. She has devoted her life to International Quaker Relief Work. She reproduced, with the permission of Bill Ricketts, a photo of one of his works <u>taken before</u> it became the property of the Sydney Museum. This was done in perfect good faith, not knowing the whereabouts of this work. It was her wish to perpetuate the Spirit of love & mankind enshrined in this sculpture. Is it too much to hope that this spirit of understanding & love, instead of distrust & suspicion, will penetrate the hearts of the Museum Authorities? …"

Penfold's ears no doubt suffered an inexplicable burning sensation as Morrison set about composing some rather apologetic letters. Hilda King was satisfied with the outcome and forgave all.

Bill did not dwell on the incident, for he was at last not only seriously planning for his next trip to the Centre, but making progress with his plans. His first act of preparation was to let his hair grow longer because, as he whispered to an Adelaide friend, *"That's how they wear their hair."*

The suppliers of the new kiln finally got it to work successfully on oil. Bill wasted no time in creating new large works for his journey, firing them at last in a kiln which did not require the constant attention of the solid fuel burners which were fed continuously by hand. It still wasn't a set-and-forget process, but it was a definite improvement. That Bill was pleased with the results is amply illustrated in a letter to Penfold written towards the end of March, 1954:

"My big oil kiln is now a success and the result from it in the finish of my conceptions has passed all I had hoped for. They are just beautiful …"

In that letter Bill offered the SMAAS the chance to purchase the works which he was taking to the Centre once he had returned. If the SMAAS did not want them, they would go overseas, *"Sweden above all, for they want all I can give them"*. Bill finished his letter urging a reply by return post, *"for I have to plan much in all I do now"*. Morrison, in Penfold's absence, made a standard reply; what's on offer, what size are they and how much will they cost? It would be four months before Bill replied.

Bill's shortage of funds is highlighted by the fact that he again mortgaged his land to the Commonwealth Bank for an unrecorded sum [but later referred to by his solicitors as "substantial"] on April 14th, 1954.

The purpose for the mortgage is also unrecorded, but it was not to fully pay off the kiln. It came to light later that Bill left Melbourne with at least part of that debt outstanding. This mortgage marks the beginning of Bill's downhill financial spiral from which he, alone, would never be able to extricate himself.

The next problem to be addressed was that of transport. Somehow Bill had been befriended by Charles Davis, Managing Director of the Mayne Nickless transport company. Bill made it known that he was short of a vehicle to take him north and Charles Davis obliged him with a retired three or four tonne flat-top Chevrolet "Maple Leaf" truck, ex-fleet number C68. Davis' generosity did not extend to supplying a driver, though, which presented a problem. At fifty-six years old, Bill had never learned to drive, so the truck was next to useless.

Enter Leo Corbet, variously described as a semi-retired stock auctioneer and agent, a real estate agent or simply a businessman, who reportedly lived in the Yarra Valley township of Launching Place. Just how the pair got together is a bit of a mystery. Bill's identified acquaintances up until that time, at least the ones who joined his mission as helpers and active supporters as opposed to the people of co-ordinating influence, were of a fey, idealistic and artistic ilk, so perfectly represented by Mary Harris. From what I could gather, Leo was a rational and formidable type who had the gift of the gab and a keen, mischievous sense of humour. He appears to have been for all intents and purposes a wag of a character, albeit a loveable one with a developed sense of justice. Asked what he remembered about Leo, Bill gave a hint of which character trait appealed:

> *"He had his own world. He was the funniest man that ever was. You'd just look at him and you'd laugh. Things he used to say—you'd just kill yourself from laughing!"*

Leo was unmarried, apparently without commitments and possibly not totally ignorant of the Centre.[3] Whether from a sense of adventure, or as a dedication to Bill's ideals, or from the simple chance of a holiday, Leo joined up as the driver and mechanical engineer for the journey to the Centre.

Bill chose a mixed selection of themes for the works he would take to the Centre for appraisal by the people whose culture he had taken to heart. He was not leaving it to chance to show the Centralian Aborigines where his loyalties lay, for most of the works he took featured his "spiritual self", shown with both adult and younger Aborigines. One piece was based on the earlier used theme of the Kangaroo Man. It differed by having Bill's upper torso, the body and tail of the kangaroo and the feet of a lyrebird, with another lyrebird leaning up against one of the legs. In one arm was cradled a possum, while in the other arm a tywerrenge was held close to the body. That conglomeration of life was Bill's sculptural manifestation of his maxim, "All Life Is One". It was also a placement of his "spiritual self" into the form of what he perceived to be an ancestral being.

In 1987 when I was in Central Australia researching this book, it happened that I found out that a Pintupi man whose company I had for a couple of days was of the maḻu [kangaroo] totemic group.[4] Without thinking, I whipped out a photograph of a work depicting the kangaroo men, with dramatic effect. On seeing the photograph he averted his eyes, clearly uncomfortable, and told me in a whisper, *"that one's business"*, meaning that it was important in some way. When Aboriginal men or women go off on "business" in the Centre, they are going off on important and private spiritual matters.

Another furtive glance from my acquaintance finally got it through to me that it would be better if I closed the album and not pursue the query. I could only wonder at the reaction Bill might have got from some sectors back in the 1950s.

There was also another "Moon Man", this time without the strange arms and legs of the Ernabella piece, and with the addition of a young girl's upper torso seeming to rest against the main head. Two larger works which were not destined for the Centre were also lined up for transport. One was similar to the work which went to the SMAAS after the Ernabella journey, except that instead of an old Anangu man sitting with Tjikalyi, it was Bill. The other was a depiction of the theme which showed Heavitree Gap in its creation. Both these works were for Mary Harris.

Along with the other assorted supplies were bags of clay totalling some 250 kg in weight, a fair indication that Bill planned to be very busy. There was a supply of smaller works for sale along the way, some with buyers already waiting in their first port of call, Adelaide. When they finally set off in May of 1954, the one critical task left unattended by Bill was the security of the Mountain Gallery during his absence. The best he managed was to have his neighbours keep an eye out, which, owing to the Gallery's natural seclusion, was anything but adequate.

Mary Harris eagerly awaited the pair's arrival in Adelaide, looking forward not only to Bill's company, but full of anticipation at receiving her first major works—the foundations of the sister-sanctuary which she envisaged Bundilla would become. She wrote in her biography:

---

3 It was reported in the *Sunday Advertiser*, August 7th, 1954, that Leo "knows the Territory from many previous visits", but nowhere else in the research did Leo's having prior knowledge of the Centre come to light.
4 Maḻu is given as the correct Pitjantjatjara spelling by Gavin Breen (IAD).

"It was a still dark evening and I sat by the fire dreaming. There was a knock at the door and I arose to answer. In the dimness I was conscious of a slight figure falling into a kneeling position with outstretched arms saying 'O, Mary'."

The next morning, after the works for Bundilla were unloaded, Mary rang one of the customers waiting on a small piece, Mrs Waters.[5]

Mrs Waters had first seen an example of Bill's work for sale in a shop and made a point of visiting him on her next trip to Melbourne. She had asked Bill if it were possible to purchase a small piece directly from him, explaining how she had seen a piece for sale elsewhere. She recalled that Bill looked aghast at the news: *"I didn't think anybody would sell one of my pieces once they had it—not even to bail themselves out of prison!"* Bill then advised her to return in a few weeks when he may have a piece for her, but finally agreed to take a work to Adelaide after she told him where she lived. *"I'll be over in a couple of months"*, he assured her. Asked where he would be staying in Adelaide, Bill said dramatically that he would *"probably camp on the banks of the Torrens River"*, only revealing that he would stay at Bundilla after Mrs Waters offered accommodation at her house.

Mrs Waters had no idea that Bill and Leo were on the move until Mary Harris' call to say that the pair had arrived in a battered old truck and were on their way to the Centre. They had Mrs Waters' piece, which would cost 7gns, as well as works for other people to deliver, but Leo was not at all keen on navigating Adelaide in the cumbersome, fully loaded Chev'. Mrs Waters offered to drive Leo and Bill around, throwing in lunch along the way. During the course of their outing, when Bill was inside a house delivering one of his works, Leo asked Mrs Waters how much she had been charged for her work. On being told he said: *"No—that's too much! I've seen him sell pieces like that for 30 shillings. I'll have a talk to him."* Not only did Mrs Waters receive a discount, but the small bust of an Anangu girl was thrown in for good measure.

Bill and Leo stayed at Bundilla for three days. Adelaide being the last major centre that they would see for an indefinite period, they purchased supplies in bulk. Bill's staple diet would be rice and potatoes, which he bought by the sackful. They also secured copies of Charles Mountford's *Brown Men and Red Sands* and Dr Charles Fenner's *Bunyips and Billabongs*. At night Bill dreamed out loud to Mary, a most faithful ally who encouraged him every step of the way. He mentioned his desire to take his fight to the world, where he was sure that good people would come forward to help him turn around Australia's thinking. He told her that he would create a Holy Mountain in the Centre, a monument which would force non-Aboriginal Australia to sit up and look at the destruction being wrought on *his* country and people.

As dear as Mary's desire was to create her sister-sanctuary to Mountain Gallery, she decided to try to help Bill as soon as he and Leo had left. She wrote a letter to the Editor of the *Advertiser* which was published on June 1st, 1954:

"Recently the most eminent sculptor of aboriginal legend, William Ricketts, passed through Adelaide on a trip to the Centre—possibly a world trip.

He left with me two magnificent works, one symbolising the creation of the Flinders Ranges. It has been suggested a suitable place to put the sculpting would be Flinders Chase.[6]

Were a public subscription raised to purchase these pieces of world renown, the monies would enable William to continue his crusade to express the oneness of life."

Mary's plea went unanswered while Leo piloted the Chev' north over some of the worst roads in Australia.

---

5 For privacy, an assumed name has been used.

6 The Flinders Chase National Park, situated on Kangaroo Island, approximately 110 km south of Adelaide. It is probable that Mary was referring to the Flinders Ranges National Park.

10 | Alice Springs Journey
   | *[1954]*

Nowadays the trip from Adelaide to Alice Springs is a simple matter of following the black ribbon of bitumen, the only hazards being the odd kangaroo, bullock or sleeping driver. In 1954 it was over 1,700 km of corrugations, bull-dust and desolation. Bill summed up all his drives to the Centre as "nightmares". Leo Corbet would later be quoted as saying, in reference to the 1954 journey: *"We were lucky nothing went wrong because I'm hopeless mechanically—I wouldn't get a third engineer's ticket on a kerosene lamp."*

The Alice Springs of 1954 was well on the way to becoming the tourist and service centre that we know today, having shaken off its "frontier town" beginnings. It started life just north of the present township as a telegraph repeater station for the historic Overland Telegraph which ultimately connected southern Australia with England. The site was chosen in 1871 by William Whitfield Mills. While cattle had reached the area in the mid 1860s, the first station lease was not granted until 1872. Prospectors and more pastoralists followed. Although Gillen, who assisted Spencer with his anthropological studies of the Arrernte, was installed as the first Protector of Aborigines by 1876, an undeclared and ongoing war for water and land rights ensued. It was decisive and mostly brutal, and continually won by the pastoralists. The more remote Aborigines whose lands were too poor for livestock were left in relative peace, disturbed only by the "doggers" and wandering prospectors.

Hermannsburg on the banks of the Finke River, some 116 km west of Alice Springs, was founded as a mission in 1877 by a group of sixteen German Lutherans, and lays claim to have been the first functioning township in the Centre. The ethics of usurping traditional spirituality and lifestyle remain arguable, but it is a fact that Hermannsburg became a haven for Aborigines who were in many cases being driven off their land at gunpoint.

It came about that the Aboriginal populations to the west of Alice Springs and Hermannsburg, prompted by a succession of bad seasons, curiosity and persecution, started migrating to centres of "civilisation". The extra influx was not considered to be in the best interests of either the Aborigines or the whites, so the Hermannsburg Lutherans established outposts at Areyonga, approximately 50 km west of Hermannsburg, and Haasts Bluff, almost 100 km north-west of Hermannsburg, as ration centres designed to stem the flow.

By the time Bill and Leo reached the Centre, the Government had taken over both the Areyonga and Haasts Bluff outposts, and had created the approximately 124,320 km^2 Haasts Bluff Aboriginal Reserve which stretched to the West Australian border.[1] To put that area into perspective, it was almost twice the size of the state of Tasmania. There was no official compulsion for the Aborigines to come in to these outpost settlements, but there was a strong temptation. For a people who previously had no concept of permanent supplies, whose lives had

---

1 The figure of 48,000 square miles was given to me by Les Wilson, one of the first superintendents of the Haasts Bluff Reserve.

for all time been ..t the mercy of the seasons and totally reliant upon the acquired resourcefulness and knowledge of their Elders, the incredible news of permanent food and water, when it reached them, proved too great for the majority to refuse. Members of the Pitjantjatjara, Pintupi, Ngaliya, Luritja and Arrernte peoples made their way in.

Likewise, the centralisation of the widely scattered groups into manageable units made the Government's chosen program of assimilating the Aborigines into the rest of Australian society much easier. Once centralised, the Aborigines could be taught the fundamentals of "civilisation", such as the wearing of clothes and the concept of working at a job to get food and clothing. They could be introduced to the different laws which governed white Australia. Introduced sicknesses such as measles and diphtheria were other major problems which could only be fought with close medical supervision, and in some cases mass immunisation; another program made easier by centralisation.

It was decided in the late 1940s that a beef cattle industry should be established on the Reserve for several reasons; to produce income to offset running costs, provide for its own meat requirements and create a venue where skills could be learned to help Aborigines' future employment prospects. Les Wilson, a Queenslander from Kingaroy, applied for and secured the position of Stock Manager for the Reserve in 1949. He and his wife, Shirley, moved to the Centre and quickly established a good rapport with the desert folk. Within a couple of years, Les was appointed Superintendent of the Haasts Bluff Reserve.

The program of centralisation provided Bill with the opportunity of encountering Aborigines relatively uncorrupted by white interference, without his having to conduct expeditions into the remote and trackless regions where such people had lived.

Like others before him who sought contact with the more traditional Aborigines of the region, the "real bush-people" as they were called, Bill had to apply for permission to visit the Haasts Bluff Reserve. He had the good sense to go as an artist seeking to model people, rather than a freedom fighter seeking to liberate a race from the bonds of a crazed white society gone wrong. Such requests were evaluated by the District Officer of the Welfare Department, whose office was in Alice Springs. Bill recalled his visits to *"the boss man in charge"*, as he put it. *"He was generally sucking a pipe"*, Bill explained, puffing out his chest and putting on his most pompous tone to recall the officer's words: *" 'I'll give you a permit to go out to the Aboriginal reserve—sign right here.' "* The District Officer referred to here is possibly Bill McCoy, who always had his pipe handy. In fairness to the officer, Bill rarely had a kind memory of officialdom, accurate or otherwise.

Interestingly, the Aborigines Protection Board in Adelaide refused Bill's written request for permission to revisit the Pitjantjatjara lands in the Musgrave Ranges during that journey, although no reason was given for the refusal. Ron Trudinger did not recall the application and speculated that Bill may have sought to enter lands away from the Ernabella Mission. Access to such country was severely restricted, even to anthropologists and the likes, which would diminish the significance of Bill's denied access. From the recalled reaction caused by Bill's first visit to Ernabella, it would not be extraordinary for access to have been denied if it had gone to Ron Trudinger's desk for comment.

Les Wilson had never heard of Bill before he was asked by his boss whether or not he had any objections to an artist coming out to sculpt the Aborigines. Les couldn't see any major problems. The Aborigines had begun to relax their concerns about photographs and their images surviving them in death, so he thought clay sculptures would be acceptable. Les recalled that Leo drove Bill out from town and made the introductions. Leo helped Bill unload his gear, set up the tent and make a camp of sorts on the settlement's fringe. When he was satisfied that all was in order, Leo drove back into town, leaving Bill to find his way at his own pace.

Shirley Wilson immediately warmed to Bill. Although he was old enough to be her father, she sensed that he needed looking after and took to "mothering" him somewhat, as Les recalled. They had him over for meals and delighted in experiencing the *"first real eccentric—a talented one—that we'd come in contact with"*. One of Bill's highlights was Shirley's banana cakes, which he raved over. They were so appreciated that, later, whenever Shirley heard that Bill was coming into the settlement, she'd be sure to have one freshly baked and waiting. *"He just loved them!"*, Shirley told me. The Wilsons, on the other hand, remember relaxing in their remote home while being entertained by Bill with his violin. To make matters more difficult for Bill, though, he had only one string left on his instrument, the other three having broken. While the Wilsons don't hold themselves to be music critics, they, like the rest of us, know what they like. And what did they think of Bill's efforts? Les summed it up enthusiastically: *"Good! He'd get a tune out—oh hell yes, no doubt about it. You could sit and listen, no worries!"* I asked Bill if he ever played for the Aborigines. *"Oh, in front of a few of them I jiggled a bit."* And what did they think? *"Very strange. They couldn't make it out."* Ultimately the violin's body sprang apart as a result of the climate and Bill finally left his musicianship behind him: *"The [violin's] remains would be in desert sands now."*

Having met Bill, Les could see no problems in letting him begin his modelling work. As busy as he was, Les could not himself accompany Bill to act as a go-between. Instead he sent one of the Aboriginal interpreters along to explain to the old bush people just what Bill wanted to do. The next thing Les knew was that Aborigines were clearing off left, right and centre, putting a good distance between themselves and the settlement camps before stopping. Les then found out why. Bill had, through the interpreter, explained that in his previous life he, too, had been an Aborigine—and although he was a white man in his present life, his spirit was still with the Aborigines. That proved unsettling enough, but when Bill went on to explain that he wanted to "capture their spirits in clay" and take them away to teach the white people, it was too much. Les had told them that mere images could not affect their spirit, and that was being accepted. But here was a whitefella with a black spirit who openly admitted that he wanted to capture *their* spirits! Les recalled:

> *"They didn't want to be mucking around with this spirit business. No way was Bill going to be getting <u>their</u> spirit and putting it in clay. They were off!"*

Les personally had to go out and explain that Bill was not going to be tampering with their spirit business, as such—it's just that he had a different way of putting things. Les had, during his time with those people, earned their trust. They accepted that he was a straight talker who would not lie to them, but he had to work a bit harder than usual to get over that one. In what sounded to me like the typical understatement of an old bushman, Les said: *"It took me a few days to get them to come back again."*

It could easily have become a repeat performance of the Ernabella trip, but Les turned the situation around. Maybe he explained that Bill was not your normal sort of whitefella. More likely, though, the Aborigines themselves came to see Bill for what he was—so widespread was his acceptance. An ex-Patrol Officer who knew Bill during that time, Creed Lovegrove, gave me his thoughts on the matter: *"Aboriginals usually take a very accepting attitude towards people like that—towards eccentrics. They don't find them difficult at all. They would have offered the hand of friendship. They're far more accepting than we are—us clever people."*

When I asked Les Wilson if he got any feedback concerning what the Aborigines thought of Bill, it appeared that he never asked—because he didn't have to:

> *"The feedback was how they used to follow him around when they got to know him. They just wouldn't leave him alone—particularly the kids. He was never left alone. He was just like a—oh—a Peter Pan or something—I don't know. But they just loved him."*

Bill became a free agent on Haasts Bluff Reserve and was trusted to look after himself without white supervision. If he was accompanied, it was by one of the Reserve's Aboriginal employees to act as a language interpreter. Les recalled that there were three principal men who acted in such a capacity; Wira, Yama and probably the most famous of the Centralian Aborigines, a Pintupi man, the late Tjunkata Tjupurrula. If you have never heard of him it's probably because he was more widely known by his "whitefella" name, Nosepeg, which was given to him in his youth because of his pierced nasal septum. The name stuck so well that everyone in the Centre, black and white, knew him by it, whereas virtually no non-Aboriginals knew him by his real name. Nosepeg is a name that is now part of Centralian tradition, and it is a name which Tjunkata Tjupurrula did not seek to discourage. Consequently, it is the name I will use here.

Nosepeg was a Centralian Aborigine who kept a foot firmly on both sides of the cultural fence. He was variously described to me as highly intelligent, quick, active, energetic, a warrior, a great thinker and very crafty. Les Wilson, after pondering on a term which might sum him up, said: *"I think they'd call him street-wise in America."*

When Nosepeg first encountered whites, he recognised that there were some worthwhile things to be had from the new civilisation—but he did not turn his back on his Aboriginality. While he progressed through all the traditional stages of his life as a Pintupi man, he kept in close touch with the other side. He learned English, and while he could speak it only reasonably, very little slipped past him when others were speaking it. Recalled Les Wilson: *"He used to sit on the outside, you know, conversations and that, and he'd take everything in. He used to get English a bit distorted now and then—but, by gee, he was never far off."* Because of his intelligence and innate abilities, he was picked to appear in and help with many films and television series, including *Jedda*, *Dust In The Sun*, "Whiplash" and "Boney".

That he could grasp what a whitefella wanted meant that he could convey the message to other Aborigines, positioning him as a very useful man. As an aside, he once danced for Queen Elizabeth II in Queensland. On his return to Haasts Bluff, he found a new house being built. Enquiring about it, Les Wilson told him that it was his and Shirley's house, to replace their old tin hut. Nosepeg disagreed. He had danced for the Queen, so it was only right that the Queen should be having the house built for him. He could not be dissuaded from the line and ultimately took it up with the District Officer in Alice Springs—to no avail. *"He was the sort of bloke whose brain was going all the time"*, recalled Les respectfully.

As could be expected, I dearly wanted to speak to Nosepeg when I was conducting research in the Centre, even though at that time I was not aware of the significance of his role in Bill's life. Bill didn't tell me that Nosepeg was his chief go-between for the Western Desert people until *after* my return to Victoria. Still, when I was there, many people advised me that if anybody could give the Aboriginal side of the story, it would be Nosepeg. At the time of my research, he would have been in his seventies, give or take a decade, but the old man proved to be far more than a match for this whitefella. Over the course of more than 1,600 km of outback travel, well off the beaten track, Nosepeg always appeared to be a couple of days in front of me. Finances and time forced me to give up before I met him, and fate did not bring us together during the rest of my stay. When, some five years later, I was finally able to get the help of an Alice Springs based man who had contact with Nosepeg, the old man proved to be vague in his recollections. Consequently, and most unfortunately, his input cannot be included here. Now Nosepeg has returned to his Dreaming, his recollections of Bill never to be recorded.

Although Bill was based at Haasts Bluff, he would go off with the Aborigines for days at a time. Sometimes he would take his tent along, sometimes not. Exactly what he did while he was away, Les did not know—but one thing he didn't do was get into trouble. One of Bill's secondary desires at Haasts Bluff was to find local clay suitable for modelling. This he did with the help of Luritja local to the area, who knew their vast land intimately. Bill did make some works from this local clay, but he did not abandon the blended clay which he'd brought along. Bill stayed on the Reserve for a month or so before Leo returned to take him and his work back into Alice Springs.

What appears to have been Bill's most personally significant encounter at Haasts Bluff was mentioned in a letter to Penfold at the SMAAS, dated July 6th, 1954. While it seems to have been written principally to clarify which works, described by him as *"my advanced period works and something new to you"*, he would be offering for sale to the Museum, Bill could not help mentioning his success. He included a photograph similar to the one shown on page 143, although the one sent to Penfold reportedly depicted the six major works he took up, whereas the one we see has only five. His comments, though, leave me with no doubts that the photo here is of the same incident.

Bill wrote:

> *"You will I feel be interested to know that the last of the old men of Haasts Bluff, 200 miles west of Alice Springs, met me in the lovely creek bed and I had the success I had worked for so long.[2] They reverently run their hands over my works and then they brought out their sacred Churingas and reverently began to chant over them. A deep understanding came over the scene and the next tribe I met was just the same and they said to me that I had made them proper happy.*
>
> *I modelled the wise & the last man of the Haast's bluff Loritja tribe in a life size figure. He must be 80 or so years old & he sang his chants to me … The picture shows us grouped around these works for the purpose of a photo …"*

Bill did not mention that the old man seated second from the left and holding the boomerang was blind. The first I knew of it was when it was matter-of-factly pointed out to me during the research in the Centre by a Luritja man who had known the tjilpi.[3] Bill did confirm it in a conversation with me during our time together. No doubt he ran his hands over the works a little more carefully than the other tjilpis. The great pity is that Bill did not have the language skills to exactly assess their reactions. Did the old men chant in gratitude to their Dreaming guides for delivering to them a whitefella who understood and would help, or did they simply chant a song from their world because, in their politeness, they knew that interested whitefellas liked their chants?

Bill would later tell Mary Harris that he was accepted as a "tribal brother" at what he described to her as "the ceremony" in the photograph.

I was sceptical about whether the tjilpis would have brought out their tywerrenges at the gathering and asked Les Wilson if he thought Bill's statement was accurate. He said:

> *"It is possible that the old men in the photo produced their tywerrenges and chanted over them in respect for their feelings for Billy's work. He may have moved them to that extent—it's hard to say. These would not be the tywerrenges belonging to a totemic group. They would be their own personal tywerrenge, handed down from father to son. The personal tywerrenges were usually carried with them if they went walk-about, or they kept them in camp—always, of course, wrapped up in some cloth or skin which no-one dared touch.*
>
> *These old men often went off on their own to a quiet spot in the bush, sitting down chanting their songs and gently rubbing their personal tywerrenge.*

---

2 If you're not familiar with the Centre, or indeed the outback in general, it should be stated that creek beds are preferred meeting places owing to the fact that they usually have a sandy bottom which, when you sit down, is kind on yours. We'll see soon enough why it's not advisable to camp in them.

3 "Tjilpi" is a Pitjantjatjara word, but it was widely understood in all the areas west of Alice through which I conducted my research. It is a kindly and not disrespectful word meaning, "old man". The correct spelling of tjilpi is supplied by Gavin Breen [IAD].

I have had old men leaving me their tywerrenge for safe-keeping in my office at the Settlement and often they would come to me for permission to sit in my office alone and chant over their tywerrenge. It was a wonderful feeling for me to be able to accommodate them that way."

Bill's statement about modelling the last of the Haasts Bluff Luritja tribe was inaccurate. Again, I turned to Les Wilson for his thoughts:

"Tjinapatunka wasn't the last of the Luritja tribe,[4] but he was certainly the oldest of the tribe and although he probably was, you might say, the spiritual leader of his particular totemic group, he was far too old to play any active part in the ceremonial activity."

Undoubtedly, though, Tjinapatunka had a great effect on Bill. He would write in a later letter to Doris Turner:

"The figure of the old man who was here before the white man came upon this scene is what I call the enshrinement of Australia for you would find his sort only right in the centre.

As he looked up to his mountain and pointed manner I saw what I came here to see. (Man meets mountain. Great thought deeds flow as a fountain.)

The old men are grand but the young men are imitation white men. That is a pity."

Tragically, it was often the case that Elders chose not to pass on their Dreaming history, lore, stories and songs because the rightful heirs to such knowledge were not considered loyal enough to tradition to be entrusted with such important information. Bill equated the Europeanisation of Aborigines with poisoning them. The principal reason for there being no young adult male Aborigines depicted in his sculptures is that, during the times of his visits to the Centre, he considered many of that age-group to have turned their backs on their culture—they were "poisoned" by white intervention. I could not get him to elaborate more. He obviously felt he'd said all that was needed.

Creed Lovegrove recalled that visiting Bill's camp one day, his eyes fell upon the small full-figure model of an Aboriginal man, about 25 cm high. The model, perfect in every way, showed the man wearing an army hat, great-coat and boots. Creed remembered one of the people with him pointing the piece out and commenting on how wonderful it was. *"No, that's not wonderful!"*, cried Bill. *"That's not wonderful! That's what's happening to these Aborigines. They come around the camp wearing these war-mongering clothes!"*

Leo helped Bill establish a camp close to the old telegraph station just north of the Alice Springs township, in the sandy bed of a gully opening onto the dry Charles River, a tributary of the Todd. The site was in The Bungalow Aboriginal Reserve, declared as such and closed to the public in the early 1930s. It was originally a settlement for those people classed as "half-castes", who were separated from "full blood" Aborigines because, having white blood flowing in their veins, they were considered to be a step up the humanity ladder—but definitely not approaching the level of whites. At around the beginning of WWII the Bungalow, as it was known, was made available exclusively for "full-blood" Aborigines, with those of mixed blood going to various hostels in the town.

The Bungalow was another area with rigorously enforced access restrictions applied to non-Aboriginals—and that included people with mixed blood. That Bill would have been

---

4 "Tjinapatunka" is the spelling Les Wilson supplied. Another spelling of the name is "Tjinapuntungka", which was written on the bottom of the duplicate transparency depicting the tjilpi. Since such spelling is phonetic, I can't say which is correct. I will use Les' spelling here.

allowed to enter the Reserve was not extraordinary, but for him to have been given permission to actually camp there for an indefinite period was unheard of. Such permission could only have resulted from an extremely favourable report and recommendation from Les Wilson. Although Les did not recall it, he said that he would have had no reason for not having made such a recommendation. Not one of the people with whom I spoke who were involved with the Welfare Department at that time could recall another white man before or after Bill being granted such permission to stay at the Bungalow. And if just one Aborigine had complained to the Reserve Superintendent, Bill, because he was not Government, would have been asked to leave. Bill stayed at the Bungalow until he wanted to leave.

Bill decided that he wanted to live like the Aborigines as well, so Leo built him a wiltja. The craftsmanship was not up to scratch, though, and Bill was rudely awakened during his first night's sleep when Leo's masterpiece came tumbling down. A more concerted effort was made, resulting in a more stable "home" for Bill. They set up the canvas tent as a studio, principally to protect the clay from the drying sun, and Bill was able to continue his work.

That Bill had not dropped the idea of creating his Cultural Centre and new Holy Mountain is shown in the August 7th, 1954, edition of Adelaide's *Sunday Advertiser*, in an article headed "Sculptor Would Fashion Native Utopia":

> "*... He is living like a native near Alice Springs—turning out masterpieces in clay and planning a native Utopia. Few white people know the sculptor here, but every native from Haast's Bluff and beyond has met or heard that long-haired Billy is making heads in clay. The little black-skinned children love him and at every opportunity invade his camp ...*"
>
> *He is ... seeking an area where he hopes to establish a unique aboriginal reserve. He wants to live with the natives and help them win back their lost culture.*
>
> *He is now doing heads of Aboriginal children. The piccaninnies sit patiently and delight in showing children their faces in clay later. Dozens of children will rush in greeting 'Billy' and delightedly identify one of the exquisite sculptures.*
>
> *Mr. Ricketts hopes to establish a great reserve in Central Australia. He needs a mountain or hilly country and water ... He would live there and the area would be an open house for natives who cared to join him.*"

Exactly what role Leo Corbet played in Bill's finding his feet in the Centre is scantily recorded. It must be assumed that Leo's input was significant, if only for the organisational abilities he could contribute. Alice Springs' local weekly paper, the *Centralian Advocate*, first featured Bill in the August 13th, 1954 edition. On the front page was an exceptionally blurred photograph of Bill modelling an Aboriginal man's head, with text that simply stated Bill's being in the area. Through the fuzz of the photo Bill can be seen smiling, looking tanned and happy in an open-necked shirt. A fortnight later, in the August 27th edition, Bill was written about in some detail, although Leo supplied all of the quotes. The article, headed "Noted Sculptor Has Plans For Native Reserve", stated that the pair were in the area for two or three months, and continued:

> "*Mr L. Corbet knows the Territory well and is looking after the sculptor who becomes completely engrossed in his work.*
>
> *The little gully in which [Bill] camps ... is like some strange fairyland. Little clay heads, each so lifelike that one swears a spirit is in them, peer from the sand and from beneath bushes.*"

In elaborating upon Bill's plan to establish a special reserve, the article quoted Leo as saying:

" '... Ayer's Rock would be ideal.'

The sculptor wishes to set his works up [in the Centre] in the same way as in the Dandenong Ranges. If Ayer's Rock was possible, it would be a magnificent National centre—alive with native traditions and myths as it is, Mr Corbet said.

Since coming to the Centre, [Bill] has not visited town. Until last weekend, few white people knew he was in the area."

Various visitors to Bill's camp at the Bungalow were told of the spectacle he could make if only Uluru were given to him. Can you imagine Uluru with monolithic bas-relief sculptures of the wise old men and women of Central Australia gazing out over the plains to Katatjuta and Mt Connor? Bill could.

After Bill was set up in a camp, Leo had time on his hands for a poke around. If he was revisiting old ground, he was looking with renewed interest. He liked what he saw; liked the history, both black and white, and nurtured a great respect for the people of the Centre. Unlike Bill's, Leo's respect also encompassed the fortitude and inventiveness of the non-Aboriginal pioneers, although he would never accept the bad treatment given to the Aborigines. The more he experienced, the greater was the Centre's grip on him.

Leo came to know an old-timer named Charles Henry "Pop" Chapman, a Territorian who'd made his mark and his money on the Granites gold fields north-west of Alice Springs; so much so that he was known as "the grand old man of the Granites". Pop Chapman, who published the *Advocate*'s first edition in May, 1947, would have been about seventy-nine years old in 1954, and an encyclopaedia of stories and yarns about pioneering the outback—just the sort of person with whom Leo would have clicked. Pop lived on a property just south of Heavitree Gap, the southern gateway to The Alice through the Macdonnell Ranges. The house was built on a small knoll which the Arrernte people knew as Alpra. After sending to Italy for a marble statue featuring an angel and erecting it prominently at his gatepost, Pop named the property "Pearly Gates" and reportedly delighted in answering telephone calls with, *"Hello, Pearly Gates—Peter here"*. By the last third of 1954, though, Pop was not in the best of health. Leo apparently spent quite a deal of time at "Pearly Gates" helping out where he could and generally enjoying the company of the old character who had a wealth of experience behind him. What's more, old Pop thoroughly enjoyed Leo's company.

Whether he knew it then or not, Leo Corbet was on an irreversible path to becoming not only a Centralian himself, but another of the Territory's characters.

Meanwhile Bill again found himself a niche within the local community of Aborigines. Positioned in the Aboriginal Reserve, living like no other whitefella known to them, his long hair giving him a rare appearance compared with other whites, Bill was not seen as a threat. No doubt due to a certain amount of spoiling by Bill, his camp became a regular drop-in place for the children.[5] This gave Bill a wonderful opportunity to capture their likenesses, albeit in a rush and often from recent memory. He wrote to Mary Harris:

"They are lovely children with a ready smile always ... I want to get about thirty of these children's heads alone besides my other works. Altogether my camp is just ground to do my work. The children model the clay I give them (that is while I model them) so we are busy."

The ploy definitely had the children sitting still for longer than usual, but no mention was made of whether he took the opportunity to teach them the fundamentals of modelling or of what they made.

---

5 The Aboriginal people I met during the research who were children at the time of Bill's visits clearly remember him best for the lollies and sweet drinks he readily handed out.

Bill worked so prolifically that it was not long before he could see the end of the stockpile of clay he'd brought along. He asked Mary Harris to contact the Potters' Club in Adelaide and organise a shipment to be railed up. In the meantime, Leo went searching and eventually turned up more local clay which Bill passed as satisfactory. It was not so satisfactory to make him cancel his order from Mary, though, but chances are that there are a couple of smaller works sitting around created from the very Centre itself.

There was no shortage of customers for the small pieces and Bill quickly found himself needing to create and fire more, if he was to keep his cash flow up. Making them was one thing—firing them, quite another. I heard stories of Bill burying sun-dried works in the hot coal-beds of camp fires or cutting the tops from twenty litre kerosine tins, placing the works inside and building fires up around them—anything to get some hardness into his pieces.

Bill fired with varying success. Two pieces I saw which were definitely created in the Centre during this period were porous in the extreme, the result of a lack of fusion due to poor firing. This was only discovered when I attempted to wipe the dust from them with a damp cloth in preparation for photographs, a normally safe procedure with kiln-fired clay. Imagine my surprise when I saw the piece absorbing water almost as fast as it was applied! The risk, of course, is that the clay might absorb enough moisture to cause swelling and, potentially, cracking. I mention this as a warning. Before dunking any of Bill's work in the washing-up water for a good scrub, do check for porosity by placing a drop of water on an inconspicuous spot and give it a few minutes to allow you to observe whether or not it soaks in. If the work is porous, simply protect it from moisture and it should remain something to be treasured and admired until you drop it on the floor.

Bill was not content with a static display for the works he'd taken up with him, or for the new pieces he was creating. Along the creek bed, over a distance of about 50 m, Bill arranged his works in such a way that they would benefit fully from the surroundings, much the same as he did at Mt Dandenong. Still not content, he and Leo hauled water from town in 200 litre drums and rigged up plumbing to those works fitted with small fountains—and the waters did flow. Under the scorching Centralian sun, surrounded by bare hills of red rock dotted with spinifex, Bill brought his works to life. The water attracted birds, so seed was purchased and put out—which attracted more birds. Another temporary sanctuary was created.

According to Bill, the Aborigines started calling him "Brother Billy". Nobody I spoke with in the Centre could confirm this, although some non-Aboriginals recalled that he would introduce himself as "Billy". Not one of the many Aborigines I spoke with in the Centre recalled Bill as either "Billy" or "Brother Billy". They remembered him as "Spirit"—not because of his spiritual air, but because of his ability to reproduce exact likenesses of their kind in white clay. The title was not recalled at any time with bitterness or superstitious awe, but simply as a matter of fact. The "Brother Billy" title was, however, picked up and taken on by both the press and many of Bill's friends down south.

Towards the end of October Bill wrote a letter to Doris Turner, with even his hardships not able to dull his wonder and happiness:

"I am doing fine and successful and I think I will be up here a few more months yet. I have been outback and will be outback again later. For the time I am on a native reserve a few miles out from Alice Springs.

Here I am called Brother Billy.

There are beautiful places here and the Standley Chasm is like being in another world. You just walk inside the mountain of rock, red colour, and with the sun at different times of the day it is just magic beyond words.

This week I have been washed out of my camp twice, for I am camped under a beautiful gum tree right in the creek bed in the lovely sand. However, it was too much so I am now on the bank with my bed hung up in the branches with ropes. It is lovely to be

*here and look up and see the many stars changing colour all the time. My works will
enshrine all this ...*

*They broadcast me often here and Darwin and I have some wonderful photos of
my work.*

*I miss the deep scent of the lovely musk and all else. Here it is the mountains of red
rock and the white gums set against the rock is just beyond words. The gums, Eucalyptus
Terininalis[6] are pure white with a scented dust you can rub off on your hands. The
butcher birds just warble and warble all day in the tree.*

Now from this red rock world I close with my kind regards to all my friends."

It was signed "Brother Billy", the form he would continue to use, and by which he preferred
to be called, for many years to come.

Bill learned a golden rule of the outback, that you never camp in a dry creek bed, in a way
which could easily have spelled disaster for him. A storm, distant or near, can suddenly turn your
idyllic spot into a wet nightmare, if not a death trap.

The first flash flood caught Bill unawares, threatening all. Bill and Leo worked frantically,
struggling through red swirling water to rescue the works and Bill's belongings. Fortunately, only
a few unfired works were lost. The rest they managed to move to higher ground. As quickly as
the water rose, it subsided and the camp was remade in the creek bed. It took a second flash flood
a few days later to convince Bill that he would be better placed permanently on the higher
ground. Relocated, Bill rigged up his ingenious aerial bed, as depicted in the photograph on
page 146. On seeing the photograph again in 1986, Bill explained: *"I was free from the snakes up
there."* The memory prompted one of his rare voluntary reminiscences:

*"I was up there one day when the Aboriginal people came and said, 'The
kurdaitchas will get you!'[7] That means men were after a certain man to kill him for doing
something. They come and told me, 'Be careful, the kurdaitchas are coming—they will
get you!' I still slept up there though."*

The kurdaitcha men on a mission of revenge were believed to have been invested with
special powers. Often it was the case that visiting kurdaitchas were there to kill a person who had
broken a Law. They killed by various means, including spearing, "singing" [performing a death
chant] or pointing the bone—the last two of which were very effective, even though science
assures that any result is psychosomatic. Their presence would send waves of unease through
whole communities. If delivered by one who knew of and believed in the kurdaitcha's powers,
such a warning as Bill's was not idle chatter.

Was it simply a friendly warning of potential danger in the area? Or was it the result of a
direct threat?

Dealing, as he was, with the oldest people he could find, Bill was treading on delicate
ground. If one of those tjilpis died soon after Bill had modelled his likeness, an accusing finger
could well have been pointed after Bill. In those days within the indigenous community of
Central Australia, there was no such thing as a "natural" death. All deaths were believed to have
been caused by foul play of some form or another. If the offender was known, and it was very
seldom that an offender could not be determined for what were considered valid reasons,
retribution had to be exacted. It obviously did not occur to Bill that the kurdaitchas might have
been after "a certain man" making spirits.

---

6 "Terininalis" is spelled faithful to Bill's letter.
7 "Kurdaitcha" has many variations of spelling, and an uncertain history. See Dixon, Ransom and Thomas, *Australian
Aboriginal Words In English*.

That aerial bed also caused Bill to be brought undone one day. It happened when a straight talking old cattleman reportedly visited the camp.[8] During the course of the visit, Bill launched into a tirade about what was going wrong in the country. The cattleman nodded in understanding about most things, including Bill's disgust at the senseless graffiti scrawled by tourists on every piece of vacant space in the Territory. But when Bill went on to the despoilers of the forests and the destruction of the trees, the cattleman grinned. He spat in the sand, then looked up at Bill's bed and the sapling poles which had been used in its construction: *"What about the trees you cut down for your hammock?"*, he asked. Bill changed the subject.

On November 6th, 1954, the Melbourne *Argus* newspaper brought news of his adventures back home via a generally approving feature article entitled, "He Dreams of a Clay Revolution". Written by Ross Annabell, Bill was described as: *"as strange a character as ever pitched his tent in the Dead Heart"*. He went on to explain that Bill: *"had renounced normal life, and turned God-inspired sculptor with a mission to spread a new religion which he believes will revolutionise the world … Had he been born 2,000 years ago, Billy would have undoubtedly become an apostle, or a saint."* Bill continued to denounce himself as the artist, insisting that God was the artist working through him. Annabell continued with what was probably a quite inflammatory statement for those days, and nowadays for that matter:

> *"Billy loves the aborigines, and claims that they live a life that is closer to God than that of the bulk of Australia's 9,000,000-odd inhabitants …*
>
> *Fiercely resentful of the way the aborigines have been treated since the coming of the white man to Australia, Billy talks of more drastic action if his works of art fail to awaken Australians to full realisation of their sins against the aborigines.*
>
> *Soon, he says, he may have to go to India and talk with Nehru to get the backing of millions of Indians on the side of the aborigines."*[9]

On November 15th, before he knew of the *Argus* article, Bill wrote to Mary Harris with a request:

> *"Of all Australia I ask you to make myself and my endeavour known to one I admire. The first man of India Pundit Nehru. I feel that he is far above the military level in the world's present plight. I too am in this fight in the realm of spirit Mary …*
>
> *Most Australians think I am doing art. That is not so, and therefore their thinking has no depth in it.*
>
> *Because I am born in Australia with some awareness of the great and noble possibilities of my spiritual life I have been looking on at all the hell let loose upon the beautiful Australian bush at the hands of the white man … Looking on and being helpless I have been forced to go through all this Australian hell and suffer it so that I would know why all this hell has come upon me. The roots of all my works go down into that hell and out of all this I try to seek the highest meaning to life itself wherein is enshrined the true meaning of the oneness and wholeness of life. That oneness means wholeness, and wholeness means to me beauty, love, wonder, a true state of health and the <u>true</u> and beautiful state of freedom.*
>
> *If people still call my work art, I tell them that I am forging a weapon to fight until the last lovely parrot is released from its cage. In this I will be both loved and hated. Most people do not understand these words of mine and they will not believe them unless they*

---

8 This tale appeared in an article by Ross Annabell which was published in the March 7th, 1956, edition of *People* magazine, which was quite a long time after Bill had moved his camp from the Bungalow.
9 Jawaharlal Nehru; 1889–1964; the first Prime Minister of the republic of India, 1947–1964.

can see them given form. So then I work so that my works being spiritual shall defend me and all I fight for ...

When I have my works all ready and finished I shall take them out of my country and ask other countries to take hold of all my works say ... and I think mostly of India ... It would be a good thing if the Indian Government took over my mountain gallery and land and build a temple there for the Indian and other students who come here.

I will be understood when I say I am going to fight because I see no repentance in the Australians as a whole ..."

Over 2,000 km away in Sydney, A. R. Penfold was worrying more than a little about Bill's situation. He had been sent a copy of the *Argus* article by an acquaintance, which he read with interest. By chance, as he was reading about Bill, he received a telephone call from Mr Williams of the Sydney office of the Victorian Tourist Bureau. Williams had recently been in Alice Springs where, by chance or design, he visited Bill's camp. Williams expressed concern over Bill's state, saying that he appeared, physically, to be on the verge of starvation, with his financial situation being no better. Penfold despatched a letter to Bill on November 16th, addressing it C/o the Alice Springs Post Office. He diplomatically offered his congratulations on Bill's achievements in the Centre and requested an account of just what Bill had produced to date. Attempting to boost Bill's financial situation, Penfold also offered to purchase anything Bill might want to sell.

The November 19th edition of the *Advocate* brought rather detailed news of Bill to the people of Alice Springs. It was, however, news which Bill would not pass on to his friends and acquaintances back home.

It appears that Bill came to know an Aborigine named Lindsay Turner who lived at the Bungalow. Creed Lovegrove very good-naturedly recalled Lindsay as, *"a bit of a larrikin of a bloke"*. Most Centralian Aborigines had never had the opportunity to learn to read or write. While Lindsay could drive a vehicle as well as anyone, a clause in the Ordinance relating to driver's licences stated that a person must be able to read and write English before a driver's licence could be issued; the result being that Lindsay was unlicensed.

Notwithstanding this minor detail [in Bill's eyes at any rate], Bill employed Lindsay to drive him around whenever the need arose. On at least one occasion Bill had been warned by Sgt Hughes, of the Alice Springs constabulary, that he could get both himself and Lindsay into trouble by letting Lindsay drive.

One evening Lindsay showed up at Bill's camp *"in a very agitated state"* with news that his father was sick and had to be taken to hospital immediately. Lindsay asked for a loan of Bill's truck, to which Bill quickly agreed. However, Lindsay's father was not sick, and instead Lindsay went and bought some beer on the sly, proceeded to drink himself into a state and then went to the *"native ward"* of the hospital in search of some female company—or as the *Advocate* eloquently reported it: *"tried to procure lubras for himself, and, in one case badly frightened one native girl in the ward ..."* The police were called and Lindsay ended up under arrest and in court before Mr J. W. Nichols, SM, on Friday, November 12th, 1954.

Mr Nichols was one of the Territory's characters in his own right. He'd been in Darwin when the Japanese bombing took place, but, unlike many other public servants who headed south, Mr Nichols stayed behind. Such was the shortage of Public Servants that Mr Nichols at one stage held twenty-three titled Government offices—concurrently! He was a physically big man who was always receiving media praise, typical examples of which are, *"one of the Territory's most respected and best liked officials"* and *"the embodiment of kindness, sociability and Justice"*.

Mr Nichols listened as a guilty plea to three charges was entered on Lindsay's behalf; drinking liquor,[10] unlicensed driving and behaving unlawfully on hospital premises. Sgt Hughes related the events leading up to Lindsay's arrest, including Bill's prior warning regarding letting an unlicensed person drive his truck. Mr Nichols told the court that he viewed the hospital incident very seriously, adding that *"it was possible that had the boy not been lent the truck, none of this would have happened"*. Sgt Hughes said that he would be having a talk to Bill about the matter, as well as going to see the person who allegedly sold Lindsay bottles of beer for the very cheap price of four shillings per bottle. Reported the *Advocate*:

> *"Mr Nichols commented dryly that if Lindsay knew where to buy beer at four shillings a bottle, perhaps they should all go see the supplier."*

Lindsay was found to be guilty as charged and sentenced to three months in jail with hard labour.

Sgt Hughes' talk with Bill resulted in him facing Mr Nichols the following Monday, being charged with lending his truck to an unlicensed driver. Bill pleaded not guilty, although he admitted in both evidence and statements that, yes, he had lent the truck to Lindsay and, yes, he did know that Lindsay was unlicensed.

Bill would have looked directly into Mr Nichols' eyes, a picture of self-righteousness and determination, with just a hint of defiance, when he responded:

> *"I place my human feelings above all things, even sometimes man-made laws—and had I not lent [Lindsay] the truck and something had happened to his father, I would have felt responsible."*

Bill then reportedly smiled at Mr Nichols and said that he liked Lindsay, adding that he still liked Lindsay. Turning round, Bill addressed Lindsay directly, saying: *"I still like you Lindsay— this business doesn't matter."*

After hearing the evidence, Mr Nichols found Bill to be guilty as charged—but said that he believed Bill's sympathy had got the better of him. Mr Nichols advised that such an offence carried a maximum fine of £100, no doubt a warning, but said that he felt a conviction without penalty, excepting costs of £1, would be correct in the case.

"When can you pay the £1 costs, Mr Ricketts?", asked Mr Nichols.

"Well", said Bill in what would surely have been his meekest little-boy-lost voice, his eyes pleading hardship and sincerity: *"it will take just about my last £1 and make it hard to continue my work—some people in Melbourne are trying to do something for me—but I suppose it must be paid."* Bill paused. Then, realising the right way for it to go from there, he said: *"However, I'd like it very much if you give me back the £1—it would help my work and my people."* Bill seized the opportunity and addressed the court in general: *"Indeed, if anyone likes they can add a few pounds on to the £1—it would help a lot."*

Creed Lovegrove also told me this tale, but he was too busy chuckling to mention Mr Nichols' response. It can be assumed that Bill paid his £1 and did not end up breaking rocks in jail.

---

10 It was illegal at that time for Aborigines to consume liquor in any form, and anybody found guilty of supplying liquor to Aborigines was subject to a mandatory six months jail term for the first offence.

11 | Finding Utopia
[1954–1955]

Bill did not complain about starvation or police persecution in the letter he wrote to Doris Turner in November, 1954. While he did mention a lack of funds which he was trying to overcome *["I do many small pieces for sale"]*, he dealt first with and so was presumably more worried about whether or not the *Herald* or *Argus* had printed anything about him, requesting that Doris send him cuttings of anything that appeared.

Readers of the November 19th Melbourne *Herald* were alerted to another of Bill's plights, this time regarding his larger works. An article headed, "'Centre' Sculptures May Be Ruined", was a vehicle for Leo Corbet's feeling that, *"Keeping Ricketts in Central Australia—and getting his work to Melbourne—were of national importance"*, and that the life-sized work of Tjinapatunka was, *"well worthy of the National Art Gallery in Melbourne"*. The general thrust of the article was that Bill should receive financial support of some sort to have his large works, at that stage only sun-dried, carefully crated and sent down south for firing. It was suggested that the only alternative was the works' destruction should Bill attempt to take the works back himself.

When the Sydney *Sun* ran an article early in December entitled "One-Man Crusade in Clay", written by Lionel Hogg, Penfold's concerns were reawakened. He had received no reply to his earlier letter. The article first brought good news about the local Arrernte peoples' reaction to Bill's work:

> *"Each morning just after dawn, the elders of the Arunta tribe walk slowly across the Bungalow Native Reserve, five miles from Alice Springs, to pay homage to the work of a strange little man with long greying hair ... They kneel in front of the sculptures, chant their song cycles, and rub their hands over them with the reverence they have for the churingas ... William Ricketts looks on happily. He knows that at last his work has been recognised ..."*[1]

Hogg went on to report that Bill had established his cultural centre and "mountain of love" on the site, which would have been interpreted by anybody who knew of Bill's history that the Mountain Gallery at Mt Dandenong had become a thing of the past. As far as Bill was concerned, such an interpretation would have been accurate. The Mountain Gallery was too small for his grand plans, but he had no hope of enlarging upon it without major backing. In a December 4th letter to Doris Turner, Bill admitted that, *"in my disgust about what people are doing to the Mountain, I stopped doing any more there ... years ago"*, because he really needed *"one third of the Dandenong Ranges for [his] great spectacle of life"*. Hogg also revealed in his article that, *"Ricketts is penniless"*.

---

1 While this quote looks similar to the description Bill himself had previously given of the Aborigines' reaction, we must assume that Mr Hogg reported from first-hand experience. He made no mention that the scene was described to him.

Unaware that Bill had posted his reply a day or two earlier, Penfold wrote again, explaining that the news of Bill's financial position caused him to be very disturbed. He again offered to be of assistance as soon as Bill got in touch. Penfold barely veiled his interest in the Mountain Gallery works, requesting information of what was happening back south and if any good works were still in situ.

Bill's letter repeated his offer of the same five works. He sent another set of photographs to make sure Penfold had an idea of what was in the collection. Bill wouldn't send the works over immediately because he planned to take them *"out back over the next six months ... to show as many native people possible"*. As soon as he returned from the Centre, though, he would take the pieces to Sydney to discuss *"their, what is called, value"*. Bill accepted Penfold's offer of financial support by airing the possibility of a £250 advance to help see him through, writing that he would have papers drawn up by a solicitor vesting ownership of the works to the SMAAS; *"a safe guard against anything happening to end my life"*. Penfold's reply of December 15th gave Bill news to make for a happy Christmas. It offered hope of the £250 advance being forwarded early the next month.

On December 22nd Bill had another little Christmas bonus; the Deptartment of Information's short documentary on the Mountain Gallery was screened in Alice Springs. Although it was the first time that he saw it, in no letter did I find his assessment of the film.

The last news Alice Springs residents received on Bill before Christmas was a December 24th article in the *Advocate* reporting that Bill had constructed a kiln at his camp, making it possible for him to at last *"bake and treat his pieces"* instead of risking a journey with them back south. Unfortunately, no mention was made of the kiln's design, but it was not large enough to accommodate the big works.

Just seven days into the new year, the Centre lost one of its favourite sons. After a *"short, serious illness"*, Pop Chapman died. I don't know how much trouble Pop had getting through *the* Pearly Gates, but on terra firma Leo made it through the Alice's Pearly Gates by purchasing the property from the two Chapman children to whom it had been left. Exactly when, I can't say, but Leo would change the name of the property. As he told a friend, *"The Pearly Gates might seem a bit presumptuous, coming from me"*. The name he settled on was Pitchi Richi, which is derived from the Arrernte language. I was given several translations, the most authoritative of which was "come and look".

Bill's new year started with him sending one of the more unusual examples of his work to Penfold. It was a delicate, thin-walled vessel from which an equally thin "veil" of clay was drawn out from one side. The "veil" was where you'd expect to find a handle, but such was its fragility that it could never confidently be used for the purpose. Opposite the veil on that piece was the sculptured face of Tjinapatunka. These were Bill's "loving cups"; so called because they had to be handled with the gentleness of a lover. When I showed Bill a photo of the work, he gasped: *"Fancy domesticating a tribe of ancient people like that!"* He studied the photo carefully, remembering how it felt in his hands before adding, with a shake of his head, *"What a pity I had to sell them"*. His thoughts had changed little over the years, because in the letter forewarning the cup's arrival, Bill wrote: *"I am hard to be satisfied with my work but this one I sent you is a very beautiful example ... I know you will treasure it for there is nothing like it in the world."* It was also a measure of the success Bill sometimes had with his home-made kilns, for the finished article rang clearly when tapped. When Penfold acknowledged receipt of the vessel, he assured Bill that *"it will be treasured"*, but could not give any definite news regarding the £250 advance.

On January 15th, 1955, the Melbourne *Age* ran a prominent page two article written by Alan Nicholls and titled, "Black Artist And White In Tragic Dilemma". I found it a disturbing and somewhat depressing piece which drew a parallel between Bill Ricketts and Albert Namatjira; suggesting that they were both, in their own way, turning their backs on their own people in preference for the other's race. Nicholls predicted: *"Though neither has fully realised it, both face tragedy."*

The word-picture Nicholls painted of Namatjira was certainly tragic. While Namatjira radiated a power, he was dirty and unkempt—his *"thirty idle hangers-on"* more so. It implied that Namatjira was not concerned at leaving his tribal life behind, although he was vehemently bitter at not being allowed to build a house on his block of land, *"to live with a refrigerator, behind an oleander hedge, like the rest of The Alice middle class"*.

Nicholls had Bill as squatting *"in the dust like a fakir, wearing nothing but tattered shorts"*. He wrote of Bill's affinity with the birds which came to his camp, *"as though he were a Francis of Assisi"*, and called him *"a latter-day William Blake"*. And he wrote of alleged troubles Bill was having:

> *"He rises now from his birds, his eyes cold with rage, to explain why he had never done a portrait of Namatjira. 'I asked him to sit', he said, 'but he just looked at me and said: How much?'*
>
> *Bill has done his best to get the aborigines to take off their clothes, telling them that their bodies are God-given temples. After much palavering round the camp fire they agreed to take them off at a price—10 [shillings] a head."*

Further on in the article, Nicholls observed:

> *"Bill is not defeated. He has only been forced to set himself a wider task. First he must restore the black man to his ancient virtue, then he must use it as an example to shame the white man. In the meantime, perhaps as a result of his tragic conflict of mind, he is working better than he ever has before."*

On that note, Nicholls went on to describe poetically the "Evening Star" and life-size "Tjinapatunka" pieces, again highlighting Bill's need for assistance to get them south for firing. If such help was not forthcoming, *"two great works of art [would] lie unseen in that blazing red gully until they crumble away"*.

When I read Bill the quote about Aborigines wanting money and I asked if it were true, he said emphatically that it was not. He told me that he had met Namatjira and admired his paintings enough to have purchased two, but never had he asked Namatjira to sit for him. Regarding the ten shillings per head to take off their clothes, Bill simply said that he had hardly enough money to feed himself, let alone pay for models. Nicholls' quote also does not fit with the picture as suggested by the Patrol Officers and Reserve Superintendents with whom I spoke. There was however an article in the *Advocate* in September, 1954, which reported that enterprising Aborigines were charging camera-wielding tourists up to £1 for the "classic" pose of no clothes, standing on one leg, with spears and boomerangs—with a regular smiling snap-shot at just one shilling.

My confusion comes from the fact that Bill largely modelled busts of his subjects, the head and shoulders only, which would not require the removal of clothes. If the article contained inaccuracies, as Bill suggested when I asked him about it, it's to be imagined that he would have pointed them out at the time. Instead, just over one month after its publication, Bill wrote to Penfold stating: *"the best article yet printed is by the Melbourne Age 15th Jan"*.

Penfold was to find out why it was that Bill had been driven to request the £250 advance when he received a letter from Bill's solicitors in Melbourne towards the end of January. Bill was being taken to court by the suppliers of his new kiln who claimed that they were still owed £418 10s 5d from an account sent to Bill on April 23rd, 1953. However, the solicitors felt that £250, although well short of the amount allegedly owed, would be sufficient to placate the creditors. The solicitors had advised Bill that he had a good case against a large portion of the claim [presumably because of the ongoing difficulties the suppliers had getting the kiln to behave], but since Bill was not to be present, defending the case was difficult. Bill had advised his solicitors of the possibility of the SMAAS advance, and since the hearing was set down for February 3rd, the solicitors thought it best to deal directly with Penfold so as to ascertain the exact picture. Penfold could not assist immediately, and advised that it would be at least February 22nd before he had any definite news.

It came to light, though, that it was not just the SMAAS who had been putting up the money for all of the purchases of Bill's works. A mystery patron, referred to by Penfold only as *"a friend who at one time assisted the Museum to acquire one or more outstanding examples of Ricketts' work"*, was no longer in a position to help. Was this "friend" patronising Bill via the Museum, or simply patronising the SMAAS? And how many was "one or more"? That I did not find out.

Quite apart from the debt crisis, Penfold took the trouble to advise Bill that he should be represented at the International Exhibition of Ceramics to be held at Cannes, France, in the coming June. Mr Williams, of the Victorian Tourist Bureau, had shown Penfold colour slides of Bill's works in the Centre, and it was one of Bill's twin-spouted tea-pots that Penfold thought would be "well-received" at the festival.[2] Bill's initial reaction was in the negative: *"When I go [overseas] with my works, I will not take __ART__ but a way of life, and the word ceramics would tend to mix things up."* It's possible that Bill's ambitions to travel overseas were further fuelled by a visit from Fred Hubbard, a Brisbane-based journalist for the respected US *Time* magazine. After interviewing Bill, Hubbard was confident enough to say that an article would appear in the internationally distributed publication as part of their February 21st, 1955, edition.

When Bill wrote to Doris Turner on February 17th, he had exciting news of big plans just ahead. He would first go north *"in two weeks"* to a new camp, but in April he planned an epic. He would return to where the road finished at Haasts Bluff and an unidentified Aboriginal friend would then take Bill out to his people in the Gibson Desert. It would require a four-week journey by camel to reach this goal and be followed by a four month long stay with true, "unpolluted" bush folk. Bill would have been bursting at the thought. At last, an epic journey to meet the true people, from which would come epic works that would challenge the world. Sadly, for Bill, it was another dream which did not come true.

Bill thanked Doris for "the money", which suggests that she was having some luck selling pieces which Bill had left behind. There were at least another three works for sale back home, which he wrote could go for *"a little less if someone genuine can not pay what I put on them"*. He had a little gripe about the hot weather, saying how glad he would be when it ended. After mentioning the visit from *Time* magazine he philosophised:

> *"If I were a mere weakling all these newspaper articles on me would make me puff up like a nice pink balloon. Instead it will help me in what I am to do.*
> *I am well and brown and it will be strange to stand in our mountain mists again and lose all my colour ... do remember me to my friends and that means more than anything my darling Lyre Bird and my ring tail possum."*

On February 21st, 1955, Penfold wrote to Bill with news that he finally had at his disposal the sum of £100 which he proposed to make available to Bill to cover the cost of the "loving cup", as well as going towards future purchases. Penfold wanted to know whether he should send the money straight up to Bill or to the solicitors, because: *"The Trustees are anxious to help you, and do not want any money that is being sent to you for your personal benefit to be handed to creditors, so as far as I am concerned, I would prefer to send the money direct to you."* Bill did not take up the offer and authorised Penfold to send the money directly to the solicitors in Melbourne. The trade-off for the advance was that Bill advise his solicitors to transfer ownership of two works to the SMAAS, on the understanding that they would not be formally valued until

---

2 If any reader has access to those slides, I would love to see them.

the Trustees examined them. Penfold also mentioned that the *Time* journalist had contacted him seeking extra information, with Penfold supplying *"much interesting information"*, as well as inviting Hubbard to view the SMAAS's Ricketts' collection. Hubbard's wife had gone down instead, but there was an air of expectation in Penfold's words about Bill's forthcoming exposure.

The *Time* article appeared under the heading of "ART" and was titled, "Oneness in the Dead Heart". Two small illustrations drew readers' attention; "Tjinapatunka" [which they spelled as Tjipuntja] sitting life-like, gazing into the distance, and "The Evening Star" maiden, head bowed wistfully, her young breasts just visible as she sank into the stone. The opening paragraph introduced Bill to a vast new international audience with the following:

> *"Few modern artists express mystical insights in vividly concrete terms because so few even try. Last week word reached the U.S. of an Australian sculptor who is trying—hard. William Ricketts' baked-clay figures may be far from great, but they are good, and the sculptor's spirit makes them news."*

There followed a description of Bill's set-up in the Centre and his personal history, both very brief. With regard to what Bill was trying to express through his work, he was quoted as saying: *"Mankind must be made aware that there is no such thing as separateness. Even the veriest grain of sand is part of the oneness of God's creatures."* Presumably as a result of the information supplied by Penfold, the SMAAS was given as the sole supplier of Bill's *"simple needs"*. Justifying the expense, Penfold was quoted as saying, *"[Bill] is undoubtedly a genius"*. *Time* poured a little oil on Penfold's high praise, finishing the article with:

> *"Not many Australian critics are aware of Ricketts, and of those who are, few share Penfold's vast enthusiasm for his art. Emotional self-expression, they complain, is absent from Ricketts' sculptures. But self-expression is only one goal of art. Ricketts, squatting beneath his wilderness gum tree to model as best he can in clay, has a loftier aim."*

The *Advocate* reviewed the *Time* article most favourably. In addition to quoting heavily from the text, they ventured their own opinion:

> *"Victorian sculptor, William Ricketts, who has now for all intents and purposes identified himself with the Centralian scene as a permanent resident, is featured in the current issue of 'Time' ...*
>
> *On the whole 'Time' has taken a distinctly appreciative view of Ricketts ... and it seems likely that this modest, unassuming man may contribute something of considerable artistic importance to the Central Australian pattern of life, as well as bringing a cultural aspect to the limited knowledge of this country held by the majority of people overseas."*

When Bill finally read the *Time* piece, his response was realistic:

> *"They did not have a great deal to say, however to be printed in it means a lot."*

The article prompted correspondence to Penfold from people the world wide, including the US, Holland, the Fiji Islands and New Zealand. They wanted to know more about Bill; whether any books about him were available, how to purchase his works or simply where to address correspondence. Penfold acknowledged these letters and personally undertook to be an intermediary in the matter of prospective purchasers. To one of them Penfold provided the following information: *"He is a very difficult man to deal with and it is only on rare occasions that he can be persuaded to part with any of his work. As a matter of fact, he rarely effects sales unless he is in urgent need of money and the present appears to be an opportune time to discuss business with him."* While Penfold may have been playing hard to get on Bill's behalf regarding the scarcity of his work for sale, it is quite probable that he had no idea of Bill's prolificness and believed that what he had written was correct.

Bill never advertised the fact that he sold regularly. Quite often potential buyers were told to come back in the near future, by which time he would have made them something "special". At other times he would disappear and return with a work, proving that it was the buyer's lucky day. Always though, there was the implication or specific request that the "lucky" purchaser should keep their good luck quiet. Bill did not want to be tied down by a rush of orders. Most buyers respected that trust, keeping their purchases to themselves, sometimes for decades. It was not the marketing ploy of a naïve eccentric. Bill knew that to stay in the race until major support came to him, he needed a cash flow. But to maintain what he perceived to be his credibility, he could not go the way of a commercial artist.

Bill continued selling small works to both locals and tourists to support himself, although it would appear that little if any of the money he earned in the Centre found its way back to Melbourne to service his debts. Debts seemed of secondary concern.

With each passing day, Bill's determination and resolve to win the battle he had declared increased and burned more intensely within him. He survived as an increasingly dense vessel of raw energy, drive and righteousness, occasionally boiling over, but never completely losing his special brand of control. He could maintain such a state of being very simply, because there was not one grain of doubt in him. He knew he was *right*, and nobody could so much as tarnish his armour. Short of someone shooting him dead, *"which had happened to every good man from Christ to Gandhi"*, as he was known to say, he would succeed.

Although Bill, in his mind, had at that time given up the idea of *the* Holy Mountain being at the Mountain Gallery, Doris' letters never failed to move him. The following condensed excerpt from a March 13th, 1955, reply to her confirms the extent of his ties and the depth of his feelings:

> *"You mention my lyre bird and that makes me so homesick. All my life in the beautiful bush is every moment alive in my spirit. In the past my inner life or spiritual life has cried to breaking point over everything that has happened in Australia. Now I get ready weapons and I will be expected to use them. So much that in the eyes of other countries, specially India, this lot in this land and the laws will never again know that same comfortable feeling.*
>
> *Beauty is the answer to everything you can think and dream about. I will single handed fight for Australia."*

The planned trip north into country on Utopia Station was repeatedly postponed. Bill kept busy and devoted some of his time to learning how to drive the truck. He entertained a couple of more important visitors one weekend in April. The Governor General, Sir William Slim, and his wife dropped into Bill's camp while they were inspecting the old telegraph buildings and were, as reported by the *Advocate*, *"keenly interested in the work"*. The article also advised that anyone who wanted to see more examples of Bill's work could make an appointment to visit Leo Corbet's property, where some exhibits were located. That snippet provides the approximate time of Pitchi Richi's first having Bill's works within its boundaries. In Bill's next letter to Doris, dated April 14th, he wrote:

> *"I would like to see the Argus with the Governor Generals visit to my camp.*[3] *I may have use for the item some time later so would you get me 4 copies in all of that Argus. I have put some stamps in to cover the cost. They told me here that the national news broadcast the Governor's visit to my place.*

---

3 Bill needn't have bothered with the *Argus* article. It said only that the Governor General intended to visit the camp.

"Now the wonderful colours are showing and the other day while I was at Jay Creek[4] I looked back over the tops of the gums that fill the creek and just the top of the range was showing near by and it was just startling to see what I could only say was burnished gold standing out above the green of the tree tops.

I shall be here until October and then I may have to come back to finish my work. I may have to leave my works here and build a kiln to harden them so that they will be alright to travel with them. I drive the truck myself now so I can go anywhere I like and next week I go to my new camp 200 miles north east. I may be there a good while if all goes well."

The next day Bill wrote to Patricia Michell, a New Zealander who, having been given Bill's address by Penfold following the *Time* article, had written to Bill. She had struck a chord within him, for he assured her that he welcomed *"letters of understanding"*. He wrote of his plans and wishes and experiences, seemingly unconcerned at revealing more than a little of himself to a stranger:

"The mountain colours here in winter time is something you cannot put into words. You can only think about the whole of it, even to the last grain of sand. Then as we think of it within our spiritual nature, we must liberate our thinking and give it outward form into works. Then if the grandeur of our works satisfies one self, then you wish with all your might to share it with all, and when I say all I mean … with every living creature."

Bill went on to tell her about his Dreaming, sometimes using nearly word-for-word sentences from past letters. On formal religion he stated: *"I am of no church for they do not impress me, but I uphold the Master's teaching at every point."* He did not identify the Master. He openly confessed his bewilderment about his place in the big picture:

"You remember your letter which says 'What a tremendous country'. And yet it is on a tiny bit infinitesimal part of the Solar System which again is as a pin prick to the outer regions and so on until I sometimes wonder whether it all really does exist.

I would like to put it in my way and that is when I look at one of my works or creations I realise how little a part it is of the great worlds or great regions that lie within your own spiritual nature. I wonder at the mystery of life but am sure that everything that ever was, is and will be is enshrined within our own spiritual nature."

Letters went back and forth to the SMAAS, with Penfold relating the interest aroused by the *Time* article. Bill had a change of heart and decided to send the tea-pot across to Sydney, much to Penfold's delight. Penfold kept up correspondence with Bill's solicitors in Melbourne, as much as anything to try to keep tabs on Bill's movements—the result of Bill's often repeated news that, *"next week I move to my new camp"*—always next week. Penfold also tried to obtain an update on what was happening at Mountain Gallery from the solicitors. All they could advise was that, yes, it belonged to Bill, although there was a "substantial" mortgage to the Commonwealth Bank. They, too, recognised a lack of security on the property and advised that they would have no objection to the SMAAS installing a resident caretaker. They also advised that in his will, Bill made a bequest of Mountain Gallery to the Nation. None of this news would have cheered Penfold. Likewise another letter from Bill, advising that the tea-pot had been despatched. The first thing Penfold would have read was a post-script in the top right corner:

"You can get a dentist if you wish to put some dental cement in the two places I fixed and then it will not break again as it is as hard as clay."

---

4 Jay Creek was another Aboriginal Reserve west-south-west of Alice.

The letter told of some firing difficulties experienced with the tea-pot, and Bill's attempt to put it through the kiln again to effect repairs. Bill was disappointed enough with the result to advise against sending the piece overseas, but was confident that it was still of an exhibition standard for the Museum. *"However if you send it over sea"*, Bill wrote, *"I would like to ask you to put a card on it to say it is one of my domestic vessels used on my journeys in Central Australia"*. Sent with the tea-pot were two more "loving cups".

It went from bad to worse for Penfold. One of the SMAAS chemists had, during a visit to Melbourne, called into the Mountain Gallery and brought back news that "a few" works on the property had been damaged by vandals. Penfold again requested from Bill news of what he intended to do with Mountain Gallery and almost pleadingly asked if there was somebody Bill could install as a caretaker. *"It would be a tragedy if anything happened to some of your beautiful objects"*, wrote Penfold.

By the time Penfold's letter reached the Alice Springs Post Office, Bill was on Utopia Station. Bill recalled that a man named Rubuntja went up with him as an interpreter and guide.[5] Bill, when telling me about Rubuntja, pointed to a sculptured head sitting with others on his kitchen bench:

> *"This man could speak good English, old Rubuntja. He's dead now, he was close on ninety, but he went. His country was Fire Country, an outpost of the Arrernte tribe, but he spoke good English. He was one of Strehlow's informers.[6]*
>
> *But his country was like all the others—bullocks romping over the whole thing. Bullock meat for cheap meat for hamburgers down the highway to Melbourne. Cheap hamburgers, cheap bullock meat—that's what the buggers have done to the country, that's what they're buggering up."*

Bill had by then learned the proper manners associated with the desert folk. He no longer made the mistake of blundering into a camp, as he had done at Ernabella all those years ago. It would be rude to walk up to a strange house, open the door and walk on in. It is the same in a society without walls and doors. You don't just walk into the middle of a group of people who may be sitting down talking. You stop a way off and wait, and observe without staring. One of the group might walk over to you, or a hand signal might invite you in. Bill hadn't meant to act badly in the past, but once he knew the etiquette, he stuck to it. He told me:

> *"I was taken in in the right way, you know. That means a lot, of course. Good manners. They understood good manners. Oh well, it was always good manners. You couldn't just rush into the camp with bad manners—they were too well trained—that was their Law.*
>
> *"The way Captain Cook and his men came in—'Here we are!'—with a gun ready. No good manners, the way they come in. Then the convicts and all the others, big bloody mob, rushed in. But the first thing they did, they rushed over their circles, their Sacred Earth Sites. First thing they did was let the bullocks in. Just like a bloody heathen rushing into my door here and saying, 'Go on, get the bloody hell [out] or we'll shoot you!' They didn't say go on, they just bloody shot. And all their Sacred Sites—just over the lot."*

Bill's attention to good manners, coupled with the inherent respect the desert folk had for the elderly [bearing in mind that Bill was not that far short of 60], allowed him to slip comfortably

---

5 The photograph of the aging bald man on page 147 was identified by Bill as Rubuntja [the spelling of whose name is my own].

6 The term "informer" might conjure up distasteful images in this land where we don't "dob in", but in its literal sense informer is quite harmless—if not admirable. The teacher is an informer to the children, simply one who provides information.

into the Utopia community. He was fortunate to form a special relationship with a highly regarded man at Utopia named, Atirantuka.[7] Bill did not rush, but allowed the experience to progress at its own pace. He did not jump straight into modelling the people he met, but instead let himself learn more of the race and culture by the best method of all, absorption. He spent just on a fortnight at Utopia before returning to the Alice to pick up his mail and purchase supplies for a six week stay back on the station property.

Bill took the opportunity to write to Mary Harris while he was back in town, telling her of his latest success in crossing the cultural bridge:

> *"I am camped 160 miles north east of Alice Springs on a wide river with flat country all round quite different to elsewhere. I am camped with the natives and they said they liked me. I will try to do a few of the old men when I go back. Every night they chant or sing. These chants or songs are all of their dreamings and every man has his dreaming plan, sugar ant, kangaroo or euro and so on right through all.[8]*
>
> *You above all people know it's my dreaming also and with all the love I can bring to bear upon this great river of thought. When I say you I always bring into the picture that great woman of America Helen Keller. How sad we cannot multiply two into one thousand million people ...*
>
> *When I said the natives chant every night I meant to add that when the fires die right down and we are in almost darkness their spirits rise just the same and I then wonder but it's easy to see and know their most precious gift comes over the scene, <u>imagination</u>."*

When Bill drove out of the Alice again, he went alone. Arriving back at the community on Utopia Station where he would be based, his confidence received an almighty boost. He stopped his truck away from a group of people and climbed down. From the group came a raised voice— *"Billy!"*, it cried. A man stood up from the crowd and began walking across the red earth to where Bill stood. In recalling the event over thirty years later, Bill's voice cracked with emotion:

> *"I was stunned. A full-blooded man—a nice man, one of these you'd just—."*

He reached out his arms as if to hug his friend from long ago, before continuing:

> *"He come out of the bunch from the camp. Well you get surprises like that. That lovely man came out, rushed out over the fields towards the Sandover River—he saw me coming up and 'Oh Billy, you're good to our people!' He said it in good English—he said it through the wind. I'll never forget that man—the way he spoke. Bumbi they call him."[9]*

It was, for Bill, undeniable proof that he wasn't being simply tolerated, he was being welcomed by those he considered as soul mates. After setting up camp and organising himself for the stay, Bill settled down to answer some letters which he'd picked up in the Alice. One had been a speedy reply from Patricia Michell in New Zealand. Bill's five-page reply was full of strength, determination and confidence. It also revealed how his Centralian experiences were being assimilated into his thinking, as the following condensed excerpt shows:

> *"My Mountain Gallery was just a mountain side when I took my mother there. Today it is beautiful just because of the way I have carved out the mountain side in such a*

---

7 "Atirantuka" is Bill's spelling.
8 Of course, every woman had her Dreaming, too—but that was women's business, about which Bill had no right to know and to which he would not have been privy.
9 "Bumbi" was how Bill guessed the name was spelled.

way and placed my works into walls of rock and earth and water from a spring above is made to run or emerge through my works or to be quite exact to run in and along and through the rhythms of my work. Rhythm is in the for in all I think of and that is where I impart to works that spiritual quality of the Aboriginal in his chanting or singing or poems of his dreamings. In his dreamings his spirit is happy."

Although he'd stated that his journey would be an extended one, Bill was back in Alice Springs a week later. He'd had a busy week, though, having constructed another kiln in the river bank near his camp. He claimed in a letter to Penfold, written while he was in town, that he'd given it a trial and achieved *"extra good"* results. This raises the possibility of Bill's having made a batch of small works for sale, which he could leave with Leo to sell. Bill apologised to Penfold for the condition of the tea-pot, offering to make another one *"in perfect finish"* for the Cannes Exhibition. But he never did get around to doing it.

The damage Penfold reported at Mountain Gallery, Bill advised, could have been by his own hand, because he "thought" he'd broken *"two or three heads off some time"*. The tone of the letter rose in intensity when, in response to Penfold's queries about the future of Mountain Gallery, Bill wrote that it was there to stay—although he didn't know into whose hands it would go. Yet again he said that he'd *"finished there years ago"*. The success he was having at Utopia fuelled his dreaming to dizzy heights; I would have thought even beyond the limits of Bill's perception of reality. His aim was *the* Holy Mountain, but now *"with £500,000 to back it up"*. This delusion was carried by his certainty that at last he had what was required to pull it off: *"I have waited all my life to have and to be trusted with enough power to do what I am to do, and by God I will do it well."* This power was coming from the Aborigines of Utopia. He still had no idea of from where the means would come.

The letter settled down to end with Bill advising that he would come to Sydney in September, "on my way home", although, he wrote, he would be quickly returning to the Centre.

Back at Utopia, Bill was privileged with being permitted to witness not just the nightly ceremonies held around the camp fires, but the more important acts of ceremony associated with the various totemic groups. The subtlety of meaning would have been lost on him, the result of his not being thoroughly educated in such matters, but he recognised and appreciated fully the spectacle and significance of the acts.

The first major ceremony he saw was associated with the men of the Sugar Ant Dreaming, and this he related in a letter to Mary Harris:

"... I was standing with the group of old men and young men looking into a small forest of beautiful white gums on the river bank.
One man sat on the earth at our feet and every now and then he would pound the earth with a heavy stick. Then, as we looked into the white gums at a distance of about 200 feet, two bronze naked old men suddenly appeared from behind two trees. Their bodies were beautifully decorated with white eagle hawk feathers, with decorated cone shapes built upon their heads and into this a long, narrow sacred churinga was standing up about three feet. As they appeared they began to dance right up to our group.
Then when they reached us the men took the tall head-dress off their heads, thus the ceremony of the sugar ant dreaming ended."

The ceremony which was most memorable for Bill, the one he referred to almost exclusively during our talks, was that involving members of the Kangaroo Totem. He recalled smatterings of it from the walk out, the ceremonies and the walk back to the camp. And every detail he remembered reinforced his belief that the Aborigines' love of country was total. For instance, towards the end of the long walk out, as they were nearing the Dreaming Site in the late afternoon, one man walked over to a rock. *"He saw a rock that was tipped over by bullocks"*, Bill recalled, *"he knew it was in the wrong place, so he went over and picked it up and put it in the right place. He knew. That is a love of country."*

Bill went on to relate the tale of what took place once they'd reached the Dreaming Site:

"It was a big rock that you'd have to walk up, and crawl up, that was all covered with ochre where they were to perform a most sacred ceremonial rite. The man that was in charge of the ceremony was Atirantuka. That's the man that I saw had the finest sense of humour. [He laughed heartily at his memory.] I'll never forget it.

It was their special kangaroo totem system symphony of life, where they held all their sacred meanings of the creation of their tribal lands. It was acted out in acts. All the grass was set on fire around so that there was light to see for the special sacred dances.

Well this man came in and lit his little fire and he put his arse in the sky and his hands on the earth—but the way he had his arse in the sky and his hands on the earth, singing the sacred song. [Atirantuka] looked at me and his face said 'Isn't that funny!' I knew they had a sense of humour.

Then he came charging up to me with the symbol in his hand, just missed my nose by a whisker, a big heavy tywerrenge symbol. Because he didn't do it good enough, [Atirantuka] stopped the ceremony. Yes, [he] stopped the ceremony because it was an offering to the spirit, the ancestral spirit, so the expert was called in and he did it supreme. So on went the whole procedure without a stop then.

Then there was a difficult dance going on in the middle of the night, with the grass on fire lighting the whole scene and the men singing—well there was a difficult dance where the dancer had to come in with his knees quivering like a humming bird, going so fast that his knees were only a blur. This was a difficult dance, but a wonderful dance. He couldn't do it well enough because [Atirantuka] who had laughed with me, he was so critical he says, 'No that man is not good enough'. So they called in the expert. He came in and done that dance with his knees going like a humming bird, a blur—you try to work your knees like that, you can't! He did it so well that [Atirantuka] gave the order for the sacred ceremony to go on.

It would be something like if a woman went to the church with the Bible and sung a hymn, but sung it all wobbly and the minister said to stop that—well it was something like that, only this was the very meaning of Australia.

The dance went right through the night. The dance was so difficult! You could have put a cup of tea on their shoulder and they'd go back with their knees quivering, they'd go back into the dark bush—well that tea would stop there, it was done so well. You ask a dancer to do that and they'd say 'you'd better give me twelve months to practice'."

When asked if he understood what was going on, Bill was quick with his answer:

"Oh no, that didn't come to me. But in the seriousness of it all, that lovely man who could laugh at it—his face literally laughed at me. I did learn a sense of humour of a good sort. The right kind of humour is very essential in good tribal keeping. I think that's so with you or me or anyone else—if you've got a good sense of humour, then you'll be very much welcome in people's homes.

[The dancing] having been done, each man scrambled up to the top of the big rock and rolled on his back on the very top of this rock to get in touch with the ochre smeared on it. That was their idea of touching the Spirit.

Then, on the way back from that ceremony at the big rock, when we were getting back towards our camp where the tribes were, one man just left the people and went out over a certain track. He picked up one of those paddy melons—a little thing about as big as a cricket ball. If you touch that with your tongue you would heave all your insides up, you would heave it out with bitterness, it was so repulsive. But he went over and just took it off the ground. He put it in his mouth and sucked the juice out of it like an orange. The Spirit had been that way towards the Kangaroo Dreaming, and so that paddy melon was alright. The juice just ran out of his mouth. It was Holy."

Bill stayed with the people of Utopia for many weeks, modelling some of the old men and conceiving creations he wished to do. One, described in a letter to Mary Harris, was a work in which roles would be reversed somewhat. Bill envisaged a work depicting a wonderful old Aboriginal man looking down into his hands, through which swept what he called *"the rock creation"*. Emerging from the rock creation would be Bill's spirit self. In the old man's hand would be a modelling stick. Was it Bill's way of expressing in his work another rebirth? Did he class his time with Atirantuka, Bumbi and the others as a reawakening of his Spirit? He never said so in as many words, but I got the feeling that his time on Utopia was as significant as any in his life.

62 *Bill with tjilpis, none of whom were identified, near Haasts Bluff, 1954. Most of the works shown are now at Pitchi Richi. Photographer unknown.*

63 *The loaned Mayne Nickless truck which took Bill and Leo Corbet to the Centre in 1954. Photo by Pat McDonald.*

64 *Nosepeg Tjunkata Tjupurrula, Bill's chief go-between for the Western Desert people. Photo by Bryce Ponsford.*

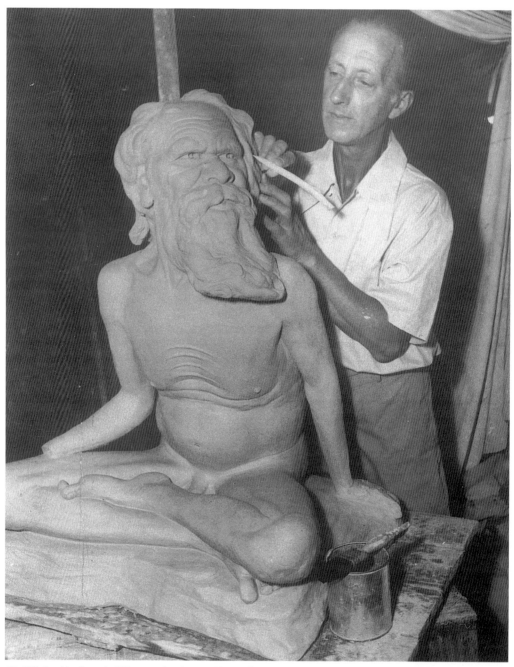

65 *Bill "working" on the Tjinapatunka piece, c. 1955. Photo courtesy of the* Advertiser.

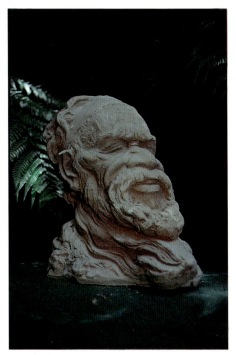

66 *The blind tjilpi from the Haasts Bluff meeting. WRS. 290 mm high.*

67 *Tjinapatunka and his dogs. Photographer unknown, c. 1950s.*

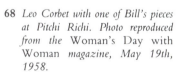

68 *Leo Corbet with one of Bill's pieces at Pitchi Richi. Photo reproduced from the* Woman's Day with Woman *magazine, May 19th, 1958.*

69 *Bill relaxes in his aerial bed at the Charles River camp, safe from the snakes, floods and kurdaitchas, c. 1954. Photo courtesy of the Age.*

70 *With young friends in the Centre. Photographer unknown, c. 1950s.*

71 & 72 *The tea-pot sent to the SMAAS from the Centre. Hidden in the base is the "child within". Unsigned, c. 1955, 425 mm high. Courtesy of the Trustees of the Museum of Applied Arts and Sciences, Sydney. Photos by author.*

73 *Rubuntja [according to Bill]. WRS collection. 300 mm high.*

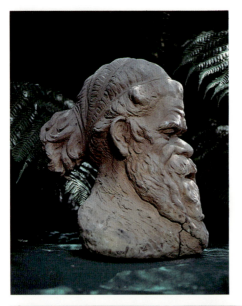

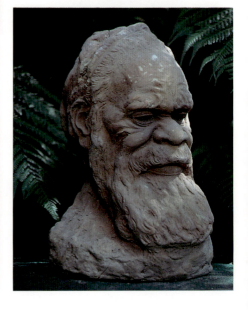

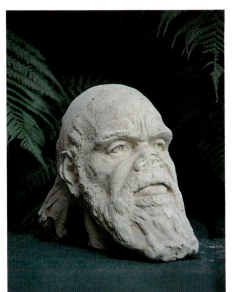

74–82 *Original heads from the Centre. WRS collection. All approx. life size.*

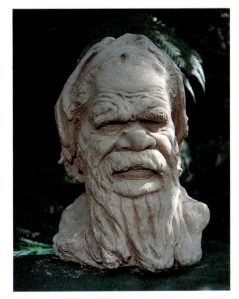

84 *Loving cup. Ins: "Wm Ricketts Alice Springs". 195 mm high. Courtesy of the Trustees of the Museum of Applied Arts and Sciences, Sydney. Photo by author.*

83 *Loving cup. Inscription obscured. 180 mm high, PC.*

85 *Self portrait. Ins: "It's a fragment of my spiritual nature. Wm Ricketts". 125 mm high, PC.*

86 *Face plaque [two children's faces on rear]. Inscription obscured. 370 mm high, PC.*

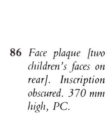

87 *Face [free-standing, two children's faces on rear]. Inscription obscured. 200 mm high, PC.*

88 *Face [free-standing]. Inscription obscured. 350 mm high, PC.*

89 *Face plaque. Ins. "Wm Ricketts". 130 mm high, PC.*

90 *Full figure male. No inscription. 192 mm high, PC.*

12 | Home, to Creation and Frustration
[1955–c. 1956]

Bill remained in Central Australia until late September, 1955. It's unlikely that he would have returned to Victoria at all, but his affairs down south were well out of order. He was acutely short of funds. The "substantial" mortgage had to be serviced and there was still the outstanding amount owed on the kiln. Mountain Gallery was a problem which would not go away. If the *right* person or organisation had come along, Bill would have given it to them—but nobody appeared. Then, of course, there was Mayne Nickless' truck to be returned. They'd loaned it to Bill for what he had told them would be three months or so, and hadn't heard anything for close to one and a half years.

Bill remained in a creative straight-jacket while he stayed in the Centre. He could conceive and execute magnificent works, but, try as he might, he could not fire his work with any degree of certainty. For every successful firing, there seemed to be countless failures. Firing the large works in Alice Springs was totally out of the question. Back in June, Penfold had gone as far as to inform Bill's solicitors that the works were deteriorating in quality to such an extent that in many cases they were quite useless for exhibition. He wrote:

> *"…The conception and sculpturing of Mr. Ricketts' work are admirable, but they soon develop bad cracks. This serious technical fault greatly reduces the value of his works … If Mr. Ricketts could improve his technique of firing, and undertake the production of a limited number of good pieces, he would quickly liquidate his debts. The Trustees are always prepared to assist him by acquiring first-class pieces. Besides, there is a good demand for his works overseas if he is prepared to sell."*

Bill would not have publicly entertained such a suggestion, but he was well aware of the shortcomings in his work. Sitting idle on the mountain was a kiln capable of taking his larger pieces. Racing around Bill's head were images of many large works which he was sure would elevate his fight to an unchallengeable position. In his mind he felt that Central Australia, the "Living Heart" of the continent, was a site from where his battle could be successfully waged. All he needed was a little support to the tune of, say, half a million pounds, a large chunk of prime real estate and a suitable kiln to fire the works. He decided to conduct a short summer campaign down south to get it all under way, after which he would acquire his own vehicle and return to the Alice.

On September 4th, Bill wrote in a letter to Penfold that all his large works were loaded on the truck ready for a departure from the Centre in "two weeks". His original undertaking to Penfold, that he would return home via Sydney to drop off the two works reserved for the SMAAS, was changed owing to, he wrote, the fragility of his load: *"I think I should play safe and take them straight back home. To go right to Sydney from Adelaide I may break many."*

It's hard to believe Bill's claim that he made it back to Mt Dandenong without breakage to any of his fired or unfired works, but that is what he wrote to Penfold. His first job was to ship a box off to the USA. One of the people who had contacted him following the *Time* article, an unidentified woman, had been successful in purchasing a piece. Although Bill had consulted Penfold about shipping, neither the work's identity nor price were revealed. Then the old Chev' truck was returned. According to Bill the men in Mayne Nickless' yard walked around it, patting the fenders and smiling amongst themselves. Bill told me it was because they loved the truck, which he claimed had been the best in the fleet. Is it possible that those men were congratulating the Chev' on simply having survived? Seventeen months outback at the hands of a mechanical incompetent is as good a test as any for a vehicle. As soon as Bill had the funds, though, he wanted to get himself a Land Rover.

After one of his spur-of-the-moment decisions, Bill confided to Penfold that the Mountain Gallery and land would have to be sold if he was to raise the beginnings of the required funds. He placed a nearly impossible condition on the sale by saying that it would have to be bought *"for the nation"*. Penfold seized the opportunity to suggest that maybe the SMAAS could purchase a selection of the *"outstanding pieces"* located in the Mountain Gallery, and urged Bill to consider bringing a collection to Sydney along with the reserved works.

By late November Bill was realising that his plans were not running as smoothly as he'd envisaged. He'd had no luck whatsoever in finding a suitable purchaser. He approached his bank to see if a second mortgage could be taken out on the block, without success. He wrote to Penfold that the banks were afraid to help *"in a splendid way"*, which suggests that he'd asked for a bit more than the property's market value. *"They are afraid to help because I am reaching a time I waited for and that is when I had the measure of power in my works I would then become the voice and spirit of the Australian bush"*, Bill wrote. He added that he would not raise that voice for another two years, eighteen months maybe, by which time all would be ready. *"Then I will be hated like every good man from Christ to Gandhi"*, he repeated.

When Bill accepted that a suitable buyer for the block would be almost impossible to find it only reinforced his opinion that the Australian public was in desperate need of salvation. He reversed his decision to sell, claiming that to do so would be a sin. *"It is now a thing of great beauty and to just pull the works out would be to destroy something sacred"*, he wrote in response to Penfold's suggestion of the SMAAS purchasing any of the in-ground pieces. *"This place must never be touched."* In the very next line of the letter, though, he reiterated his plan for another *"great Holy Mountain"*.

Bill was pinning his hopes on a favourable response from the Indian Government, as there had been no reply at that stage to Mary Harris' letter. His feelings would have been mixed when, at last, Mary contacted him with news that India had finally responded. Mary's letter had somehow found its way to Dr Verrier Elwin, D.Sc., F.A.S., F.N.I., the Adviser for Tribal Affairs with the North East Frontier Agency. He was based in Shillong, in the state of Meghalaya; in that part of India which sits between Burma and Bangladesh. Dr Elwin wrote to Mary:

> *"Thank you very much indeed for your letter, for the remarkable pictures as well as the most interesting letter from William Ricketts. I have shown them to a number of my friends here and they have been deeply interested and excited by the unique and wonderful interpretation of tribal life that he has made.*
>
> *I have myself lived among the tribal peoples of India for over 20 years but my medium of interpretation has rather been poetry and literature. I can therefore understand fully the life that he has laid and the ideals which he follows.*
>
> *I am sending your letter and all the enclosures to our Ministry of External Affairs, which is the Ministry that deals with all international matters, and I hope very much that they will be shown to the Prime Minister who, as you know, has always had a deep and an affectionate interest in the tribal people not only of India but the world.*

With kind regards and with many thanks for giving me the chance of contact with this unique and remarkable man."

There must have been a certain amount of frustration on Bill's part, as it had been over twelve months since he asked Mary to write to India. Had her letter been passed around for all that time, or was this simply the first response she'd received to many letters? At least her request was now going to the right people, which must have given Bill a little joy. He relaxed a little in the knowledge that there would be a short wait before India came to his aid, rather than suffer the daily disappointment of hearing nothing. In his eternally optimistic mind, there could be no outcome other than a successful one. It was just a matter of time.

Mary could not contain herself. She promptly put pen to paper and wrote a letter to the editor of one of the Adelaide newspapers, stating that the Indian Government had "discovered" Bill's work, having seen photographs which were sent over. She didn't mention that it was she who forwarded the material, but she did challenge the Australian Government to recognise *"the work of this genius"*.

Bill's desired Christmas departure for the Centre was postponed, re-establishing the by now usual pattern for his time-table based largely on incredible hope. In an attempt to gain access to possible funding from the general public, Bill arranged a loose exhibition at Mountain Gallery featuring the works he'd taken to the Centre, as well as some he'd actually created while he was up there. It would be an open exhibition lasting until he left again to head north.

Early in the new year of 1956, Bill heard from somewhere that Penfold might be retiring as the Director of the SMAAS. On January 13th Bill wrote to Penfold, asking if it were true, and asking if Penfold still wanted a work to show at the second Cannes exhibition. Bill also moved his proposed visit to Sydney forward to March. The reply Bill received from the SMAAS was written by Mr F. R. Morrison, Acting Director. Morrison informed Bill that Penfold had retired on December 31st, 1955. Penfold was gone without even saying goodbye, and Bill had lost his most influential patron, confidant and promoter. Penfold did not cut all ties with Bill, but it was never the same. Likewise, Bill's relationship with the SMAAS. There would be spasmodic contact, but nothing like that generated by Penfold in his capacity as Director.

Bill set to work transforming his experiences and inspiration of the Centre and its people into the permanency of clay. The rebirth concept described at the end of the previous chapter was one of the first to be executed. It changed somewhat from his original idea, but the end result and general impression were the same.

The work features at one end the upper torso, arms and head of a bearded Aboriginal patriarch; his arms angled out and slightly down along the work; his hands, with fingers spread, appearing to push something away. The illusion of pushing is enhanced by the tensed and sinewy modelling of well-muscled arms. The Elder's head is inclined down, giving the impression that he is looking along the same line as that which his hands are pushing against. Following this line are the work's rhythms, and suddenly it can be seen that the old man is not pushing, but bracing himself against the out-pouring of an energy force.

This energy force, represented by the rhythms, sweeps down and up to the other end of the piece, where we see Bill's stylised "spiritual self", full figure and naked, arms arching up over his own head to embrace the heads of Aboriginal children and his totemic animals, the lyrebirds. Bill is flying, being carried along on the projected energy of the Aborigine. Bordering the end towards which Bill is being propelled, but outside the energy blast, are tywerrenge shapes and the heads of Aboriginal children, the history and the future of a race. But Bill is not propelled forward as a mere white man, for now on his chest appears four cicatrices—the physical sign of his initiation "in spirit" into Aboriginal Australia. This signifies a major change in his perception of his place among the Aborigines, for until this period the chests of Bill's sculptural "spiritual selves" were clear of such scarring.

One of the first questions I asked Bill when I first met him informally in 1983 concerned his initiation scars, and whether or not he was *truly* initiated. He replied, *"I was initiated into the tribes of Australia, in Spirit"*. That was his way of saying, no, not actually physically initiated, but in his Dreaming, yes.

The concept described above became another favourite of Bill's, as there were at the time of writing at least four similar works in the Melbourne area alone, with another in Alice Springs. It's most likely that there are more which have not yet come to my attention.

Bill let his expectations exceed his capabilities again in March by informing Leo Corbet that he intended to return to Alice Springs in the near future, with a stop in Adelaide to hold an exhibition at the Adelaide University before bringing the show through to the Alice. Leo jumped into the preparations, prompting a front-page article in the *Advocate* which forewarned the locals of the event to come. They waited, and waited—and waited.

The desire to leave the Mountain Gallery behind to create *the* Holy Mountain did not stop Bill working for its expansion and recognition. On April 11th, 1956, the Melbourne *Herald* published an article headed "Lone Crusader of the Hills Gives In," written by R. J. Howard. Not quite the headline for an article about a determined fighter, and it became worse— but one should never underestimate Bill's occasionally masterful strategies. Howard started his piece:

> *"A 10-year-old battle in the Dandenongs is over. It ended recently in a beautiful little fern gully somewhere between Kalorama and Olinda. Fifty-one-year-old[1] sculptor William Ricketts stood in the bed of the gully and shook his fist at the southern horizon. His blue eyes blazed and his long, sandy hair danced in fury.*
>
> *'You win!' he shouted. 'But you'll rue the day.' It was the capitulation of a lone crusader. Billy Ricketts had lost."*

Howard gave a brief history, as he knew it, claiming that the block had been Bill's home from 1937 *"until last year"*. He told of Bill's success, the interest shown in his works by both public and press nationally and internationally, but how, instead of going for the fame and money, Bill wanted *"to turn the Dandenongs' hillside into a great 'cathedral' to the 'Supreme Being'"* and follow his conscience into a battle against the *"spoilation of the Dandenongs and the vandalism of mankind"*. Howard went on:

> *"But it was the intrusion of suburbia that proved too much ... 'I'm going back to the Dead Heart,' [Bill] said. 'No man with a soul can live here and watch this area strangled.' 'The estate agents have got that land,' [Bill] said softly. 'They don't care who gets it, as long as the price is good.'"*

Then Bill made a lunge straight for the heart-strings:

> *"'Things have gone from bad to worse. More and more trees are being chopped down. They come here shooting the birds I've trained to eat off my shoulder. My little possums have crawled back here to let me see them die. They've been maimed with traps.*
>
> *'Won't anyone help me?' [Bill] suddenly thundered. 'I've appealed to many people. I think I could stay here and turn this into a glory if they saved the little fern gully next to here. It's for sale soon and they'll move in there with their roads and axes and cars. Please ask the Government or some organisation with a soul to add the gully to my land. It's my water supply, too. I haven't the money to buy it, but it would make this a glorious reserve for the nation.'"*

---

1 At least he was consistent.

Thousands of kilometres away, in India, a file containing Mary's letter and the associated material on Bill was being passed between many hands, slowly making its way to the desk of Prime Minister Nehru. It seems that everybody who saw it was impressed, arousing an unprecedented interest in the Australian sculptor with high ideals and dreams. I did not sight Mary's letter, but it appears to have suggested that Bill, although a white man, was a member of the Arrernte "tribe", and at least part of the support he required was a grant of £2,000 for the purchase of his own truck.

Nehru joined the ranks of those captivated by Bill's work and desires, but, for what appears to have been reasons of diplomacy, was unable to intervene in the way Bill wanted. After making his decision and sending the file back to Dr Elwin, Nehru directed his Ministry of External Affairs to suggest to the Australian Government, via the Australian High Commission [AHC] in New Delhi, that assistance for Bill might be gained in Australia. On June 1st, 1956, the AHC contacted in turn the Australian Department of External Affairs.

Under a heading of *"Request to Indian Government for Financial Assistance for Brother Billy (Arunta Tribe)"*, the AHC outlined the request made on behalf of *"Brother Billy of the Arunta Tribe (a white man whose former name was William Ricketts)"*. They stated that: *"As the Indian officials dealing with the matter were impressed by the photographs of Brother Billy's work, they thought that conceivably some public authority or private benefactor in Australia might like to take some action."* The AHC also indicated that they desired to inform the Indian authorities if, in due course, assistance was provided to Bill. The Australian Department of External Affairs did their homework and, after ascertaining where the "Arunta Tribe" came from, passed the matter on to the Department of Territories—who in turn passed it on to the Director of Welfare in Darwin, Harry Giese.

Harry Giese had at least heard of Billy Ricketts, but this "Brother Billy" was new, as was Bill's having sought assistance. So he, in turn, requested from his officers in Alice Springs some information about Bill, which he could send back up the line. Finally, on August 1st, 1956, a letter containing information about Bill left the Northern Territory on its way to the AHC in New Delhi, via Canberra. It was prepared by J. C. Archer, who, after clarifying that "Brother Billy" was indeed the William Ricketts known to the Welfare Department in the Centre, went on to report in paragraph 3:

> *"For your information, Mr. Ricketts has never been known to officers of the Welfare Branch by the name of Brother Billy and he is certainly not a member of the Aranda Tribe. Mr. Ricketts is an artist of considerable ability and his modelling work in clay is of a very high standard. However, he is, to say the least, eccentric in his behaviour and obsessed with the idea that he has been placed on earth to restore nature, through the Aborigine, to its wild state. He portrays in his art the white man as an evil spirit who destroys nature by burning and cutting down forests for his own use."*

Bill never knew of the exchange, but it highlights a fatal flaw in his approach to securing funds. No doubt every Welfare Officer in Central Australia knew that Bill was waiting for money to come from somewhere so that he could start his Holy Mountain Dreaming, but Bill had not written one letter to any specific Department asking for support, so the funding issue was never considered. It was a problem he suffered for the rest of his career. Even when talking face-to-face with a potential philanthropist, Bill would not say: "Will *you* help?" Instead he would beat around the bush saying something along the lines of, "If only some good person or organisation would give me the help I need, I could do this or that". With a few significant exceptions, the person opposite Bill or reading the article about him would nod and agree, without seeing themselves as that good person or organisation. Bill could not even bring himself to write to India with a direct request. He got Mary to do that for him.

Mary received news of Nehru's decision in a letter from Dr Elwin dated June 28th, 1956, although the knock-back was not as devastating as it could have been:

> *"I am afraid it has taken a long time to send you another letter ... but our Prime Minister is a very busy man and it was not possible to show him the photographs and tell him about Brother Billy earlier.*
>
> *I am glad to say, however, that the Prime Minister has seen the photographs of Brother Billy's sculptures ... and his letter and was greatly impressed by them. He admires his artistic ability and feels that this collection of mountain sculpture may, one day, be of the greatest value. Had Brother Billy been in India he would have made every effort to help him. Unhappily there are all kinds of difficulties in the way of giving any practical assistance to someone outside India. It is, I am afraid, just not possible for India to purchase property in Australia in the way suggested.*
>
> *But I have been asked to write to you and send the Prime Minister's very best wishes to Brother Billy and to tell him how much he appreciates his work and how grateful he is that it was brought to his notice.*
>
> *If there is any other way in which we could give some help or encouragement to Brother Billy, I hope you will let me know."*

When Bill finally read Dr Elwin's letter it would have served to further reinforce his views about Australia going wrong. To Bill it would have been obvious that Nehru and his Indian Government wanted to help, but the Australian Government would not allow it. With a conviction stronger than ever, Bill knew he would have to travel to India to enlist the support he knew they would provide. His immediate task, though, was to continue fashioning the weapons for his fight.

A motif which came to feature regularly and significantly in Bill's work resulted from another experience he had with Atirantuka and his people at Utopia. Bill was taken along with a small group of Aboriginal men to a sacred place for people of the Emu Dreaming. The leader of the group carried a small fire-stick. They wound their way first through hilly country, which became progressively steeper and rougher, before they eventually stopped at a signal from the leading man. At that point everybody in the group, including Bill, had to remove their clothing. *"That was the Law—that you have not a stitch on you when you come to this holy place"*, Bill explained to me. That done, the leader fanned his fire-stick into greater life and, when it was flaming well, held it up above his head and led the group single file into a deep gully between the mountains. Deep inside they came to where the sides had been sculptured by the Dreaming ancestor or by erosion, depending on your beliefs. Bill recalled: *"All the way down between the mountains ... all the caves were as though they took out a big emu egg—out of the caves all the way down. You never saw anything like it."*

It was not so much the site of the Emu Dreaming which impressed itself upon Bill's mind, but the little fire-stick and its flame, which Bill interpreted as a symbol of Aboriginal Law. He told me with utmost conviction:

> *"Not the parliament law, but <u>the Law of the tribe</u>. That little fire that that one man was holding ... wasn't just a little fire—he was holding your soul as a living flame. You've got to put that down! The soul was a living flame."*

The seemingly insignificant little fire-stick featured in various ways, but most often Bill placed it emerging from the centre of the concentric circles which he used to signify a Sacred Site. I think it was Bill's way of saying that at the very centre of the Dreaming was the Law, never to be challenged and never to be broken. It was a dramatic departure from Bill's feelings towards parliamentary and common law for which he had, in the main, little respect.

Back in Alice Springs Leo was settling into his new life very well. He'd bought himself a Land Rover and was pottering around out-of-the-way places searching for relics left over from the pioneering days. Leo had decided to gather a collection of Centralian memorabilia which could be exhibited in what he planned as an outdoor museum at Pitchi Richi. His easy charm opened many doors for him on the outlying stations, with station owners and managers directing him to the old rubbish dumps and occasionally letting him loose in their sheds. It was a very relaxed affair, with no rushing around or deadlines. If there was a yarn to be had, Leo would yarn. If there was nobody to yarn with, Leo would scrounge.

Gradually, though, the Pitchi Richi collection grew into something that tourists considered worth taking a look at, and Leo was only too happy for them to do so. Leo also hosted various art exhibitions and workshops at Pitchi Richi. In August 1956, there was an exhibition of oil paintings by the landscape artist, Robert Johnson, the proceeds of which went to the Australian Inland Mission [AIM], as well as a pottery workshop conducted by the Victorian ceramicist, Roy Cook.

The year 1956 was a big one for Melbourne. The Olympic Games came to town, swelling the population with visitors from all over Australia and the world. Bill's connection in the Commonwealth Bank, who he recalled to have been Mr Dowling, arranged for Bill to stage an exhibition in the bank's Melbourne head office for the duration of the Games which commenced in November. A large portion of the main banking chamber was reportedly transformed into an Australian bush setting, throughout which Bill's works were placed to great advantage.

The bank exhibition was not the only plan Bill had for the Olympics. An unsubstantiated story which popped up several times during the research concerned Queen Elizabeth II, who was coming out to open the Games. Bill saw this as an ideal opportunity to meet her and have a whisper in her ear about what was going wrong with the country—maybe even drop a hint that the Mountain Gallery could do with a bit of support. So he went to work creating a piece worthy of Her Majesty and informed an official [possibly Melbourne's Lord Mayor] of what he had in mind. Apparently the official thought that it was a wonderful idea, thanked Bill for his generosity and said that he would organise for the piece to be picked up. The official assured Bill that the Queen would be told who made the piece when it was presented to her. Bill pricked his ears up at that and explained that *he* was to present the piece to the Queen, and that this would have to happen at the Mountain Gallery.

How else, Bill thought, would she recognise the Gallery's worth and pronounce a Royal Decree that it should be supported? Terribly sorry, said the official—plans and all that. It would be presented by an official or not at all. Bill, with his nose pushed firmly out of joint, informed the official that it would be the latter: and totally unbeknown to Elizabeth II, she missed out on a unique gift.

Doris Turner accompanied Bill down to the city for the Bank exhibition opening, and recalled that the layout was simply beautiful. Bill's banker acquaintance gave an opening address and introduced Bill to the gathering to say a few words. Bill started off calmly, but as he went along he built up steam. His speech became more passionate, his anger came to the boil and away he went on a roller-coaster of vitriol and disgust. Somewhere in the tirade the Australian Prime Minister, Robert Menzies, copped a blast, and another, and another until Bill was positively threatening him with all sorts of unpleasantries.[2] Finally Bill wound down and a peace settled on the exhibition, which left viewers to quietly contemplate the works and absorb their subtle thought-provoking messages.

Very soon after the exhibition opening, Doris received a telephone call from a highly-placed member of the Melbourne Police. After it was established that she had accompanied Bill to the exhibition and that she was a close friend, she was given some extraordinary advice:

---

2 Non-violent, of course.

"I couldn't believe it—it sounded so funny. 'Please restrain him.' The Melbourne Police asking me to please restrain him!"

Bill continually searched for a way to gather the funds which would enable him to realise his dream, without success. His legion of supporters kept growing, though, coming from all walks of life—ordinary working class people, academics, prominent Melbourne business figures and all kinds in between. Bill's unfailing ambition to stop the destruction of animals led to an increasingly strong relationship with the Wild Life Preservation Society based in Sydney; and in particular, with Mr Jim Brown, a leading figure in the organisation. The moral backing and encouragement given by such people provided the ground swell of support that kept Bill going, because while it grew it proved to him that an ultimate victory was achievable.

These supporters and other admirers of his work provided Bill with a healthy enough cash flow through sales, enabling him to live at a level of his choosing. That he chose to live modestly seems to have been his admirable choice.

A recollection that Doris Turner had from around that time was what she perceived to be a shift in Bill's motivational emphasis. *"He became less interested in the physical characteristics of his work, and became totally involved in the spiritual side of it all"*, she told me. This recollection ties in with Bill's own actions. As far as he was concerned, the physical qualities of his works had triumphed when the Centralian Aborigines had accepted them. The only way of increasing their "power" was to broaden and deepen the spiritual message. More often than not, the spiritual messages contained in the works were accessible only to Bill and the fortunate few who were given direct interpretations by Bill. The general viewer was left to fathom out their own meanings, making it a more personal experience. Bill provided the spark, but the viewers were left to add their own fuel and in doing so create their own personal fire of thought.

13 | News From the Mountain and Beyond
[c. 1957–1958]

Two people who had come into Bill's life were actively working with him towards the production of the Mountain Gallery's first independent publication. Boyd Coutts, B.A. Dip.Ed., a local hills' resident and friend, had offered his services as an editor for Bill's writings. To W. Grevis-James, a very capable photographer, fell the task of recording Bill's new works. Bill wisely had Grevis-James photograph his pieces prior to their firing. While this missed out on any subtle colouring which glazing might add, it captured the works at their pristine best, free of any heat distortion or the firing cracks which inevitably occurred. The results were admirable, and a collection of material was slowly accumulated.

By April, 1957, Bill had decided it was time to settle his account with the SMAAS, to whom he still owed the two works which they'd reserved and towards which they'd advanced £100. On April 9th, F. R. Morrison looked at a letter addressed to the "Director, A. R. Penfold". The distinctive hand-writing left no doubts as to who the letter was from, so Morrison, who had by then been appointed as the new Director, opened and read the following:

> *"I have at last sent a large box with the work you picked out from the pictures while I was in the Nth Terr. This is the work the natives liked best of all I took to them. You have the picture of it and I have written on the back of it. You were generous to advance me £100 to help me in my trouble or better to say to help me do the right thing for Australia.*
>
> *I will leave for the Nth Terr again on May 25th and I need a large sum of money to do it and whatever the museum can pay for it will be a help towards my fund. I do hope you will be pleased with the work. There may be a couple of hair marks from the kiln. You will receive the box in three days."*

Morrison consulted a staff member, Mr Brown, about the work and sought his opinion. Brown was of the opinion that if the work was offered for sale, they should return it. He obviously did not feel that it was of a standard which would add to the Museum's already impressive collection. Morrison considered the letter again and, in the knowledge that money had already been paid, wrote a reply in which he advised that the museum would be glad to accept the work for exhibition. In what appears to have been the first draft, he added that he would investigate the possibility of a contribution towards Bill's proposed journey; but he must have had second thoughts. In the end he sent a brief letter simply accepting the work and wishing Bill well, but not inviting a response.

Regarding Bill's statement that he was off to the Centre again, I found no evidence that he went. We will see that by late 1958 Mary Harris had at least two more of Bill's major works at Bundilla; but they could easily have been freighted over to Adelaide, rather than Bill delivering them himself.

Ten kilometres from the Mountain Gallery, on the outskirts of Belgrave, a remarkable Koorie named Bill Onus had established a souvenir shop which was fast becoming a must-visit spot in the hills. The star attraction was Onus himself, who gave boomerang throwing displays outside the shop. It was not simply Onus' boomerang making and throwing prowess which made him an attraction. In the days before Aborigines were granted citizenship in their own country, there was a Koorie owning and operating a successful business. That alone would have made him a novelty.

According to his son, Lin, Bill Onus was born in southern NSW in 1906. He lived at the Cummeragunja community on the Murray River, opposite the Victorian township of Barmah. It was a known safe community for Koories, who endured frequent raids by Police looking to abduct children of mixed blood. When the Police fronted up at "Cummera", the safest course of action for Koories with mixed-blood children and any other Koorie who did not want to endure the bother of a Police raid was to slip across the Murray, which is the border between NSW and Victoria, and out of the jurisdiction of the NSW Police. When the threat had passed, they simply slipped back home again.

Bill Onus, like many NSW Koories, came across the border one day and stayed, leaving his homelands behind because of persecution.

Onus worked his way around and ended up living in Balwyn, employed on the Melbourne wharves as a clerk—no small achievement in itself. In his spare time he made and sold boomerangs. His "lucky" break came one day when he was driving his car and a fire engine smashed into him. The luck was that he survived to ultimately receive an insurance pay-out. With money in the bank, Onus set his mind on buying a little shop and going into business for himself. Not being a citizen, though, there were difficulties not only in securing a loan, but in his buying land. Eventually he found a backer, overcame the considerable obstacles before him and purchased his shop near Belgrave. He called it "Aboriginal Enterprises".

Bill Onus also applied himself on the political fringe, as Lin explained:

> *"In the very early days Dad was involved with an organisation called the Australian Aborigines' League, set up in 1938. He was heavily involved in that for years. It was Sydney-based originally, then a sister-organisation was formed in Melbourne. Dad was quite a leading force behind it at the time.*
>
> *When you look back on the types of meetings and see the sorts of resolutions that came out of them, people held a lot of store in petitions to the Queen and the likes—'we respectfully beg' and that sort of stuff. By today's standards they were actually very tame, but at the time they were quite revolutionary. Occasionally there'd be some sort of feature article or story where some journo' would go along to a meeting, and invariably they'd remark upon how well dressed the people were or how clean they were or how well spoken—serious stuff."*

Lin believes that his father and Bill Ricketts may have first met at the Healesville Sanctuary, outside which Bill Onus would sometimes sell his handicrafts. Lin thought that Bill Ricketts may have occasionally sold his small works at the same venue, although I found no other evidence of this. Lin does not recall Bill accompanying Onus to any political meetings, but he clearly remembers the strong friendship which developed. Lin recalled of the ensuing relationship:

> *"My father was fascinated by Bill in those days. For example, when people, say in Aboriginal Affairs, first approach you and they want to give you a hand, you're always very suspicious of what their motives are. Are they anthropologists, are they this or that? Bill transcended all of those sorts of things. I think it was just a common respect."*

Bill Onus would often drop in at the Mountain Gallery on his way home; sometimes to pick up extra stock of Bill's small works for the shop, but mostly just for a talk and to indulge their mutual love of classical music. Lin's first memories of meeting Bill stem from accompanying his father on some of those visits. As a young boy, though, Lin soon lost his fascination:

"Once I'd explored a place once or twice, it didn't have the same fascination for a youngster. You know, thirty or forty times a year—it used to get a bit tedious. Often during the winter months it would be quite dark when we got up to the place, and the shack was very cluttered—clay everywhere—but it was always very warm in there. Even on a freezing day, it was always warm.

They used to get into these amazing raves that would go on for hours and hours. I'd want to go home, I'd want to have tea or something like that—but they would talk and talk and talk, on and on and on. I'd be there blatantly yawning. Unfortunately, I don't remember what they would talk about.

I would hear what Bill was saying but never pay attention to it. It wasn't, perhaps, until I got into my thirties that I finally listened to the words that he was saying. Stuff like the commonality of humankind and that sort of thing—the things he was talking about way back, people were unable to see it—conservation and looking after the environment, people didn't even know about it. Those post-war years were really quite rapacious.

His words really had significance, but it took me twenty years to twig to it."

By mid-1957, Leo Corbet found himself embroiled in a little environmental battle all of his own. Across the road from Pitchi Richi an enterprising chap by the name of Johnny Rhonberg had commenced a small quarry immediately adjacent to Heavitree Gap, for the purpose of supplying crushed rock for road-building in the vicinity. Since it was on the opposite side of the Macdonnell Ranges to the Alice Springs township, the majority of locals didn't give the quarry a second thought. Leo, on the other hand, had two gripes. Firstly, his peaceful life was no longer so, what with regular explosions to loosen the stone and a rock-crushing plant grinding away all day for five or six days a week. Secondly, and more importantly, Leo could see what was going to happen to the Alice's most imposing natural feature, which Heavitree Gap surely is. The southern gateway to the town was being defaced in what Leo saw as a criminal way, and he wanted to stop it.

Leo expressed his concern widely, to no avail. He could not convince the authorities or the townsfolk of the potential disaster which he saw happening. What would they call it after a few years of quarrying? Heavitree *Gaps*! In the end he consulted a "legal friend" and formulated a bold plan. The pair discovered that the quarry had been commenced without a mining lease on the site. Leo armed himself with pegs, went across the road and staked out a significant portion of the Macdonnell Ranges, which happened to include the quarry, as a claim for his intended gold mining lease. That done, he asked the local police to *"eject all those people who are interfering with my mining lease"*.

The quarry was by no means given up without a fight. The case went to court and was adjourned at least once. It was patently obvious that Leo had no intentions whatsoever of seriously working the lease, but he had a legal edge which ultimately saw him win through. The quarrying at the site stopped forever. He reportedly maintained the lease for many years after his victory, strolling across the road to scratch around for the mandatory one day a year which he was required to "work" it. That it was a popular win is evidenced by newspaper reports which were published around the country, an example of which was the Melbourne *Sun's* July 7th, 1957 article headed, "Purple Hills of Alice Reprieved—Blasting to Stop at Quarry".

It was a round one victory to Leo, but Johnny Rhonberg didn't stop there. If he couldn't quarry the rock, he'd build a caravan park in front of it. Leo had to finally admit defeat when two large public toilet blocks were built outside the caravan park, marring his view of the Macdonnells. He brought in a bulldozer and had an earth bank pushed up on his northern boundary. A grove of Desert Oaks completed the screen. From the inside, Pitchi Richi had at least the illusion of seclusion.

The book on which Bill and his associates were working was finally published in late 1957 or early 1958. Its twenty-four pages were approximately A4 size, titled simply, *Catalogue—Sculptures by William Ricketts*. The earthy brown cover featured a line drawing of the sculptured bust of Tjinapatunka. Grevis-James' stunning black-and-white photographs, which were printed leaving him totally unacknowledged, took up eleven full pages, with one photograph from Bill's previous Central Australian trip making twelve illustrations altogether. Six featured sculptures incorporating Bill's "spiritual self" in varying degrees of prominence, and one was a portrait of Bill pretending to work on the model of a child's head. Only one of the illustrations did not include the images of Aborigines—a piece depicting Bill's "spiritual self" as a kangaroo man in whose arm was cradled a lyrebird. This kangaroo man was standing between the trunks of two trees which had branches terminating in human hands, one of which was holding a mother possum with her baby on her back.

The book's first illustration depicted a work which Bill would have me photograph again in 1986 for his last publication, *Australiandia*. It was an inscribed piece, across the top of which were the words, ***"Our fathers faith That ALL LIVING THINGS Share in the Same eternal Breath of Life that Lives and endures in the works of our Brother Billy"***. The lower half of the work shows the concentric circle motif, from the centre of which emerges a single hand grasping a flaming brand. Around the outside of the concentric circles are sixteen separate groupings of curved lines, which the caption claimed were the equivalent of signatures, inscribed by old men of the "Aranda tribe". I was unable to verify whether or not that work was actually signed in the Centre as Bill claimed.

In the first block of text Bill explained that:

> *"The meaning of my works is spiritual and basically they need no words to explain them. They are able to stand on their own feet; but people so often ask me my intentions in my works. To quicken your understanding, I wish to convey to you in words that will attempt to inform you of my innermost sanctuary of spirit, where I dwell at will and breathe outward my prayer into my works."*

In the foreword, Bill gave his first printed introduction to himself:

> *"To the oft-asked question, 'What made you come to this mountain and express the aborigine thus?' my only possible answer is—*
>
> *For the purpose of my development, my creator worked through the Australian aborigine to get hold of me.*
>
> *In thankfulness for having been shown the way to a fuller and finer life, I accept responsibility and power to create as a sacred trust. That is my innermost experience.*
>
> *As I try to understand the deepest meaning of life, I have become inspired by a unique growth of love for the Australian Bush.*
>
> *Because of that powerful love, I have become an integral part of my environment: Bird, animal, forest, mountain, desert, rock, water—everything, everywhere, at one time. I am linked indivisibly with all of them. In this way I have come to know that separateness is the enemy of true religion.*
>
> *As I have dared to know what wholeness of life means, I have come to know that greatest form of love which is enshrined in beauty, wonder, health and true freedom.*

I have tried to show you all this in my largest work: 'Alchera'.[1] ('I, Atirantuka, have known my Brother ever from the Alchera.') I am able to speak to you from my innermost self in works and words, despite the grim, naked reality that I have been brought through. I have witnessed the unspeakable cruelty and brutality which has been let loose upon the innocent Australian Bush at the hands of far too many white people. For me, this tragedy will have meaning for the rest of my life.

I have shown you all this in my work: 'The Burnt Tree'. From the bottom of that black hell my unique growth of love spreads out its roots into all living things.

Thus my Creator has put into my hands weapons of the spirit, and I know that I am expected to use them in defence of the Australian Bush.

'A righteous anger, with God in the very centre of my works'—these shall remain my watch words."

Contributors added to the publication's text their own views of where Bill fitted in.

Ted Strehlow, at that time Reader in Australian Linguistics at the University of Adelaide, quoted from his work, *An Australian Viewpoint*, in an attempt to express the love and respect of country which the Australian Aborigines embraced. In concluding, he offered his opinion that Bill was, *"the only white man that sought to express that same oneness of Man and Nature, both living and inanimate, in his creative work"*. Strehlow's closing statement was that Bill's work *"expresses Australia"*.

Boyd Coutts, the publication's unacknowledged editor, contributed two pages of text in an attempt to make Bill more accessible to those struggling to grasp the message. He explained that: *"When [Bill] speaks about saving the 'Bush', that is what he means. He is not thinking in terms of National Parks. He loves a tree as a living thing, but he loves equally the indigenous animals and people of this country."* Further into his piece, Coutts attempted to put Bill's anger into perspective:

"When Ricketts speaks of weapons and fighting, his meaning is wholly spiritual. Sometimes the vehemence of his expressions is frightening—but so must the prophets of old have spoken. They were not lukewarm. Their task was superhuman. They knew this, and acted accordingly.

In his own way, Ricketts is a modern prophet. He seeks nothing less than to turn a heedless generation from its ways of coldness and indifference into the paths of understanding and warm sympathy for all things having a claim on man's protection."

Mary Harris wrote a fey piece which gave readers the benefit of her insight into Bill's works: *"Truly the imprisoned splendour flows in Ricketts' creations, as water flows, as the tree roots move in the darkness of earth and reach their branches to the heavens. And all the while, like a cloud of witnesses, little child faces appear in rock and tree, suggesting the harmony of all creation."* Unquestionably soul mates, Mary and Bill. It was followed by a transcript of Helen Keller's letter of thanks to the Victorian Committee, mentioned on page 83.

Next came a page of text printed under the heading, "Atirantuka Speaks", implying that it was a transcript of Atirantuka's words. The piece went:

"The most brutal crime committed against the Australian Bush at the hands of the white fellow is the burning of the holy forests and the destruction of the native animals that live in them.

---

1 The current correct Arrernte spelling for the word "Alchera" is "Altyerre". [Gavin Breen, IAD.] It refers to that period in the spiritual past which is often called the Dreaming.

The fire that burned the forests has burned deep into the soul of my Brother, whom I, Atirantuka, have known ever from the Alchera. It was from the centre of the burning holy forest that my Brother received the law of every tribe, including the Victorian tribes who suffered so greatly when the white man came.

The tribal law is symbolised by fire—suffering. Suffering is the fire stick in my Brother's hand.

White fellow, my people regard even the desert places as holy. Before you can reach the heaven spoken of by your churches you must find the heaven in your own land, in the beautiful spectacle of life as it still exists in the Australian Bush.

When you, as a white Australian, can learn to feel at one with the loveliness of our land, you will not want to destroy or pervert that loveliness as you do when you deprive beautiful birds of their rightful freedom by keeping them in cages.

As a nation, you are indifferent to the burning and killing that destroy the bush. Now your indifferences become stupidity when, in the name of science and defence, you are taking away more land from the aborigines and dispersing the wild creatures.

Do you understand that in the end you are creating weapons that shoot at freedom itself? My Brother was given great spiritual power when he received the law of every tribe, and he will use that power in defence of the Australian Bush, now being swept away in this last onslaught of the white man's indifference and folly.

A pure imagination, born to man in a state of pure freedom, and wrought in fire, is to be desired above all things. Therein lie the sources of health, beauty, great love, and wonder and freedom themselves. The life of man is one with these things. Anything that separates man from them can only be evil, which you are told to resist.

Does it mean anything to you that my Brother is determined to fight this evil of man's separation from beauty, freedom and love? Will you not help him in this fight?"

Atirantuka was, according to Bill, an Eastern Arrernte man, born and bred in the arid desert regions of Central Australia. His concept of a forest would have been a scattering of large gums lining a water-course or a scrub of mulga. His people had from time immemorial used fire as a land management tool. He would have had restricted access to the "white" education system, so his grasp of the English language would have been limited. Would such a man have composed the preceding statement?

I'm sure that during Bill's time at Utopia, Atirantuka would have spoken of his concerns about the whites' lack of respect for the land. It's most probable that Atirantuka gave Bill his blessing to go and speak on his behalf. But I had to express my doubts to Bill about the validity of Atirantuka's eloquent plea and other writings claimed by Bill to have been given to him by Aborigines. Bill finally told me that that's what they wanted to say—what they would have said if they had a better command of the English language.

I'm left feeling that the "Atirantuka Speaks" passage is largely Bill's. My guess is that Bill took such action in desperation. If he could have white people believing that so-called "primitive" men had a firm grasp on the right path for humanity, maybe non-Aboriginal Australia could be shamed into modifying their views. Unfortunately, in my mind, it sets a precedent for doubt. Which of the words that Bill attributed to Aborigines are their's, and which are Bill's?

The very next block of text in the publication showed that Bill was not above admitting that he offered his interpretation of things said to him by the old men. Referring to a work he'd taken to Central Australia in 1954, one depicting his "spiritual self" cupping the faces of two children which were portrayed to be emerging from the work, the whole of which was standing in a tywerrenge shape, Bill wrote:

"This picture was taken at my camp in Central Australia. One wise old Aranda man, after speaking with the other old men, picked up some sand from the creek bed and said, as it trickled through his fingers—'Numbakulla made this. He made mountains, trees; He made everything.' Then he turned to me and to the old men, and pointing to my sculpture … said—'No man made that'—meaning that I was moved by the spirit of Numbakulla in making it. To find confirmation of this fact was one of the reasons I went to Central Australia."

There followed a listing of eleven examples of Bill's work to be found at the Mountain Gallery but which were not illustrated in the publication. The fifth listing was: *"Pertalchera (Perta-rock)—Dwelling place of the spirits. This is the happy name given to the rocks, the waterfall, the tiny creek, and the many spirit figures in various nooks and places at the back of the Mountain Gallery."* I never saw this area, but those who did tell of a truly marvellous place—a veritable fairyland. The works found there were all miniature, dating back to the time when Bill was limited in the size of the works he executed because of his small kiln. They also dated from the days when Bill applied incredible detail to his small creations, with stunning effect. It was apparently an area which could be walked around a score of times, and each time something new would be found that had been missed before. It was a fascinating delight to children and adults alike—quite another world where the imagination could run freely. More than anywhere else in the Gallery, it was a delicate area. And that was to be its downfall.

Bill sent his catalogues far and wide. Mary Harris helped him by sending them even further. She renewed her contact with Dr Verrier Elwin in India by forwarding one to him early in 1958. Elwin's letter of thanks was most appreciative. He wrote: *"I was particularly moved and thrilled by his own Foreword which expresses so beautifully what I myself feel in a much less perfect and developed way. His final words, 'A righteous anger, with God in the very centre of my works,' are a challenge to all 'civilised' people throughout the world."* Just what Bill wanted them to be.

Leo and Pitchi Richi [and, therefore, Bill's works] were back in the national eye in May, 1958, when the magazine *Woman's Day with Woman* devoted two full pages to the man who was fast becoming a character in a land of characters. The article's author, Ailsa Craig, portrayed Pitchi Richi as a haven, with its citrus and fruit orchards, swimming pool and endless cups of tea for the weary traveller. Leo was, *"one of the few men in the world who had managed to translate a youthful ideal into concrete fact"*. Craig wrote of how Leo had dreamed of a life *"where making money didn't matter, where he could live simply, but graciously, on next to nothing and help people for the sake of helping them, asking no reward but their thanks"*. At Pitchi Richi, she reported, he'd finally found it. It had become a drop-in centre, whether Leo was at home or not. All the makings for a cuppa and biscuits were permanently on hand—all you had to do was make it yourself. His good-humoured hospitality was rewarded with a constant stream of presents from around Australia and the world. Craig wrote that the magazine's gift was going to be a big kettle, because *"the one he has now isn't nearly large enough for the incessant cups of tea he makes for guests"*. Leo was enjoying himself.

Back on Mt Dandenong, Bill was feeling that his luck wasn't running as well as could be expected. More and more people were coming to him, but that one major sponsor failed to materialise. He was accumulating funds, though. In what amounted to desperation, he was relying more heavily on the sale of small works to boost his coffers. Although he never admitted it, not even when he was standing next to a pile of them, Bill was relying more and more on reproducing his small works with the aid of plaster casts and moulds. From what I've been told, there is quite a deal of skill involved in producing good moulds, and I can only speculate that Bill learned this skill way back in his early days at somewhere like the Crows' porcelain factory. He almost certainly used moulds throughout his career, a conclusion borne out by the many near-identical pieces originating from the similar periods. The only differences were the finishing marks, which Bill added by hand after the piece had been given its basic form. He kept this practice a closely guarded secret, disclosing it only to a handful of close acquaintances. He felt that such reproduction was hypocritical in the extreme.

There he was, a fighter for the spirit of a land, a man who wanted to disassociate himself from the idea of artist or sculptor so that attention could be concentrated on his "mission" and "vision"—there he was popping out moulded works for the purpose of raising filthy money.

It didn't occur to him that the painstaking finishing touches created originality. Nor that the very act of firing and glazing the pieces resulted in no two being identical. And he obviously didn't stop to think that most of his customers were not buying an investment art-work—they were buying a little piece of Bill's philosophy, a "concrete" reminder of the little man who had moved them to thought. No, the idea of moulding remained abhorrent to Bill; a shameful practice which must remain a closely guarded secret. He felt that if word of it leaked out it would shatter any hope he had of succeeding in his battle. His righteous purity would be degraded and cheapened.

I guess this is a good indication of the misplaced emphasis he put on the physical characteristics of his sculpture. Maybe he couldn't see that it wasn't just his sculpture which drew attention. After all, by that time there would have been others in Australia who could match his skill at the physical act of making the features in a lump of clay. Nobody, though, could come close to his passion, his imagination, his vision—or his absolute sincerity to his chosen cause. And because he could not see these facts about his position in the scheme he'd created, he suffered the most horrible of inner turmoils. He lived with a lie, and he could only justify it to himself with the knowledge that his ultimate goal was worth it.

Bill's immediate goal was to raise the funds which would allow him to continue his fight and to somehow secure the Mountain Gallery in such a way that its safety and integrity would be assured. He had to remove the responsibility of it from himself to free his mind and energy for what he saw as more important matters. The Wild Life Preservation Society in Sydney seem to have agreed to take on the responsibility of Mountain Gallery, but before they would touch it, Bill had to free the property from its binding mortgage. References in letters to Mary Harris suggest that a sum of £400 was still owed to the Commonwealth Bank. I can only presume that it was pure mismanagement on Bill's part which kept him in debt to the bank, or possibly his feeling that the Commonwealth Bank, then being Government-owned, should discharge the mortgage as a contribution towards his fight.

By this time, Lou and Dorothy Atkinson's Churinga Nursery was up and running. Although she did not recall the exact date, or even the year for that matter, Dorothy recounted a visitor she had who threw her into a bit of turmoil.

There was a knock at the Atkinson's door one day and in answering it Dorothy recognised Edith Bolte [later Dame Edith], wife of the Victorian Premier, Henry [later Sir Henry]. Mrs Bolte had come to ask Dorothy for a favour; she had twelve people sitting in taxis up on the road in need of refreshments and wondered if Dorothy could arrange a cup of tea for the party? Dorothy didn't know which way to look. She was not licensed to serve refreshments to the public, but did that include a direct request from the Premier's wife? In the end she apologised, explained her quandary and said that she just wouldn't dare. Mrs Bolte accepted the refusal and asked where she could take her party to entertain them? *"Well in the first place, you can take them over to see William Ricketts"*, Dorothy told her. She knew that Bill's place was not pristine, recalling that the *"dirty old hut"* and general mess was, in a word, dreadful, but she also knew that it was special. Dorothy recalled:

"Mrs Bolte listened to me and she took her twelve people over there, and talked long to William. She came back—it's quite a walk—and she said, 'I have never been so impressed in all my life. Why isn't something being done for this man?' I said,

'I don't know—I do all I can'. And she said, 'I'm going home to speak to my husband'. And she did."

There was to be no immediate response, at least on a public level, from any discussions about Bill between the Boltes.

In the November 19th, 1958, edition of the *Australian Women's Weekly*, an article about Bill entitled, "Artist Sculpts Spirit of Bush", was published. Written by an unacknowledged staff reporter, the article appears to have been wholly the result of Mary Harris' efforts; she was reported to be Bill's publicity agent. There were two significant items of interest. The first, written in the sub-heading, was that Bill had recently given his property to the Wild Life Preservation Society of Australia. The second was that he had recently bought a new three-ton truck. Bill was quoted as having said:

> *"This four and a half acres of forest at Mt Dandenong (which I paid for by instalments) I have given without payment to the Wild Life Preservation Society to be maintained in perpetuity as a sanctuary for Australian flora and fauna. Now I need the help of friends. To carry the responsibility and the heavy task placed upon my shoulders I need money. I have given this property to the nation, so I must depend on the nation's support to carry out my work."*

That statement was inaccurate. Bill had agreed to hand over the property and the WLPS had agreed to take it, but he had not discharged the mortgage. The fact that he'd bought a new truck, which cost far in excess of the £400 he owed, gives a firm indication of where his priorities lay.

The main thrust of the article was that Bill needed funds for his next Centralian "crusade", and that he was offering four large works to the City of Adelaide, *"on condition they are placed in the city's public sanctuary for native art, trees and flowers on the banks of the River Torrens"*. In other words, the works would have to go into Mary's Bundilla Sanctuary. One cannot help but feel there was too much optimism in the plan. The article also reported that Bill was hoping to set out for the Centre at the end of November, 1958.

Bill had planned to be up in the Centre at the beginning of the 1958 winter. He had fulfilled a long-standing dream to facilitate that journey by purchasing a brand new Land Rover for the purpose. But Bill's lack of practicality thwarted his plans. He'd gone out and bought a short-wheel-base Land Rover utility. While it would have been an eminently suitable vehicle for traversing Centralia's open spaces, it was totally unsuitable for transporting his load of clay and sculptures up there.

Mil Roche had the Austin truck franchise in Upwey early in 1958. He recalled the day that he received a phone call from his friend, Alf Turner [Doris' husband]. Alf explained that he needed help convincing Bill Ricketts that he couldn't drive up to Central Australia in a SWB Land Rover loaded with one and a half tons of sculpture. Mil recalled that when he first set eyes on Bill's Land Rover it was sitting back with its front wheels barely touching the ground. After talking to Bill, Mil advised him that at the least, he needed a three ton truck. It took some time, but eventually Bill saw reason in the argument. The most heart-breaking fact for Bill was that, although he'd had the vehicle for between six and eight months, the Land Rover had just ninety miles on the clock.

Mil ordered Bill a new three ton Austin truck and had it custom-painted a special light green at Bill's request. Instead of simply trading in the Land Rover, Mil took it upon himself to sell it privately to minimise Bill's loss. He recalled that the biggest problem he had was convincing potential purchasers that the speedo reading was accurate. Then Mil, an engineer, and Alf Turner set to work modifying the truck's tray to suit Bill's needs. They put a solid roof over it and canvas sides that could be rolled up as required. At Bill's request, they also installed seats along the inside of the tray, in case Bill had any passengers to transport in the Centre.

The last job was to teach Bill how to drive the Austin. Although Mil had driven trucks all his life, he did not refuse the help of mate, Ed King, who was a professional truckie. Mil rolled his eyes and had a laugh at the memory:

> *"We wheeled Bill up and down that mountain side in fear and trembling a hundred times. He was hopeless! But eventually—eventually—through perseverance and many, many hours, he got the hang of it."*

The confusion over the Land Rover's failings and the modifications to the new Austin meant that Bill was not ready to leave until summer—and that was the wrong time of year. He did have at least one trip up to Sydney, where he stayed with Jim Brown of the WLPS; presumably to further negotiations regarding the WLPS's takeover of the Mountain Gallery. The rest of the time until the following winter Bill devoted to making new works to fill up his newly acquired space in the Austin.

14 | Return to the Centre
[1959]

Bill was ready to leave for the Centre in April, 1959. He'd bought a caravan to take along as a more adequate studio than the tent had been previously. In his enthusiasm, Bill loaded as much modelling clay, food and executed sculpture as he could. On the morning of his departure from Mt Dandenong he eased into Alf Turner's garage for petrol. Doris recalled the shock Alf got when he saw Bill's rig. The weight was such that every spring on the truck and caravan was flattened. Alf immediately ordered Bill to go home and unload things until his springs were again pointing up the right way. Bill complied, but events will show that his rig must still have been grossly overloaded.

There was a stopover in Adelaide where an exhibition on the lawns of St Peter's Cathedral had been arranged by Mary Harris. The Quaker Meeting House adjoined the Cathedral grounds, providing Bill with a handy camping spot.

The exhibition, which was open for viewing by May 2nd, was by most accounts a raging success. Large crowds came, reportedly in their hundreds, to see the twelve larger works Bill had on show and to listen to what he had to say. He had many small works for sale, which were much sought after. Mary Harris related in her unpublished biography the profound effect Bill's speech had on one young woman: *"She went to the market in Adelaide and spent every penny she had—£14—in buying caged birds. She took them to the hills above Adelaide and set them free."* The exhibition continued for about a fortnight. When finished, members of the Society of Friends helped Bill pack up in preparation for the journey north. Mary described the scene:

> *"It had been a strenuous morning loading great works, some of which took three men to lift, into the waiting truck … A black-robed figure passed us and smiled: it was the Dean and he had given these inspired works, so heavy to handle, his blessing. But it was a woman, fair haired and ever helpful, who conceived the idea of applying to the nearby Children's Hospital for a hand-truck to carry the works from lawn to roadside.*
>
> *I heard the quiet answer of a man who wrenched his back in lifting: 'It is an honour to handle such works.'"*

After all was loaded and the area swept clean of the packing straw and leaves which had been dragged around, Bill picked up that Mary's mood was somewhat sad. She told him that she was distressed by an "incredibly ignorant and vulgar" review which had appeared in the previous evening's paper.

The Adelaide *News* had published in its May 15th edition a review by Geoffrey Dutton titled, "Nature Becomes a Ham". It was the one bad review about Bill which I sighted during the research. It read in part:

> *"Modestly tucked away ... by the cathedral lawns, an ego as vast as the Northern Territory is at present displaying itself in the clay sculpture of William Ricketts. Above the chubby torsos of aboriginal children and clusters of pesky possums, born aloft on a cloud of congealed ectoplasm, rises the slender but powerful chest, the noble profile, and the billowing mane of a white man called Brother Billy.*
>
> *Apparently he is a close relation of William Ricketts ... We are ... modestly told ... that 'For the purpose of my development, my Creator worked through the Australian aboriginal to get hold of me.'*
>
> *The question is: Was Mr Ricketts worth getting hold of? For some of his ideas and his imagination, yes; for his love of the aborigines and of Nature, yes; as a sculptor, no ...*
>
> *Mr Ricketts always gives us the same ham actor in the part of the spirit of Nature or of the bush. It is the sort of figure you'd pay sixpence to have a shy at in the Aunt Sally stall at a country show ..."*

Bill told Mary not to worry about the review, just to forget about it; implying that it did not concern him at all. But it did worry him, which is only natural. Other people from that time say that an almost visible grey veil came over him. A photograph published in the *Woman's Day with Woman* magazine [June 22nd, 1959] shows Bill sitting in his truck at the time of the exhibition. I don't know if it was taken before or after Dutton's review, but it shows a positively tight-lipped, stern-faced and humourless Bill, which he would later describe as an *"awful monster in a motor"*.

In the article by Rita Dunstan published with that photograph, Bill was made out to be off to establish his Holy Mountain somewhere. He was quoted as having said: *"I have cried enough. If I should cry any more I should go mad. I only want now to fulfil the purpose of my life and bring peace and love to the whole of life through my holy mountain."* Rita Dunstan then wrote: *"Mr Ricketts said his aim could be accomplished if 25,000 people gave £1 each to finance the establishment of the mountain meeting-place."* The Mt Dandenong sanctuary was described as merely the seed of the mountain to come. And again, it was reported that the Mt Dandenong property had been signed over to the WLPS. Bill was quoted: *"Now I have given it away as I give everything away. I never want anything for myself."*

Bill was reported in several articles as being hopeful that when he finally reached the Centre, he would be able to have Ted Strehlow accompany him on a journey to the Aborigines, so that Strehlow might be able to accurately translate the response generated by the truck-load of new works. As far as Bill was concerned, the Aborigines were to be his only critics, and, with Strehlow's help, their reactions would be made known.

Mary wrote of the farewell meal held at the Friends' Meeting House in her unpublished biography. She referred to Bill as looking like Leonardo da Vinci's Christ in the Last Supper painting: *"Brother Billy sat at the far end of the table against the light. Sitting in this position his face was shadowed against the light which enveloped him."* Further on she wrote: *"The unity of the Last Supper drew us together. A Last Supper is not conceivable without its Judas. The Judas of the twentieth century may be an ignorant and irresponsible journalist, seeking in the attempted destruction of a man's life and spirit his thirty pieces of silver."*

Poor Mr Dutton; exercising freedom of the press, getting nowhere near his thirty pieces of silver, and forever after enduring the wrath of the most formidable Miss Mary Packer Harris.

There was one other legacy of the interest aroused by the St Peter's Exhibition. Very soon after Bill had left Adelaide, Mr Martindale approached Mary Harris on behalf of the Adelaide Junior Chamber of Commerce. The Junior Chamber International had organised an international exhibition, with exhibits from eighty-nine countries, to be held in a museum at Nathanya, near Tel Aviv. The Australian chapter wanted to purchase a piece of Bill's work to send as their contribution. The piece they chose featured one bust and several faces of Aboriginal children.

Ted Strehlow wrote a small essay to accompany the piece on its journey, describing it as a "poem in stone". John Rundle, National President of the Australian Jaycees was reported as saying that the piece *"should be an admirable ambassador for [Australia] to the world"*.

On Bill's first night out of town he scribbled off a quick note to Lou and Dorothy Atkinson. He gave his address as, *"Somewhere along the road 150 miles north of Adelaide"*. Bill had either put the bad review behind him or put it out of his mind altogether, writing:

> *"My works were shown on the lawns of St Peters Cathedral. The success was <u>complete</u> and it was more than an ordinary success. Now I am on my way to the natives to get a unique success. On the Cathedral lawns it was as if a beautiful wild flower was raised up and the people came and did drink deep of the pure nectar. I will write later on and let you know how things go."*

The next letter the Atkinson's received was not quite so full of good news. Bill found himself undertaking the drive of a life-time, one which he would describe as, *"a thousand mile nightmare"*. Still a relatively inexperienced driver at the age of 61 years, the drive north in good conditions would have been a test. As Bill's luck would have it, the conditions were anything but good.

His first test was the kilometre after kilometre of deep, bone-jarring corrugations in the road. Those who haven't experienced it personally can never know its full horrors. Imagine, if you can, driving over small, narrow speed-humps, about 10 cm in height, spaced every 40 cm apart for hundreds of kilometres on end; with bad sections irregularly thrown in to keep you awake. Your whole being is immersed in the sickening sound and whole-body feeling of your vehicle being slowly, but surely, shaken to bits. A fine, talcum-like dust fills the air, because you can't go fast enough to provide an adequate ventilation of fresh air. You can try to build up speed in an attempt to "get on top" of the corrugations, but the abuse to the suspension becomes extreme, inviting a major mechanical failure. Steering at these speeds becomes a finely-tuned attempt to merely aim in the right general direction, with a constant and real risk of shuddering off your chosen path, the road, to whatever fate awaits. You try it, but ultimately you must slacken off and drive slowly, up and down every corrugation. The dust clogs every pore in your skin, fills your hair to the point where it feels like brittle straw, fills your eyes with a permanently abrasive irritation, mixes in your nose, your mouth and your throat to become a clogging red mud. Sweat runs in red rivulets over your body.

Add the tension of knowing that the most precious part of your cargo is kiln-fired clay, vulnerable to the knocks and jolts which constantly assault and threaten everything from the tyres up. If your imagination is fertile, you now know the beginnings of what Bill went through for the first 800 km of his journey up the infamous old Stuart Highway to Coober Pedy.

Somewhere north of the opal town Bill picked up a hitch-hiker, a Pitjantjatjara man who'd had enough of the high life in town and was heading back to his homeland. Bill wrote in letters describing the journey that the man was sick with an influenza, which Bill promptly caught.

Then it rained. In some places it was the best rain had in four years.

Rain transforms outback roads just as quickly as it transforms dry outback river-beds. Bill suddenly found himself driving on slippery surfaces in a two-wheel-drive truck which responded mercilessly to the conditions, the heavy caravan only adding to the confusion of his endeavour. As the table drains filled, sections of the road became long lakes of red-brown water which hid any obstacle. Bill could only apply his whole being to the task of staying on the road and maintaining forward motion. When he tried to slow down quickly, the trailer's inertia wanted to push the truck around in a jack-knife. If he had to gather speed to get through a particularly bad patch, the trailer would respond as a dead weight, leaving his drive wheels to spin uselessly.

At some point an awareness of a change forced itself through the effort of driving and the fast-overtaking influenza. Bill could not work it out, but the awareness would not leave him.

Finally he realised what it was. As he wrote to Doris Turner: *"I stopped for something to eat and I found the caravan gone."*

With visions of his caravan overturned and wrecked, its contents strewn about in the mud and being ruined by the rain, Bill found a place where he could safely turn around and drove back *"five miles"* before he found it. It was not overturned or wrecked—it was sitting patiently on the road, being inspected by three men whose Land Rover was parked nearby. When Bill stopped and got out, one of the men strode over, extended his hand and said to Bill: *"I've been wanting to meet you for years!"* In the middle of nowhere, in the depth of adversity, fate had delivered to Bill a supporter waiting to help him out. The caravan's coupling had jumped off the tow-ball and the caravan had slid to a graceful halt. It was a simple matter of hooking it back up. After thanks and farewells, Bill set off again.

The conditions continued to be atrocious. Bill slipped and skidded and spun his way north with a determination nourished by visions of the haven of Pitchi Richi and Leo at the end of the road. Later in the journey, though, Bill suffered another set-back. He lost control of the truck and started sliding towards the edge of the road. Before he knew it, he was past the point of no return. In the soft mud on the road's edge, the truck foundered and was dragged further into trouble by the caravan's dead weight.

They were stuck. What must have been in excess of five tonnes of bogged truck and caravan, and two men struck by influenza, one of whom was in his sixties. For two hours they sat in the glorious silence of the outback, wondering what they were going to do.

Again, fate was kind to Bill. The sound of a heavy vehicle's laboured approach soon gave way to the vision of a bus struggling through the treacherous conditions. It stopped adjacent to Bill and out piled a load of Church of England tourists. The Minister came down and happily shook Bill's hand. He lived in Olinda and had been to the Mountain Gallery on many occasions. Next came the bus driver, happy to be meeting Bill for the first time. He, too, knew the Gallery well. The whole bus-load knew of Bill. As soon as all who had cameras had captured the event on film, they were only too happy to be of help. They jumped into the muck and heaved and pushed and coaxed the truck and caravan back onto the road. More photographs and then farewells, and a bus-load of smiling faces set off again on their own journey, satisfied with their success in rendering assistance.[1]

Bill continued on for what he wrote was another *"200 miles"*, fighting all the way and in constant fear of becoming bogged. At times he decided that the road was impassable, so he took to the bush, screaming the motor at maximum revs to keep going—and just getting through. More long lakes of water with unknown bottoms. Some of them he went through, some of them he went around, and although he came perilously close, he did not get seriously bogged again.

The stresses inflicted upon the truck sought release. The draw-bar tore through; its metal ripping away not from the chassis, but tearing through the middle. Again Bill was stuck on the side of the road, and again fate brought help. How they achieved it Bill did not say, but a welding plant was trucked out from a nearby cattle station and the draw-bar repaired *"stronger than before"*.

Finally the hitch-hiker directed Bill off the main road and guided him into an area of the North West Reserve to what Bill described as a *"large group of Pitjantjatjara people"*. In a letter to Mary Harris, Bill wrote: *"It was just as if a million years had gone by and I had just returned to them."* Despite his sickness, Bill unloaded three works to show those people. He claimed that one man *"with a bad leg"* came forward. As a child, the man had spent time in hospital in Adelaide and spoke *"lovely English"*. Bill claimed that the man told him that all his people knew him, and would help him. Bill knew where he would return as soon as he was well enough.

---

1 Unfortunately, nobody came forward during my research with a photograph of that situation. Maybe in the next edition.

Back on the road again and north to Pitchi Richi. Bill was sick, weak and worn out. He wrote to Doris that he felt *"a complete wreck"*. But eventually he reached his goal, Pitchi Richi, and the reassuring face of Leo Corbet. Bill stopped and got out. As low as his spirits were, as relieved as he was to be at his journey's end, everything in his being sank to new depths when he looked to the back of his truck. The bolt holding the tow-ball had snapped and the caravan was, again, gone. Bill went back with Leo, fresh thoughts of a twisted roadside wreck swirling through his fevered mind. They found the caravan upright and intact about 16 km out of town. They hooked it up to a new tow-ball and drove back to Pitchi Richi. The nightmare was over.

The journey can now be done in one long day, or two easy days. Going by the dates on letters and the information Bill wrote in them, it took him around two weeks to complete the journey. It left him badly physically weakened, although his resolve remained untarnished. He did do at least one job, though, before allowing himself the time to recuperate. He sent a quick letter off to the Aborigines Department of South Australia, requesting permission to return to the group of Pitjantjatjaras he'd met in the North West Reserve.

He was confident that it would be only a matter of weeks before the approval came through. For the next two weeks Bill suffered ulcerous sores on his legs where they had been knocked during the trip, forcing him to rest up. The rain had gone and Bill was able to sit in the sun, feasting on oranges and other fruits from Pitchi Richi's gardens, marvelling at the flocks of birds around him and listening with delight to the tales Leo had to tell. The best tale of all, and one which would be retold by many a passing journalist, was about the birds at Pitchi Richi. It went something like this.

The rains which had caused Bill such distress were desperately needed. In many places there had been a four year drought—there had been no good rains since Bill's first visit to the area. The drought had devastating and widespread effects, but of immediate concern to Leo were the starving birds which flocked to his property for the abundant water. Leo took to spreading a little seed out for them, but as quick as it hit the ground, it was eaten. So he contacted the local bakery and made arrangements to sweep the floors of crumbs every morning, which usually gave him about half a bag full. He needed more food to do the job properly, so he wrote letters to four major newspapers down south, explaining his plight and asking them to publish a request for some bird seed. *"I hoped some of the old ladies who kept canaries and love birds might oblige with a few packets"*, he was later quoted as saying.

A week or so went by and just when Leo was beginning to think the worst of his request, a Trans Australia Airlines [TAA] delivery van wheeled into his drive. The driver jumped out and told Leo that he had one tonne of seed in the back, with another two and a half tonnes waiting at their freight terminal—where did he want it? It turned out that TAA had offered to fly the seed up free if people dropped it off to them, and the response spoke for itself.

Not long after that the Alice Springs Postmaster rang up and frantically told Leo to get in there quick. Leo arrived at the Post Office to see the cause of the Postmaster's concern. Bags and packets of bird seed, all addressed to Leo, were strewn all over the place. The packets that were leaking all over the floor and through the postal sacks had brought in what nearly amounted to a mouse plague—and they were busily making their homes in the sudden land of plenty, with no regard whatsoever to the sanctity of the Royal Mail. Leo backed his Land Rover up and hastily shovelled the mess into the tray, throwing back the letters that got caught up.

The seed continued to come in and Leo busily spread it out, resulting in thousands of birds, chiefly the pink and grey galahs, centring their lives around Pitchi Richi.

There had been a letter waiting for Bill when he arrived. It was from one of his sisters and contained news that Mr Gardener had left Bill's place. It suggests that this Mr Gardener, who is not known to me, was left as caretaker, but had decided not to continue with the vocation. Bill wrote to Dorothy and Lou with a request that they move some of the more portable pieces of sculpture inside his house for safety.

By June 10th Bill was ready to move out bush, except for one problem. *"Something went wrong with me during my journey"*, he explained in his letter to the Atkinsons. Apart from the ulcerous sores he'd arrived with, he was getting more, having only to touch his legs to have *"sores start to run"*. He ended up having to get treatment from a doctor and was ordered to rest up for a while longer. So as not to waste his time, Bill thought it an ideal opportunity to make a batch of small works for sale. To this end he asked Lou Atkinson to go into his house and collect five plaster moulds, giving specific instructions [including very poor sketches] about which ones he wanted and where they were to be found. He asked that they be put in a box addressed to Leo, and sent by air to the Alice. One short sentence in the letter shows how uncomfortable Bill was with the concept of moulding—*"Don't put my name on the box"*, he wrote.

Bill planned to make small works not only for sale from Pitchi Richi, but to send back to the Atkinsons as well. In letters to follow he expressed greater fear about the security of his Mountain Gallery, specifically identifying more works to the Atkinsons that he requested be put inside his house. He predicted a stay of at least twelve months in the Centre. In one letter he joked at what would be waiting for him on his return:

> *"I suppose my house will be a fungus garden by then. Last summer when I went to Sydney I came back and as I opened the door a large fungus looked up at me to say welcome, and anyway it will save me painting the ceiling white."*

Bill expected the permit authorising him to enter Pitjantjatjara lands to arrive any day. When he was fit enough to travel and the permit still had not arrived, he made the decision to go *"out a bit"*; which suggests to me a visit to the Jay Creek Aboriginal settlement which was some 42 km from Alice, on the road to Hermannsburg. It would have been close enough for Bill to regularly drop back to Pitchi Richi.

On August 11th, a Melbourne *Age* journalist wrote a small piece commenting on Victoria's *"systematic preservation of irreplaceable things"*, citing the historic mansion, Como, as an example. The journalist went on to cite Bill's property as irreplaceable, explaining that she or he had recently visited the *"extraordinary open-air gallery"* on Mt Dandenong. The journalist wrote:

> *"Ricketts, whose work has excited international notice, was travelling Central Australia when I called. He had taken with him many of his pieces ... but dozens of the exquisite examples of his work remain. The danger is that, if Ricketts were not to return, for any reason, the gallery might eventually be lost. And we could not afford to lose it."*

The piece was aimed at the powers which might be able to protect the future of Bill's Gallery. Unwittingly, though, the piece alerted any opportunist *Age* reader[2] to the fact that there were dozens of good Ricketts' pieces unguarded and open to the public, just waiting to be *admired* within the grounds of Mountain Gallery.

The month of July, 1959, saw Albert Namatjira die and be buried near Mt Gillen. The official causes were pneumonia and a heart condition, although others would say that Namatjira died of a broken heart. At the time of his death he was just ten weeks out of detention for having shared a drink of alcohol with some friends and relatives. Namatjira, having been granted citizenship, was legally allowed to have a drink himself. The privilege did not extend to those Aborigines close to him. He was caught, and the mandatory sentence of six months imposed. The great man whose art captured so sensitively the country of his birth was reduced to being a common criminal for sharing a drink with friends. That, the story goes, was the beginning of his end.

---

2 Of course, the general opinion among *Age* readers will be that there is no such beast.

A new settlement was in the process of being established at Papunya, approximately 40 km by road north-west of Haasts Bluff settlement. It was to take over from Haasts Bluff settlement the role of accommodating the large numbers of Aborigines who were coming in from the bush. Haasts Bluff would continue as the operational centre for the cattle industry established on the reserve, and a number of Aborigines would remain there, but the majority were moved to Papunya. The *Advocate* reported in its August 21st edition that violent riots had occurred at Papunya, initially sparked off by a traditional pay-back killing. At the end of the melee, two Aborigines were dead, with at least nineteen Aborigines injured. On the day following the riot a search and seizure resulted in over 200 traditional weapons being confiscated by the Welfare authorities. The incident was a major flare-up of what appeared to be continuous conflict between the various groups who found themselves living in unusual proximity.

Within Pitchi Richi Leo had somehow managed to get the Governor of South Australia to plant a eucalyptus tree, after which Leo prepared a plaque of sorts to commemorate the event. Whether it was at Leo's request, or as a result of Bill not wanting to be outdone in the environmental awareness stakes, it came about that Bill also planted a eucalyptus and made a commemorative plaque as a record. The plaque he prepared bears the words, **"With this lovely tree I planted thoughts of beauty to be. William Ricketts on August 20, 1959"**, and featured the small faces of three Aboriginal children. Bill fired the plaque in another home-made bush kiln constructed at Pitchi Richi which used some kind of drum as the firing chamber. That the plaque was intact with no signs of deterioration when I last viewed it in late 1987 confirms the success of at least some of Bill's Centralian firing endeavours.

Bill worked around Pitchi Richi, spent time at Jay Creek and even went up to Utopia for a spell, but still no word came about his permit from the Aborigines Department of South Australia. He wrote that his works were an instant success with the old Aboriginal men who saw them, but he almost always referred to heading **"300 miles"** south to his new-found Pitjantjatjara friends. By November, 1959, Bill had decided to head back out to Haasts Bluff settlement.

About one month into his stay at Haasts Bluff, Bill suffered yet another serious medical set-back. At some point he and an Aboriginal friend were unloading one of the larger sculptures. The friend lost his grip during the lift, leaving Bill to bear the full weight on one shoulder until his friend recovered his hold. The effort would have been extreme, because Bill would not have been seeking assistance unless he was sure that there was no way he could lift the piece himself. That was a fixed part of his character. It was three days before the full strain of the accident brought him to a halt. He was experiencing such acute pain in the shoulder that he could not raise his arm. The pain was so great that he took himself to hospital in Alice Springs, where x-rays revealed a calcium formation on the bone at the top of his arm.

This build-up, he was told, had been forming over many years, the result of continuous heavy lifting. The stress of being suddenly overloaded at Haasts Bluff had caused associated soft tissue damage, but Bill was told that such a flare-up had been inevitable. He was under the care of Dr Bromwieh,[3] who decided not to operate on the arm unless it was absolutely necessary. For a time Bill had to attend the hospital on a daily basis for heat treatment and physiotherapy, with additional exercises prescribed for the intervening times. The threat of an operation, which had the potential of laying him up for many weeks, would have given the hospital staff an exemplary patient.

Forever the optimist, Bill wrote to the Atkinsons that his accident had come at as good a time as could be hoped for. Summer was by then asserting itself with the weather becoming **"really hot and boiling and windy"**. With still no word on the North West Reserve permit, Bill decided to stay and work at Pitchi Richi over the summer, or at least until the heat abated. Bill made another request to the Atkinsons to help him in his work. He carefully described the whereabouts of some pink clay which he used in the colouring of his pieces. He directed them to

---

3 This is Bill's spelling, as recorded in a letter to Mary Harris written on November 20th, 1959.

a stash stored *"between those logs where the four lights are"*, or to *"the base of that big work with seven old men along the base"*. Bill advised that they would see the hole where he'd reached in to extract the clay. He wanted *"just a little, about as much as you can put in your two hands"*. The Atkinsons did their best, but were rewarded with a letter telling them that what they'd sent was *"just common stuff and no good"*.

Bill again directed them into the alcove in his old house, going as far as to sketch them a very rough map in an attempt to show them where his stash of clay was located. When they finally found it, they were to: *"Blow the dust off and maybe a little yellow clay hanging on to the pink clay so take that off. Use a torch and you can see it."* With directions like that, how could they fail?

In his letters to the Atkinsons, Bill always enquired after his *"darling lyre birds"*, and continually asked Dorothy to remember him to them. Judging by Bill's comments, Dorothy always told him of their latest news. When he learned that Dorothy had seen the beginnings of nest-building activity by one of the hen-birds, Bill could only wish that his dreaded weeds, the blackberries, were thick enough to *"keep out the unwanted ones"*.

A letter from the Atkinsons in December 1959, brought the news that Bill had been dreading—works had been stolen from the Mountain Gallery, and money taken from his wishing well. In his reply Bill tried to get the Atkinsons to identify just which works were gone, but it would appear that they were not as familiar with all the works as Bill would have hoped. He ended up asking them to tell him the positions of where they thought works had been removed from, claiming that he would then know exactly which piece had been there. As anxious as he was about the sculptures and the *"devil agents"* who stole them, Bill made sure to thank the Atkinsons for *"watching over our darling sister in life, our Lyre bird"*. He did not contemplate returning home straight away, though, writing that he would see them *"next year winter time"*.

15 | Mountain Gallery "In Ruins"
[1960]

The theft about which the Atkinsons informed Bill was by no means the first at the Mountain Gallery. Doug Harkness, the local Olinda Police Officer prior to and during the 1959–60 episode, recalled that theft from the site was ongoing, largely facilitated by Bill's complete lack of attention to, or at least inability to provide, security.

Harkness used to call in regularly to visit Bill, just to say hello and see that things were going all right for him. Then, all of a sudden, Bill would be gone without a word of advice to the local constabulary. The very nature of the Gallery was a potential thief's delight—totally screened from the road, and plenty of bush to hide in should somebody else come along. Harkness would still call in when Bill was away, but it was almost a waste of time. As Harkness told me: *"The only way to protect it was to have somebody there all the time."*

While theft may have been an ongoing occurrence at the Gallery, it accelerated dramatically after Christmas, 1959. The Gallery's popularity had increased to the point where an almost constant flow of visitors was entering it. That theft became mixed with vandalism is not surprising. Once the readily moved works were gone, people started on those pieces fixed into the earth and onto rocks. Force would have to have been used to get such pieces, and that would have found any weaknesses formed during the inconsistent firing, resulting in broken pieces lying on the ground for the next person to trip over. The Gallery was transformed from a place which inspired a reverent silence to a smash-and-grab yard.

I spoke to one man, Ian, who had known and respected the Gallery since the mid-1940s, when he was first taken there as a twelve-year-old. He recalled a day sometime in the late 1950s when he visited the Gallery with his girlfriend, and the long conversation he had with Bill, during which Ian explained how much he was looking forward to being able to purchase his own piece of Bill's work. Bill disappeared inside his hut and returned with a miniature bust of an adolescent Aboriginal girl. He gave it to Ian, saying that it would cost £7, which Ian quickly said he did not have. *"That's all right"*, said Bill. *"Just post it care of the Mt Dandenong Post Office—I'm sure I'll get it."* Ian did not betray the trust.

Ian vividly recalled his next visit early in 1960—the day he walked in and found the scene looking like a battlefield. He was horrified and filled with revulsion, and, being the only person in the grounds at the time, was overcome by a sense of desolation. As he walked around—this man who had loved and respected the Gallery for fifteen years of his life, and to whom Bill's trust had been extended with no questions—Ian's eyes came to rest upon one of Bill's beautifully sculptured heads lying on the path at his feet. Temptation caught him as he bent down and picked up the head. He felt a sudden, overpowering urge to take it home, deceiving himself that he would be giving it refuge. He had stood up before the full realisation of what he was about to do hit him, and then his revulsion increased tenfold. Ashamed and embarrassed, he placed the work back on the ground and left. Twenty-six years later, when I spoke to him in Adelaide, his voice still filled with emotion and disbelief in recounting the tale.

Ian put the work back because of his long association with the Gallery. Another person with no such affiliation could quite easily have kept walking with the work. As the year, 1960, progressed, so too did the destruction.

When Bill wrote to Mary Harris early in January telling of the Atkinsons' news, he said, *"Something will have to be done quickly"*, but offered no suggestions. He did give her a reason for not wanting to return home immediately, though: *"I am doing good work here, far above [anything] I have ever done."* The other good news was that his arm was at last healed *"back to normal"*. On January 20th, Bill wrote to the Atkinsons enquiring after the lyrebird chick, the nest-building having apparently been a success, and forewarning of a parcel containing small works for sale soon to arrive at the Croydon railway station. Lou was asked to send up more pink clay: *"the same amount only send it ordinary mail because I am not in a hurry for it this time"*. The only reference made to the Gallery's security came in the form of:

> *"It is a pity someone will not stay as caretaker in my house. I have not the money to make it better to live in. I will I think hand over the title of the land to the Wild Life preservation society then I will not have to pay Lilydale rates of £6-6-0."*

Despite the still hot weather in the Centre, Bill decided to go out bush again in early February. He stocked up with provisions, loaded the truck, hooked up the caravan and set out for the new settlement of Papunya. Not far into the 200 km trip it began to rain. Bill's all-too-recent memories of the nightmare of driving the wet outback roads prompted him to turn around and retreat to the security of Pitchi Richi. While waiting for the countryside to dry out, he sent off another letter to the Atkinsons, dated February 13th.

He informed them that he had written to the WLPS in Sydney requesting that they take over the Gallery, *"and make it law to be held as sacred trust for all time"*. Bill would explain it better when he came down *"for a few days"* in October, further proving his intention to separate himself from any responsibility regarding the Gallery.

He hoped that the WLPS might be able to get a married couple to live rent-free in the house, which he saw as the only answer. Bill told the Atkinsons that they could put up a sign in the Gallery directing people to Churinga, presumably so that small works could be purchased. He also forewarned them of a couple of people he'd spoken with in the Alice who would be calling in to purchase larger works, which he described.

He wrote that he would wait until Tuesday, three days off, before trying to go out again, intending to stay for a few weeks, after which he would at last:

> *"... go south-west 300 miles to the Pitjantjatjara. These people know me. They know me in that burnt tree. I did that work long before you came up there and in my native conceptions I am to do this burnt tree will be known as (The miracle fire dreaming of William Ricketts) and the native conceptions have and will have their roots in that terrible and beautiful thing."*

How must Bill have felt when he received the letter from the Aborigines Department of South Australia a few days later? His relief at receiving it would have turned to disbelief when he read that he was refused entry—and rage when he read their reasoning:

> *"The aborigines in this area either reside at Ernabella Mission or live as near primitives on the Reserve, and permission to enter the Reserve is only granted where it is of some benefit to the aborigines or if considered of National importance."*

It would have proved to Bill, beyond doubt, just how blind and ignorant the Government was. Couldn't they see, he would have asked Leo, that the very reason for his working in such a way was to be not of *some* benefit to Aborigines, but to *greatly* benefit the race? And to imply that his work was not of National importance! It was of *International* importance. With everything that had gone wrong so far during the journey, it was a slap in the face that he really did not need. But in no way would it have got him down. He would have seen it as a concrete attempt to thwart his awakening of a Nation's consciousness—and that would only have made him more determined to succeed.

As soon as the roads were passable, Bill headed out to Papunya.

The Papunya settlement Superintendent at the time was Harry Kitching, who had first come into contact with Bill at the Bungalow Reserve in 1954–55. Kitching estimated the Aboriginal population at the time of Bill's visit to be between 400 and 600 adults, of whom about 150 were employed working in the settlement kitchens, gardens and sewing rooms, and the cattle enterprise, which included fencing, yard-building and the maintenance of the smaller settlements on the outlying bores. That unfortunately left a significant surplus of idle people, and, as Harry Kitching explained, it was the idle hands that were Papunya's greatest source of unrest.

Arnold Probin was employed as a Farm Manager at Papunya at that time. When I asked him what his duties were, he shook his head and said: *"I stopped fights. Oh God, there was always a fight going on somewhere."* There were fights for all sorts of reasons, but the worst Probin recalled were the fights between the women which sometimes got totally out of control. Probin recalled having to, at times, step in and physically remove a combatant:

"I'd have to grab the woman and take her off to hospital and get a Largactil down her—a quietening medicine. We had to try and get them and pacify them. But you had to watch that they didn't bite or scratch your eyes out—'cause they would bite you. They would attack you and I'd have to put their arm up behind their back—but I wouldn't hurt them—but I had to get them to the hospital to get a Largactil down them. Having been in the Navy and being on patrol and all that, it wasn't hard to do. But I really did have to watch that they didn't attack me."

Another man involved in the sometimes chaotic goings on was Dr George Tippett, Medical Officer in charge of Native Health and the Aerial Medical Service in Alice Springs. He had a big job:

"I went round to all the settlements, all the cattle stations and it was my job to know where every black-fellow was in our territory, then when I found them I would send out my—well they call them community health sisters now—and she would go and actually live on a settlement until she had everyone listed and named and cross-indexed so that we could find out where the tribes were moving around. We were looking to vaccinate them, find what disease was amongst them—leprosy, yaws, tuberculosis—I was involved in an anti-T.B. campaign that went up through there. On top of that we did the general practitioner service, ran the radio sessions, sent planes out to people who needed to be brought in, were very involved with infant welfare because of the appalling death-rate that there was at that stage.

Of course back in those days it was the middle of a drought that went on for years and years and the general condition of the Aborigines was very bad. The Government set up settlements and the Aborigines came in from their nomadic life and lived on the settlements, intermingled and cross-infected each other. There was tribal violence as different groups came together who were very much strangers to each other. They were fed out of very generous government feeding programs, but it completely stopped their own

91 *Rebirth at the hands of the Elder, as described on page 155. A similar piece remains at the WRS, while another was sold by Bill to raise funds for Animal Liberation. Approx. 1800 mm wide. Photographer unknown.*

92 *Mary Packer Harris at Bundilla with the piece, Billy & Tjikalyi. Photographer unknown.*

93 *Inscribed work claimed by Bill to bear the "signatures" of 16 men from the Centre. WRS. 560 mm high.*

94 *Bill Ricketts and Bill Onus, c. late 1950s.*

96 *Bill in the Mountain Gallery. Reproduced from* Woman's Day and Home *magazine, August 3rd, 1953.*

95 The Enshrinement of Ricketts in Churinga. *WRS collection [now has very bad firing cracks]. 1400 mm high.*

97 *An early* Brute. *Photo by W. Grevis-James. WRS [remains of]. Approx. 800 mm high.*

98 *Face plaque. Ins: "Wm Ricketts". 120 mm high, PC.*

99 *360° piece featuring men, women, children and Bill's self portrait. No inscription. 580 mm high, PC.*

100 *Child's face, possum and pitchi bowl. Ins: "Wm Ricketts". 60 mm high, PC.*

102 *Bill with unidentified friends near Papunya. Photographer unknown, c. 1950s.*

101 *Bill called this the "monster in a motor" photo; taken shortly after Geoffrey Dutton's bad review of the St Peter's Cathedral exhibition. Reproduced from* Woman's Day with Woman *magazine, June 22nd, 1959.*

103 & 104 *With unfired works in the Centre behind the 3 t Austin. Photographer unknown, c. 1950s.*

105 *Bill with unidentified friends near Papunya. Photographer unknown, c. 1950s.*

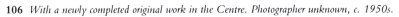

106 *With a newly completed original work in the Centre. Photographer unknown, c. 1950s.*

107 *Bill as a tree spirit. Pitchi Richi. 1970 mm high.*

109 *Ted Hemsley, past manager of Pitchi Richi, and the remains of a kiln Bill constructed there.*

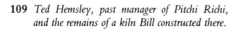

108 *Rear of a Pitchi Richi piece showing construction detail. 575 mm high.*

110 *Emu Dreaming children. Pitchi Richi. 1060 mm high. Photographer unknown.*

111 *Moon-Man and young girl. Pitchi Richi. 380 mm high.*

112 *At Pitchi Richi. 880 mm high.*

113 *At Pitchi Richi. Ins: "With this lovely Tree I planted thoughts of beauty to be. William Ricketts on August 20, 1959". 380 mm high.*

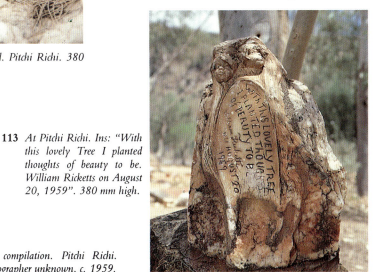

114 *Bill with a 3-piece compilation. Pitchi Richi. 3070 mm wide. Photographer unknown, c. 1959.*

116 *Mary Harris and Bill at Bundilla. Photographer unknown, c. 1950s.*

115 *A miniature* Evening Star. *Ins: "William Ricketts Mt Dandenong". 300 mm high, PC.*

118 *At Pitchi Richi, an unidentified local appears proud to be photographed with the likeness of Tjinapatunka. Photographer and date unknown.*

117 *Leo Corbet and unidentified helpers working at Pitchi Richi, c. 1960s. Reproduced by courtesy of Douglass Baglin.*

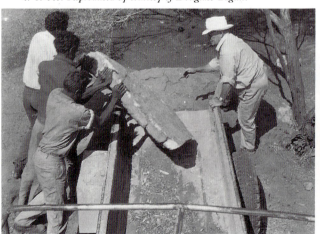

119 *Double-sided piece. 120 mm high, PC.*

120 *Spirit of the rocks. 120 mm high, PC.*

121 *Head only. 85 mm high, PC.*

122 *Double-sided piece. Ins: "Within is the spirit of our race and culture. Without separation throughout the whole of creation. To the girls & teachers of the Wilderness. 1953. I liberate." 350 mm high, PC.*

123 *The original Earthly Mother at Bundilla en route to Mt Dandenong. Photographer unknown, c. 1960. WRS. 590 mm high.*

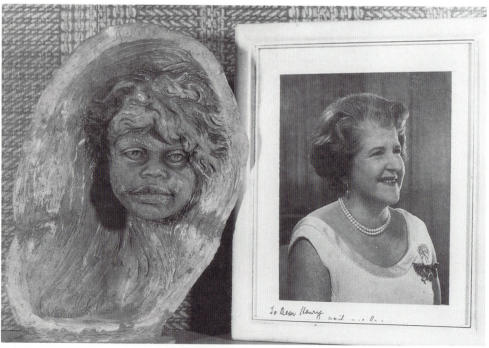

124 *Dame Edith Bolte and, presumably, her gift from Bill. Courtesy of Sir Henry Bolte.*

efforts to get food. Once they saw they could get food for nothing sitting outside the settlement, they wouldn't bother to hunt for it.[1]

There was certainly a big health problem because of the concentration of infection. And then of course there came the cohabitation between people of the wrong mixtures and there was a lot of fighting went on.

They also ran into the very bad example that was set by many of the white people who were amongst the artisans who were building the new settlements. So their first contact was with the white fellows—or prolonged contact—was with a group of people whose social behaviour was not of the standard that they probably experienced on the land, which was probably quite high because of the desperation of survival. But they were those who were overpaid and over-fed, too much booze—it was a big problem. The building of the settlements made a very big contribution to their experience of bad social behaviour."

I should clarify that Tippett was referring to some of the building crews being a bad influence, and not the actual Welfare staff themselves. As can be seen, though, despite the best of intentions and great effort on the part of the Welfare Branch, life was not always rosy at Papunya, nor, presumably, at other settlements of the kind.

Harry Kitching recalled that Bill set up his caravan away from the main settlement compound, as opposed to in it: *"He just wanted to be alone—that was one of the things with him. But he was never any bother."* Bill for the most part restricted his contact to the older men. Although there were still people like Nosepeg around who helped Bill bridge the gap, Kitching recalled that more often than not Bill would show the old tjilpis his works and get his message across that he wanted to model their features. When I asked Harry Kitching if there were ever any troubles with Bill's actions, he told me:

"No, nothing like that at all. Nobody ever complained to me about it. Oh I would have picked it up [if there had been problems]. The old men would have been on to me like a shot. But there didn't seem to be anything like that at all. He just showed them what he'd done, and there was a bit of respect for him for his age as much as anything else, and he wasn't worried about chasing little girls or things like that, so they tolerated him. There were no worries with him."

The only little boys and girls Bill was interested in chasing around were the Pitjantjatjara children, but it was only to model them. Kitching recalled how taken Bill was with their fine features and sun-bleached blond hair, claiming that he could always pick out the Pitjantjatjara kids in Bill's work.

Bill had his mail forwarded out to Papunya from the Alice. The Atkinsons were keeping him informed as to what was going on at the Gallery, and the news was not good. In one of their letters they included a news clipping published in late January or early February, the heading of which would have taken Bill's breath away—"Art Centre in Ruins". Bill read on:

"Among the ruins of a desecrated sanctuary at Mt Dandenong, a beautifully scripted plaque[2] *ironically reads: 'They shall not hurt nor destroy in all my Holy mountain.' A constant stream of visitors—art lovers, nature lovers and the just plain curious—pause*

---

1 Indeed, what rational person would go tramping off into the desert to spend a day foraging for food when you could just as easily conserve your energy in the shade, safe in the knowledge that a meal would be there at the end of the day? Besides, the whitefellas had plenty of food to share. If it ran out, the Aborigines would have then shared their food.
2 This plaque had been painted by Mary Harris and given to Bill.

at the plaque and leave shaking their head. For this is the sanctuary of William (Billy) Ricketts—and vandals have taken over.

Billy Ricketts, internationally acclaimed sculptor and eccentric, has not lived in the little log cabin on the sanctuary for nine months. When he left ... the sanctuary was left open to his friends and anyone else who wanted to come and admire his work. Then about Christmas time the vandals came to Mt Dandenong. Since then a growing wave of theft and desecration has spread across the sanctuary."

Bill scribbled off a quick note to the Atkinsons urging that somebody be put in his house rent free. His anger boiled to rage when he wrote: ***"I would like to shoot those dirty low things for what they do."***[3] After telling them that he would write again soon, he sent the letter away—and then went away himself to do a little bit of research and thinking. His next quick note asked for two copies of ***"that article"***, and went on to reveal the extent of his research:

"I understand that word eccentric means off balance.

Well that well meaning person who wrote that article and others who think likewise are going to be shown on a world wide scale who is eccentric and who is the normal man walking through the work of creation with reverence for life."

Bill had obviously gone off and asked somebody at Papunya what eccentric meant, which would no doubt have placed that person in a spot of embarrassment, because they were all referring to Bill as an eccentric at the time—though not maliciously. Bill was given a pretty narrow definition of the word's meaning—and he was none too happy with the definition he received. The pressure was building up within him over the senseless goings on at his Mountain Gallery and a small part of his steam was let off in another letter to the Atkinsons, dated April 17th. It is another example of the extreme in Bill, beginning with the familiar line:

"I don't have to tell you that every beautiful thing from <u>Christ</u> to this present day has been murdered and from now onwards I and my works (a way of life) shall be on that list for murder ... This vandal thief and murderer all in one sits in high and low places all over the country sheltering himself behind that beautiful thing (A British way of life) ...

The greatest works of my life which I shall now do in the near future will reveal and express only one thing the greatest thing <u>Reverence for life the whole of life</u> and that means the Australian bush life expressing itself as unique Australia ... In the greatest works ... the old men and the others of the native tribes will be used to express that reverence for life ... I make the ancient native the missionary ..."

To make these ***"greatest future works"***, Bill could not sit writing letters. He needed the people to present to *his* uncivilised world—he needed his missionaries. Word came into Papunya that some bush folk had walked into the Mt Liebig camp, just over 50 km to the west. These were the people Bill sought most, those untarnished by white culture. He unhooked the caravan, loaded provisions and somehow found a man to guide him out.

Bill made the Mt Liebig camp without any problems and found the group of people he was seeking. He thought that they were Pitjantjatjaras who came up from their country 320 km to the south to meet up with the members of the Pintupi. Maybe they learned that the people they sought were living at Papunya, or maybe the harsher conditions to the west drove them in—Bill

---

3 Non-violently, of course.

did not remember. He did remember that one woman among the group stood out as if a vision. She had strong features, a strong body, was strong in character and spirit, was clearly confident and self-assured—but she carried all of these qualities in a totally unassuming manner. To Bill she epitomised the strength of a race, this mother of the Earth. Indeed, he saw this woman as the human representation of the Earthly Mother. He somehow asked for and received her permission to model her, and he proceeded to re-create in clay one of the most serenely powerful women you're ever likely to see.

After a time the group decided to set off again en route to Papunya. Bill tagged along, possibly even giving them a lift in his truck. Exactly what happened was lost in time, but somewhere along the way Bill ended up well off the main road [if those tracks could be referred to as such] and into a bog up to his axles. When the truck found its hole, much of the load was upset, including the freshly-made model of the wonderful woman. The model disintegrated. The group did not go off and leave Bill stuck, but stayed with him. They waited for help, during which time Bill was able to re-model the woman. The wait lengthened into days, and Bill's food and water dwindled.

Dr George Tippett had somehow missed out on hearing that Bill was camped at Papunya. He would surely have made the effort of introducing himself had he known, because George had been thinking about Bill. Back in his youth, as a brash young engineering student, George and a student mate stumbled into an exhibition of Bill's work being held in the basement of a building in Swanston Street, Melbourne. It was such an out of the way affair that George doubted whether anybody but those who were lost would have found it.

He recalled the scene from the mid-1940s:

"There was Bill surrounded by his Aborigines. I remember particularly the one where Bill rises out of the tree trunk, surrounded by figures. I asked him what on earth it was—and Bill, posturing, looking very much like the figure in the tree trunk himself, and throwing his arms up and saying how he felt his spirit rising up out of the earth, part of the earth and part of the people who are also rising up out of the earth with him—and I thought that was the greatest load of bull-shit I'd ever heard in my life. But I went away puzzled by it.

Then, after I'd studied medicine and had the job as Medical Officer in Alice Springs, the more I learnt about Aborigines, the more this picture of Bill rising like the Phoenix from the ashes in the burnt stump came back to me. I was seeing more of what he was all about."

So with Bill bouncing round his mind every now and then, George Tippett was flown from settlement to camp to station trying to keep a grip on the health of a widely scattered group of humanity. He remembers that he'd been given another task to worry about. A family had set out from Alice Springs on foot, heading west, with a plan to set themselves up somewhere with a small herd of sheep and goats in a self sufficient manner far beyond the limits of settlement. The word was spread to keep a lookout for them, just in case they ran into difficulties.

The pilot was flying George in a round about way from Areyonga up to Papunya, and George was keeping his eye out for the Coppicks, as well as any groups of wandering bush folk who he could add to his list of lives to look after. He spotted instead a stationary truck where he would not have expected a truck to be. They circled it and saw no movement, but took a fix on its position with the idea of returning in a vehicle from Papunya.

George got a couple of people to run him back out in a Land Rover and sure enough, there was Bill, his bogged truck and the small group of Aborigines. It was a fairly simple matter of extracting the truck from its predicament, but neither Bill nor the group were the best for wear. I asked George if Bill had shared out his supplies:

"He would have given them whatever he had, that's for sure. I think that's why Bill was short—he's that sort of guy. The way things were for them out there, they'd have been those sorts of guys, too. But there was nothing much to share.

Not only that but [Bill] had a very bad attack of bronchitis and seemed to have quite a lot of respiratory trouble."

Back at Papunya George Tippett prescribed some medication for Bill and arranged for him to be looked in on by staff members. The wives of both Harry Kitching and Arnold Probin were involved in keeping an eye on Bill, taking him meals and medicines. Harry Kitching recalled that even when he was ill, Bill paid more attention to his work than anything else. And that, apparently, was the only time Bill caused Harry any worry.

Interestingly, while Bill wrote of other troubles in the letters back to his friends, I did not sight one word in reference to the trauma just described. Bill still remembered the event over twenty-five years later, though; the time when he found the Earthly Mother, and when the "flying doctor" pulled him out of the bog.

In the meantime, the Atkinsons had been trying to fathom some way of protecting what was left at the Mountain Gallery. Try as they might, they could not get a caretaker into Bill's hut. It was apparently quite unfit for habitation, not to mention the fact that the power had been cut off. Bill wasn't about to pay £5, *"just to have the electric light turned on. I asked them to contribute free a little light, three of four shillings a week, and they refused"*.[4] The only possible solution they could come up with was to physically relocate all the remaining works to their property. The problem was that many of the works would require at least three people to lift them, and others were cemented firmly in the ground. They would need help. Dorothy wrote to the Lillydale Shire Council, advising them of the destruction which was taking place and asking for suggestions.

It seems that some time in May, 1960, another concerned admirer walked the paths of the Mountain Gallery. Mrs Edith Bolte returned to see for herself what was happening, and she was dismayed. Her companion on that visit was Ms J. Andrews, who recalled the event:

"I can see to this day us walking down that path where now that entrance is built, and her saying that 'This should be protected'. Because it was all so rustic then and a-la-natural—and it was all the vandalism you could see—everywhere."

Dame Edith Bolte passed away before I could speak with her and Sir Henry Bolte did not permit me a personal interview before his death, although he did finally consent to answer a list of written questions. I sent twenty questions, to which he responded with an average of eight words per question. Consequently, I cannot elaborate greatly on the inner workings behind the actions which took place, actions which remain unique in Australian history.

Sir Henry informed me that it was not uncommon for his wife and him to compare notes at the end of the day, which is presumably how Dame Edith brought the situation at Mountain Gallery to her husband's notice. Sir Henry did not investigate the matter himself, but relied *"entirely on [his] wife's judgement"* when he initially directed his Premier's Department staff to look into what could be done to safeguard the remains of Bill's Gallery. To this end the Premier's Department contacted the Lillydale Shire Council in an attempt to ascertain what would be the most appropriate action to take.

The Lillydale Council also received a letter from the WLPS which urged some form of action to protect Mountain Gallery. On May 26th, 1960, the Council replied to Dorothy's letter expressing their desire to help preserve what statuary remained on Bill's property. Thinking that

---

4 Taken from an undated letter to the Atkinsons written at Papunya. I was not able to exactly place its chronological position by the contents.

the Atkinsons had the authority to relocate the works to their property for safe keeping, the Council offered to assist with their removal. It was by no means an ultimate answer, but at least Bill would have something to work with when he returned.

Dorothy wrote to Bill informing him of the interest that had been aroused and telling of their plan to save what was left. After all her effort and worry, Bill's response could only have left her dismayed:

> *"Those works must not be removed. If they did that to all the big works then the place would be a complete wreck. I did it for Victoria and that is all I can do is to then give it to the people ... the National Parks will or may do something not for my works but they have a duty to the Lyre Birds ...*
>
> *To take those big works out would mean they would have to be torn out and what a terrible sight it would leave ... So my sanctuary will be a monument to what could have been done. I will see you about October."*

Dorothy wrote to the Council and informed them that the plan was off due to direct instructions from Bill. The Atkinsons could not simply stand by and watch the continuing destruction, though. They went over and brought what they could carry themselves back to Churinga, preferring the possibility of suffering Bill's wrath when he returned rather than let him experience the total heartbreak of having lost everything.

Bill occasionally let his rage show, but for the most part he did not reveal how traumatised he was in the letters back south. In a letter to Ola Cohn, written during his stay at Papunya, Bill told of subtle changes which were taking place in his relationship with the Centre's Aborigines. *"For the first time I have been able to look them right in the face"*, he wrote, explaining that *"before this journey they did not like me looking hard at them."* He praised his caravan for the protection it gave from the flies and heat, and told of the frantic rush he found himself in, having on average only three sittings of ten minutes duration from the people he sought to model. Of the vandalism, Bill's only comment was that he would call in and see Ola in Melbourne before heading up the hill to *"see what the mad devil lot have done"*.

By early August Bill was feeling that he was ready to leave the Centre. In a letter dated August 10th, he informed the Atkinsons that he had written to the Lillydale Council offering to *"give the whole thing [Mountain Gallery] over free. Then I said How much money will the body give towards my life work"*. He also indicated that the WLPS in Sydney had advised him that he would do better to get *"someone close at hand to look after"* the Gallery. It could well be that the WLPS realised the magnitude of the task Bill had requested of them; that being their taking over the Gallery. Bill made no mention of his latest plan to escape the nightmare which awaited him back south. This plan he kept as a guarded secret, shared it would seem only with Leo Corbet.

Three letters surfaced when I salvaged the rotted and mouldy mess in Bill's "spare room"[5] that revealed his intention of leaving behind all that awaited him at the Mountain Gallery—the debts, the destruction and the heartbreak. For how long he planned to be away is not recorded.

Bill had a supporter, Christine, whose home city was Copenhagen and whom I know only from letters uncovered in the "spare room". She seemed to have been an avid traveller, with the pair first having met some time in the late 1940s or early 1950s when Christine was in Australia. She was quite taken with Bill, his work and his vision, and on returning to Europe had at least a couple of articles published which featured the Mountain Gallery and its creator. In 1951 Bill had sent Penfold a copy of an article published in Norway, and although the author was not identified I suspect it to have been the work of Christine. The pair kept up frequent correspondence, with

---

5 The room which was originally his bedroom in the new house which was built.

Bill requesting from the Centre in 1955 that Doris Turner hold his mail until his return—with an exception: *"Any one from Sweden send them on to me. They are good to me."* [6]

Back to the three letters indicating Bill's intention to leave, the most revealing of which came from the manager of Fleetways Transport and Agency Pty Ltd, of Melbourne. The letter, dated September 6th, 1960, was sent to Bill at "Petchi-Rechi" in response, they wrote, to a September 2nd letter from Bill, *"regarding the shipment of Clay heads to Copenhagen"*. Bill was informed that Fleetways would value the works at £100 for Customs purposes, and he was requested to supply all identifying information and serial numbers for the vehicle, which would have to be verified by a Customs official to avoid any trouble on re-entry. It was not stated if Bill had informed Fleetways that there would be a re-entry, or if they presumed it. They had ascertained that Bill had booked on the freighter, *Korea*, in October.

The second letter was from the Department of Immigration, Melbourne, also in response to a September 2nd letter from Bill. They advised that Bill leave *"the medical side of your departure until you are in Melbourne"*. The third letter, dated September 25th, was written by Leo and was meant to introduce Bill to someone called Frank. The last line in that letter read: *"Hope you can help him re the necessary medical certificate etc."*

Quite obviously, Bill was preparing to leave the country. The secrecy of his intention, especially his not having mentioned it to the Atkinsons, makes me wonder whether or not his plan included returning to Australia. Loaded on the truck were the seeds for a new Holy Mountain. Did he plan to abandon the destruction and debts and disorganisation to start afresh somewhere else altogether? Bill could not tell me—he said that he did not recall the event at all.

As advanced as his plans to leave were, Bill did not drive straight to the docks. He changed his mind and went instead to the Mountain Gallery and a scene of devastation. His Gallery was shattered. His house had been broken into and ransacked. Dorothy recalled: *"There was no way he would go into that hut. He walked all around it but wouldn't go in. So he went away and found sheets of corrugated iron and made himself a humpy. There were evil spirits in the old house ..."* It was the same with some of the works which the Atkinsons had saved. Dorothy said that Bill: *"gave me a lot of works that were smashed up by vandals—a lot of the ones in [Churinga's] garden, they've all been patched up and stuck back together. He gave them to me because they were full of evil spirits—all right for me to have them, but not him!"*

Bill wrote to Ola Cohn shortly after his return: *"My place is in ruins and the brutes took my original works I did up north seven in all* [7] *... My house is unfit to live in so I camp along the path ..."* His dismay at seeing first-hand what had become of his dream and what little respect people had for his vision renewed his longing to flee. He wrote to Ola: *"I only want to get away from the place now."* But something stayed him. Something caused him to remain amid that scene of waste. The only thing I can think of that it may have been was knowledge of the fact that the Premier's Department was seriously looking into a rescue package.

---

6 I realise Copenhagen is not in Sweden, but Christine moved around, and she was Bill's one regular correspondent from that part of the world.

7 These were from Bill's Ernabella journey in 1949–50 and constituted the first models from real life he made of any Aborigines.

16 | Rescue and Resurrection
[late 1960–1962]

By November 22nd, 1960, the Victorian State Government was reported as being actively involved in negotiations to purchase and preserve the Mountain Gallery. The Mt Dandenong Reserve Committee which managed the Mt Dandenong Arboretum, whose members included the then Minister for Agriculture, Mr Gilbert Chandler; Mr Borthwick, MLA; and Mr Keith Fraser, lobbied hard for the case of a Government takeover. Premier Bolte was quoted in a Melbourne *Herald* article as saying: ***"It is hoped that Mr Ricketts will be able to restore the gallery to its former state ... It might be possible to persuade Mr Ricketts to continue his work at the gallery."***

Bill was not so easily convinced—or he was playing hard to get. On November 26th the *Herald* ran a more substantial piece about Bill, written by Kenneth Joachim. Its headline was a screaming quote from Bill which read, "I'm Going Back to the Desert!" In describing Bill, Joachim wrote: ***"He looks and talks—as always—like an artist in agony. Only this time it is worse."*** Joachim could not draw a comment from Bill regarding whether or not the Government had made a firm offer to buy the Gallery, nor whether Bill would be prepared to sell. After quoting the US *Time* magazine's description of Bill as a mystic, Joachim wrote that Bill ***"proved he could be a mystery as well—even about the two men who visited him separately while I was there and drew him aside to talk long, earnestly and in undertones"***. Further along Joachim wrote that Bill wanted his Holy Mountain to be not at its present site, but in Central Australia.

The rationalists among Bill's supporters had to convince him that here at last was the opportunity he'd been waiting for. While it was in no way as grand as Bill's visions of the Holy Mountain being a crowning glory on Mt Dandenong, and while it would not transform the mountain as a whole, which would have meant kicking all the residents off, letting the bush take over their homes and taking the television transmission towers to the dump, Bill would at least have the backing and support of a State Government. His Mountain Gallery would be guaranteed a safe existence in perpetuity. He would not have been an easy man to convince, but at long last they had him come around to what really was his best option—if not his only option.

On January 7th, 1961, Bill sat down with the Atkinsons and read through a Draft Agreement between himself and the State, which was to be forwarded to Mr A. J. Fraser, Minister of Forests and State Development. The agreement was the culmination of many discussions with many people, and designed to lay the groundwork for the transfer of Bill's property to the National Parks Authority, after which the property would be dedicated as a National Park.

Bill was to receive £800 as a loan from the Government, at a fixed interest rate of £1 per year, to be repaid at Bill's convenience. This money would first be used to clear the mortgage on the block, after which money could be spent by Bill in continuing his work on the property. Once the transfer of land had been effected, the State would take steps to, ***"erect a suitable residence, of a type to be agreed upon, together with a suitable studio and kiln for the purpose of*** *allowing [Bill] to continue [his] work and to, as far as possible, restore the sanctuary to its original state"*. Bill was to retain the right of occupancy for the rest of his life and be paid the sum of £200 per annum, which he could use at his discretion. The property was to be officially known as, *"William Ricketts' Mountain Gallery Sanctuary National Park"*,[1] and Bill agreed to provide suitable *"supervisory control"* over the property.

The summer of 1960–61 saw the Atkinsons sit down and reassess their own position. The excessive heat of the time had cost them much of their nursery stock. They found it a heart-wrenching experience to watch their business wilt and die in front of their eyes. During a round-table discussion of the problem, it was Dorothy's son, David, who floated the idea of incorporating a restaurant and tea-room into the business. No doubt the decision of the Government to step in and support Bill increased their awareness that the property's position was a prime one. Unable to find any objections to David's suggestion, they decided to go ahead and give it a try.

On January 10th, 1961, Mr Fraser publicly announced that the State Government would definitely be running the Gallery, adding that Bill had already commenced his task of restoration. Fraser also appealed to the people who had removed works from the Gallery during Bill's absence to return them during a twenty-one day amnesty period. The warning was given that after the amnesty period had expired, people found to be in possession of the "easily recognised" works would be prosecuted. Dorothy Atkinson recalled that while several works were anonymously returned, the bulk of the stolen pieces, including the original busts and heads of the Ernabella people, remained listed as stolen property.

After much deliberation it was decided that the responsibility would be better given to the Forests Commission [the Commission], rather than the National Parks Authority. The Commission was well-established in the Dandenongs and could provide the labour and equipment necessary to help Bill rebuild and further the Gallery. That the Commission had never been involved with anything even remotely similar was a recognised problem.

More talks ensued which attempted to further clarify what should happen at Bill's property after the takeover. On April 18th, Fraser sent a letter to Bill expressing his appreciation for Bill's *"public spirited offer"* to transfer his land to the Forests Commission for the sum of £1,198.9.11.[2] The letter confirmed that once the transfer of ownership had occurred, the Commission would begin its work of securing the property and preparing plans for the buildings which had been decided upon through consultation with Bill. With the Commission handling the task, the official title was shortened to "William Ricketts' Mountain Gallery Sanctuary" [the Sanctuary]. Fraser also mentioned the probability of a Committee of Management being appointed for the Sanctuary.

The next day, April 19th, 1961, Bill signed over his Title to Queen Elizabeth II, and on the day after that the mortgage documents were finally stamped as being discharged. Bill had at last "given" his land to the people, was free of debt and, at the tender age of sixty-two, he could begin the task of rebuilding the Sanctuary. However, he had not given up hope of *the* Holy Mountain, and, in his mind, *the* Holy Mountain did not necessarily have to be on Mt Dandenong.

The Commission set about establishing a Provisional Advisory Committee for the Sanctuary until such time that a Committee of Management could be formally constituted. To this end the Commission Chairman, Mr A. O. Lawrence, contacted people whom he knew to have a sincere interest in Bill and the Sanctuary, requesting that they consider joining the temporary Committee. Those asked were, in the main, drawn from the Mt Dandenong Reserve Committee. New additions were the Atkinsons, Doug Harkness in at least an advisory capacity

---

1 I would hate to guess what processes and discussions were involved in arriving at this official title, but it can be assured that they were protracted.

2 Unfortunately, it is not recorded as to how such a neat sum was determined.

and Jim Westcott, the Commission's District Officer based at Kallista, upon whose shoulders would rest the unenviable task of being the intermediary.

Although Westcott had been living in the area since 1955 and had no doubt driven past the Sanctuary countless times in the course of his duties, he had no knowledge of the Sanctuary's existence prior to his becoming involved. He told me that he had quite a job to find it when he had to. *"Who could imagine that a thing like Ricketts' was a Forestry job?"*, Westcott recalled, looking back on the Commission's involvement. *"But they had enough gumption to realise that this was something out of the ordinary for Victoria."* As the man at the "doing" end of the Commission, I think it was as much Jim Westcott's precognitive realisation of the Sanctuary's intrinsic worth that resulted in Bill receiving such extraordinary help on the practical level.

In theory, the task at hand for Jim Westcott was fairly straightforward. Working together with Bill, the Sanctuary had to be secured to prevent further theft or damage, after which it had to be cleaned up, restored where possible and added to in preparation for an official opening at some time in the future. The only trouble was that it had to be put into practise. It became a very slow process.

One of the first tasks tackled was reconnecting the power and cleaning up Bill's old house to get it to a point where he would live in it. Then a front boundary fence was constructed using simple barbed wire to give the appearance that the property was secure. As for the fencing of the other boundaries, that is a long and exceedingly drawn-out tale.

The ground works were not so easy. As Jim Westcott recalled: *"It was in a bad state. The vandalism had been pretty crook—arms had been broken off, legs snapped off, heads of the little animals and other works snapped off. It was a mess."* Bill decided that many of the works were beyond repair, which saw them taken out of the ground. Well may you ask, where are they now? Even though those damaged works would become and remain the property of the State, all but a few "walked" out of the grounds and into private collections. The oil-burning kiln was barely serviceable, but Bill nevertheless set to work creating new pieces to be incorporated in the grounds.

The actual ground works were done principally by the Commission's Olinda gang. Bill was by no means an easy man to work with; apt to change his mind about a project at the last minute, no matter how much work had gone into the job beforehand, quick to jump on the person who accidently damaged a plant and ever ready to corner somebody and impart to them his views. It resulted in a couple of workers becoming downright negative toward him. As Westcott recalled: *"There were some fellows I never sent up there. They'd say: 'Put Billy down there and we'll flatten him!' But that's how it went."* Generally speaking, Jim remembered the crew who did most of the initial work as a great bunch of blokes who operated with absolute forbearance.

Just to give some idea of the antics, I'll share an anecdote told by Jim Westcott concerning some of the boulders which can be seen throughout the Sanctuary, on which many of Bill's works are mounted. It started with my attempt at irony, suggesting that they must have had some fun:

> *"Oh, enormous amounts of fun! For instance, he'd want a gigantic stone, one that weighed tons, in a certain spot—but without any scrub touched at all. Now, I don't know how anybody can get stones of that size into there without damaging a little bit of scrub, but my fellows went as close to doing it as anybody ever could.*
>
> *He'd see a rock, maybe five miles away where somebody was widening a road or something, and he'd say, 'Oh, I've got just the place for that'. So we'd send a truck and loader around, and we'd get the rocks and take them up to Billy and ask him where he wanted them. Well he'd say, 'Down there'—pointing to the most inaccessible spot you could think of. And my blokes did it, too, thanks to Charlie Chamberland, my Olinda foreman— a _damn_ good man. He went to no end of trouble.*
>
> *You see, we were still using hand winches in those days, big drum winches.*

So we'd anchor a couple of these to the butts of a couple of trees, tie the rock like a Christmas present so that it couldn't escape, and just let it—well, it went down the hill on its own!—but we steadied it with these winches. No bulldozers or front end loaders, it was all by hand—and with an absolute minimum of environmental impact. Of course, our biggest worry was that one of these things would take off down the hill, because you'd never stop them.

Then when you got it down there, you'd have to place it properly. And sure as hell, Bill would want the bottom up to the top or something, so there'd be half a day of juggling the bloody things around. Oh yes, up to ten men—one holding a <u>bush</u> out of the way! [He burst out laughing, out of control, until we both were wiping tears from our eyes.] *Like, you can laugh about it now—but sometimes it was different then."*

A new house for Bill was under constant consideration. Bill already had the site picked out, in fact he'd chosen and had much of it levelled years before. His nephew, Jim Valentine, was staying up at the property some time in the 1950s when Bill told him of a plan to build a new house. Bill led the way up to a steepish bit of ground with some exposed rock which, after good rain, became a small waterfall. Bill liked the idea of having this intermittent waterfall nearby, so the pair marked out a house site and began levelling. Jim was unsure where Bill went, but he left the property for an extended period, telling him that, if he liked, he could clear the spot and cut the hill out a bit. *"He said he'd appreciate it"*, Jim recalled: *"Well I did clear a big patch for him—levering big logs and boulders away—all by hand! He came back and said, 'Oh, that looks good', but that's as far as he went. He'd changed his mind!"*

An article in the February 6th, 1962 edition of the *Age* reveals that Bill had begun his process of stirring up attention in an effort to get things moving more quickly for him. The article, in the "News of the Day" column, first stated that Bill needed a Land Rover *"for hire or for sale cheap"*, so that he could head back up to the Centre for a couple of months. Bill wanted to go back for some more life studies which could be incorporated into the new large works which he would create when he had the new electric kiln at his disposal. There were two blatant inaccuracies in the article which could only have come from Bill's comments to the article's author.

The first was that the Government hadn't yet kept its promise to *"take over the sanctuary and statuary"*, which implied that they were reneging on their publicly proclaimed offer. No doubt that statement caused a little heart-burn for those in the Commission who had been trying their bureaucratic best to keep Bill happy. The second inaccuracy was that the Walkerville Council in Adelaide were *"extending a sanctuary for him there, first started by Miss Mary Harris"*, which suggested that Bill might have another place to go if the Government didn't get their act together.

As we will see, Bill would use this tactic quite often. While it often roused the public's interest to varying degrees, it most certainly roused the ire of more than a few within the Government which was, in effect, feeding him.

With all the discussion that took place, it is small wonder that a plan for Bill's house was not decided upon until April, 1962, when tenders were finally called for the construction of the new buildings and the installation of a new electric kiln. Little did the Commission architects and costing clerks realise that even at that late stage, Bill would have a few "minor" alterations up his sleeve. It was also around this time that the final moves were being made to have the Sanctuary become officially reclassified from Crown Land to a Permanent Forest. The significance of this reclassification is that whereas Crown Land can be alienated by simply going through the Lands Department procedures, a Permanent Forest would require an Act of Parliament before it could be taken away from the State or changed dramatically by, for instance, the clearing of its flora. In effect, the reclassification provided the best possible protection the State of Victoria could give.

As Jim Westcott described to me, it became untouchable. The actual date of reclassification was given on the final Agreement between Bill and the Commission as June 6th, 1962.

Bill took time out to write to Ted Strehlow in late April or early May, principally to get some Arrernte translation for new plaques he was making. Along with a little news of the latest creations, Bill told Strehlow that the work on his new house was set to begin. Strehlow's reply of May 9th was full of congratulations for the progress at the Sanctuary. He informed Bill that he had accumulated funds for a winter of research in the Centre, concentrating on filming and recording the ceremonies of the Arrernte. He noted that *"time is fast running out for this kind of work"*, and expressed sadness at seeing his *"old friends going, one by one"*. Strehlow drew a similarity between his work and Bill's, noting that they were both creating: *"things that physical death cannot destroy; & these are things that can inspire the generations of men & women that will come after us. This is the hope that we have in our present labours, the satisfaction that we may derive from our present creations."* There was one major difference, though. Whereas Strehlow was collecting material which would be studied *after* the original custodians had gone and the ageless continuity of that custodianship was dead, Bill was actively seeking to inspire the efforts required to keep that continuity alive.

Bill bought into another fight at the end of June. He'd heard that a party from the British Museum were coming to Australia for the purpose of collecting specimens. Outraged, Bill wrote a letter to Dorothy Atkinson in which he asked that a request be brought before Mr Borthwick, head of the provisional advisory committee. Bill wrote, in part:

> *"The British Museum is to come here to invade our wild life. The wild life is involved in the true quest for a true state of peace, wonder, beauty, a true state of freedom, love, and a love of country that can only be God like ...*
>
> *I and my native relations accept the challenge that if the British Museum come here to kill and destroy, then I shall ask for sanctuary in another country where the head man will give me and my cause all the help in his power. I shall take all my life's work among my native people, including large works just completed, with me to that country ... I give one week for Victoria to decide between that lot from England and I and my native friends ..."*

Bill repeated his threat in a lengthy no-holds-barred letter sent directly to the Premier. He wrote, in part:

> *"I and my Aboriginal relations were shot, poisoned, kicked, shoved and then packed into a museum ... Silly people used to come in look at us laugh then shake their heads ... Good people came in and with shame on their faces went away ... Believe it or not but as the big white fellow museum boss stood there saying to himself how nicely [he] has us all fixed up our spiritual nature took on forms of great beauty and purity and we just simply moved past the big white fellow museum and out and here we are in the sanctuary at Mt Dandenong. Of course the big white fellow museum boss could not notice us being liberated ...*
>
> *The innocent untouched pure Australian bush [is] the great miracle of God. Within the great miracle of God the law of our people is contained, and the roots of our whole man goes down into this spiritual soil and sustaining power ... We are linked with wild life in this way and we are very sorry to see that the white fellow cannot comprehend this let alone carry it in his heart. The white fellow has tried to break this law and in doing so has left the hall mark of the brute upon the Australian bush everywhere all because little children have never been educated to grow up with a deep love of country a reverence for life the whole of life.*
>
> *No man can explain life but where these and all word end our works begin ... we*

want to express all this in the Holy Mountain ... and how glad we would be to give you
this freely in a mountain spectacle.

My beautiful Lyre Bird is now on her nest right against my house here and if I went
out and killed her put her into a glass case and asked people to come in and look
I would be doing the same ugly criminal thing as the museum people ... Now I shall
prepare to go everything here on this great task is now stopped."

The Premier's Department acknowledged receipt of the letter on July 3rd, but Premier Bolte took it upon himself to send a personally handwritten letter to Bill, dated August 7th, 1962, in an attempt to head off a potentially embarrassing situation:

"... I am concerned that you have taken this matter so strongly to heart. I realise
that you have an antipathy for museum collectors, but they are hardly in the category to
be described as a 'bunch of killers'.

I think it is important that you should know that the Government is far from
enthusiastic about the proposal & that at the moment no authority whatsoever has been
given for any of the proposed collecting to be undertaken in this State. Until such time
that the party arrives in Australia & we know precisely what they require, there will be no
thought to issuing any permits. The attitude of our Fisheries & Wildlife Dept is wholly
protective & conservative & I can give you my Personal assurance that the museum
collecting party is not going to be allowed to enter upon a wild rampage. The people of
this State & of the City of Melbourne in particular, have been deeply stirred by the
nature, the Spiritual meaning & the deep sincerity of your work at Kalorama [sic]. You
would be doing a very great disservice to the many thousands of people who are your
supporters & admirers if you walk out of the place as you apparently have a mind to do.

The extent to which the public becomes aware of your work will expand rapidly with
the developments now in progress at your sanctuary.

You have a far greater hope of ultimate attainment of your noble objective by
continuing the struggle among an ever-widening circle of friends and supporters than by
abandoning it at this stage. On behalf of the people of this State I commend you on your
great endeavour & wish you continued success."

Confident in the knowledge that Victoria, at least, was safe from the clutching hands of the British Museum, Bill threw a few bags of clay and provisions into his truck, hooked up the caravan, and set off for what would be his last journey to Central Australia. He called in to see Mary Harris on his way through Adelaide and told her of all that was progressing with his Sanctuary. They struck upon the idea that, since Bundilla had its own complement of Bill's work, there was no reason that the Victorian Government shouldn't provide similar protection there. Mary would write to the Minister of Forests, Mr Fraser, with the suggestion. In Alice Springs Bill suggested that Leo do the same.

It was very much a flying trip for Bill, lasting only until late September, but he managed to accomplish much. It was also the trip during which Bill captured, to my mind, one of his most enduring images.

It is not an image in clay, although the theme had been and would continue to be expressed many times in that medium. It is a colour transparency, slightly over-exposed, out of alignment and out of focus, but priceless in its content. It is a camp scene from the Centre. In the foreground there is red earth, white camp-fire ash and a big, well-used billy can. In the background, beneath a cloudless blue sky and surrounded by desert scrub, a partially obscured Aboriginal man and a skinny camp dog. The photograph shows Atirantuka and Bill clasping hands over a smallish clay work which featured the burning flame of Law. Both men were without shirts; Atirantuka's lean and sinewy brown frame contrasting sharply with Bill's pale, yet surprisingly solid and well-muscled torso and arms. On Bill's face is the hint of a smile and an expression which showed him to be as relaxed as I ever saw him. And why not? He was with "his" people, in their quiet and embracing land. At that instant, his fight was a world away, and he was content.

Bill told me that he took the photograph himself, using the borrowed camera's self-timing device. He said that he set it, placed it on the red dirt and rushed back to seat himself next to Atirantuka. The pair reached over and joined hands, as Bill recalled, *"just as the camera went off"*.

In two of the three letters I sighted which Bill wrote back to the Atkinsons during that trip, Bill contradicted my impression that he was experiencing moments of peace while out in the camps. He wrote that it was, *"hard going out here and tension comes on me in doing my work but I soon come round when I come back to the quiet and peace of [Pitchi Richi]"*. He wrote in the next letter: *"It will be lovely to have the quiet of my forest after all this up here. It will be like going onto a calm sea."* Nevertheless, I still see a relaxed man when I look at the photo of Atirantuka and Bill.

The second of the letters from that trip contained a unique account of Bill clandestinely committing to memory the face and expression of Atirantuka for later inclusion in his work. He wrote to the Atkinsons:

> *"My last camp in the gidgee tree scrub was something I will not easy forget.[3] The air was yellow with bull dust, my small camp fire with one native and three dingoes around it was a dimly lit scene to see something of the highest importance. The native was my friend Atirantuka mentioned in my book, two full blood dingoes and the third dingo was myself.*
>
> *My native friend one leg under his bottom and one knee under his chin was on one side of the small fire. Two dingoes and I the third dingo sat on the other side of the fire with one leg under my bottom and the other knee under my chin. Every now and then I got a full look into the face of my native friend to gather in the impression I needed. I was so cunning a dingo that my native friend did not know I was doing this although he flashed his eyes every now and then just wondering.*
>
> *He also said something about my work that left no room for misunderstanding.[4] Then of a sudden the dingo grabbed a tin of milk just opened and off with it. I grabbed from my native friend with his lovely face and head and a dignity dead true all I needed and off to my Mountain sanctuary I went."*

Do we take it from that account that Atirantuka did not want his image recorded in clay—or was Bill witness to an expression which he would never see if the modelling clay was out? Twilight by an outback camp-fire is a special time when it is just as easy to slip into a state of reverie as deep contemplation. To observe somebody in either state is to see them at their unconscious best. Add the light of a flickering camp fire and the effect is captivating. If that was the scene, it is easy to imagine Bill wanting to remember every detail.

When by mid-September Bill was ready to head home, he tried to secure free passage with the railways as far as Port Augusta, even writing to Canberra with his request, but the result was negative. If he wanted his truck and himself railed south, he would have to pay. His indignation burned bright when he wrote to the Atkinsons forewarning them of his arrival back home: *"Millions of pounds are wasted up here, lots of it goes through the hotels. [Pitchi Richi] sanctuary is impressive with my works and is known very well overseas and the railways benefit from this, but it's no to me."* Bill sold his caravan before leaving, but whether he drove back or paid for the rail is not recorded.

---

3 The gidgee is a small acacia tree, *Acacia cambagei*, if Bill's identification was correct.
4 The great pity is that Bill did not relate what Atirantuka said.

17 | A Mountain Bureaucracy
[late 1962–1964]

Back at Mt Dandenong the new house was well under way and Bill became quite creative in his fresh thoughts about what additions or minor changes could be made. Most were accommodated, but one day not too long after Bill's return from the Centre the builder strolled over to the Atkinsons and told them that he'd had enough. He was going away to his other jobs until after Christmas. Enquiring as to what the problem was, the builder informed them that he'd just started on the fireplace surrounds when Bill intervened with news that he wouldn't accept the plans as they were. There was to be a mantelpiece over the fire, and Bill apparently didn't want something where *"people would lean smoking their cigars"*. He had a sculptural conception in mind.

Dorothy persuaded the builder to wait while she contacted the Commission Head Office and spoke directly to the Chairman, Mr Lawrence. Dorothy recalled that he dumped it straight back on her, asking her to work it out between themselves. Whatever the outcome, Lawrence would smooth it over with the building inspectors and authorise any change in the budget.

Bill went ahead and created the unique sculptured fireplace surround that remains intact in the display room of his house. It was the perfect setting to incorporate the flame of Law theme, at the very top of which is the upper torso of an old Elder created to be gazing down on anybody in the room. Bill also composed a sentence to be incorporated within the piece: *"In loving my country I am burning like a consuming fire."* Not content with that, Bill wrote to Ted Strehlow requesting an Arrernte translation for the sentence. Strehlow sent Bill the words, "PMARA NUKANAKA ERARERAMALA JINGA URA LJIRTJA MBULANAMA", which he told Bill he'd turned around so as to avoid abstract nouns. The word-for-word English translation which Strehlow provided for the Arrernte was: "Country my loving I fire flaming/consuming am burning."

Mary Harris had by this time completed her manuscript, "The Holy Mountain of a Crusader in Clay: A Book of William Ricketts", and submitted it to The Legend Press in Sydney. The Director, John Brackenreg, wrote to her on January 22nd, 1963, rejecting the manuscript on the grounds that Mary's *"kind of descriptive text matter"* was not in line with their usual publishing. He did not reject the notion of a publication featuring Bill, though. He had in mind *"an edition of dramatic photographs of his sculptures, together with any autobiographical notice he would like to have printed"*. If Mary was stung by the rejection, she did not show it. As soon as she received Brackenreg's letter, she wrote to Bill with the alternative book proposal, praising The Legend Press' previous publications in an attempt to warm Bill to the idea. With utter selflessness, she wrote: *"I do hope a really wonderful book may be the outcome."* Of her manuscript's rejection she offered: *"My book is too much in story form: I myself should say a spiritual pilgrimage."*

Mary also wrote straight back to Brackenreg to express her support for his proposed publication. In his reply Brackenreg informed Mary that he had friends who were very close to

Premier Bolte and he suggested that he may approach Bill with the proposal through Bolte the following month when he visited Melbourne. Brackenreg praised Mary for being *"most kind about the whole thing and certainly [putting] the work of William Ricketts above all else ..."* Where the subsequent negotiations went from there I cannot say, but to my knowledge The Legend Press did not publish a volume featuring Bill or his work.

The new kiln decided upon by the Public Works Department was a large electric model, with the inside firing chamber's dimensions measuring approximately 1.8 m × 1.2 m × 1.5 m high. It would prove to be one of the Sanctuary's physical mysteries as a result of its design and positioning.

The whole kiln is essentially in two pieces—one stationary and the other mobile. The ceiling, two side-walls and rear wall are stationary, supported by legs to stand some 75 cm from the ground. The floor and front wall of the kiln are mounted on a frame supported by four large metal wheels which run along sections of railway line. This set-up makes it possible to roll out the floor section so that the kiln can be loaded without restriction, after which it is simply keyed back into place to form a sealed chamber. The mysterious aspect of the arrangement is that the kiln as a whole is located behind large, locked, barn-like doors in one section of the new house, with only the railway lines protruding out into the public's view, and with nothing to suggest their purpose.

The kiln was expensive, at around £5,000, but right from the start it proved to have shortcomings. Initially it had a start-up temperature of 100°F, with the capability of rising to 1,250°F on a fine day. A change in the weather could see it fall back to 1,100°F. Such fluctuations adversely affect the firing process. The main problem was the start-up temperature. The moisture in wet clay must be slowly drawn out of the mass to a point where it is totally dry. Too much heat causes that moisture to become steam within the clay mass, with the result being, at best, cracking to various degrees or, at the worst, total disintegration through explosion. Bill's works often varied in thickness from a few millimetres up to thirty centimetres. Only a very slow and gradual drying process would work for such pieces. Throwing them straight into 100°F was not acceptable, regularly producing poor quality finishes.

It was ultimately determined by Dr Tauber, a ceramics engineer from the Commonwealth Scientific and Industrial Research Organisation [CSIRO], that *"the wrong type of kiln had been installed for [Bill's] type of work"*.[1] Many changes were suggested and made to the kiln, but it was never replaced. Major changes in the kiln's function modes were still being made as late as 1986, with new firing schedules continuing to be formulated through until the kiln's last firing when Bill was alive.

The formal Agreement between Bill and the Commission was signed on June 12th, 1963. It did not vary greatly from the Draft Agreement of January 7th, 1961, although it did set down points in greater detail. Bill's token payment from the Commission was revised from £200 per annum to £4 per week, giving him an extra £8 per annum.

The most significant clauses in the Agreement concerned the ownership of works already at the Sanctuary and of the future works to be created. The Agreement noted that Bill had previously agreed to, *"repair and maintain the existing sculpture work on the said land"*,[2] and *"... produce further sculpture work for the purposes of the Sanctuary ..."*,[3] and *"transfer the property in such sculpture work to the Government of the State"*.[4] In the next section of the Agreement, under the heading *"NOW THIS AGREEMENT WITNESSETH as follows"*, the matter of ownership was further clarified in part 3(a) which stated: *"It is hereby agreed and declared as follows—That the sculpture work at present on the said land and all future sculpture*

---

1 As recorded in the October 13th, 1964, Committee meeting Minutes.
2 As stated in part III(b)(i).
3 As stated in part III(b)(ii).
4 As stated in part III(b)(iii).

work produced by the vendor thereon for the purposes of the Sanctuary shall be the property of the Government of the said State."

That seems to be pretty well cut and dried, but it caused quite a bit of bother over the years. Quite simply, it boiled down to stating that all works in the Sanctuary at the time of the Government takeover became the property of the State. That was unqualified and all-encompassing—with no exceptions. It then said that any works Bill created in the future "for the purposes of the Sanctuary" would also become the property of the Government. That part was left wide open and Bill, under the specific terms of the Agreement, had a free rein to maintain ownership over whichever *new* works he wanted—providing he decided that the work was not going to be "for the purposes of the Sanctuary". Bill could make works for sale or to give away as often as he liked, providing, of course, that he upheld his original commitments to furthering the Sanctuary.

The Government blundered in a monumental way by their failure to maintain their custodianship of the works which were in the Sanctuary *at the time of the takeover*, and which were by the terms of the Agreement the property of the State. This does not apply to just the Bolte Government, but every State Government which has followed. It is a sad fact that works which became the property of the State in 1961 have been leaving the Sanctuary continually. Bill gave them away, or sold them, and others "walked" away without his knowledge. The trouble was that they were not Bill's to give or to sell. He had entrusted those older works to the care of the State—he had already given them to the people. Because of the various governments' inattention and apparent disinterest, historic and irreplaceable works have been lost to private collections throughout Australia and probably the world.

It would have been so easy to go through and catalogue every work in the Sanctuary at the time of the takeover, damaged and intact. We will see that it was suggested, but never fully acted upon. It would then have been a simple case of updating the catalogue with every new piece created for the Sanctuary. At regular intervals, an equally simple stock-taking would have identified any loss. At the time of writing, there is still no complete catalogue of every work within the Sanctuary.

An Official Advisory Committee to replace the provisional variety of 1961 was not put together until April 1964, with their inaugural meeting being held at the Atkinsons' house on April 20th. The Committee consisted of Lou and Dorothy Atkinson, Jim Westcott, Mr L. Bakacs and Mr Ralph Wilson. Bakacs and Wilson were long standing friends of Bill's and both brought to the Committee a wealth of business and organisational acumen. Also present at the inaugural meeting was the Commission Chairman, Mr A. O. Lawrence, who started proceedings with an address to the members.[5]

He described the Committee as being *"small and hand-picked and where nobody represents any organisation or is being paid"*, and their role as being *"to advise the Commission on matters of policy and detail relating to the executive management by the Commission of any particular thing in view"*. Lawrence went on to say:

> *"We are now in the early stage of the modern phase of the Galleries. As a Commission we are at a loss with regard to these Mountain Galleries, having never handled anything like this before, and we would like to make a job of it to our credit. We have ideas and recognise that we have in this Gallery works of inestimable value, and we think that, as the years go by, this collection will prove more valuable still."*

The first significant matter raised for discussion was funding, in particular Bill's newly adopted policy of free spending. He'd apparently ordered, without authorisation, £600 worth of

---

5 This information is taken from the official Minutes of the meeting, in which dialogue is attributed to various "speakers". While it is almost certainly not verbatim, the Minutes are nonetheless official, and will be quoted here.

slate paving for the paths within the Sanctuary. It was unanimously agreed that he should be curtailed as subtly as possible. The aim was to get Bill to restore and progress the Sanctuary to the point where he was ready to present it to the public. *"We do not want to stop him in the portrayal of his views in sculpture or in his ideas"*, Lawrence said, *"but one thing that is inflexible is the budgeting; once there is an approved budget then that is the finish."* It was a case of letting the creative juices flow freely—as long as they flowed within budget.

The ownership of the works cropped up several times during the meeting, with Wilson most actively pressing for clarification on the matter of the Commission's policy. Lawrence admitted that at the time there was no *"balance sheet"* kept on the place and later he stated that while it was not spelled out in the Agreement, Bill was supposed to mark works prior to firing them if he wanted to retain ownership. Asked how the Government could identify works which were their's, Lawrence responded that he wanted works marked to identify them. Wilson suggested that a photographic catalogue could be compiled and is recorded as stating that, *"You must have this inventory"*. No reaction from Lawrence was recorded in response.

Leo Corbet's possession of many of Bill's works was discussed, with suggestions made to have a Crown Law injunction being placed against their sale. Before any such legal action, they decided to consult Bill for some facts. The production of a new souvenir catalogue received some mention, and although the Minutes did not say as much, the job of organising them seems to have been given to Wilson at the meeting. Lawrence said that the Commission would fund it, and although tenders would not be called for such a job, they would like to know in advance what the costs would be. It was hoped that the souvenir catalogues would raise enough funds to cover the cost of administering the area.

One matter that seemed to cause some consternation was Bill's desire to invite some of his Aboriginal friends to the official opening of the Sanctuary. Lawrence was recorded as asking, *"Would the Department of Natives' Affairs allow this?"* A resolution of that meeting was that the number of Aborigines coming down should be limited to three, and that their names should be ascertained so that permission could be sought to have them transported down for whatever period Bill sought to host their visit.

The other resolutions of note were nos 9 and 10, the first of which read: *"Recommend that the Commission send up a photographer forthwith to photograph all the existing works in situ for the purpose of cataloguing and identification of all works on the property ..."* Resolution No. 10 stated: *"To prepare a catalogue of existing works, and a catalogue of works for sale. Collate a brochure on William Ricketts' Works at his Mountain Galleries, Mt. Dandenong, and Mr. Wilson to seek out Mr. Hetherington, the journalist, in this regard. Mr. Wilson will take preliminary action about the brochure with the idea of having it ready for the spring opening."*

My copy of the Minutes came from the Atkinsons' collection of papers relating to Bill. A sheet of paper with Lou Atkinson's hand-written notes was with the Minutes. The second hand-written note on that sheet read: *"Mr Lawrence said at the meeting that there would be no restriction on what [Bill] did with sculptures that were not seated into position in the sanctuary."* It would seem, if the Minutes are anything to go by, that the significance of the older works and broken works was disregarded or not realised at the time. The Committee and the Commission apparently concentrated on looking ahead to what they could help create in the so-called "modern phase" of the Sanctuary.

At the Advisory Committee's meeting held on May 19th, the matter of the "Aborigines' visit" to the opening ceremony was considered. Bill was not to be persuaded in limiting the number to three individuals. He wanted to invite six people down; four Arrernte and two Pitjantjatjara. Bill had made it known that he wanted to drive up to collect them personally and then drive them home again after the opening was done. The Committee resigned themselves to the fact and decided that the Commission be requested, through Jim Westcott, to make the necessary arrangements with the respective South Australian and Northern Territory Departments responsible for Aborigines. The Commission would also be asked to cover all associated costs.

Having Aborigines to the opening was recorded as being "still in abeyance" at the June meeting, but came up for further discussion during the July 16th meeting, at which the Commission Chairman, Mr Lawrence, was present. The confusion and consternation caused by the issue is amply illustrated in the following excerpt from the Minutes, under the sub-heading *"(Aborigines from Central Australia)"*:

> *"Mr. Lawrence: The Commission must keep out of this officially. I seriously doubt if the Commonwealth Aboriginal Welfare Board will allow this to happen. There is a lot to commend the idea of having aborigines to provide atmosphere but we must be practical. From the human point of view, what advantage are six aborigines going to get? From the administrative point of view, we cannot have anything to do with it. The whole responsibility will fall on us—there would be personal accident risks involved, and if one absconds through panic or for any other reason it would be very awkward.*
>
> *Mr. Baskett:[6] ... The authorities concerned would need to be assured of their security and other details of the visit—how they will be housed while here, etc. Then there is the question of these people coming from Central Australia and Northern Territory to a cold climate.*
>
> *Mr. Lawrence suggested that we do not antagonise Ricketts or upset him in any way by saying that we are opposed to the idea. Leave the whole thing to rest on the basis that* he *has to get the permission of the Commonwealth Aboriginal Welfare people before he can move six aborigines. We would be criticised to the limit if we attempt this, and therefore we cannot be associated with the project. We have no objection personally or departmentally to the attendance of the aborigines here but we cannot be officially associated with it. Don't convey to him in any way at all that there is an objection—he is to break through the barrier himself.*
>
> *Mr. Lawrence is prepared to address a letter to the secretary of the Commonwealth Authority dealing with this and state the story simply of what Ricketts requires; while the Commission has no objection to the proposal it will not take any responsibility whatsoever financially or in any other way with regard to the proposed movement of these people ..."*

It would seem that no credence was given to the possibility of having Aboriginal representatives from Central Australia to the Official Opening as an exercise in race relations. After all, it could hardly affect the self esteem of Centralian Aborigines to learn that facets of their culture were being embraced by the whites in one small pocket of mountains next to a major city far to the south-east of their country. Bill's organisational abilities were known. By leaving it to him, it was as good as guaranteed that no Aborigines would attend the Opening. So they left it to Bill.

Back to the May Committee meeting, though, where matters of importance were being addressed with more clear goals in mind.

Leo Corbet had been down to Victoria the month before and had met with the Atkinsons while he was visiting Bill. The works at Pitchi Richi were discussed, which resulted in Leo agreeing to have his Will changed so as to ensure that the works would come back to Mt Dandenong when he died. The Committee took it one step further, passing a motion that a legally irrevocable Agreement between Leo and the Commission be entered into: *"declaring that the works of Wm. Ricketts at present under the control of Corbet at Pitchy Richie become the property of the Forests Commission of Victoria and shall be returned to the State of Victoria upon*

---

6 Mr Jack L. Baskett, Estates Officer of the Forests Commission, whose significant contribution to the Sanctuary is discussed in Chapter 18.

the death of Corbet, and that this agreement precludes any sale of these works prior to the death of Corbet unless with the approval of the Forests Commission of Victoria, and that these works of Ricketts' at Pitchy Richie be catalogued, photographed and described in the Agreement, and that the committee regards this matter as urgent."

Considering the Commission's and the Committee's apparent lack of interest in some of the works within the Mt Dandenong Sanctuary, the intensity of feeling for the Pitchi Richi collection was surprisingly high.

The May Minutes also contain a motion of Wilson's which was passed concerning the main entrance to the Sanctuary. Wilson thought that the Commission should be requested to place a large boulder on either side of the entrance, on to which Bill could place works. It was reasoned that such a concept would be not only more aesthetically pleasing than a formal gate, but more economical as well. When Mr Bakacs approached Bill with the idea, Bill thought it a good one and held onto it. It was finally realised that such a main entrance would in no way contribute to the Sanctuary's security. A more formal gate was accepted, but Bill decided to have the *real* entrance within the grounds. It consists of two huge boulders, each flanked by a smaller boulder. Walking through the centre of the geomorphic quartet, you pass beneath the likenesses of a pair of dignified Aboriginal men whose outstretched arms show the way within. It is not hard to imagine them as a pair of guardians, there to *admit*, rather than welcome, the visitor to the Sanctuary beyond.

The most significant motion to come out of the June 16th Committee meeting, proposed by Mr Bakacs, was *"that the committee recommends to the Forests Commission that a historian be seconded to write the complete history of Ricketts' life and works as far back as can be ascertained"*.

Mr Lawrence addressed the issue of a biography when he attended the July meeting, with record being made that the Commission was keen on the idea. The issue was clouded by knowledge of the existence of Mary Harris' manuscript which nobody had sighted, even though a copy of it was known to be in Bill's possession. Lawrence suggested that before anything was done, Mary's manuscript should be assessed, after which research could be carried out into the periods which were found not to be covered.

In her attempt to give access to Bill's life and work, Mary Harris had unwittingly squashed the slim chance of a professional historian being commissioned to prepare an authoritative biography based on fact rather than whimsical fancy. The Committee waited at least two months, possibly much longer, before sighting Mary's manuscript. When at last it was sighted, it would immediately have been recognised as a totally unsuitable basis from which to start serious research. The matter of a biography was never mentioned in the Minutes again.

Had Mary's manuscript not existed, the question of a biography would have been considered fully when the idea was fresh and strong. The Commission may or may not have made adequate funding available for comprehensive research. But if they had gone ahead with it, the story of Bill's early days would definitely have been significantly more complete. This is because the great majority of Bill's life story existed only in memories of people who had known him. In 1964, many of the major players in Bill's life were still alive, as were his siblings. The oral histories from such first-hand witnesses and contributors to Bill's life would have been invaluable to a more complete history. Over twenty years later, when the research for this biography was commenced, the great majority of those with first-hand experience of Bill's early days were gone. An opportunity lost.

While the Committee and the Commission were grappling with the issues raised during the meetings, Bill was working frantically towards having the Sanctuary presentable enough for an Official Opening. He wanted it to be some time in the spring of 1964. His task was being greatly hampered by the continuing problems with the kiln. In the Committee's August Minutes, Ralph Wilson is recorded as having said that Bill was experiencing a 33 per cent "casualty rate" as a result of the kiln's operation, and noted that *"all the time that work has to be done again Ricketts could be doing something else"*.

To Bill's credit, he struggled along with the kiln and the firing failures—conceiving works and planning in his mind where they would be set, creating them and working in with the gangs organised by Jim Westcott to finally have the new sculptural groups become an integral part of the forest Sanctuary. A major difference between the placement of the new works and those placed previously by Bill was that the new works were there to stay. *"Some of those great big works set back into the hillside—you wouldn't believe the amount of iron-work that's behind them to tie them back"*, Jim Westcott informed me. *"We went to no end of trouble to key them all into the soil. An enormous amount of iron!"*

Bill informed the Committee shortly before their September meeting that he was ahead of schedule with the ground works and would be ready for his Opening by the beginning of November. The Opening was eventually set down for Sunday, November 8th, at 2.30 p.m. and the Commission was advised accordingly.

Bill's new Will received a mention at the September meeting. Jack Baskett was attempting to organise it through the Public Trustee's office. It was recorded in the Minutes that the only items of value which Bill owned at that time were his Austin truck [which was by then unregistered and up on blocks at Alf Turner's garage] and three original paintings by Australian artists; one of which was by Albert Namatjira. It says a lot about Bill's priorities and selflessness that at the age of sixty-six his material wealth amounted to so little.

Good news came via the Literary Review of the Saturday, October 10th, edition of the *Age*, in which John Hetherington featured Bill in the series of profiles known collectively as "Uncommon Men".[7] Although Hetherington had known and supported Bill for some years, he and Mr Clive Turnbull lunched with Bill for three and a half hours a month earlier, on September 10th, during which, no doubt, much of the profile's content was obtained. The profile was illustrated with a line drawing by Louis Kahan, winner of the 1963 Archibald Prize for Portraiture.

Hetherington opened the profile:

> *" 'All life is one', Billy Ricketts says. 'Men are clamouring for peace, but peace for men alone can never be. It must be peace for everything. Reverence for life whole is the only hope.' "*

Hetherington skilfully picked through Bill's life in an enlightening and revealing way. He looked at the "crusader in clay" description which had been used for years and offered: *"... he is less a crusader, seeking to force his ideas on people, than an evangelist, trying to persuade men to see the truth of life as he sees it"*. Hetherington also revealed, less than one month before the Grand Opening of the Sanctuary, that Bill still held onto his dream of *the* Holy Mountain which, Hetherington conveyed, would *"draw to it the best minds from every part of the world"*.

> *" 'Any little child brought to that holy mountain would go back and never be the same again', [Bill] says. 'The children are the hope. They can be led to understand, and through them this belief [that all Life is one] could be spread to all men.' "*

Hetherington's profile was undoubtedly the best ever published. While it contained inaccuracies [purely, I suggest, as a result of Bill's inaccurate answers to questions], Hetherington tapped the essence of Bill's philosophies and aspirations and presented Bill to readers in such a way that Bill could have only dreamed for.

A rush leading up to the Opening came upon all associated with the Sanctuary. Within the grounds Charlie Chamberlain, his son Peter and fellow Commission worker Boris Esmond made

---

7 The profile was reprinted in Hetherington's book, *Uncommon Men*, published by F. W. Cheshire Publishing Pty Ltd in 1965. "Billy Ricketts: Evangelist in Clay" begins on p. 159.

final touches under Bill's hectic guidance. It still looked very new, compared with the Sanctuary which you walk through today, but it was no less unique a place. Invitation lists were made and sent out, speeches prepared and local authorities forewarned. A special police courtesy squad was arranged to help control the traffic, because at that time there was no car park below Churinga. The Commission provided parking attendants for the day and sent out special vehicle identification stickers to invited guests.

If the Atkinsons had a smile when they received their vehicle identification sticker, what must they have thought when the following invitation arrived in the mail? *"The Minister for Forests, The Hon. L. H. S. Thompson, MLC, and Members of the Forests Commission and their wives would be pleased if* **Mr. and Mrs. L. H. Atkinson** [their names were hand written] *could find it convenient to join them in AFTERNOON TEA at the home of Mr. and Mrs. L. H. Atkinson, Churinga Nursery, Mt. Dandenong Road, Mt. Dandenong after the Official Opening of the Mountain Galleries Reserve by the Minister on Sunday next."* Obviously, some people were not thinking too clearly down at Head Office.

Somewhere along the way Dame Edith Bolte, who was supposed to officially open the Sanctuary, was replaced by Lindsay Thompson. I did not find out the reason, but speculate that by the time a decision was made on an opening date, Dame Edith's schedule was booked up.

Sunday, November 8th, 1964, finally came and the guests arrived to be shown through the Sanctuary before the Opening ceremony began at 2.30 p.m. A small podium had been erected near the main gate.

First to take the stage was Cr Maurice Seymour, representing the Lillydale Shire Council. Cr Seymour's association with Bill went back to the post-WWII days when people like Hilda King and Ola Cohn were playing such a supportive role in Bill's life. Seymour told me that he based his address around the quote, "We oft forget by which base means we did ascend", knowing that Bill would not bother to mention or thank those who had assisted him along the path to that Official Opening. In recounting his association with Bill, and sharing what history he knew, Cr Seymour was able to mention the names of those who he knew to have been major players.

Next to speak was A. O. Lawrence, Commission Chairman. Lawrence spoke of the work which had been done to re-establish the Sanctuary, praising the Commission workers for their efforts and forewarning of the expense of maintaining the Sanctuary and bettering it in the future. Lou Atkinson spoke on behalf of the Advisory Committee, expressing great pleasure at seeing the Sanctuary at last being officially opened and Bill's work recognised publicly. He added: *"We believe this venture will be greatly appreciated by many people not only in Australia, but overseas as well. I would like to congratulate the Government through the Forests Commission for such a fine effort in making this possible for all time."*

Bill was then introduced to the gathering. As Seymour had predicted, Bill looked to the future and did not dwell on the past, except in mentioning his relationship with Australia's Aborigines, especially his friends in the Centre. He described the day as an important one, adding: *"Now I have something concrete on which to base my crusade, which is to fight against the corruption the white man brought to this Aboriginal land."* I did not find a transcript of Bill's speech, if indeed one exists. I've no doubt, though, that it was fervent.

Finally Lindsay Thompson took the stage, where his speech to the guests included: *"The Dandenongs have always been a source of inspiration, as can be seen by Mr Ricketts' work, which shows a highly individual, imaginative and religious mind. In this highly mechanical age it is refreshing to see such individual work which does not mimic others. It is the work of a creative hand and should be treasured and admired by the nation."* After making a special appeal for the public to conserve their heritage, Thompson declared the Mountain Galleries Reserve officially open. The Sanctuary became the people's—and not one Aborigine was there to witness it.

18 | International Crusade
[late 1964–1966]

It had taken all of thirty years, but at last the Sanctuary was a permanent feature of Mt Dandenong. Bill could have relaxed, confident in the knowledge that the works he created for placement in his forest would be secure. The increasing flow of visitors would take his message away to be spread throughout Australia and the world. His ideals were guaranteed a voice in an ever-increasing support base. But the victory of Government support and recognition was merely an old obstacle overcome. After all, he'd been advocating Government protection of his Sanctuary for almost as long as he'd been on the mountain. Bill had said on the opening day: *"Now I have something concrete on which to base my crusade ..."* As far as Bill was concerned, the crusade could begin in earnest.

Mr Bakacs reported at the December 1964, Committee meeting that Bill had stated his desire to journey through Europe with some of his works to conduct a one-man crusade. The Atkinsons had pencilled a note next to the Minutes' reference that Bill still wanted to travel to India as well. The Minutes record the Committee's opinion that Bill: *"would have to have somebody (who has the time and money) with him to assist and guide him; he is such a naive, simple man that he would, by expressing his opinions, invite trouble. Also his art is singular and perhaps would not be appreciated in some countries."* Bill would not have entertained the idea of a minder for a minute. A one-man crusade was just that—not one man plus minder. But the Committee were not attempting to nobble him. They knew that the simple truth was that Bill would be out of his depth if he landed in Europe without somebody to help with the practical aspects of getting by in a foreign country. Unaware that he had any supporters in Europe who could fill such a role, the Committee members unofficially adopted a plan of subtle discouragement whenever Bill raised his desires for overseas crusading.

One facet of Bill's vision which was being pursued by the Commission, with enthusiastic encouragement from the Committee, was the expansion of the Sanctuary's boundaries into adjacent privately owned land. The Victorian Government had been actively engaged in a buy-back of land throughout the State for some time, with one of the driving forces on the ground being Jack Baskett. Jim Westcott recalled Baskett's contribution with respect:

> *"He was a great personal friend of mine, and he deserves a damn lot of praise for what he did in the Dandenongs—for all this buy back of land that you hear so much about. That started [in the Dandenongs] around 1960. But Jack and I had been friends for a great many years—he and I were buying land back for the Commission right up in the north-east, a hell of a lot of land. He went to no end of trouble in buying land back for Ricketts—we'd split titles or anything."*

The 1890s carve-up of land in the Dandenongs had been done principally on paper, with no regard for the topographical features. While the initial clearing was devastating in its completeness, land which was too steep to be of practical use had in many cases been left to grow wild. Excessively steep blocks might only have had a house-block-size piece of land maintained. The Government sought to connect what remaining forest and regrowth it could purchase in a bid to regain some of the Dandenongs' former glory. Their most noticeable achievement is the western slopes of the ranges which, when viewed from Melbourne, appear almost complete in their cover of forest.

When Bill's property became State owned it was only a continuation of existing policy to attempt to add what bush surrounded the block. The one difference was that the newly acquired land was added to the Sanctuary to become permanent forest, rather than reverting to ordinary Crown Land. It was in this way that the natural spring which supplies the Sanctuary's water was ultimately protected. Bill watched as his Sanctuary grew to fourteen acres at the time of the Opening, ever hopeful that eventually his boundary would reach the actual peak of Mt Dandenong, already owned by the State. If the peak became his, it would then be possible to create *the* Holy Mountain of his dreams.

Bill was outraged when, early in 1965, he became aware of plans to further develop the summit of Mt Dandenong as a public vantage point, complete with restaurant. Bill knew that if the development went ahead, any chance of his being able to build a temple on the peak would be lost. Full to the brim with indignation, he wrote a letter to the editor of the *Age*, which was published under the heading "Sculptor's Plea for Mt Dandenong":

> *"When I approach the high point of Mount Dandenong I am full of high expectation. When one looks into that wonderful view from the summit, one is conscious of peace and freedom—the richest reward this lovely mountain peak offers to everyone. Now the ugly mind has come upon this scene, and threatens it with bulldozers …*
>
> *To create a motor park and roads around this lovely mountain will be to encircle it with poison and kill its beauty. Any plan that panders to the motor car and would put a liquor-selling place on the mountain-top is a devil's plan. The motor car is not only killing people but also annihilating our wild life and beauty. If this monstrous plan is put into effect, then I shall leave this mountain, but that does not mean that I shall run away or make mere words my weapons. I mean business."*

Had Bill put forward a detailed proposal outlining his plans for the summit, he would surely have received some support. Whether or not it would have been enough support to see his plan become a reality is doubtful—but at least he would have been in with a chance. Unfortunately, a detailed proposal was not Bill's way of working.

Unbeknown to the Committee members, Bill was busy on another front. The subtle discouragement of his ambitions to "crusade" overseas had been ineffective. He was sending away letters in an attempt to organise a tour—or have a tour organised for him. He was also attempting to solicit the help of any overseas tourists who visited the Sanctuary. This is evidenced by a February 15th, 1965, letter from Sidney Zuckert, a New Yorker to whom Bill had explained his eagerness to tour the USA. Zuckert wrote the letter on a flight from Melbourne to Sydney the day after meeting Bill, to advise him that another American, Philip Crowe, Director of the World Wildlife Fund [WWF], was in Melbourne for a short time. Zuckert felt that Crowe might be able to interest the New York based WWF in sponsoring Bill on a tour of the USA. Zuckert's next letter, dated March 16th, was written in response to a letter from Bill which was waiting when Zuckert arrived back in the US. Bill had missed Crowe in Melbourne and asked Zuckert to contact Crowe in New York. Zuckert indicated that he was waiting on Bill to forward photos and biographical information so that he in turn could pass them on to "art people" he knew.

Apart from simply presenting his dreams to the host of fresh minds he would find there, the USA offered vague hope of some extremely wealthy sponsor getting behind Bill to provide him with the funds necessary to create *the* Holy Mountain in Australia. Across the Pacific from the

USA was another country full of fresh minds, the USSR. Bill knew there would be little chance of funds from the USSR, but he did count on the support of the people.

Bill had always been sympathetic toward the USSR, initially because of the great Russian composers who had been an inspiration for most of his life. As Bill's ideals became more well known and his prominence increased, visits from Soviet diplomats were not uncommon.[1] When children in Soviet schools were introduced to Australian artists, Bill was included with the likes of Albert Namatjira and Katharine Susannah Prichard; although this could have been an attempt to highlight the inequalities which existed in this capitalist country. Then there had been a tour of the Sanctuary by Soviet athletes during the 1956 Olympics. The relationship which existed between Bill and the Soviet Embassy in Canberra was strong enough to warrant Bill's receipt of invitations to official functions.

The early 1960s saw Bill hosting small delegations from visiting Soviet ships which docked in Melbourne. In March, 1964, the Soviet bulk grain carrier *Perekop* was loading wheat, but delays resulted in the ship remaining in port for some six weeks. In an attempt to relieve the crew's boredom, a request was published in local papers asking Melburnians to consider hosting visits by members of the crew. Bob and Florence Felstead heeded the call and made themselves available to entertain, and be entertained by, crew members of the *Perekop*. Along with the meals at their home and on board the *Perekop*, the Felsteads took crew members away for days of sightseeing.

They called into the Sanctuary on one outing, only to be told that visitors were not permitted until after the Opening. Mrs Felstead, a long-term admirer of Bill's work, wrote to him explaining the situation and requesting an invitation so that the Russians would not miss out on the experience. Bill was more than happy to comply.

A visit was arranged for Sunday, April 12th, 1964. The party consisted of Bob Felstead, First Officer Ivan Ivashko, and the Second and Fourth Officers whose first names only were recorded respectively as Boris and Igor. The ship's Captain Sidorenko passed on his apologies for not being able to attend owing to his commitment of having to stay aboard the ship on weekends. Ivan Ivashko was also the ship's camera-man and resident journalist, which led to him having several articles about Bill published in the Soviet Union after his return. One article headed "White Brother" was published in the Odessa newspaper, *Znamia Kommunizma*, which Ivan told Bill had a readership of two million people. It related Ivan's first meeting with Bill. The following are excerpts from that article:[2]

> *"I always wanted to tell you about my Australian friend ... Bill Ricketts ...*
>
> *We met in April 1964 ... Gum trees of the fairytales. Mount Dandenong. A narrow path leading to the gate ... behind the gate a neat little house. A slender, not tall man with a friendly smile was greeting us. When we were shaking hands we saw his serene grey-blue eyes. These eyes spoke of his soul, his shyness and confidence of strong personality. He is sixty years old and looks much more younger[3] ... Ricketts asked us a lot of questions [about] our age, and birthplace, about our education and hobbies.*
>
> *We came into the house ... Near the open verandah—a clear spring. A lot of birds are singing near the house and they all know their master and greet him. We wanted to see the sculptures but Ricketts is busy with dinner. It was a masterpiece cooked by the host himself. And only after dinner Ricketts began to show his works to us. Near the window there are some bas-reliefs of aborigines which were made specially for us. Then*

---

1 I contacted ASIO, Australia's secret intelligence organisation, but they would neither confirm nor deny if there was a file on Bill within their data bank.

2 These excerpts are taken from what was described as an "Unofficial Translation" by the USSR's Australian Embassy staff who provided Bill with a translation of the article. The translation was recovered in the "spare room".

3 Of course, Bill was heading towards his 66th birthday—but he was obviously holding up well.

we see unfinished sculpture of a young aboriginal girl—delicate, pensive and a little bit tired …

Suddenly Ricketts switches on the music—music by Rimsky-Korsakov, so touching to Russians. Ricketts speaks about the importance of music in his work and how proud we are to hear that Russian music … helps Ricketts to create his masterpieces. What is in common with Russian music and aborigines forced to live in deserts? It is the love of everything beautiful and hatred to cruelty … Each sculpture is a memorial to the aborigines who fight for the right to live, to work, to be equal to the white people …

Ricketts stresses that it is the aborigines who taught him to work with selflessness. 'You know, Australian aborigines are people of special courage, they are strong as water and wind and patient as rocks.'

… Quite recently I received a letter from Billy where he writes that he is going to visit the Soviet Union and my town Odessa …"

Bill's prediction that he would visit Odessa was premature. Bill had written to the Soviet Embassy on April 5th, 1965, requesting help in arranging a tour of the Republic, but the initial response in a May 11th letter from I. Volkov, the Second Secretary, indicated that there would be no speedy decisions. Volkov informed Bill that he had sent a letter to the Union of Soviet Artists as an introduction to Bill. *"Now we shall wait for their reply"*, Volkov wrote, adding: *"It will be very good if we have an album with the photos of your works (we were talking about when we visited you) as soon as possible since they … will need it before taking a decision."*

The brochure, entitled *A Living Voice of the Living Bush*, was completed in July, 1965. Ralph Wilson was responsible for the production of the high-quality booklet of twenty-two pages. That Wilson's hands were quite full with running his own successful business made his undertaking quite extraordinary. When asked why such an obviously busy person took on such a responsibility and commitment, his answer was simple: *"I believed in [Bill's] philosophy, and I thought that it was worth the work. I believed in him. Because we were lithographers, having quite an under-standing of the transparencies and reproduction, we could arrange all of [the brochure]."*

Wilson's one condition on becoming involved with the project was that neither his nor his company's name be associated with the finished product. *"I'm a person who's very publicity shy"*, he explained when I queried him about that decision. But he was not shy of hard work.

Wilson chose the firm McLaren and Co., who he considered to be the best of Australian printers, to print 5,000 copies. Lindsay Thompson, the Minister of Forests, provided a brief foreword. Bill had asked Ted Strehlow to write an essay to form the majority of the text, but when it finally arrived, it took Wilson and his staff some time to get it to a standard with which they were satisfied. *"It had to be edited"*, Wilson explained, *"not in context—but it had to be sent back a lot of times. For a professor of linguistics, it was rather surprising."*

Bill's contribution to the text was a barely changed copy of that which was published in the earlier catalogue, including the "quoted" words of Atirantuka.

Strehlow's text occupied six pages and proved to serve as a good introduction to Bill's work, although it did not attempt to go into Bill's personal history. Strehlow opened what he termed his "appreciation" by quoting from the inscription found at the entrance of the sculptural group generally known as "The Shrine": *"All living things everywhere are forever one with us."* He stated that it not only summed up Bill's philosophy but that it was an excellent summation of the Central Australian Aborigine's totemic beliefs. He went on to summarise those beliefs and gave an overview of how well Bill's sculptural conceptions equated with them—but he went to pains to point out that Bill was not simply illustrating borrowed themes. In Strehlow's opinion, the Aboriginal beliefs were a "liberating agent" for Bill's own creative forces. The one small problem I had with Strehlow's text was his referring to Atirantuka as *"the most articulate spokesman"* of Bill's Aboriginal friends, thereby endorsing the "Atirantuka Speaks" quotation. I have expressed my thoughts regarding that quotation earlier. Strehlow, who knew the Arrernte as well as, if not better than, any white person, either believed the quote to be accurate or he was pandering to his friend's dreaming. Still, the text is well worth reading and can be found nowadays in Bill's *Australiandia: Land of the Holy Spirit*.

When John Hetherington reviewed *A Living Voice of the Living Bush* for the *Age*,[4] his opening paragraph read:

> *"Anyone who tries to write about Billy Ricketts finds himself struggling. Ricketts belongs in no known pigeonhole; he cannot be presented in terms which fit ordinary men, nor can his work be discussed in the slithery jargon of the art dabblers."*

Hetherington finished his review by praising Strehlow's as the text of one who "understands" Bill.

The Commission had produced the first Sanctuary pamphlet at the same time as the brochure's completion. It contained the briefest of biographies as well as a simple map detailing the Sanctuary's location. There were two changes to be made when the pamphlet's second edition came out. The Committee picked up that the cover was incorrect by stating the location as Olinda, and Bill *"was not happy about his mother being mentioned in the script"*.[5] That may seem surprising when Susan Ricketts' contribution is recalled, but when we look at the actual wording of the pamphlet, Bill's reasoning becomes clearer. Referring to Bill's move from the city to Mt Dandenong, the pamphlet stated that Bill was *"accompanied and inspired by his mother ..."* Bill would have objected to the inference that he was "inspired" by Susan, for he maintained right to the end that he was helped and inspired by no person—*"not even my mother"*.

Another source for Bill's discontent to surface during this period was the Commission's intention to introduce an entry fee at the Sanctuary. Bill was of the opinion that his message, as expressed within the Sanctuary, should be freely available to the public. He was adamant that he had been verbally guaranteed that no entry fee would be imposed during his lifetime. The Commission argued that the costs of maintaining and improving the Sanctuary had to be offset. Bill believed that rather than forcing visitors to pay, they should be given the chance to voluntarily donate money towards the Sanctuary's upkeep. He cited the funds that he had raised over the years through his wishing-well. A compromise was reached by getting Bill to construct another vessel to receive donations. A six month trial period was allowed to ascertain whether or not the generosity of patrons would be enough to fund the Sanctuary. When it became apparent that public generosity would not suffice, the decision to implement an entrance fee of two shillings also resulted in the construction of the gatehouse and the employment of ticket-sellers.

Such problems did not take Bill's mind off the most important task of that time—his overseas "crusade". Mary Harris had involved herself, probably at Bill's request, by soliciting help from Quakers in the USA. To this end she had been corresponding with Rev. Tobias, who lived in Philadelphia. I found no letters from Tobias to Bill, but the references made in correspondence between Bill and Mary suggest that Tobias had passed on news to Mary which was encouraging enough to have Bill believing that it was only a matter of time before firm plans were in place to accommodate him.

The story was similar with the WLPS in Sydney. After formally agreeing to support Bill with his proposed US tour, Jim Brown, in his capacity of Hon. Publicity Officer, was given the task of attempting to encourage the WWF, through Philip Crowe, to handle the organisational responsibilities in the US. Brown wrote to Crowe early in November, 1965, explaining who Bill was and what his needs would be while in the US. Brown wrote that the arrangements and costs associated with landing Bill, his truck and sculptures in the US would be handled from Australia, but there was a need for exhibition venues to be arranged throughout the States. Brown suggested

---

4 The *Age*, October 9th, 1965.
5 As recorded in the July 18th, 1965, Committee Minutes.

that funds could be raised from entrance fees to exhibitions, as well as from the sale of small works which Bill would take for the purpose. Bill would need only enough money to sustain himself during the tour, and to pay for his return to Australia. Excess funds could be accepted as donations to the WWF. Brown finished his letter by requesting that Crowe contact Bill direct to further the matter.

I sighted no letters from Crowe, but Bill, in his optimism, was sure that moves were under way within the WWF to arrange his tour. So confident was Bill that he wrote to Tobias in Philadelphia advising him to contact Crowe so that the arrangements could be better co-ordinated.

Bill continued his planning and wrote to the US Consulate in Melbourne seeking assurance that there would be no trouble with his touring the States in his truck. The US Vice Consul, Don Kienzle, replied in a letter dated December 31st, 1965. Bill was informed that there would be no duty incurred against his truck or sculpture, as long as the Customs officials were satisfied that all would be exported from the US at the conclusion of Bill's tour. Regarding the sculptures, the Customs officials had to be satisfied that they were all original works of art and that none would be sold during the tour. A non-immigrant visa would be issued after Bill had supplied a valid passport, a travel letter showing his travel itinerary and a bank letter stating that Bill would be taking sufficient funds to cover anticipated needs. Of course, Bill had neither an itinerary nor sufficient funds.

The Austin truck had to be resurrected for the journey, with the job going to Alf Turner. The list of work to get it back to road-worthy condition was impressive. Apart from the replacement of all electrical components and all fluids associated with the engine and transmission, the Austin needed new headlights, clutch, flywheel, speedometer, brake and radiator hoses, water pump, windscreen, exhaust muffler, battery straps and [as evidence of how fine Bill cut his driving clearances] two new side-view mirrors. The total cost came to £65 6s 5d.

Bill had his proposed tour publicised on January 27th, 1966, when the *Age* published an article titled, "Hills Artist Plans a Crusade". The unacknowledged writer of the piece told that Bill was leaving around April for the USA and India, *"and possibly other countries"*, for an unspecified period of time. Ever ready to use publicity to his advantage, Bill gave his reasons for going as being directly related to the proposed developments in the Dandenongs aimed at creating a major tourist attraction. *"The plan is just one more step toward the destruction of the Australian bush and Australian wild life"*, Bill was quoted as saying. The writer explained that Bill would be seeking support for his Holy Mountain, and although Bill did not know which mountain would be transformed, he said that Mt Dandenong could be used, *"unless the bulldozers get there first and wreck it forever"*. The writer added that on reaching America, Bill would *"drive to Philadelphia where friends are waiting to launch him on what could become a nationwide crusade"*.

Not content with this coverage, Bill sent a letter to the editor of the *Age* which was published on February 7th, stating:

> *"... Although I have high hopes of the response in the United States to my dream of establishing a holy mountain in Australia, I am no less hopeful of gaining powerful support in India—that wonderful country which has given the world so many great thinkers down the centuries.*
>
> *The late Mr Nehru knew of my work here and told me in a letter that if I were in his country he would give me all the help in his power. On this trip I hope to see his daughter, Mrs Gandhi, the new Prime Minister. I have reason to suppose she shares her late father's enthusiasm for my beliefs, notably my central philosophy that all life is one."*

How Bill was planning to tour India on that trip is a total mystery. No correspondence surfaced which so much as hinted at any pre-planning. The contents of his letter to the editor was suspect. Apart from Verrier Elwin's letter to Mary Harris which contained suggestions that Nehru may have helped Bill, had Bill been in India, there is no evidence of Bill having received a letter direct from Nehru. Similarly, on the evidence available, all that would have given Bill reason for supposing Indira Gandhi shared her late father's enthusiasm would have been his optimism.

It would appear that the Committee did not concern itself greatly with the reported news that Bill was leaving on his "crusade", although they may have become aware that their subtle discouragement had failed to change his mind. It's quite possible that they felt safe in the knowledge that by leaving it to Bill to organise, the venture would never become a reality. They would have known that Bill had been "planning" an overseas tour for many years, but his impracticality and lack of sound organisational ability had always kept his feet on Australian soil.

Early in March 1966, Bill received a letter from another New Yorker whom he had met in the Sanctuary, Mary Bailey. Bill had written to her with the news that he would arrive some time in April and requested that she do what she could to organise exhibition venues. While Mary Bailey admitted that it was totally beyond her field of experience, she was able to pass Bill's request on to a friend, Jeanne Miles. Miss Miles, herself a painter who knew the ways of the New York art scene, was immediately impressed by Bill's work and philosophy and had happily agreed to do what she could to help.

Miss Miles' first action was to contact the Australian Ambassador to the United Nations, Mr Shaw, who advised her to contact the Australian Consul-General in New York, Sir Reginald Sholl. Sir Reginald advised her that he had not the authority, funds nor personnel to assist in organising a tour for Bill. He passed her on to the Australian Ambassador in Washington, Mr J. K. Waller. The best that the Ambassador could offer was to suggest that Bill write to him directly requesting assistance, after which possible plans could be developed. But it would all take time to arrange. In an attempt to give Bill some idea of what he was attempting to break into, Miss Miles explained that there were some 9,000 practising artists in New York, all of whom were seeking exhibition space. It was almost a plea when Miss Miles wrote in her letter to Bill: *"If it is at all feasible, a much later date than April would give us more time to make arrangements …"*

When Bill read those letters, it's most likely that he would not have been terribly worried by the contents. Firstly, his plans had been delayed a little, which gave them the time they required. Secondly, 9,000 mere artists were no competition to one man on a holy crusade. Once the people with space in New York saw what he had to share, he would go to the top of the list. And thirdly, such matters paled into insignificance when compared to the problems he was having with that barbarian next-door-neighbour!

The episode is best summed up in Bill's words, written in a letter of March 7th, 1966, to the Committee which started, "Dear friends":

> *"A little while ago the man who has just bought that lovely water fern gully joining this sanctuary cut off my water supply by putting in his own catchment. I took it off and flung it down the creek. He came in ready for business with me. I told him to put his pipe in down below the catchment basin for this sanctuary. He did so. Now yesterday my water supply was cut off again. I went up to see he put in a grand scheme right above the catchment basin for this sanctuary. I took this off and flung it down the creek. This will lead to conflict …"*

Bill was calling in the troops to help protect his water rights, and the rights of occupation held by his lyrebirds whose territory included the fern gully. Bill went on to explain that during his thirty-three years on the property, a progression of "couldn't care less" men had occupied the adjoining land. It was time for the Government to resume the gully and sixty-six feet on the other side. Bill ended the letter with his familiar ultimatum: *"If he stays I leave."* That Bill was not reported as being jailed or hospitalised suggests that the Committee were able to effect a compromise solution between the warring parties.

Bill received and had translated another letter from Ivan Ivashko during March. It was basically a belated thank you for the brochure which Bill had sent over, but also contained news that due to illness, Ivan had been unable to appear on television with the "new" tale of Bill's works. Ivan's wording suggests that Bill had already been presented to the television audience of Odessa at least. Looking at the brochure, Ivan wrote, brought back many memories of the "magic Dandenongs". The letter was filled with praise and understanding, increasing in tone to the point where Ivan wrote: *"In one of the Australian papers one writer calls you a Don Quixote, tilting at the windmills of the 20th century,[6] but to me you seem like Jesus, come down to the Australian soil, to lead into the light those aboriginals, who once were undoubtedly masters of the fifth continent."*

It was by no means the first time that such a comparison had been made. Over the years countless people had in one way or another compared Bill to Jesus, most often in private, but occasionally in a more public way. Mary Harris, in her unpublished manuscript, had described the meal before Bill's 1959 departure from Adelaide as being like the Last Supper, leaving her inference clear for all who read the text. And it was her hope that many would read the text. In 1961 Bill had received a letter from an admirer in Kew who requested that Bill make a small work for her:

> *"Have you ever thought of depicting yourself on a crucifix … It may seem startling at first.*
>
> *I know the outraged indignant voices of some would be raised. But, startling as this idea in clay might be, you have given your life to teaching as He did. You have lived among white men and not been touched with their corruption and greed. You, too, have been poor. But you have kept alight a steady burning flame to guide others. You seem to be in touch with the infinite. I have heard harsh criticism of your work over the years, but, also I have heard others who came in contact with you speak of the inspiration you have given. Many have come away feeling deeply disturbed in their thoughts. Not only a feeling of guilt at their own selfishness, but realising they were breaking up the world they had and did not value at its real value. So many have loved you for what you have done for them. For, maybe you have not expressed it in words in your own mind, but you have been showing the world a practical, a tangible proof of the power of faith and indestructible beauty and truth and simplicity.*
>
> *I know you do not make small pieces of your work now, but would it be too much for me to ask you to make this crucifix as a small and private order for me at a price, and because of a friendship of nearly twenty years. It would make a very lonely person very happy. And no one would treasure it more than I. I ask you very humbly. I ask it as one of your disciples …"*

The expression of such devotion to Bill was not uncommon. Bill started off with a developed sense of self-worth. Without it he could never have persevered on the path he chose. Along that path his sense of self-worth was reinforced and inflated time after time, year after year, decade after decade, by people who saw him as, rightly or wrongly, the physical manifestation of the conscience of a nation, or a world, which was not squeaky clean. It's doubtful that any person could remain immune to such consistent praise and glorification. Bill came to believe that he had a power unmatched—a power that really could bring about change for the better. He came to call it his power of love. With such a power he was supremely confident that he could take on the world. A great many of his supporters maintained that it was not a delusion.

On April 6th and 14th, 1966, Bill had his smallpox vaccinations. Somewhere along the way he had secured free passage for himself, his sculptures and his truck to New York with the US

---

6 From John Hetherington's "Uncommon Men" article—"… a great-hearted, modern Don Quixote tilting at 20th century windmills …"

shipping company, Farrell Lines. It is not recorded who organised it, but it was a coup for Bill which made his plans irreversible.

On April 19th, 1966, the day that Bill's first passport was issued, the Advisory Committee met. Within the Minutes it was finally recognised that Bill's journey was probable. There was also a letter tabled in which Bill offered the services of a friend to act as a live-in caretaker, without payment. Although Bill did not spell it out, the Committee knew that Bill was referring to his absence abroad and recorded it. The letter, therefore, served as notice of his intention to be away from the Sanctuary. After some discussion it was decided that *"the trip should be stopped, or at any rate postponed for some time"*. They were fearful for Bill's welfare and unsure about the security of the works Bill planned to take away. The Commission was informed and made a mistake in their haste.

On April 26th, H. G. Murphy, Secretary, wrote the following letter to Bill on behalf of the Commission:

> *"It has come to the notice of the Commission that you are proposing to visit North America at an early date and that you are actively engaged with arrangements to that end.*
>
> *While the Commission would not, of course, intrude upon your wishes in this respect, it regrets the necessity of the tour and retains some misgivings as to your welfare. The Chairman has asked me to impress upon you the very great importance of making a firm arrangement in advance, which will ensure that some person or organisation will meet you on arrival and provide essential advice, particularly in relation to traffic laws.*
>
> *I am also required to point out that under your agreement with the Commission you are required to give it at least 30 days notice in writing of any period during which you will not be in residence at the Sanctuary.*
>
> *It has come to the Commission's notice that it is your intention to take some pieces of sculpture with you to North America as examples of your art. You are informed that the Commission can not allow this to happen. Under clause 3(a) of the terms of your agreement with the Commission, all sculpture work produced by you for the purposes of the Sanctuary is the property of the Government of Victoria. Even if you adopt the view that the sculptures which you propose to take with you were not produced 'for the purposes of the Sanctuary', the Commission has an equity therein and will not be prepared to forgo that equity.*
>
> *I am instructed to stress with you the great importance of your appreciation of ownership of the sculptures and to advise you that any attempt to remove sculptures from the Sanctuary could lead to an unfortunate situation."*

When Bill received that letter his rage seemed to shake the very foundations of Mt Dandenong. He mobilised, first giving his notice of resignation from the Sanctuary to the Atkinsons and then contacting the newspapers. The Commission, meanwhile, sent a letter to the Crown Solicitor seeking advice on taking out a Court injunction to stop the removal of any sculptures from the Sanctuary.

April 30th saw an article in the *Age* titled, "Official Brush Troubles Gentle Artist", written by John Macdonald. It put both Bill's and the Commission's case forward in a reasonably balanced way, citing Bill's wish to take his message and his sculptures abroad, but incorrectly pointing out that an agreement existed which made the sculptures Government property. Bill was reported to have said that the works would be returned no matter what happened, but it was also noted that Bill had *"no return ticket and little money"*.

One week later, on May 7th, the Melbourne *Truth* scented scandal and weighed in, boots and all, with an article titled, "Bill Will Fight For His Statues". In the first paragraph Bill was quoted as saying: *"I will push the wretches into the sea. I will punch hell out of them.[7] They will*

---

7 Non-violently, of course.

not possess my soul." After stating that Bill intended to take twelve of his sculptures overseas, the letter from the Commission was reprinted verbatim. The journalist admitted that when he first approached Bill with questions regarding the fight over the sculptures, Bill replied, *"I don't want any trouble—no coals on the fire".* It apparently did not take much coaxing to have the fire raging inside Bill, with him being quoted as saying: *"When any man points a gun at your head it is dictatorship. This man would take possession of your soul ... My soul is in my work— it is spiritual. I must take it overseas."* *Truth* sought comment from the Commission, but all Mr Murphy had to say, apart from pointing out that an agreement existed, was, *"We have referred the matter to the Crown Solicitor".* He would not comment further, saying that, *"The matter is sub judice".*

The Crown Solicitor's response was circulated through the Commission's upper echelons on May 9th. It stated quite simply that unless any of the sculptures Bill proposed to take could be proved to have been made for the purposes of the Sanctuary, neither the State nor the Commission could enforce their ruling.

The Commission immediately adopted a conciliatory attitude. A meeting was arranged between Bill, L. Thompson, the Minister of Forests, A. Benallack, the Commission's Deputy Chairman and Lou Atkinson. The exact date of the meeting is unclear. My copy of the typed *"notes of interview",* prepared on June 20th by Mr Benallack, record that the meeting was held on May 5th, well before the Crown Solicitor's response was received. But reference to the May 7th *Truth* article is made in the notes, showing the May 5th meeting date to be inaccurate. It is more than likely that the meeting was convened after the *Truth* article and after the Crown Solicitor's response—and, therefore, after the Commission knew that their letter to Bill was indefensible.

In his notes Benallack recorded that Thompson explained to Bill that the Commission's actions had been prompted by concern for Bill's welfare, and an attempt was made to get Bill to see the logic in postponing his trip until such time as definite plans were made. Bill, safe in the knowledge that the Commission was on the run, also adopted a conciliatory approach, although no less definite. He is recorded as having been "horrified" by the *Truth* article, but adamant that his plans were irrevocable. Bill explained that he had to *"honour a promise and fulfil a pact"* made with Aborigines in Central Australia. He had told them that he would take their struggle to the world, and that was just what he intended to do. He could not give any indication as to how long he would be gone. Thompson offered to arrange for a testimonial from the Premier, with Benallack recording:

> *"Mr Ricketts stated that this would be of no use to him as he knew he could succeed on his own personal qualities and that the mission would be a success. The question of money did not cause him any concern as he was certain that his mission could bring in millions and the goal of his holy mountain would be achieved in spite of all the opposition which had been put in his way."*

On May 16th, Thompson forwarded to Bill a testimonial to Sir Reginald Sholl, urging him to make use of it if the need arose. Thompson closed his letter to Bill with *"personal good wishes for a successful trip".* On the same day, Thompson prepared a letter to the editor of the *Truth* in which he explained that there had been a great deal of misunderstanding, adding that *"at no time was it the purpose of the Forests Commission to injure the feelings of this highly sensitive and talented man".* Thompson assured the *Truth* that the matter was amicably settled, and that Bill was leaving with not only Thompson's best wishes, but the personal testimonial to the Australian Consul-General in New York as well. Thompson did not send his letter to the *Truth*, opting instead to telephone them that same day to explain the matter personally.

Bill had won the fight, but he did not really know why. For the rest of his life he was fearful that at any time the Government could step in and exercise their rights of ownership over any of his works. For the rest of his life he remained totally confused about what the Agreement really meant. At different times he would go to great lengths to try to "get around" nonexistent obstacles. He would forevermore class the Government in general as an adversary.

As far as the US tour went, though, Bill had nothing standing in his way; although it remains a mystery as to how he got around the requirements to have his passport endorsed with a US entry visa stamp on May 25th. On June 6th, Bill's truck, reportedly loaded with four and a half tons of sculpture [which is a good effort considering it was rated as a three-ton truck] was loaded aboard the freighter, *Australian Isle*. Bill had decided not to board the ship in Melbourne, but to join it instead in Sydney. On June 24th, Bill was issued with his international driver's permit.

As the day of Bill's departure drew near, his friends and acquaintances wondered how it would go for him. They knew only too well Bill's practicality, or lack of it, and their joy that he was fulfilling his mission was tempered by thoughts of a mishap. One friend, Ms Rojo, spoke to Bill by telephone to wish him well and request that he take good care of himself. Knowing Bill's temperament and knowing that the US might prove overwhelming, she said to him: *"Do you know that if you really can't take it any longer, you can be home in two days?"* In recalling the moment, Ms Rojo told me: *"He nearly fell through the phone, and I could feel that he had been terribly worried, subconsciously, that he might find himself in that position. He thanked me most profusely, as if I'd just suddenly invented [international plane travel] for his benefit. I knew it had registered."*

Such worry, if indeed it was there, was vastly overshadowed by Bill's plans for positive action. Another with whom he spoke at length prior to leaving was John Hetherington. Bill wanted Hetherington to explain to the people just what he was doing, and how important his mission was. Bill assured Hetherington that people were awaiting his arrival in New York, and that they would launch him with an exhibition there, as well as organise exhibitions throughout the USA. Bill explained to Hetherington:

> *"If I can get even one influential man on my side in the USA, someone who can make his fellow countrymen listen when he tells them, 'This man Ricketts has brought a true message from Australia,' then I shall be satisfied. I want to rouse the American people. I must rouse them. I want them as allies in my battle against this criminal destruction of our environments and the wanton killing of living creatures which goes ceaselessly and senselessly on ... The Americans are my starting point."*

Bill went on to tell Hetherington that after America he planned to go to India, possibly throughout Europe, and definitely Russia. How he would get there and for how long he would be away, Bill could not say. But he would certainly come home as soon as his mission was over, if only to fight to have the Government reclaim the fern gully. Bill explained his views on the resumption:

> *"The white man is not surrendering some piece of property that belongs to him when he declares a fern gully, a hillside or some other piece of Australia a sanctuary. The whites acquired this country from the true owners, the Aborigines, by force. It was a theft, and is no more valid than any other theft. I am trying to wake the conscience of the white man in Australia and throughout the world. I have made some headway, and I believe the victory is in sight. All I need is a little time."*

Hetherington took his notes and went away to write the latest story of his friend. It was published in the *Age* on July 12th, but not before an unacknowledged author had another article published in the *Age* on July 9th. It was a dark piece of writing full of doubt as to whether or not Bill was doing the right thing by going overseas. An unnamed "friend" was quoted as having said: *"He is not equipped to go out into the world. But we could not stop him, he is determined."*

126 Bill "working" in the original hut. Photographer unknown.

127 Bill by the seaside. Photographer unknown, c. 1964.

125 Crowded paths outside Bill's original hut, c. early 1960s. Courtesy of the Age.

128 An example of the sort of work which was in the WRS prior to the State take over, but is not there today. Reproduced from Australasian Post, April 7th, 1949.

129 *Bill and the lyrebirds which he adopted as his totemic animal. Courtesy of R. E. Lord, c. 1960s.*

130 *The new house shortly after its completion. Reproduced by courtesy of Douglass Baglin.*

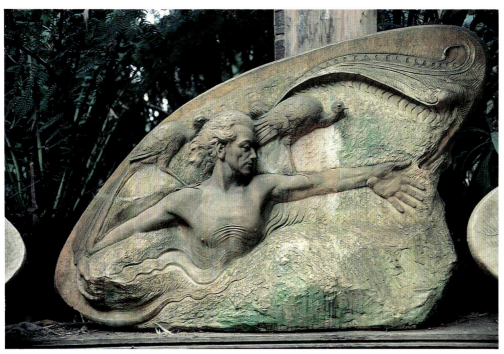

131 *A much travelled piece featuring the lyrebirds. It was given to Mary Harris, shown by her all over Adelaide, and finally purchased by Bill to give it a permanent home in the WRS collection. 950 mm high.*

132 *Another example of Bill's inclusion of lyrebirds in his work. WRS. 1750 mm high.*

133 *Bill and Atirantuka at Utopia, c. early 1960s. Bill claimed that he took this photo himself.*

134 *Bill with a camp dog and dingo in the Centre. Photographer unknown, c. early 1960s.*

135 & 136 *With unidentified friends near Papunya. Photographer unknown, c. early 1960s.*

137 *At the house of Rino Petrini, near Knoxville, USA, with unidentified people. Photographer unknown, c. 1966.*

138 *Getting acquainted with the locals at Cherokee, North Carolina. Photographer unknown, c. 1966.*

139 *Never one to follow the rules, Bill hops out of the car to be photographed with a black bear in the Great Smoky Mountains National Park. Photographer unknown, c. 1966.*

140 *Now part of the WRS collection, the five parts of this group were taken to the USA as part of Bill's 1966 exhibition. 6600 mm wide, 2650 mm high.*

141 *Bill used water to represent a flowing of life and spirit. WRS. 1450 mm high.*

142 *Child group at the WRS. 2000 mm high.*

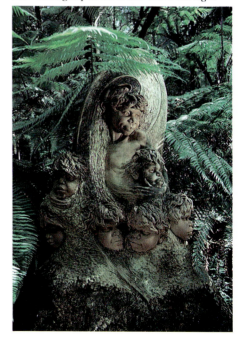

143 *Amy Osborne was the model for this piece. Amy was a Western Desert woman, but was "kidnapped" as a child by the Government under the assimilation policy because she had mixed blood. She met Bill at the WRS in the late 1960s and was a firm friend for many years. Amy has returned to her Dreaming. WRS. Sculpture 900 mm high, whole setting 3950 mm high.*

19 | The USA Tour
[1966]

The day finally arrived; Thursday, July 7th, 1966, and Bill prepared to embark on his first ride in an aeroplane. Lou and Dorothy Atkinson drove him to Essendon Airport, and at 2.00 p.m. they watched the plane fly off, bound for Canberra. If there was any fear in Bill's heart, it quickly turned to child-like joy. The next day he wrote to the Atkinsons telling them: *"Nineteen thousand feet up it was in another world right above the snow white clouds as far as you could see. It was just like looking into a fairy story."*

Bill was picked up in Canberra by Jim Brown and driven to the Brown's home in Wahroonga, a northern suburb of Sydney, where he was a guest for two days. The Browns went to great lengths attempting to get Bill to see the sense of letting the Americans first look upon his work as aesthetically pleasing pieces of art, after which they could be introduced to Bill's philosophical message. Bill's denial that he was an artist or sculptor was, they reasoned, more likely to confuse people rather than attract them. Gradually they persuaded him to at least think the matter over. For all of the discussion about the ways and means of best getting the message across to the Americans, the highlight of Bill's stay with the Browns was a tour of the Ku-ring-gai Chase National Park's waterways, guided by the head ranger in the park's motor launch.

On July 11th, Bill was welcomed aboard the *Australian Isle* by Captain Don Hanford and the ship put to sea bound for Brisbane, its last port of call in Australia. Calm seas prevailed and Bill enthusiastically slipped into his first experience of ocean life. As the ship neared Brisbane he wrote a quick letter to the Atkinsons in which his joy and wonder was obvious:

> *"A lovely good morning to you from the top deck of the ship. The sun shines, a calm sea, and a gentle breeze, and a great endless timeless scene all around makes this a wonderful journey. The ship is so clean, cabins and beds all wonderful and the food wonderful. The steward is a splendid man and he makes all a delight to sit at his table."*

Two days in Brisbane and then the *Australian Isle* put to sea again for a three and a half week voyage to their next landfall, Cristobal, at the far end of the Panama Canal. Bill had nothing to do but put his feet up and dream of the events to come. Mt Dandenong was a long way off, even from his thoughts. Fortunately, his Sanctuary had been left in good hands.

Jim Westcott had authorised that two Commission employees, J. Naughton and P. Chamberlain, move into the studio and live there for the duration of Bill's tour. Bill's talk of touring extensively in the entire northern hemisphere had Westcott worried, because the workers living on site had to be paid an added "camp allowance". Westcott also had to ensure that he had men on the grounds over every weekend and public holiday. The Olinda gang foreman, Charlie Chamberlain, was given direct responsibility for ensuring that there was at least one Commission employee on the grounds for the full twenty-four hours a day. Lou Atkinson became the "honorary overseer" because it was reckoned that he knew better than anyone what would upset

Bill least when he finally returned. The result was that, as well as running his own business with Dorothy, Lou had to run across the road whenever a decision was needed regarding ground works, plant rubbish removal, path construction—almost anything that went on within the Sanctuary. It was nothing new to Lou, or Dorothy. They had put more time into helping Bill than any other people: time that was invariably given freely.

The August edition of the US publication *Sunrise*,[1] featured an article about Bill titled, "Brotherhood in Sculpture", but it would appear to have been purely coincidental to Bill's imminent arrival in the US. The article's content was derived from Hetherington's "Uncommon Men" article and Strehlow's appreciation in *A Living Voice of the Living Bush*, with photographs lifted from the latter. No mention was made that Bill was to tour the US.

On August 2nd, Bill entered the northern hemisphere for the first time in his life. Captain Hanford ceremoniously presented him with a certificate emblazoned with a smiling King Neptune and a buxom mermaid, stating that Bill was *"duly initiated into the mysteries of the Order of the Trident, having crossed the Equator, and, hereby and forevermore, is a member of the brotherhood of the Nautilus"*.

It would have tickled Bill's fancy no end. The next day he sat down and wrote to the Atkinsons, giving his address as, "Pacific Ocean". The first line read: *"From the vast expanse of the ocean and just above the equator line I write to say it is a wonderful journey."* The ship was still "lovely" and Bill was delighting in watching the flying fish getting themselves out of the *Australian Isle's* way. He speculated that when the ship docked at Veracruz for two days, after the passage through the Panama Canal, he might fly up to Mexico City, *"because I may not be this way again"*. After Mexico City he would write to tell them if he had *"a senorita to bring back"*.

There was another quick letter from Cristobal on August 9th, *"after passing through one of the Earth's wonders"*—which Bill thought the Panama Canal to be. And the journey was still "wonderful" with Bill going as far as to say, *"I just had to see all this"*. And still there was more to see! Bill's letter of August 13th, written after leaving Cristobal, reassured the Atkinsons that there were no hurricanes or storms in the Gulf of Mexico to spoil the so far perfect and "wonderful" voyage. He was still effervescent about the Panama Canal, but he wasn't too sure about Cristobal:

> *"Cristobal is very poor with West Indies negro people speaking Spanish, living in Spanish like houses, very old and the place smells bad. With my cabin friend we went through Cristobal midnight until four a.m. and we visited a night club to see the girls singing in Spanish and dancing and one of the girls dropped off her dress to dance naked with men near the stage, cheap and ugly. We got back to the ship safe but were told by the police that it was not safe to go in one part. The police carry revolvers here ..."*

Just prior to departing from Cristobal a parcel of letters came aboard for Bill. One of them, he wrote, was from India, written by the father of a Melbourne-based friend of Bill's.[2] The letter told Bill that when he arrived in India, all would be arranged for him. Bill closed his letter with, *"this is a wonderful journey"*. As an indication of just how high his spirits were, Bill included a letter for the Committee as a whole:

> *"It is my pleasure through the chairman of the sanctuary committee Mr and Mrs Atkinson to convey to the Forest Commission Victoria my heart felt thanks for their wonderful co-operation in loading my motor truck with the works. The packing of these*

---

1 Theosophical University Press, Altadena, California.
2 This friend was Vijayadev Yogendra, who is introduced more fully in the next chapter.

works was done very well and the calm seas on this journey means a safe passage for this truck and contents.

In a very wide appreciation I remain your ever ready friend and servant ..."

The *Australian Isle* docked in Veracruz where Bill opted not to fly to Mexico City for a visit and maybe a pretty senorita to take home. From Veracruz across the Gulf of Mexico, into the Atlantic Ocean and up the east coast to their first US port of call, Charleston, South Carolina, where they docked on August 19th. Another 1,100 km voyage to the north and the *Australian Isle* docked in Port Newark. Bill had reached his destination.

On August 22nd the truck and sculptures were unloaded, and the dream took a sour turn. The Customs officials questioned whether all of Bill's works would be re-exported. Bill innocently explained that all of the major works would definitely be re-exported, but if he could sell some of the smaller pieces along the way, which he'd brought to help cover expenses, all well and good. Not so, thought the Customs people. There would be duty payable on any work that was sold, and since Bill could not say which works would be sold, a Customs bond would have to be put up on the whole exhibition, which was estimated to be valued at US$7,180. Although he told the Customs people that he had only A$700, Bill in fact had a total of A$1,200 with him, which converted to approximately US$600, making it impossible for him to pay any Bond. It should be said that even if Bill did have sufficient money, it's unlikely that he would have paid any bond on principle. He had come to give the Americans a great gift of realisation—and there was no way that he should have to pay *them* to accept it.

Bill told the Customs that he was as good as a representative of the Australian Government, explaining how his Sanctuary had been taken over and was being fully funded by the Victorian State Government. In an attempt to sort out the problem, Customs officials contacted the Australian Consul-General, Sir Reginald Sholl, asking if he was prepared to give a Federal Government guarantee of a Customs bond. Sir Reginald, who had heard nothing about Bill since Jeanne Miles had contacted him months before, was at a loss. He had to tell them that he had no authority to guarantee a bond, and he could not certify that the exhibition was Government property sent for public exhibition in the US. The result was that Customs impounded the truck and sculptures until the matter could be sorted out, charging a storage fee which, fortunately for Bill, Farrell Lines paid.

Bill's next blow came when he realised that there was nobody there to welcome him in New York. Nor were there any planned exhibitions to launch him on his grand tour.

Alone in a city more dense than he had ever dreamed possible, Bill took a room in the Carteret Hotel on West 23rd Street. He recalled that even in the little room of his own, for which he paid US$10 per night, he could not escape an intense feeling of claustrophobia. He told me of one night when he woke up desperately afraid that the building and city were going to come crashing down on him. He had to fight to get his mind to think of something better, his forest home thousands of kilometres away, before he could go back to sleep. By day he walked to his only sympathetic acquaintances at the offices of Farrell Lines in Whitehall Street. There he would pick up any mail waiting for him, and talk about what he must do in the US.

Then back out onto the streets where he got *"lost in a damned jungle of concrete—up to the sky"*. He could not believe that concrete, steel girders, rivets and bolts could be turned into such a monster. Far from being the Big Apple, New York became his private nightmare.

One day he called into a bar: *"I wanted to have a drink of brandy—a little wine mixed in— I felt cold."* Bill remembered the bar as a dark place with small lights, and, even then, only half the lights were turned on. He waited at the counter in the gloom, and waited—and waited. Maybe the bar-keeper didn't see him, but that's unlikely. Maybe Bill, dressed strangely in green from his beret to his cloth shoes, looked like a person who wouldn't have had the price of a drink in his pocket. Whatever the case, Bill did not speak up. He turned and went back onto the streets.

The next letter the Atkinsons received was written one week after Bill had landed in New York:

> *"This time I write from a big noisy and not so nice place.*
>
> *This is a monster of a place, just a lot of people adding up figures. I will be terribly glad to get out of this into a more American place. I will go to Washington on Monday to see someone in the Dept of State to see if my first showing of works can be in Washington. I am told it's a lovely place of history ...*
>
> *Every now and then a motor goes screaming through followed by an ambulance or something else so it is not so nice ...*
>
> *I miss the fragrance of my lovely bush so you know I will get back as soon as possible. However you know I and those killers in Australia can not exist alongside one another. One of the two must go and so long as I can stand up to this and my success comes in the right way I will stand over them and tell the Prime Minister what I intend to do. That would have to be done.*
>
> *My venture here in the USA must be done very smooth calm and not to reveal to America just what I intend to do. The only aspect I will tell them is this:*
>
> *'It is through the spiritual life expressed in these works that I am endeavouring to impart to you the approximation of the ultimate in Human's true place in Wild Life conservation in Australia. What I hope to achieve from this venture is a Holy Mountain or <u>Mountain of Remembrance</u> set in a wilderness area in Australia where the best minds of our conservationists in Australia and the world can be brought to bear on the most urgent quest of our time.'*
>
> *So long as I can succeed in USA then I can proceed to my task and tell those killers ... that if they are not stopped then I shall make myself a historical figure, in short I am saying they will be thrown out ...*
>
> *My powerful <u>love</u> informs me to do all that I have said to you and how people could help if they could send money to help start up my venture without leaving it all to me. My task alone is very heavy ..."*

Bill took himself to Washington, visiting the Department of State and the Smithsonian Institute, but he was seeking the impossible in wanting an exhibition to be organised at short notice. The night of Tuesday, August 30th, was spent in room 731 of the Hotel Washington; a luxury which relieved him of another US$14.30. Three days later he was in Canada, his passport stamp bearing the location, Blackpool. Bill later wrote to the Atkinsons that he had been to Montreal, but did not mention why he went up there. If it was to organise an exhibition, he was unsuccessful.

Back in New York Bill continued to attempt to solve his predicament. He finally found his way to Sir Reginald's offices, but found no joy there. Sir Reginald explained that he had not the funds, personnel nor authority to take on such a task as organising exhibitions or a tour. Bill suggested an exhibition in Central Park, into which he'd wandered and which he thought would be suitable. Sir Reginald contacted the Commissioner of Parks, only to be told that owing to the threat of vandalism, as well as the high competition among artists, the general policy was against exhibitions. Sir Reginald would explain all of this to Lindsay Thompson in a letter dated September 22nd. He also expressed a willingness to help, for he personally knew Bill's work and felt that it would be well received in the US, but in reality his hands were tied. Sir Reginald observed that: *"[Bill] is a difficult man in some ways to deal with, and completely unpractical. When last I saw him he was threatening to depart for India."*

In the offices of Farrell Lines the staff were doing their best to work out what they could do to help Bill. Mr Lewis, one of the heads of the New York office, had also been to see Sir Reginald, only to be told that they may have done a disservice to Bill by bringing him to the

US when there was nothing arranged. Somebody in the office came up with the idea of putting the *New York Times* onto the job, which saw Bill being interviewed by journalist, Richard Shepard. The result was an article titled, "Sculptor Brings Word From The Bush", which appeared in the September 11th edition of the widely read newspaper. The photograph illustrating the article showed Bill standing in front of a series of photographs depicting his work. Somehow the photographer had even persuaded Bill to take off his beret.

The article opened by telling readers: ***"Four and a half tons of sculpture in a three-ton truck, all from Australia, is sitting on a Port Newark pier waiting to go somewhere, anywhere, and be seen."*** It did not mention that the truck and works remained impounded by Customs, who were still waiting for the bond to be paid. Bill had explained away his predicament as being the result of a simple misunderstanding, which saw him interpret an ***"expression of interest"*** as an invitation. ***"I am not dismayed"***, he was quoted as saying: ***"I am not the artist coming here to sell. None of these large pieces are for sale, just some of the little ones."*** The article presented Bill as a conservationist, come to America with a pure message of conservation: ***"I want to show how close a man can get to his environment."***

Over 1,000 km to the south-west, in Knoxville, Tennessee, Rino Petrini read the article with interest. Petrini, an expatriate Australian, had visited Bill's Sanctuary many times when living in his home-town, Melbourne. The next morning he burst into the office of his employer, Bill Lacy, Dean of the University of Tennessee's New School of Architecture. He told Lacy that a golden opportunity was there for the taking—the premier US exhibition of Brother Billy Ricketts' sculpture, there in Knoxville. Lacy had never heard of Bill, but he recalled that he ***"became very excited by the prospect without truly understanding why"***. Petrini was given permission to invite Bill to Tennessee under the School of Architecture's sponsorship. He wasted no time in telephoning Bill at his hotel with the news.

Even after what he described as ***"a very good article ... in the New York Times"*** which aroused considerable interest in addition to Petrini's telephone call offering an all expenses paid exhibition in Knoxville, Bill could not be happy. He wrote to the Atkinsons on September 16th with news that, ***"for the time being everything has fallen through"***. His worry was money, and he wrote that he would contact John Hetherington with a request that an appeal be launched for public donations to fund his US venture. Bill wrote of an interview he'd taped "yesterday" with the "Australian Broadcasting Commission", during which Bill read a prepared statement similar to the one he'd sent back to the Atkinsons in his previous letter.[3] As far as he was concerned, he was promoting the cause of conservation ***"single handed"***, so it was not unreasonable to expect the people who would benefit from his fight to help fund his way. Bill remained confident that ***"once my first showing of these works is done then it will proceed"***. On top of it all, Bill was homesick: ***"Autumn is now starting here, but how I miss my bush."***

Once it was confirmed that the School of Architecture would sponsor Bill's exhibition, Sir Reginald was contacted and asked to negotiate the release of Bill's truck and works from the Customs. It was not recorded in the letters or documents I saw as to how he achieved this, or under what authority, or if a bond was paid, but by September 20th the truck and works had been released.

After Bill flew to Knoxville on September 21st, things took a definite turn for the better. He stayed with Petrini, who lived on the Alcoa Highway, some 8 km out of the city. Petrini's was one of three houses set on a large bush property overlooking the Tennessee River. After the crush of New York, Bill at last had the breathing space he so desperately needed. Bill was taken on a trip to the Great Smoky Mountains National Park; over 207,000 ha of wilderness in the Appalachian Mountains which straddle the border of Tennessee and North Carolina. The drive took him through forested mountains rising to 2,205 m, across clear streams and down to the

---

3 It is not known if this interview went to air in Australia; or indeed, if it was the American Broadcasting Corporation [also ABC] which interviewed him.

town of Cherokee, located in the Cherokee Indian Reservation. During the day Bill was promised by a Ranger that when next he came, he would be *"taken deeper by track into untrodden parts to see the big black bears"* which survive within the sanctuary of the Park. Bill was revitalised by the greenness of Tennessee and he had regained his stature so much that when Dean Bill Lacy met him, the image which remained in his memory was that of *"an elderly Green Beret"*.

The School of Architecture secured exhibition space and co-sponsorship at Knoxville's Dulin Art Gallery, with the show planned to run between October 5th and 23rd. A problem arose in getting Bill's works to Knoxville. Bill would write to the Atkinsons that his truck was too overloaded to negotiate the mountains which would be encountered en route. Of course, he may have been reluctant to undertake the drive because he was terrified by the prospect. It was one thing to drive up to Alice Springs on a rough, but deserted, road.

The thought of taking on New York's traffic, followed by 1,000 km of towns and cities, all on the wrong side of the road, might just have been too much for Bill to contemplate. It ended up that Bill further depleted his funds by contracting the Acme Van Company to transport a selection of the works he'd taken over, leaving the truck and the majority of the works in storage in New York.

Publicity for the show began in the Knoxville *News-Sentinel* on September 22nd, with Bill being reported as *"Australia's leading sculptor"* and the people of Knoxville informed that they were privileged with the first show of Bill's international tour. An update article appeared in the *New York Times* on September 28th which overviewed their previous article. It mentioned Petrini's and the New School of Architecture's involvement and gave the location and dates of the show. Additional local promotion included specially printed invitation cards touting Bill as the *"Foremost Sculptor of Australia"*, news releases and an active word-of-mouth campaign.

The activity did not stop in Knoxville. A small band of people were attempting to solicit support and sponsorship for Bill in other parts of the USA: people such as Fae Hinkley from Portland, Oregon, who was busy sending letters of introduction all around Oregon and California. Others were attempting to interest organisations such as the National Broadcasting Company to consider making television shows and short documentaries about Bill. It all combined to set in motion a small ground swell of support, but one which appeared to be gaining momentum.

On October 3rd Bill wrote confidently to the Atkinsons:

"Just a short note to say my event (Australia's event) is to start up this Wednesday.
I have just been told that the Ports Authority of America will stage my works in the very building of the La Guardia Airport, 15 miles out from New York.[4] This is lovely with a huge water fountain in front.
So it now seems that I shall proceed onwards after such a rough start off. Many good people are close to me here so you need not be alarmed as to my well being.
I should come out right as regards money, success means that all that will be taken care of."

On the day of the Opening, October 5th, the Knoxville *News-Sentinel* published an article heralding the show. This time Bill was presented as a *"sculptor and crusader ... an intense conservationist ... seeking to communicate through his sculpture the Australian Aborigines' primitive beauty and love of country ..."*

Bill's doubts were openly expressed, quoting his statement:

---

4 I did not sight any official confirmation of this exhibition booking, nor any correspondence from the American Ports Authority.

"I have been told that Americans are good-living but materialistic people, but I have to make up my own mind. The Americans who visited my sanctuary in Australia said the finest and most understanding things about what they felt there. I feel quite sure that I will not find the people here so materialistic."

As to why he concentrated on Australian Aborigines to express his ideals, Bill was quoted:

"They're not primitive, just materially backward; the white man is materially progressive, but spiritually backward. The Aborigines have a complete sophistication about spiritual things."

While the *News-Sentinel* reported that Bill had brought *"five and a half tons"* of his sculpture to town, they also wrote that only Bill's "original" works would be shown. This is supported by the few photographs I saw of the exhibition which featured, principally, original heads from his Centralian journeys, and not the reported nine newly created major works.

The show opened at the Dulin Gallery to an invitation-only audience. Exactly what went on has proved to be yet another mystery. Bill's version of events was never any more than brief, but it was invariably filled with revulsion and disgust:

"It was a booze party. The night came when the opening was supposed to be [and] the place was in a stupor of drunken orgy when I got there. The night opened— [he leaned over and imitated someone vomiting]—*women and all, spewing their hearts up."*

Bill would then say that instead of addressing the gathering and presenting his prepared speech, he opted to stay on the footpath chatting to passers-by. Bill's version of events was not, however, supported by other accounts.

Bill Lacy recalled that the show opened *"to an enthusiastic, if provincial, audience"*. He did not mention a wild party or that Bill failed to be present at the Opening. Rino Petrini referred to the show as *"a great success"* and an *"extreme success"* in his letters to other possible exhibition venues and the Immigration Department. At some point during the first week of the exhibition Bill presented Lacy with a small work as a thank you, which suggests that Bill was not displeased. It was not until October 17th that the first proof that things were going wrong surfaced, and that was in a letter to the Atkinsons:

"I've just sent a letter to say I had reached the end. My event seems to inform you and other good Australians that this materialistic world does not want to see or listen to such a message I brought. That is an ugly prospect for all good people and all life.

I now ask you Dorothy. Please do not mention a word to anyone what has happened. I will return on the first ship leave my truck with some friends here and send for it when I have the money to pay for it. If people ask just simply say I did what I wanted to do and am now satisfied.

Do not even mention this to Jim Westcott. I will write next week to say if I will return straight away or if something has happened."

It is unlikely that Bill shared his distress with Rino Petrini, for the day after Bill wrote the above letter, Petrini wrote to the Immigration Department requesting that Bill's visa be extended. Petrini stated in that letter that Bill was *"due to show his work in Oakridge, Tennessee; New York, New York; and Portland, Oregon"*, adding that he could provide evidence to support his claims. This may have been wishful thinking, speculating that evidence would be available by the time Immigration requested it. The day after, on the 19th, Bill wrote a letter to the Atkinsons which leaves no doubt as to the degree of his distress:

> *"I have reached the end—my money is gone and if America can not give my mission a chance then I have to get back home.*
>
> *Can you send what Jim Westcott has of my £4 a week allowance and if you have any money from small works sold. Can you send this straight away.*
>
> *Australia has looked on while I set out to do the most important work to save what is left in Australia of Wild Life. I cannot ask the shipping company to take my truck back for nothing so it will just have to be all abandoned. My truck is in New York 800 miles from here. The works were brought here by trailer at high cost and now I have to get them back again.*
>
> *If you can sell that Namatjira painting for 150 dollars let it go. A lot of pocket money went in bad handling. For instance 200 dollars was thrown away in wrong handling of my works. I hurt my arm and had to go to hospital for two days and so my money is gone. Do not worry, just send what is possible.*
>
> *If John Hetherington asked through the press for about two thousand of my friends to give one dollar each, then Australia may do the rest.*
>
> *There are many good people here thinking and working for that which I stand. My works showing finish this Sunday week that is the 23rd and if the airport request from them has fallen through then I shall have to return.*
>
> *In that case I shall have to ask through John Hetherington for some friends to lend me 2,000 dollars to get me and my truck back.*
>
> *I cannot borrow on that forest sanctuary any more so I now have to ask.*
>
> *If nothing comes my way by next Sunday 23rd then I must get these works back to New York where my truck is then get back somehow to Australia. Australia has looked on and left it all to me ..."*

There was no mention of the rudeness of a drunken party as being the source of his discontent, just the strong suggestion that the people of Knoxville were not picking up his dream and taking it to their hearts. After two months in the USA, the majority of which was spent in a cloud of uncertainty, Bill had reached a point where his dreaming was not enough to carry him through. He needed to be bailed out, and in his frustration he was laying blame everywhere for the tour's failure.

There were, possibly, other contributing factors to Bill's failure.

The USA was then a country at war. America's involvement in Vietnam had by that time cost the lives of more than 5,000 US Service personnel; the number of dead then rising by almost 100 per week. Just under 20,000 Americans had been wounded in Vietnam in the first nine months of 1966 alone. But the war did not stay in Vietnam. On September 22nd, in the same edition that first told of Bill's coming to town, the Knoxville *News-Sentinel* published a photograph of two *"armed vigilantes"* checking out a *"suspicious"* car in Clyde, California. The caption read, *"Private Protection"*. The car was "suspicious" because it was thought to contain anti-war activists. The paper did not criticise nor even question the fact that armed vigilante groups were operating against protesters.

Throughout the United States citizens were being forced to make decisions on whether or not it was right to become involved in a remote war which was costing lives. By the *News-Sentinel's* standards, it was clearly un-American if they thought it was not right. On an environmental note, citizens were being told that US Forces were attempting to defoliate huge swathes of the demilitarised zone between North and South Vietnam in an attempt to expose Viet Cong supply lines. Americans simply had to accept it as a fact of war.

Into that rarefied social atmosphere came a disorganised old man advocating peace, love and harmony. He was not so much talking about the war, but his ideals were not dissimilar to those of the "un-American freaks" who were being sought out by groups of armed vigilantes. That same old man even suggested that the white people of the country that God was being constantly asked to bless were the spiritual inferiors to a mob of stone-age Aborigines from Australia! Is it really that surprising that Bill was not raised high on American shoulders and loved as a man of vision?

Then there were the separate but similar comments of three US citizens with whom I spoke about the failure of Bill's US journey. When they found out that Bill's one and only exhibition venue was in Tennessee, all three nodded a knowing nod and claimed that they were not surprised—their simple reasoning best summed up by, *"Well, that <u>was</u> the South"*.

We can only guess at what the outcome might have been if Bill had first been introduced to the un-American protesters who were themselves riding the 1960s' rising wave of "peace, love and harmony".

Bill had the Acme Van Company transport him and his works back to Port Newark, where he set about trying to organise a trip home. The pressure became too great, though, and Bill remembered the advice of Ms Rojo—he could be home in two days by air, and home was where he desperately wanted to be. On the morning of October 31st, Bill telephoned Lou Atkinson to ask for money to be sent over to pay for his air fare home. As a measure of Bill's desperation, he asked Lou to pass his request through to the Minister of Forests. Lou told Bill to sit tight and he would do what he could. A week passed before Bill telephoned Mr Bakacs with a request for $400 to make up the air fare home. Bakacs contacted the Commission with the news and informed them that he would personally pay half of Bill's return fare if the Commission came up with the other half. It took a further two days for the Commission to agree, by which time Bakacs was attempting to organise passage for Bill and his goods on a Maston Line vessel. That booking could not be confirmed for a further two days.

On November 8th, two days after Bill had phoned Bakacs, Dorothy Atkinson received a call from Bill at approximately 6.00 a.m. He told her that he wanted to come home, and he wanted to come home the next day—would she get him home? Dorothy was unaware of any other arrangements being made, but promised Bill that she would arrange it somehow. He would have to wait just a little longer, though. She promised him that by the end of the day she would write an air-mail letter to him with news of how he would be brought home. He just had to sit tight for a few more days.

As soon as businesses opened, Dorothy was on the telephone trying to make the arrangements. She recalled that she spent the best part of the day ringing around, desperately trying to get Bill home. Finally she got back to Farrell Lines. She recalled: *"They said, 'You want a miracle!', and I told them that I thought they could have a little miracle for William, surely?"* In the end they relented, giving her the date that Bill and his truck and works could be picked up at Port Newark for passage to Australia free of charge. Dorothy sat down and wrote Bill his air-mail letter, giving him all the information that she was sure would make him one happy man. She posted the letter in the afternoon and slept soundly that night, confident that she had done very well indeed.

It's not too hard to imagine how Dorothy and Lou must have felt when a telegram came the next day which stated: *"Bill Ricketts flying home this afternoon will arrive Melbourne Friday morning Nov 11th. B Rogan."* Bernice Rogan was, according to Bill, the manager of Acme Van Company, and she had apparently taken Bill under her wing to a large degree while he was in the States. This included giving him credit on the transport and storage of his truck and sculptures, as well as loaning him the money he needed to fly back to Australia, including a taxi fare, a helicopter fare to the airport, and $30 "pocket money".

When I spoke to him about the incident, Bill had no recollection of the trouble and disruption he caused by flying back as he did. He landed in Sydney on November 11th and telephoned Dorothy to tell her what time he would be arriving at Essendon Airport that afternoon. Dorothy organised a lift to the airport, but on arriving and checking the passenger list of the plane Bill was supposed to be on, she could not find his name anywhere. She waited for the plane to arrive, but still no Bill. She did not know what to do, so she waited, confused and worried. Presently a light plane taxied up and out jumped the sole passenger, a little man with a green beret. *"He came over with his arms out"*, Dorothy recalled: *"He was safe again."* She did not even worry him with queries about how he came to be on a plane of his own. Sometimes it was best just to accept events as far as Bill was concerned.

Of course, the saga of the US venture did not end until Bill's debts were cleared and the truck and works came back to Australia. The full details would require another half a chapter to relate, and while there are points of interest, it is basically a tale of bureaucratic dealings.

Complications arose firstly because of Bill's desire to return to the States after more solid arrangements were made for him by a number of American supporters who were keen to see him tour. When that fizzled out, Bill wanted to take off for the rest of his world tour from the States, his reasoning being that the truck and works were already in the northern hemisphere. That plan, too, died of natural causes. Then a sticky problem arose when it was realised that Bill had sold or given away some ten works of varying sizes. That brought the US Customs into the fray. The frustration sometimes showed, as in Sir Reginald Sholl's letter to Commission Chairman, A. Lawrence, dated January 30th, 1967:

> *"... let me assure you that I am personally concerned at the effect on the good opinion which Americans have of Australians by Mr Ricketts' thoroughly unbusinesslike handling of his affairs and the unpaid debts which he owes ...*
> *... my personal view is that it has been a most unfortunate affair for all concerned. Ricketts gained some favourable notoriety for his work, but the whole visit lacked organisation and business direction. Anything you can do to terminate the thoroughly unsatisfactory present position will be a good thing for Australia and Victoria."*

Finally, though, after almost one year of very patient work by the Advisory Committee, the Forests Commission and Sir Reginald in New York, Farrell Lines brought the truck and works back to Australia, free of charge, aboard the *Australian Surf*. The last hiccup was the works being held in bond by Australian Customs in Sydney. After that was cleared up, the *African Moon* brought the works on their last leg home to Melbourne in late October, 1967.

20 | Planning the Crusade No. 2
[late 1966–1970]

The story that Bill brought home to Australia was a little less than accurate, for reasons he kept to himself. Bill's account became public via an article published in the *Age* on November 30th, 1966. Titled, "Home—With A Deep Breath", Bill was first quoted as saying, ***"Life is once more an ecstasy"***. Whether it was due to misquoting or misinformation, Bill was reported as having personally driven his truck to the University of Tennessee where: ***"At the front porch I realised they were making a guzzle party of it inside, so I pocketed my eight-page speech and went away and talked to some passers by."*** Bill was then reported to have decided to fly home. The article finished with: ***"He has an invitation to visit the Yoga Faith Centre near Bombay—when he recoups his fortunes."***

While a return to the US was in Bill's mind, his principal desire became a tour of India. Money, or a lack of it, had been his chief worry in the United States. It was possible that he could have weathered his personal storm of uncertainty had he been well cashed up. It was the constant threat of completely running out of funds that caused Bill to panic and head for home. His trip to India would not suffer the same fate. No matter what, Bill would be sure that he had what he considered to be ample funds before setting off again.

He did not have to wait long before his latest ally for a tour of India sent promising news. Vijayadev Yogendra, an Indian-born man, was at that time the Principal of an establishment called the Yoga Education Centre in Melbourne. It would appear that he had known Bill for less than a year, but Vijay [as he is known] had quickly recognised Bill as one worthy of his respect. Shortly after meeting Bill at the Sanctuary, Vijay published in the *Yoga Pracharak: Bulletin of the Yoga Education Centre*,[1] that the theme which Bill expressed: ***"represented a basic and intrinsic cardinal principle in Yoga governing the fundamentals of Yoga behaviour. 'The love for life', that is the love for living and sustaining carrying, respecting and upholding life, this was the main theme of our discussion with Mr Ricketts. We could not agree with him more when he suggested that our children should have this love, respect and care for life …"*** On learning of Bill's desire to tour India with his works and philosophy, Vijay became an active supporter of the idea.

When Bill's return from the USA became public knowledge, Vijay wrote of his latest achievement during Bill's absence: ***"I had a meeting with the High Commissioner of India and I have already introduced your work to him and I am sure he must have sent a note to the Government of India."*** Such news, although indefinite, would have fuelled Bill's fervour immensely.

The two major changes awaiting Bill at the Sanctuary were a gatehouse under construction and the appointment of a permanent warden. Jim Westcott had been actively trying to find the right person to be based full-time at the Sanctuary, but Bill's idiosyncrasies had proved to be an obstacle. Westcott recalled:

---

1 Volume II, April, 66/9.

"I tried sending different chaps up there to look after the place. After a week or two they'd say, 'Oh cripes boss, I can't stand that place—take us out of there for goodness sake!' I'd say all right, and pick another one. Up he'd go and the same thing would happen. After I'd made about four or five false starts with others, I sent in Ron Olver. He took to it like a fish to water—took to the whole thing. Most importantly, Billy took to him."

Olver had been with the Commission for only five years or so, having progressed to the point of being the leading hand for one of the Olinda gangs. He would end up occupying the position of Sanctuary warden for almost twenty years, until he retired, and somehow avoided the "burn-out" usually experienced by those closely associated with Bill over a long period. Olver recalled:

"I never knew of William Ricketts until 1964. Before that I never knew that he even existed. At that stage all the forestry boys just called him the madman. We'd have to go up there and do work—you'd look up and Bill would be standing behind a tree, just looking at you, what you were doing, and this sort of caper. A lot of them just refused to even go up there and work up in the place, 'Don't want that bloody crap-artist bastard looking at us'.

I worked pretty good with him, more or less. We got on very good together, the whole time. We had our little differences and that—he'd say he wanted it done somehow, and I'd say, 'All right, if you want it done that way, well you do it your bloody self—I'm having nothing to do with it, you do it'. He'd go away and come back, 'All right Ron, you do it your way', so we'd get along that way. To stand and argue with Bill was no good, he'd reckon you were against him. But he'd come round and see the folly in his ways, and everything would go all right."

It was probably that gruff, no-nonsense approach with Bill that saw Olver through. Olver largely avoided frustration by simply not involving himself in what he considered to be fruitless projects. But he could not insulate himself completely. On the one occasion that Olver consented to be interviewed for this book, he made it clear that his full recollections of his times with Bill would not be made public while Bill was alive. His explanation for why he did not want to contribute fully to this authorised biography was:

"If he's still alive and it was published and somebody come up to him and started quoting back things to him, and he starts carrying on—I don't want him to think that I told all these tales on him!"

The irony is that Bill survived Olver by several years.

Rather than begin organising details of his tour with the Indian Government, Bill first concentrated on raising the funds to pay for it. He had only two avenues of approach—donations and the sale of works. While remaining ever-hopeful of large donations, Bill knew that to be sure he had better start his own funds coming in. He envisaged raising the bulk of his money through the sale of small works and saw no reason why he should not use the two new assets available to him—Ron Olver and the soon-to-be-completed gatehouse. Whether Bill or Olver took the proposal to the Committee is not recorded, but the Committee's response, as recorded in the meeting Minutes for February 14th, 1967, is quite clear: *"The committee is unanimously agreed that it is absolutely against Mr Ricketts' idea of Commission employee Olver being employed in making hundreds of small moulded heads for sale at the gatehouse."* Bill dropped the idea of a production line, but went ahead on his own, producing the small moulded works by the hundreds, often telling buyers that they were contributing to his holy mission to India with their purchase.

The sale of these works would prove to be another sore point in Olver's memory. Olver was of the opinion that Bill was selling too cheaply and offered to price the works and have them sold from the gatehouse, where Olver's wife was eventually employed. Bill agreed, although he quite often thought that the prices which Olver put on the works were too high. Olver constantly had to tell Bill that he was undervaluing himself by putting low prices on the works, although he could never quite convince Bill of the fact. The crunch came one day when two visitors enquired at the gatehouse about the prices of the works on display there. When told, one said to the other that they should go up and see Bill. Shortly after they returned down the hill with a newly acquired work which they proudly showed off as they departed. Olver recalled:

> *"I went up to Bill and says you just sold a piece to those blokes who've just gone out. 'Oh yes, he was a friend.' I said, 'He was no friend—you didn't even know him. What price did you charge him?' He looked at me with that sheepish look he gets, told me the price, and I said, 'Right Bill, from now on you sell your own works—you're not making a fool of me. People think I'm making money out of it, or the Commission. Count me out.' "*

The works continued to be sold through the gatehouse, but at Bill's much reduced prices.

There were also new major works to be conceived for the tour and to this end Bill contacted Strehlow with a request for copies of photographs depicting male Aboriginal elders which Strehlow had taken on his earliest official expeditions to the outback regions west and south-west of Alice Springs in the mid to late 1930s. The images of those old men would be used in some of the new conceptions, with Bill no doubt thinking that such "pre-contact" Aborigines would add a purity and power to his works. Strehlow obliged with eighteen black and white reprints early in 1967.

Of major concern to Bill was that the Commission might stop him from taking any major works away to India. Of course, under the terms of the Agreement, the Commission could do nothing of the sort, but Bill would never believe it. Before he began work on the large pieces, he had to find out where he stood with the Government.

On March 9th, 1967, Bill wrote to inform Lindsay Thompson that for the next year he would be creating works to take on a tour of India. *"Indians here are preparing this for me"*, he wrote. Bill sought an assurance that neither the present nor any future Government would demand the return of those works while he was away. Bill threatened that if the Agreement allowed any Government to force him to return the works, then he would have to leave the country, explaining that *"Freedom spiritual is my quest"*. In another letter to Thompson of the same date, Bill explained that he would repay the Commission whatever money was involved in getting his works back from America, adding that *"I shall tell my American friends who are trying to organise all for me that I shall not return to the USA"*.

It is a wonder that somebody did not whisper into Bill's ear that there was nothing in the Agreement to stop him from taking new works overseas—but it is just as likely that if somebody did, it would not have filtered through—so convinced was he that the Government had ultimate control of his works. It's probable that only a letter of very careful explanation from a Minister or Premier would have changed Bill's mind, and that is precisely what Bill was asking for. It was a fact that the few who knew of the Agreement's wording were of the opinion that Bill was less likely to encounter difficulties if he remained in Australia. With the US experience still fresh in their minds, the opinion was that it was definitely in Bill's best interests to remain confused, in the hope that he would abandon the desire of an international crusade.

Thompson, fully aware of the terms of the Agreement, replied to Bill on March 29th. He wrote that before he could discuss the matter with his fellow Ministers, he would need more information. Thompson wanted to know the object of the tour; who was organising it, with copies of letters, invitations and so on required; whether the National Government or any State Governments in India had undertaken to arrange the tour and, if not, how would it be organised on a Governmental level; the proposed duration of the tour; what the estimated costs would be from Australia to Australia; and how Bill planned to raise the funds required.

Bill's answers to the questions, although spreading over three pages, were typically vague. The only solid piece of information given was Vijay's name and address. Thompson had the Commission Chairman write to Vijay on April 5th in an attempt to have his questions answered. After stating the Commission's fears regarding Bill's proposed tour, the Chairman requested of Vijay: *"… whether you have established contacts in India … whether you would be able to organise effectively a visit to India … and whether you are of the opinion that he should go to India at all at this stage."* I somehow doubt that Vijay's reply was exactly what the Commission and its Minister was looking for. Dated April 14th, it read:

> *"… I would like to state that efforts are being made to invite and receive [Bill] to India along with his work. As yet I have not heard from India.*
>
> *It is true that I have written to some well placed people in the political and cultural life in India, drawing their attention to the work of Mr Ricketts and his philosophy. I must add here that we are greatly impressed with Mr Ricketts' sincerity and devotion to his work. We feel that at this stage, when Australia is trying to promote greater understanding between herself and Asian countries as per the statement of Prime Minister Holt, a visit by some of its cultural messengers and fine minds could go a long way in promoting a healthier relationship between various countries. I am sure this would not be inconsistent with your own thinking.*
>
> *… Yours for greater cultural understanding.*
>
> *P.S. As Mr Ricketts' work and thought has [the] message of peace and goodwill—it leaves me wondering why no efforts are being made to sponsor his trip from here."*

If the Minister of Forests or a Commission official gave a written response to Bill's queries, I did not see it. Nor did I find any evidence suggesting that a written or verbal response was given. Again, it is just as likely that the Commission left Bill's queries unanswered in the hopes that he might change his plans due to the uncertainty.

Back in the USSR, Ivan Ivashko was doing his level best to spread the word of Billy and so prepare the Soviet people for a tour. Ivan had received many letters from readers of his articles requesting more information about Bill and the proposed tour. By the end of June 1967, Ivan had appeared three times on Odessa and Ukrainian television networks with stories about Bill. Ivan wrote: *"I am taking great pains in trying to acquaint the greatest number of Soviet people with your art, your deliberation in the struggle to uplift the standard of Australian Aborigines."* Ivan was also lobbying the Ministry of Culture of the USSR to support a tour by Bill, preferably during the period of the 50th Anniversary *"of our homeland"*.

Towards the end of 1967 Bill became aware that India's Prime Minister, Indira Gandhi, would be visiting Australia early in 1968. He saw the visit as a perfect opportunity to introduce his Sanctuary, work and philosophy to India's leader, and so set about trying to have it arranged that his Sanctuary be included on her itinerary. Bill initially asked Vijay to see what he could do, explaining that Indira Gandhi's father, Nehru, had once expressed support in a letter. [Bill was still referring to Verrier Elwin's letter to Mary Harris years before.] Vijay planned to put together a submission to send to the Indian High Commissioner in Canberra, to which end he asked Bill to supply copies of any relevant documents that would support the case. How Bill got around not producing the fabled Nehru letter, which Vijay specifically requested, I do not know. Vijay did pull off a coup, though, by personally taking the Indian High Commissioner, A. M. Thomas, and the Commissioner's wife up to meet Bill and experience the Sanctuary first hand. This is evidenced by a note of thanks from Thomas to Bill, dated October 24th, 1967. While the note did not mention Gandhi's forthcoming visit, Thomas was full of praise and expressed a readiness to spend more time with Bill when next he was in Melbourne.

Bill placed his request to host Indira Gandhi before his local Federal MP, who in turn passed the request through to the relevant people in Canberra, but it turned out that her visiting the Sanctuary could not be arranged. Bill did succeed in meeting Indira Gandhi during her tour and presenting her with one of his sculptures as a gift, but at the time of writing the details of the meeting were not known to me.

When the truck and works finally arrived back on the mountain from the USA, Bill had the disappointing experience of finding his vehicle in very poor order. There were various dents on almost every body panel, the canvas drop-sides had been badly ripped and the cabin lining had been torn, making it look like a wreck. The engine was not in running order, the battery had split in half, the front bumper bar had been torn off and thrown in the tray, and the track rod and drag link had been bent to such an extent that the vehicle was unsteerable. The tail-shaft, too, had somehow been bent so badly that it had to be removed before the truck could be towed up to Olinda. It was not a major worry for Bill, though. The three-ton Austin had proved to be inadequate in the US, so he had decided to get a larger capacity vehicle.

Bill was again featured in a Soviet newspaper early in 1968, the result of one of Bill's small works being exhibited in the Vladivostok Art Gallery. The piece had been presented to the Soviet scientist, Yuri Gorovoi, who met Bill during a visit to Melbourne by his ship, *The Lyre*, which was attached to the Pacific Ocean Scientific Institute of Fishing Industry and Oceanography. The small article was illustrated with a photograph of the Gallery's Director, Nina Ilchuk, holding the piece which depicted in relief the bust of a Centralian Aboriginal male.

In June, 1968, Bill received a letter which would have both overjoyed and dismayed him. Dated June 15th, it came from Miss Usha Bhagat, Social Secretary to Indira Gandhi. It acknowledged an earlier letter from Bill to the Prime Minister and went on to state: *"She was glad to meet you and thanks you for the sculpture you presented to her."* Bhagat mentioned another request made on Bill's behalf which had previously reached the Prime Minister, and wrote: *"On enquiries made here we learnt that it may be possible for the Indian Council for Cultural Relations [ICCR] to offer you hospitality for 2 or 3 weeks, if you come to India on your own ..."* Bill was then advised to contact the ICCR Secretary in New Delhi to make further arrangements.

Bill classed it as a direct invitation from Indira Gandhi herself, and for that he was overjoyed. But a visit of two or three weeks? How could he ever hope to spread his message throughout India in such a short time? Still, the initial obstacle was overcome. He had his invitation from India's leader, and the minor problem of the tour's duration could be overcome later. Bill wrote to the ICCR immediately, but their reply of July 29th was a bit ahead of his plans. They wanted dates so that arrangements could be made—and Bill was not ready to supply dates. When the ICCR had heard nothing by October 9th, they again wrote requesting the dates of Bill's tour. Bill replied that he was not ready, advising them that he planned to come over sometime in October the following year. The ICCR acknowledged the date and asked to be informed of a definite date well in advance.

Bill stepped up his fund-raising campaign by distributing his small works farther afield. One of the places he sold from was the Victorian Tourist Bureau in Melbourne. Such was the success of his initial trial there that a letter was sent by Mrs Orford to Bill requesting more. Orford had priced the works at $8.00, $12.00 and $25.00, depending on their size. She wrote: *"... I feel that we can sell many more of your works, so any time you have the time you may like to add a few more small children's studies to our display which is now so sadly depleted ..."*

The Advisory Committee meeting Minutes of October 15th, 1968, reveal that Bill was still fretting because of his uncertainty regarding the conditions of his Agreement. It was noted that he wanted the Agreement reworded to include a clause guaranteeing him the right to take his works out of the country unhindered. The Minutes also recorded: *"[Bill] has tried to get a visa stamped by the American US Consul, but this was refused. Neither the Chairman of the Forests Commission nor the Minister are prepared to assist him. The Indian Government will only look after him once he has arrived in India, but he will have to find his own fare, a new truck etc to get there."* If Bill was going to tour India, he would have do so without the assistance of the Advisory Committee or the State Government of Victoria.

With support seemingly guaranteed by the Indian Government, although not defined, Bill decided to up the ante and apply more pressure for another of his obsessions. By the beginning of 1969 the Commission had purchased the fern gully adjoining the Sanctuary, but only to a distance of some 20 m beyond the watercourse. However, Bill was still greatly upset by his neighbours' land management practices, mainly because of their clearing of undergrowth and use of chain saws. The chain saws' noise shattered the forest's peace and drove Bill to distraction—as did the regular incursions by roving domestic dogs, cats and adolescents who set rabbit traps and occasionally went shooting in the gully.

Bill had, back in April 1967, written to the Minister of Forests suggesting that the two neighbouring houses be purchased and then rented to Aboriginal families, reasoning that Aboriginal families would respect their surroundings. The Minister passed the suggestion on to the Aboriginal Welfare Board, but nothing ever came from it. Now Bill again took his problem, and his threat, to the papers.

The January 11th, 1969, edition of the *Age* carried an article by John Messer with a large headline proclaiming, "Ranges Sculptor Threatens To Leave 'Noisy' Gully". It was illustrated with a large photograph showing Bill standing defiantly, legs apart, arms hanging by his side in the attitude of a gunfighter from the wild west, strong hands ready to draw. He was not staring into the camera, but over and beyond it—not confronting the reader, but the world. The article covered Bill's distress over the noise coming across the gully, quoting him as having said: *"The gully is now ruined. The lyre birds do not wish to go there now, and I also shall not go there again."* Bill was reported as considering a move to a *"mountain nature reserve north of Sydney"* as well as planning to leave for India on October 1st. *"Mr Ricketts said that … the gully had been progressively wrecked by the noise from the neighbouring property and the development associated with it"*, Messer wrote. Readers learned that when Bill met India's best thinkers, *"he would tell them the truth about Australia"*. There was no mention of how Bill proposed that the noise problem be overcome. Apart from introducing the concept that noise pollution in the Mt Dandenong area was undesirable, it was not really clear as to what Bill hoped to achieve from the publicity.

Time was running out for Bill to make a decision on the major works he wanted to create for the tour. Apparently on the advice of unidentified but ill-informed friends, Bill acted. He wrote a long letter to the Committee Chairman, Lou Atkinson, in which his frustration and confusion over the whole matter of the works' ownership was painfully obvious. He opened his letter with: *"When I looked into the once beautiful forest gully my vision then 36 years ago was that the most beautiful thing in the world would be created here. One place on earth where no man, not even my self, would say this belongs to me or us."* The letter went on to explain how Bill had asked two Government Ministers to alter the Agreement's wording, although nothing had eventuated: *"They thought my spiritual life (God life) would be better as a puppet show—pull strings to have fun with."* Bill told Lou that he was paying for the cost of operating the kiln to *"protect the spiritual life in the works"*. He went on to say that the $8 allowance paid to him by the Government every week barely covered the cost of the food he provided the wild life. He complained about what he perceived to be the downfall of the area through development. He complained about the Government not buying the two houses across the gully. As things went, it was a pretty eloquent plea, for Bill.

I sighted no letter of response to Bill's demands, nor any suggestion that a response was made. It's pure speculation, but I suggest that Bill was verbally informed, if not promised, that he didn't have to worry because nobody would stand in his way regarding taking his works out of Australia. He was still not told exactly why he didn't have to worry.

Bill continued planning his tour with no apparent change of pace. He sought further advice from various people in Australia and overseas in an attempt to determine an itinerary. In May Bill received a letter from a friend, Mary Beasy, who had just completed an organised overland tour from Calcutta to England. As he read of her adventures, he realised that here was an opportunity of getting first-hand information of the conditions he would encounter in India. As he read on, Bill struck upon the idea of following her tracks through Pakistan and the Kyber Pass to Afghanistan, on through Iran and Turkey, turn right at the Black Sea and follow it around to Ivan in Odessa! What easier way than a cross country drive could there be of getting to Odessa? Bill wrote back to Mrs Beasy, requesting information on all she thought he should know. Her reply contained many notes of caution, warned of the bad roads and troubles encountered when crossing borders, and repeatedly asked if Bill would have a travelling companion—but nowhere did she advise him against the trip. She obviously knew Bill well enough to know that it would have been a waste of time. Not surprisingly, the idea never became a reality—but it was a good effort for a man nearly seventy-one years old to contemplate such a drive.

A letter from the ICCR dated June 13th, 1969, offers a hint of evidence that Bill had been granted an audience with the leader in exile of the Tibetan Buddhists, the Dalai Lama. Earlier correspondence from Florence Cockerill, who was associated with the organisation, World Union [with headquarters in Pondicherry, India], had hinted that an audience was in the process of being arranged. However, I failed to sight anything conclusive. Usha Razdan's June 13th letter from the ICCR stated that she was working out the costs of Bill taking his truck to Dharmasala, in the Himalayan foothills, the home of the Dalai Lama. Razdan also wrote, *"Letter from H. H. Dalai Lama is returned herewith"*. This clearly indicates that Bill was attempting to meet persons at the highest levels of religion and spiritual awareness in his quest to gain support for his fight in Australia.

Bill had repeatedly postponed his arrival in India, from October 1969, to November, but he finally felt confident enough to book his passage for some time in May 1970. He did so, then wrote to the ICCR on September 5th, 1969, informing them of his plans. For reasons not given the ICCR advised Bill to postpone his arrival until after October 1970, which he did.

Bill found himself in an awkward situation which was probably the result of his high volume marketing strategy to raise funds for the Indian tour. Somehow the ever-alert ears of the Taxation Department got wind of Bill's income-producing ventures. A quick check would have revealed that the name William Ricketts had not appeared on their desks for many years—possibly not since the early 1930s. An investigator was sent up to assess the situation. Dorothy Atkinson was over with Bill when what she recalled as a *"very official man with his hat and briefcase"* came in to the Sanctuary. Was it a sixth sense which warned Bill that something was amiss with this latest visitor? Dorothy recalled many years later:

> *"He went up to William and said, 'I suppose you sell a lot of sculptures here?' Behind this man were signs on old bits of cardboard—$25, $12—right behind him! 'Oh no,' says William, and I'm standing next to him thinking, 'You silly gonk!'— because there were signs everywhere! And William said, 'You wouldn't <u>believe</u> the trouble I have—sometimes I have to go right down to the gate with people just to <u>give away</u> these works after they've been kind to me.' "*

It was not long afterwards that Bill received a notice saying that the Taxation Department was owed $1,844, although how they would have arrived at the figure is anybody's guess—no records or receipts were anywhere to be found. Distraught, Bill went down to the Atkinsons with his tale of injustice. There he was, having given his all to the people of Australia, and the Government had the damnable bad manners to ask for money. Dorothy recalled that Bill was in *"a frightful state"* because, he told her, he didn't have the money to pay and was concerned with being sent to jail. [Of course, Bill had many times that amount salted away for the Indian trip, but that money was for a mission.] Lou contacted the Forests Commission to see if they could help— and they could not. Then he contacted the local Federal MP, John Jess, who somehow negotiated an incredible reduction to $750.

Bill still didn't like the idea of paying, but he was astute enough to recognise the difference between $1,844 and $750. He ended up contacting a South Australian couple who he knew to be keen collectors of his work. He told them of the abhorrent reason for his needing $750 and asked if they'd like to purchase a medium-sized work that he'd recently completed. They jumped at the offer, giving Bill their cheque for $750.[2] Forwarding money on to the Taxation Department must have slipped his mind.

The Advisory Committee were also busy doing a little plotting. Back in 1964 it had been reasoned that Bill could do with a separate studio in which to do his sculpting. The reason was simple enough—hundreds of kilograms of wet clay inside Bill's house was making a terrible mess. Bill had objected to the idea, not wanting to ruin another little bit of his forest for such a luxury. Over the intervening years Bill's house had suffered greatly because of his working habits, and the Committee planned to use his proposed period of absence productively by preparing a little homecoming surprise. The November 18th, 1969, Committee meeting Minutes record a passed motion to accept plans for the workshop, *"but no word of this should leak out before … Ricketts goes overseas"*.

Another prominent Indian to offer his support and respect to Bill was Guru Nitya Chaitanya Yati. The pair appear to have met in 1969 when Nitya was on lecture tour of Australia. Nitya had done much to organise matters for Bill once he'd landed in India, including arranging drivers and helpers, and had invited Bill to exhibit his works at a gathering called the World Conference For Peace Through Unitive Understanding, to be held near Ramanthali, Kerala State, in November, 1970. On December 26th, 1969, Nitya wrote to Bill from Kerala State with news that he was preparing three articles about Bill; one each in English, Hindi and Malayalam, to be published in the north, central and south of India. He did not write in which publications the stories would appear, only that his desire was for a wide coverage of the reading public. Nitya went on to write:

> *"After fixing your date of arrival in India kindly write to me. I have informed my friends in Bombay to provide for you whatever help you require. Jahangir Art Gallery is the right place for exhibition. My friends will look after all that … My love to you and the beloved lyre birds of your sanctuary. When I write this a honey-sucker mothering two babes is looking into my eyes with great assurance. The place it has found convenient to build its nest is my doorway. Every time I look at the bird I think of you."*

At some time during this period Bill went out and purchased a new truck; a green four-ton Austin. Ron Olver recalled that Bill tried unsuccessfully to get the required Heavy Vehicle licence so that he could legally drive it:

> *"Yeah, Bill had tried to get a licence to drive it, but they just knocked him back. Seventy-one or two [years old]. But he used to drive it round—in fact he was the only man I've ever seen drive from Olinda and turn up that driveway in one hit! Tearing round the corner and straight up the drive in that great big four-ton truck!"*

Mary Harris had been quietly campaigning for some time for the beautification of the Howie Reserve, which separated her home, Bundilla, from the River Torrens. She had

---

2 Those purchasers forget just how long it was, but years later their bank manager telephoned them asking what he should do with a grubby, mouldy cheque for $750 which had just turned up!

persuaded Bill to donate a major work for placement in the Reserve and received enthusiastic support from officers of the Corporation of the Town of Walkerville, the municipality in which her home and the Reserve were located. By the beginning of 1970 a base had been constructed to receive Bill's work, but it was not until March of that year that Bill drove his truck to Adelaide to set the piece in place.

It was, indeed, a major work; depicting the almost life-sized upper torso of a male Aboriginal Elder, as well as children's heads and possums moulded into the form to give the impression of the adult overseeing the future. Bill called it, "Pmaranuka: My Country".

The official unveiling of the work took place on March 31st, with the Mayor of Walkerville, E. C. Scales, conducting what was reported as "a short ceremony". It was a dream come true for the aging Mary Harris. It was her wish that Bundilla be preserved intact as a permanent sanctuary after her death.

The addition of Bill's work to Howie Reserve complemented the works already within the grounds of Bundilla, bolstering her hopes that Bundilla and the Reserve become one. Sadly, the Howie Reserve piece became another example of the futility of placing Bill's clay works in public. It survived intact until late 1984 or early 1985, when vandals took to the head and shoulders of the Elder with a blunt instrument, smashing it to pieces.

The remains were gathered up and transferred to the Council Works depot. Bill was contacted and asked if the work could be repaired, but he did not respond to the request. As far as Bill was concerned, "Pmaranuka" was finished. The Council eventually contracted Artlab Australia[3] in July, 1992, to conserve the work. Amber Rowe, Objects Conservator, took up the challenge and spent approximately fifty-nine hours on the conservation. Although large sections of the face, the left shoulder and shoulder blade, and the lower back were missing, Ms Rowe successfully located the twenty-seven surviving pieces into a special Araldite resin. The completed process, while not attempting to disguise the repairs, regained "Pmaranuka's" former glory. In late 1992, it was again unveiled to the people of Walkerville. Now, though, "Pmaranuka" resides safely within the walls of the Council Chambers, incorporated into a water feature for all to enjoy.

As well as the work for Howie Reserve, Bill took to Adelaide a small exhibition for showing at Bundilla. It consisted of some of the new works he had created for the Indian tour, as well as three short films about the Sanctuary which had been made over the years. These films were shown through Bill's newly acquired 16mm projector. It would appear that Bill used the journey to Adelaide as a dummy run to gauge how he would go in India. What he didn't bargain on was Mary's reaction to one of the new works.

Called, "The Brute", is was another clay manifestation of Bill's hatred and rage. It was the repetition of a theme which he'd been creating since at least 1934, but it was unequalled in its depiction of horror. It showed a big, heavily muscled white man holding a rifle in each powerful arm—arms which terminated in claws. One of the rifles was complete with a telescopic sight. [Bill had apparently tramped the streets of Melbourne looking for a firearms shop with sporting rifles in the window to make the extremely crude sketches from which to work.] This man's face was contorted in a frowning scowl, a cigarette butt protruding from his snarling lips. It was the very face of hatred. His hair was cut in a militaristic crew-cut style. On his head sat a three-tiered crown of large calibre bullets. From just below the "brute's" deep chest emerged tentacle-like protrusions which terminated in three-toed claws. This "brute" did not walk through the Australian bush on his irreverent killing spree—he slithered and clawed his way along. Around the "brute" was a tragic wasteland littered with the corpses of Aborigines, kangaroos, possums, koalas and lyrebirds.

Not content with this visual horror, Bill had prepared accompanying plaques into which was inscribed the "brute's" creed:

---

3 ARTLAB AUSTRALIA, 70 Kintore Avenue, Adelaide 5000.

I AM
As a nation
THE BRUTE IN AUSTRALIA
Two hundred years ago I landed here
And wrote the law of the land on
The end of a gun barrel and
Arsenic of poison
EVER SINCE
I have been shooting and looting
Raping burning and poisoning
Trapping birds and animals
Millions of koalas, possums
Lyre birds, everything the
Aboriginal people
Regard
As Sacred.

I AM
The one who
Collects tax blood money
From the sale and use
Of the so-called sporting gun.

I AM
The same one
Who starts all
Bush fires going.
I live by this
Indescribable cruelty
And I will have
More and more of
It every year.

I AM
Parasite and Destroyer
Paid much money to kill off
Australia's wild life and
Grab their environments.
I lead science and technology
And paid to regard nothing as sacred.
I hate and revolt against
The highest life and in my
Fury will trample tear or
Crucify any divine power
That has the presumption
To offer to make life
Pure and
Luminous.

Mary Harris was horrified by the "brute". She would not let Bill unload it into her yard, and reportedly did not even want the truck to be parked on her footpath while the "brute" was inside. Why, she pleaded, had Bill spent his precious energy on such a hateful, evil expression? Why didn't he concentrate on the beautiful images which had been proven to evoke love and respect?

Bill had to express his righteous hate and rage. It was a part of him. He knew this and accepted it. He even went as far as treasuring it, because without it he would never have sought to strive for bettering this country in which he lived, and which he loved. To know what was good and right, he had to know what was evil and wrong. And in knowing that evil, he had to occasionally let it out. The latest "brute" had been unleashed, and it carried a powerful message. Bill was quite prepared to let the "brute" take to India his interpretation of the state of Australia.

Bill returned to the Sanctuary and continued his planning, but his frustrations boiled over again on April 24th. Bill spoke with the *Age* journalist, John Larkin, on that day and had again expressed his dismay at the surrounding development and associated noise which was ruining the Sanctuary. He told Larkin that he would leave the mountain when he returned from India. Before he departed, though, he would give the people of Melbourne an opportunity of viewing the works destined for India. Larkin wrote in his "Briefing" column the next day that: *"The public will be able to see [the works] tomorrow week. Mr Ricketts said he thought he might say something to the people at 3 o'clock in the afternoon."* Unaware that Larkin's article would be published the next day, Bill wrote to Lou Atkinson on April 24th, beginning his letter with evidence that there had been a leak:

> *"It has come to my notice of a new building or workshop to be put in here.*
> *I want to now advise the committee that I will no longer be in need of such. I leave for India soon and I shall not return to this sanctuary. I will advise the press next week that I will not speak next Sunday, being the day for people to view these works.*
> *I shall not now speak because of the likelihood of a chain saw concert in the heart of this sanctuary … I will not take part in any talk to alter anything. I just want a little time left in peace."*

Things were not looking good for Bill's visit to the USSR. Ivan Ivashko had been suffering from poor health, principally due to recurring kidney problems. So ill was he that he could not manage to personally accompany Bill around his country. This apparently created problems. Also, Ivan was not able to get around to the various Government Departments to hurry up bureaucratic proceedings, resulting in, at best, desperately slow progress. In a letter dated May 19th, 1970, Ivan did have one major reason for joy, though. He had been visited by a group of Soviet sailors who had recently returned from a voyage which included Melbourne as one port of call. The sailors had been taken up to see Bill, and Bill had sent a present for Ivan back to Odessa with the men. Ivan was greatly moved to find the present to be a self-portrait by Bill—so much better than a mere photograph.

Bill also received another letter from Nitya in May. It began: *"My dear Guru William, May I address you so. You represent a love and kindliness that underlie the teachings of all Gurus …"* Such a greeting would surely have raised Bill's hopes for a successful Indian tour a hundredfold. At last he was associating with people who recognised him for the teacher that he thought he could be. Nitya informed Bill that he was writing to at least five centres to have them prepare for Bill's arrival with the exhibition. He also reaffirmed his efforts to ensure that Bill had a driver waiting in Bombay, as well as helpers to move the works *"to where ever you want to take them"*. Things were flowing smoothly.

Having been informed which works Bill would be bringing, and at last receiving a definite arrival date in Bombay, the ICCR wrote to Bill on July 18th to inform him that papers had been lodged with Indian Customs officials for final clearances. On July 31st the ICCR sent another letter stating that all they required to complete their formalities was a cost, insurance and freight value of the sculptures. Attached to that letter were copies of letters from the Office of the Chief Controller of Imports and Exports, the Department of Revenue and Insurance and the Ministry of Commerce and Industry. Each of these letters set out what conditions the ICCR and Bill would have to abide by for the duration of Bill's tour. It boiled down to Bill being given a maximum of six months in India, with the ICCR having to take full responsibility that the works would be re-exported before the six months expired. To this end they had to put up bonds and pay insurances. Also, the truck and exhibits could only move around India to exhibitions sponsored by the ICCR—Bill was not to show his works anywhere else. The letters all made references to the truck as being included in the ICCR's responsibility, unless it was imported under a valid carnet de passage. Miss B. Banerjee, the author of this latest ICCR letter, had taken the trouble to underline every mention of the truck. Bill had been advised months before to take out a carnet de passage on his truck, but Miss Banerjee was still making sure that Bill was aware of his responsibility.

The truck was packed up and shipped off ahead of Bill. Ron Olver recalled that it looked like a travelling circus, with trestles and tables and planks tied to the sides and roof. Finally, on September 5th, 1970, at the age of almost seventy-two years, Bill boarded the Air India flight for his second journey away from Australia's shores. There was a stop in Singapore before his arrival at Bombay's Santa Cruz Airport at 2.00 a.m. on the morning of the 6th. As he'd been told to do, Bill took the Air India coach to the Bombay city terminus where an ICCR representative met him and took him to the ICCR's guest room. The adventure could begin.

21 | The India Tour
[1970–1972]

The Indian adventure started with Bill catching an influenza which knocked him to the point where he had to seek medical treatment. While in the grip of his illness, he was informed that as a result of some mishap, all of his trestles, stands and tables had been off-loaded "somewhere near Singapore", as he wrote to the Atkinsons. They would not be shipped on to Bombay until October 17th. As it turned out, those problems were secondary to the one which arose when the truck came to be cleared through Customs.

Bill had not followed the ICCR's direction to obtain a carnet de passage, reportedly valued at $10,000, from the Australian Automobile Association. The refundable carnet would have allowed him to import and later re-export the truck without attracting any Customs' duty in India. Bill had worked hard to accumulate enough money to see him through the trip, but he had not calculated on an extra $10,000. He didn't have it, so he couldn't pay it. Indian Customs officials, however, were diligent. If the truck was not covered by some sort of bond, it would not leave their yards. The ICCR was already putting up bonds and sureties to cover the works, not to mention paying out for insurance, exhibition space, accommodation and other sundry expenses associated with the tour. They did not see it as their responsibility to also cover the truck which they'd asked Bill to look after.

It slowly dawned on Bill that the regulations would not be overlooked, no matter how pure the intent of his travels in India. Stuck in a stalemate, he wrote to Nitya, whom he thought to be at the Gurukula Island Home in Kerala State, in an attempt to solicit help. The letter read, in part:

> *"I am stuck in Bombay with everything. My truck with all my work inside it is held by Customs. The Customs will not release the truck and have made charges and complications and it now seems hopeless for me to wait in India.*
>
> *I spent all my money to get here with my big truck (Rs. 85,000.00) [approx $11,333]. I have enough money for food and to pay my way along.*
>
> *Please can you ask the Prime Minister Mrs Gandhi to instruct the Customs to give me the truck so that I can show my work and the films to India. If nothing can be done then I must return home and send my truck back …"*

Bill then wrote home to the Atkinsons. While mentioning the problem with Customs, even speculating that if the problem could not be sorted out he may have to return home, the general tone of the letter was much less distressed than that which went to Nitya. Bill went on to relay his observations:

> *"Five million people here and it's colourful—everyone is dressed differently from the west. Sacred cows are led past you on the foot paths or they sit down there. These cows have lovely eyes and are such gentle creatures.*

This big city like all cities now with motor cars—it is not to my liking so I look forward to be out of it. There are all kinds or groups of people and they seem to get along somehow.

If all is straightened out for me then the next time or perhaps soon after I will write to you from an Indian forest with monkeys helping me to write to you but my heart is deeply in love with the Australian bush and what has been done to it breaks my heart ..."

Bill was confident that his problems would be sorted out, speculating that his first showing would be in New Delhi on October 25th. Bill planned to travel to New Delhi in "a week", where he hoped to sort out the Customs problems.

When Bill's letter reached Gurukula Island Home, Nitya was still overseas organising the forthcoming World Conference for Peace. The conference, at which Bill had been invited to exhibit, was to be held at Gurukula for ten days, beginning on November 11th, 1970. When the conference President, Dr Nataraja Guru, was given Bill's letter he wrote directly to Indira Gandhi. While Nataraja Guru knew only the details which Bill had included in his letter, most of which he repeated in his letter to Gandhi, he nonetheless made an eloquent plea for the Prime Minister to give her attention *"to the question of making it possible for Mr Ricketts to have no avoidable difficulties, so as to save him from the frustration which would seem otherwise to be a natural consequence".*

While this was going on Bill received an unexpected publicity boost throughout Australia. On Saturday, October 3rd, the *Australian* newspaper ran "The Brute of Australia" as a front page feature for all to see. A large photograph of the "Brute" was flanked by a slightly edited version of the "Brute's" creed. Adding enormously to the "Brute's" power was the *Australian*'s incorrect exaggeration that it was a *"four ton monolith"*! Awesome stuff.

Bill made his way to New Delhi where he continued to be accommodated in a guest room supplied by the ICCR. He attempted to see the Prime Minister personally, but, as he would later recall, *"she was too busy"*. As could be imagined, all of Bill's attempts to clear his way through the bureaucratic red tape failed. But that did not mean that he was having a rough time of things. The ICCR supplied Bill with a car and driver so that he could at least get about and see some of the things for which India is famous. In a letter to the Atkinsons dated October 18th, Bill told of a journey to Agra, some 185 km south of New Delhi. There he was "staggered" by the architecture of such places as Fort Akbar and the four and a half centuries old Taj Mahal: *"Indians and others just stare in wonder at all."* By the enthusiasm expressed in the letter, there is no doubt that there was one aged little Australian doing his share of staring as well. Of New Delhi, Bill's most enduring memory was of a trip to a zoo where he saw his one and only tiger—a huge, white Bengal tiger. Bill would have loved to have gone on an elephant safari into one of the National Parks where tigers could still be seen in the wild, but, as he told me: *"I sort of didn't have the money to splash here there and everywhere. I had to squeeze in."*

In the letter Bill expressed his wonder at the profuse evidence of history which he said was *"everywhere all over India"*. He went on effusively:

"In many parts you see small hills rise up from the road and there is the bare remains of an ancient city with stone doorways standing upright a few feet from the base ruins and monkeys living there. My host driver stopped the car for me to see the monkeys.

I think one of the monkeys was a communist for he was talking to the other monkeys on the eternal beauties of communism. This monkey had his behind facing me and I'm sure it was not the sunrise, but red enough for it to be."

The letter to the Atkinsons also contained an update on the state of affairs regarding the truck:

"My truck is to be released from Customs but because of a mistake by customs in Australia I got into real trouble here. It is because people here are very friendly to me that the release of my truck without payments is now going on. Members of parliament and highest government officers are doing all for me ..."

Bill speculated to the Atkinsons that within a week or so the truck would be released, and his first exhibition in Bombay could begin, after which he would travel to Gujarat where "friends" associated with the World Union were working with tribal peoples around Vedchhi. Bill may have been over optimistic, or maybe he was buoyed by the optimism of his advisers, but the facts did not reflect Bill's speculations. He languished in New Delhi and Bombay right through until December, suffering another bout of influenza during that time, before anything positive took place regarding the truck's release. Ultimately it was the ICCR who came to his rescue by undertaking to put up a bond of Rs 142,150 [approx. $16,062], redeemable only if the truck and all works were re-exported within a six month period. The truck and works were ultimately cleared through Customs on December 28th, 1970. On the following day Bill was issued with an open letter of introduction from the ICCR's regional representative in Bombay, J. P. Pathak:

*"We have the pleasure of introducing MR. WILLIAM RICKETTS of Australia, who is travelling with his truck, containing huge size sculptures made by him. His visit to India is being sponsored by the Council on the kind advice from the Prime Minister's Secretariat, New Delhi. Mr. William Ricketts is as simple as a saint and his mission to India is to convey the spiritual message for the preservation of wild life. **Sculptures are for exhibition, not for sale.**[1]*

Any assistance afforded to him will be immensely valued by Mr. Ricketts and highly appreciated by the Council. He may kindly be allowed to move freely across the various State boundaries and may be granted all necessary concessions, exemptions of octrois and road taxes, etc., since he is visiting India as our honoured guest."

Although Bill had been repeatedly told of the conditions to which he must adhere while touring India, J. P. Pathak thought it wise to again spell them out before Bill set out on his odyssey. This Pathak did in a letter dated December 30th, which he delivered to Bill by hand and which he carefully went through with him. The letter read:

"Now that you are all set on your journey across India, I take this opportunity in wishing you every success in your mission.

While you are travelling I have to request you to kindly take care of the following necessities:

1. *The truck and sculptures and all other fittings are under Bond and they have to be RE-EXPORTED within 6 months. You have, therefore, to ensure to keep every piece of the items, even if they are broken, and show them at the time of re-exporting to Australia.*
2. *[This dealt with the insurance organised to cover the truck, sculptures and fixtures, and advised what to do in case of damage, theft or accident.]*
3. *Keep to the schedule of your proposed exhibition as per the dates given below:*
   Pondicherry—10th January to 24th March, 1971.
   Delhi—3rd April to 17th April, 1971.
   Gujarat—22nd April to 6th May, 1971.
   Bombay—8th May to 22nd May, 1971.

---

1 This last sentence was hand written, appearing to have been deemed a necessary afterthought.

4. Since the sculptures have been exempted on the understanding that the Council will be holding the exhibitions at every centre, please make sure that the [ICCR's] name is mentioned as the main sponsors of your exhibition in all centres."

Before leaving Bombay, Bill received a publicity boost through an article in the English language weekly newspaper, *Blitz*. The article, published on January 2nd, described Bill as *"Australia's living legend"* and told that he was on a pilgrimage to India, *"a lone crusader against the white man's hell-fire in Australia"*. The article went on to report that Bill was there to gain the spiritual support of the Indian people, which would be of enormous help to his fight back in Australia. Bill had chosen India for his crusade because: *"... he thinks that like the Australian Aborigines, the Indians are people who accept the unity of life in whatever form it comes."*

With the help of a driver, Bill headed straight down to Pondicherry on India's south-east coast. Although the straight-line distance is only a little over 1,000 km, the journey took six days to complete. Bill was heading for the Sri Aurobindo Ashram, to where he had been invited by the World Union organisation. His first showing was to be held in the community of Auroville. He had reached his destination by at least January 15th, 1971, which is the day he wrote back to the ICCR in Bombay to inform them of his safe arrival. Their letter of reply wished Bill well and informed him that his Bombay exhibition dates had been altered to run from May 18th to May 31st.

After Bill had settled in he took the time to write back to the Atkinsons:[2]

"My first showing in India is now going on. I am eight miles out from Pondicherry, out in the bush. A vast native area over looking the blue ocean of the Bay of Bengal. My works are on show in a big hall of native style, sides open and roofed with thatched grass and banana leaves.

This area is part of Aurobindo Ashram, a world leading spiritual centre. The Ashram itself is in Pondicherry. The Mother of the Ashram, now 92 years, is looked upon by all as the divine Mother and she has drawn people from many countries to come to live here in this area to dream & think & work for the dream city of the world where all the world's troubles will not exist.

There are many French couples, Australian, American & others here and a few children born here. They all live in native style huts of thatched roof—electricity and all conveniences.

My showing opened on Sunday with no fuss and no newspapers. My visitors are of the right kind from the Ashram in Pondicherry and it is these right kind I seek in India and I will receive a message to be directed right back to my Aboriginal people, which means all Australia as we knew it before the white man started to move in.

My fight now starts and as my spiritual success mounts up the killer with his gun and the rest of it is going to be told that Australia is no longer Crown lands ..."

At the time of his writing that letter, Bill was still planning to keep to the schedule as set out in his letter from the ICCR, although he was not looking forward to the 3,800 km drive to New Delhi, if for no other reason than the high cost of petrol. But his mind would soon begin to change on the matter of heading north. Very quickly Bill found himself enveloped in a crush of like-minded people. Bill could speak his esoteric language of the spirit and get, in return, looks of appreciation and understanding. In Australia it was more often the case that he was rewarded with blank looks of incomprehension; but there, in an Ashram in southern India, he fitted in perfectly.

---

2 This letter was totally undated, with no envelope kept from which to obtain a postal date. The contents, however, clearly show that it was the first letter from Pondicherry.

If Bill's first letter from Auroville to the Atkinsons had been positive, his next letter of February 18th, written on green paper hand-made at the Ashram, was the outpouring of a man engrossed. A note at the beginning told: *"My plans now changed to all south India. I will go north perhaps in August. My mission is now about to unfold in public with newspapers etc. Australia is now entrusted in my hands <u>alone</u>."* Bill was ready to change his plans dramatically, including the pre-arranged itinerary and time limit of his tour. The main letter began:

> *"All that I ever thought of, dreamed of, has now come true.*
>
> *In this lovely tree filled Ashram garden where I am with all these works & films a divine destiny is reaching out into its depths, its width and height and Divine might. Out of India's sustaining deep spirituality has come the everlasting arms to surround me with love and respect, and the depth of understanding given so freely to me every day stretches right back to the Vedic Rishis people of Ancient India (India's wisdom). The same understanding of wisdom belongs to my Aboriginal people in Australia so you will understand how wonderful it is when Indian people detect all this in these works. No words can fully reveal what all this means except that I knew that I had to come to India to receive all this.*
>
> *My health is fine and strong so that I can speak back to these fine Indians as they surround me with a speech that is also strong.*
>
> *I was asked to address the Ashram gathering and this was completely successful. The governor was here and All India Radio is to come with important people. Saturday 21st I have to address the students of this Ashram.*
>
> *This Ashram is a world Spiritual centre radiating its message to the world and in this Ashram you find people from many countries and all of them playing their part as teachers & workers. It has drawn these people from all over the world by the great teachings of two of the greatest souls upon the earth—Sri Aurobindo (now passed on) and the Mother now 93 years and she is looked upon as the Divine Mother and not only Indians but all those people from other lands look upon her as the giver of Divine guidance to everywhere. I am to meet her on Friday 26th. Many of these folk from many countries … most of them full of disgust at what is going on in their own countries almost worship the Mother here …*
>
> *The Ashram is a big arrangement with its education centre the best in the world because each individual is educated separately not like the west with the teacher standing over a big number in a class like a dictator who pumps into them what was pumped into him without any regard to bring forth a divine race.*
>
> *This paper is from the Ashram paper making works and there are all else that makes up part of Pondicherry but all right down to the ordinary worker almost worship the Mother of the Ashram.*
>
> *Indians look upon that work The Gun Brute of Australia in the right way so it has now taken its right place and groups of little Indian children & teachers are now being taught what cruelty & brute force is in charge of Australia and I will put on the same big boot as Jesus did when he turned the tables of the money changers and sellers of doves.*
>
> *I will have a driver to take me to south Kerala & elsewhere.*
>
> *I dress as an Indian and I eat Indian food. My midday meal is brought to me so you now know I am alright but the fragrance of the Eucalyptus earth is terribly missing. However I have much to do before I can smell, touch, feel, hear, taste all that I am allied to and I dare not at the moment try to think just where and when I may be asked to go because my only theme I have dedicated my life to is Wild Life Preservation through a divinised earth and this together with people poisoning the earth known as pollution has created a race against time so I shall leave my mind open.*

As this flower opens more and more to the light then I shall tell you more of it.
Please give my friends my love and that I shall bring them the message from India."

This letter, apart from amply illustrating that Bill was luxuriously immersed in his surroundings, contains the first mention of the Rishis. Almost anybody who spoke with Bill after his return from India would have heard him speak of the Rishis, for he took them very much to heart.

The Rishis date from India's pre-history. They were the ancient poets and seers upon whose wisdom the Veda, the most ancient sacred writings of Hinduism, were compiled. Bill, accepting as he did the theory that Aboriginal Australians are descendants of Veddoid immigrants from the region of southern India, paralleled the ancient wisdom of the Aboriginal Dreaming with the ancient wisdom of the Rishis of India. It was this perceived spiritual overlap which made Bill confident that the modern day Indians would be able to fathom the depths of his message and in so doing give him the spiritual support he desired. The degree of acceptance shown him by the Indians would appear to indicate that he was right.

Bill had written to Mary Harris as well, telling her of life with the people of Aurobindo Ashram. She wrote back brimming with joy that Bill was finding success, telling him: *"I am with you in the Ashram with people of all nations. I love your atmospheric description so—I feel I could paint it …"* She could not help but mention the 'brute' though: *"I am glad about the gun brute being presented in the <u>right</u> environment, where there is <u>peace</u> and <u>reason</u>. The press here presented him in an abominable way—a hymn of hate weighing 4 tons! Well you know what the press is! Ted Strehlow said all the Brute represents is true, but wrongly presented to the public all by himself can evoke wrath …"*

Bill continued to bathe in the sea of like-minded folk at Auroville and Aurobindo Ashram, drawing more strength from the experience daily. He met the Mother and received her blessings, although he did not personally get a great deal from the meeting. All he was able to recall when I asked him about her was that *"she was French … she was old—not very active—very still. She died soon after"*. The conversation apparently did not progress to great depths, and did not last long. But she recognised in Bill a true purpose, and for that she blessed him. And within the society of Aurobindo Ashram, the Mother's blessing counted for much.

As a way to show that his message was being received, Bill was given a hand-written statement, prepared on an Auroville letterhead, to take back to Australia on behalf of the people of the Ashram. It read:

"We the Indians from
Sri Aurobindo Ashram
and from all over India
send our deepest spiritual
love and respect
to the Aboriginal people
of Australia through
William Ricketts
who has made himself a loving
brother of not only the Aborigines
but also of the Indians.
His sculpture has brought
to India the spiritual message
from the Aboriginal friends and
has made us feel one with them.
THE ALCHERA AND THE BRAHMAN
ARE ONE AND THE SAME."

Bill wrote to the ICCR office in New Delhi on February 19th, telling them that he felt the trouble and expense of getting to New Delhi for the pre-arranged exhibition might not be worth it, especially since he was due to stay there only a short time. He suggested that he stay in the south and raised the possibility of an extension of the deadline for the re-export of the truck and works. The ICCR response came from Bandona Banerjee, dated March 4th. She wrote that the Council had no objections to Bill staying in the south, but strongly indicated that it would be best for Bill to stick with his planned visit to Gujarat, where exhibitions could be arranged in Ahmadabad, Surat and Valod-Vedhi. She advised Bill that the ICCR's Bombay representative, Mr Pathak, was doing all he could to arrange for a low cost exhibition in Bombay, after which the truck and works could be re-exported. She wrote: *"... the exhibits and your truck are to be definitely re-exported before June 1971 (Ministry of Finance etc have not agreed to extend the time limit) ..."*

Bill immediately contacted Nitya, who was then in New Delhi, with the bad news and requested that he somehow get the various Government departments responsible for setting the deadline to extend his stay.

Although somewhat concerned by the prospect of an early departure from India, there was much to keep Bill happy. As the time drew near for his departure from Pondicherry, Bill thought it only fitting that he make some sort of contribution to the people of Aurobindo Ashram. Not only had they evoked his great respect for what they were doing, but they had returned it in kind. The best Bill could offer them was one of his works, and the best place for it to go was in front of the Ashram's library. Bill set to work with helpers and secured one of his major works to the ground with concrete and reinforcing. I do not think he forgot the golden rule as set down by the ICCR—that he was not to sell or give away any of his works. Bill was acting on a higher principle than that which determines the rules of Governments. Of course, that would not make it any easier when the time ultimately came for a head-count of the works for re-export.

Aurobindo Library's librarian, Medhananda, composed the letter of thanks:

> *"Dear Friend,*
> *We appreciate very much your generous gift of one of your beautiful sculptures, and are happy to accept it as a donation to the Sri Aurobindo Library.*
> *'A thing of beauty is a joy forever.' It will be a reminder to all of us of your presence in our midst, as well as a continuous message about the oneness of life from Australia to India."*

Nitya wrote back to Bill [still at Pondicherry] on March 13th with news that he had personally been to see a secretary in the Finance Department's office in New Delhi. He was apparently successful in his negotiations because he advised Bill that all he need do was write direct to the Minister of Finance, stating all the details and advising exactly what he would like the Government to do regarding the re-export time limit. Nitya wrote that *"the Government should do [it] for you"*. Nitya also gave the name of a woman in New Delhi who would *"take you to the Prime Minister"*, if Bill went to the capital. Nitya confidently concluded the letter with: *"There is nothing to worry. Everything will go fine."*

Bill was receiving many invitations to show his work and films, as well as speak to gatherings. Typical of these invitations was that from M. Venkataraman, Head of the Madurai University's Department of Mathematics. He had seen the exhibition and heard Bill speak at Auroville. On returning to Madurai, Venkataraman spoke with acquaintances about what he had seen and been impressed by, and it was agreed to invite Bill to exhibit. On March 12th Venkataraman wrote to Bill saying: *"... it would be good if our students here are given the opportunity to listen to you and see your exhibition. The Gandhi Smarak Sangrahalaya, the Bharatiya Vidya Bhavan and the Sri Aurobindo Circle here have agreed to co-sponsor an exhibition of your sculptures at Madurai—at the premises of the Gandhi Smarak Sangrahalaya. I shall be happy if you can make it possible for you to be here at Madurai for a few days before you go back from Pondicherry."* Just how many exhibitions Bill had is not recorded. It is the same with his exact movements around southern India. The one thing about which there is no doubt is the widespread acclaim and support he received while in the region.

From the Aurobindo Ashram in Pondicherry Bill made his way to Kerala State on India's south-west coast. He was heading to Sasthamcottah and the World Parliament of Religions, which Nitya had played a large part in organising. It was scheduled to run between March 24th and April 3rd. It was a large conference addressed by more than fifty speakers representing various religious faiths, both East and West, with speakers and delegates coming from all over the world. Nitya had invited Bill to be present with his sculptures, although Bill was not mentioned in the official program. The drive to Sasthamcottah was not without mishap. Bill later wrote in a letter to the Atkinsons that, early one morning, the truck *"went into a big hole in the road"*, the result being unspecified damage to three works and the total destruction of another.

It was the time immediately before the monsoon season, often referred to in tropical Australia as the "build-up" to "the Wet". If the conditions in southern India are similar to those of northern Australia, it is a time of oppressive heat and high humidity. Well into his seventy-third year, Bill found the climate difficult. It was an extreme change to his temperate mountain home in the Dandenongs, and vastly different to the dry heat he'd experienced in Australia's Centre more than a decade before. He set up his exhibition with the assistance of willing helpers, but when the time came for him to address the gathering, his body failed him. With typical vagueness, Bill explained the events to the Atkinsons in a letter written some six weeks later:

> *"… I started off but I could see I was not getting through the language barrier and this made me a little excited or uneasy and this in the tropical heat. I went back to the big lake side room set aside for me and I felt queer so they called in a real nice doctor who nearly took me to hospital. My temperature was much too high. He got to work with what he brought liquids put on my forehead. Next day I was much better … "*

Once the weather broke and the rains started, Bill said that the climate became much more tolerable, going as far as referring to it as *"lovely and cool"*. Whether to aid his convalescence or just to show him around the land in which he was staying, Bill was taken further south to the Lake Periyar Game Reserve. There he was taken on a cruise in a motor boat through a tropical wonderland. He wrote back to the Atkinsons that: *"… we did not see any tigers only elephants deer and bison.*[3] *However I hope to go to the other sanctuaries and find a friendly tiger."* Almost twenty years later Bill still recalled the cruise with child-like enthusiasm, telling me: *"We saw the deer, right across on the tops of the mountains. Then we went right along where the elephants were having a wash—putting their trunks under and squirting one and other—big elephants! That was a big sanctuary."* And, almost twenty years later, Bill still recalled—with regret—that they did not see a tiger at Lake Periyar.

After Sasthamcottah Bill travelled to the Jnana Ashram, near Vyasagiri, in the Trichur District of Kerala State. Bill had an exhibition there, but he stayed on for much of the monsoon season. It was from Jnana Ashram that he wrote back to the Atkinsons with news of his ill-health and the journey to Lake Periyar. That letter also contained proof that he had found a fair degree of contentment:[4]

> *"I am here in this lovely Ashram right out in the country. The trees here are cashew nut banana coconut and other tropical fruits. The monsoon rain season is here but the climate here is lovely and I am in good health.*

---

3 Are there bison in India?
4 The letter was undated, but the contents suggest that it comes from late May or early June, 1971.

The tropical heat just before the present rain season is trying. One cannot work all the day. Most people lay down a good deal. Now that the Yogi guests are all gone home there are just a few of us.

My room is in the forest with electric light and a hard board bed.

We all have our meals in the main Ashram building. We sit on the floor feet drawn in like Buddha. Each one of us has a piece of lovely fresh banana leaf in front of us. Our rice is put on this and three or four lots of vegetable curry is poured on. We just use our finger tips to pick up the rice and curry and now I am expert & like it. Rice three times a day.

The swamis in their tan cloth robes are real fine and their thinking and understanding to life is the same as my self. I have been here six weeks and will be their guest for about another month...

It is never cold here. Most men just wear a loin cloth like Mahatma Gandhi did. I dress in Indian clothes of white. The water here is lovely from the hillside so I have a lovely shower. I am in good hands so for another month you can think of me with a banana leaf and my finger tips mixing up the curry into my rice. The leaves are discarded after meals.

I drive the truck and through narrow village streets packed with bullock carts and everything else. When I passed the police on traffic points I smiled like a stale mullet and all went fine.[5] The patient little bullocks in their ancient little carts are dear little animals and keep on in their ancient ways & they are everywhere. They plough the soil in the same ancient way.

Too many people everywhere, that is the curse of the environment—now it's a few with science & technology, a larger curse when there is no love in it."

With the date of the truck and works' re-export fast approaching, the ICCR began to get a little anxious. Bill had apparently written to the ICCR [New Delhi] with news that he had written to the various Government Departments requesting an extension. Bandona Banerjee contacted these Departments to ascertain for herself the situation, only to be told that nobody had received Bill's letters. She wrote a short, but pleasant, letter to Bill on June 1st requesting copies of the letters he had sent. It isn't recorded whether or not Bill forwarded the requested copies of letters in his reply, but he did drop a bit of a bombshell by telling them of his donation of the piece to the Aurobindo Ashram.

The ICCR response was headed "Most Urgent". Usha Malik, a Program Officer, expressed "surprise" that Bill had disregarded his undertaking not to give away any works, especially when the ICCR stood to lose part of their Rs 140,000 bond as a result. Bill was informed that it was a *"very serious matter"*. Malik also requested that Bill arrange for whichever Institution was organising the rest of his visit, if an extension was granted, to take over the responsibility of the surety and bond against the truck and works being re-exported.

Just two days before the original time limit for the truck and works' re-export expired, there was further intervention. On June 21st the ICCR sent Bill the following telegram:

"CONTACT IMMEDIATELY PATHAK BOMBAY REGARDING INSURANCE PREMIUM PAYABLE FOR EXTENDED PERIOD BY YOU AS COUNCILS FURTHER FINANCIAL RESPONSIBILITY IMPOSSIBLE (x) INFORM TELEGRAPHICALLY REGARDING BOND TRANSFER..."

It would appear that Bill had received his one year extension, but that the ICCR were not too keen on continuing their role of responsibility. In the letter that followed the telegram, Usha

---

5 Bill's "stale mullet" smile was given because he did not have a driver's licence for India—the smile of a guilty man!

Malik also requested that Bill do something about arranging the return of the work which had been donated to the Aurobindo Ashram.

If Bill did anything about the question of some other organisation taking over responsibility for the bond and surety, nothing came of it. It is a fact that the ICCR remained the nervous guarantors of the truck and works for the whole time that they were in India. Bill's 1971 response to the matter of the donated work was reprinted, in part, in a letter sent from the ICCR to the Forests Commission in 1973:

> *"Only one work was given to the Ashram and I can only express regret over my mistake. To get that work returned to my keeping it would now have to be taken down with a hammer and then all I could show Customs would be a heap of bits and pieces. It is so well concreted to a base that all the bottom half would have to be broken away bit by bit or piece by piece and then with the hope that the top half with the figures could be saved. If Customs say this has to be done then I shall inform the Ashram of my mistake and break it down with the small hope that something of the top half can be saved."*

Bill made it clear that he would reluctantly abide by the conditions, but only if the ICCR or Customs were ruthless enough to, in effect, order the work's destruction. A good example of Bill's style of diplomacy.

While at Jnana Ashram, with time on his hands, Bill was struck with whatever impulse it is that leads to the creation of new works. To this end he contacted V. G. N. Panicker, manager of the New India Ceramics Ltd in Feroke, from whom he ultimately purchased some 230 kg of clay. Bill was informed by Panicker that his company would also be able to fire any completed works. A July 10th letter to Bill from Joy Thomas [who had written an article about Bill for the newspaper, *Deepika*] requested that Bill keep her informed of his activities, *"especially of the works you had done about Kerala and Keralian"*. If it was the case that Bill had begun depicting Keralian people and spirituality in his work, it would have represented the first change in his subject matter since beginning his career in clay more than half a century earlier. It would also serve to illustrate what great effect the Indian experience was having on Bill.

It was around this time, late July or early August, 1971, that the Department of Taxation in Melbourne gave up waiting for Bill's $750 and decided to take him to Court over the matter. Ron Olver recalled his meeting with the police who fronted up at the Sanctuary with the Summons:

> *"Yeah, the police came up with a bluey—a summons for taxation. [Bill] was in India, and I just said he was in India, I don't know where he is, he's travelling in India and I don't think anybody knows where he is. I knew exactly where he was, because I'd just got a letter from him—but I said that I couldn't give any information on him at all. I said he left here at such-and-such a date, when he'll be back we don't know. The copper said, 'Well in that case we'll just have to take it back and say we don't know where he is'.*
>
> *It wasn't long after that a report came out in the paper—how it got there I don't know—whether the taxation or not, but it was put in that he'd died in India. His death notice and all, in India. I wrote a letter back into the paper then to say that he wasn't dead in India."*

I did not sight the article or Olver's letter. It appears that many people did read the article at the time, but did not read the subsequent letter, because rumours ran rife about Bill's reported death. Both the Atkinsons and the Sanctuary staff were kept busy assuring Bill's concerned admirers that he was, indeed, alive and kicking in India.

 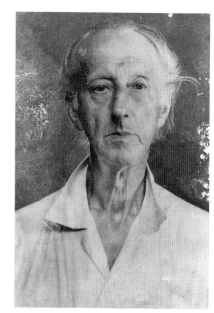

144 & 145 *Bill at the Taj Mahal [c. October, 1970] and, right, the photo for his new passport [c. April, 1971]. For a period of just over six months, his appearance had changed dramatically. Photographers unknown.*

146 *An exhibition in India; location unknown. Photo by Vidyavrata.*

147 *At the unveiling of* Pmaranuka: My Country *in Howie Reserve, Walkerville [page 251],Bill explains the work to Pippa Dormer. Courtesy of the* Advertiser.

148 *The vandalised* Pmaranuka *before it was relocated to the Walkerville Council works depot. Photo courtesy of Mary Wilding.*

149 *Prof. Ted Strehlow addresses the Open Day at the WRS in 1973.*

150 *Bill at the 1973 WRS Open Day.*

151–153 *The* Earthly Mother *group [above] at the WRS, and [below] detail of the same group. 4000 mm wide, 2150 mm high.*

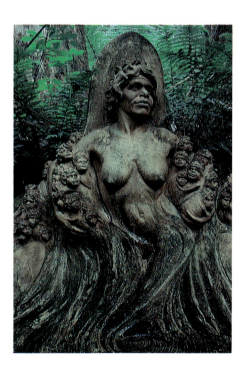

154 *One of several meticulously created raised-letter plaques at the WRS. 890 mm high.*

155 *Snow—a rare and beautiful, but damaging, visitor to the WRS.*

156 *Where is it now? I photographed this piece, set in the earth and therefore the property of the State, at the WRS in 1983. When I returned in 1986, the work was nowhere to be found.*

157 *Bill feeds an orphaned ringtail possum in what was once his bedroom. He would transform the room by bringing in branches, fern fronds and hollow logs whenever he had a possum to care for. The story goes that it was for a baby possum that he first moved his bed into the kitchen.*

158 Thorny Devil Pmara Kutata *[Sacred Earth Site]*. WRS. *7000 wide, 3100 mm high.*

159 *Curiously enough, this piece is known within the WRS as Long Beard. 3300 mm high.*

161 *What Bill would have put on the summit of Mt Dandenong, given the chance. WRS. 800 mm high.*

160 *Bill called this group, Life Harmonious. WRS. 2000 mm high.*

162 *The Pitjantjatjara Elder created after the Erna-bella journey. WRS. 1000 mm high.*

163 Betrayed *has symbolism which leaves little to the imagination. WRS. 2350 mm high.*

271

164 *Dignity is all pervasive within the WRS's characters. 1700 mm high.*

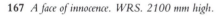

167 *A face of innocence. WRS. 2100 mm high.*

165 Possum Pmara Kutata. *WRS. 4200 mm high.*

166 *A face of disrespect, the* Brute of Australia, *whose creed appears on page 252. WRS. 1650 mm high.*

168 *This shot shows almost all of Bill's kitchen, where he lived. I sat on his bed, my back against the wall. His stove was to the right, his fridge to the left; the rest of his "home" is in the photo.*

169 *The mobile floor and front wall of the electric kiln. [Brief description page 207.]*

170 *The whitefella Dreaming.*

When the Atkinsons wrote to Bill [a letter which I did not see] at Jnana Ashram with news of his reported death, Bill responded in a letter full of fighting spirit:[6]

> *"Yes I was dead but that was before I came to my Holy Mountain forest ... Now I am alive and my guidance in my Mountain forest for forty years alone is now of very great wonder to me that because I was dead then to become alive as soon as my hands touched the earth.[7]*
>
> *It is all the more a great wonder now I am in India. India has confirmed what I and my Aboriginal know to be true. Yes dead true.*
>
> *If I went through Australia with these works and especially the two I have executed in this Ashram then the so called Christian Religion would have rejected me in the very same way they rejected my people the Aboriginal and in doing that they helped the white man to destroy [Aboriginal Australia's] way of life but not the spirit.*
>
> *I hold this spirit and its expression in the Earth Nature and in this Earth Nature the Divine is the secret centre and it is the aim of Nature to lift the Human into the highest Consciousness.*
>
> *Organised Religion has led people away from the Earth."*

Bill went on to forewarn the Atkinsons of a booklet soon to arrive by ordinary mail. He asked Dorothy to hold its contents as "sacred" and not to release it to anybody, including the press, until such time that he reached Bangalore for his series of exhibitions. *"Dorothy from now onwards be on guard of anyone wanting information to know this or that"*, Bill wrote, adding in conclusion: *"I know my position in Australia the moment they know who I am and not the artist or anything like it. I am a fighter same as Mr Gandhi said of himself."*

The booklet which Bill had sent back to Australia was *Kaivalya Sudha*, Jnana Ashram's magazine. It was a special issue, the *Yoga Vedanta Souvenir*, produced after the occasion of their fourth Retreat and Yoga Training Camp. Within its pages was a reprint of John Hetherington's *Uncommon Men* article about Bill. As an introduction, though, the magazine's anonymous editor wrote:

> *"The write-up that appears below is about Mr William Ricketts (Billy Ricketts) who is currently camping at Jnana Asram. He is an inspired crusader, who has given expression to his innate experience of the unity of existence and the Divinity of life, through many captivating masterpieces of sculpture, which were exhibited in the Asram campus till the break of the monsoon ...*
>
> *The people of Australia, his country, do not appreciate or recognise the mission of Mr Ricketts. His philosophy is the same as of the ancient Rishis of Bharat. It is 'life is divine: hence live in tune with the Divine that expresses in all the things around us. Live with and in nature without destroying it'. It is all 'Essence' in his words: 'Satta' as we call it.*
>
> *Like inspiring and elevating music, his pieces elevate and enthral the sensitive spectator. One has to see it to know what it is.*
>
> *His plan is to go to Bangalore after leaving the Asram. He feels that Bangalore would be the doorway through which he could enter the hearts of the people of this country.*
>
> *What he expects of the people of this land is their understanding and support of his mission (or crusade) which is as profound and at the same time as simple as the 'love and respect for life and nature that is Divine'—'Essence'.*

---

6 This letter was post-marked August 30th, 1971.
7 Copied verbatim, it is a hard sentence to get through—but, with a little effort, the meaning of it can be gleaned.

India would be able to do this easily, as the very core of our culture, philosophy and religion is the same—that is.

SARVAM KHALU IDAM BRAHMA
All this is Brahman

Our loving help will be the strongest weapon for Mr William Ricketts to win the understanding and support of the white people of Australia, who are yet to learn the 'Divinity of all life'."

The bit which Bill did not want disclosed referred to his philosophy as being the same as the Rishis. This surprise he wanted to keep until the right moment—the fact that he had come to India only to learn that what he was preaching was the same as had been preached in India's pre-history by the Rishis.

Bill had a couple of stops to make before reaching Bangalore. He left Jnana Ashram late in September, heading for Feroke and the New India Ceramics company so that he could fire his works. In 1988, Sri V. G. N. Panicker wrote me a letter in which he did his best to recall the events which took place sixteen years previously:

> *"He was allotted a room in the corner where he worked and made a big piece—my memory is it was about life size—of some original inhabitants of your country under torment by the later invaders and this work was rushed for exhibition along with other art pieces and photographs at Gandhi Griham, Cherooty Road, Calicut.*
>
> *The works had probably not dried completely—this being the rainy season and came out after firing partly cracked and some pieces disintegrated. Besides the firing was in a semi continuous kiln, where the draft and temperature could not be controlled accurately ...*
>
> *I am now 73 years and I remember vividly Mr Ricketts' short associations with us and I have a personal regard for the great artist and thinker. He upheld the cause of the downtrodden much in the manner of Gandhiji ..."*

Panicker wrote that the works which were too badly damaged to be shown in the exhibition, as well as an unspecified number of unfinished works, were placed in a store room after Bill left for Calicut. They were kept for fourteen years, until 1986, when they were at last dumped. Unfortunately they have now all disintegrated.

Bill received publicity prior to his arrival in Calicut through an October 2nd article in the *Mathru Bhumi* [which Bill would later describe as Calicut's main newspaper]. Titled, "Artistic Works Which Reflect the Oneness of Universe", it opened with: *"It is 'Thathwamasi'— the Rishis philosophy of oneness of the part and the whole—that inspires the Australian artist Mr William Ricketts. The aim of his life is to express the unity in diversity of the universe through his artistic works."* It went on to outline Bill's beliefs in such a way that would have made him very happy—and Bill had pulled no punches in his describing of what was going on in the land down under. The article went on to state [no doubt using material gained from Bill]: *"Standing behind a screen of culture and civilisation, the Australian white man mistunes the melodious harmony of the universe. This destructive tendency saddens Mr William Ricketts ... his heart is deeply stirred at the merciless policy of the white man of Australia ..."* In his attempts to bring about a stop to such barbarism, Bill was creating works with a *"heavenly appearance and expression"*. His influence, however, came from the *"religious faiths of the hill-tribes of Middle Australia"*, who, the article clearly pointed out, shared the belief of oneness.

Bill's exhibition in Calicut was his first outside the Ashrams and retreats, which were more sanctuaries full of gentle minds. But in Calicut, Bill was exposed to the masses in general. He would write to the Atkinsons: *"Calicut city opened its arms to me, my first public appearance in India and I was treated as though I were a king."* He did not stay for more than a couple of weeks and was soon on the road to Bangalore; once capital of the State of Mysore, now capital of the State of Karnataka—and in 1971 a bustling city of more than 1.5 million people.

Bill's arrival in Bangalore was in no way unannounced. Many of the swamis, gurus and influential people with whom he had come into contact had written to various well-placed people and officials in Bangalore, alerting them to Bill's imminent arrival. It meant that Bill arrived not as a strange, vagabond Australian artist, but as a mystic personality already well known to many of the south's spiritual and intellectual minds. The support and encouragement Bill received is reflected in the letter of October 21st, 1971, sent to Indira Gandhi under the letterhead of the "Sukrtindra Oriental Research Institute and N Govinda Pai Memorial Library", which listed half a page of Doctors, Professors, Religious leaders and Government officials [past and serving] as its patrons, office bearers and members.[8] The letter read:

> *"Respected Mother of India,*
> *We wish to draw your kind attention that a great personality ACHARYA WILLIAM RICKETTS stayed in Kerala and now the said (Rishi) personality is staying in Bangalore City.*
> *We believe that he deserves all co-operation from the government of India to make his mission all success.*
> *We further request that the Govt. of India be pleased to instruct the Govt. of Mysore to give his all-necessary help in his venture.*
> *May, Bagawan Sri Ramakrishna, Holy Mother Sri Sarada Devi and Swami Vivekananda bless him in his venture so as to enable him to inculcate the spirit of world brotherhood."*

Bill wrote to the Atkinsons on November 3rd, giving his address as "C/- Information and Tourism, High Grounds, Palace Road". A note on the top told that he was *"in the beautiful Park grounds and trees ... right in the city of Bangalore's government place"*. Full of optimism, Bill wrote:

> *"I have been in India fifteen months and all this time and from one to another a wonderful thing has been building up for me quietly and gently ... everything is opening out. The moment I reached Bangalore I became a guest of the State of Mysore.*
> *It is the Divine gates opening out gently and quietly to the message I guard deep down in my inner most life. I shall not say much more except Bangalore the lovely city of trees and trees in every street will give to the world my Aboriginal people's message, but that will be in December when as arranged now my works and films will be shown in Bangalore's famous ancient gardens and in a section that to me is an enchanted forest.*
> *So I ask you to wait until that time and then the meaning and mystery of my life will be unfolded by India.*
> *As you will see in that letter [from Pai to Indira Gandhi] where I am now spoken of as <u>Acharya</u> William Ricketts. You will understand how the Indian people know me from that word Acharya. A-chary-a means in an Indian word the deepest wisdom of India from the Ancient Fathers of India's wisdom the Rishis people who lived in forests not eating meat and lived with all living tigers and all else in harmony.*
> *Swami Poonanda here said to me, 'You have come to India with an Indian mind and that is why we love you'.*

---

8 Bill reprinted this letter in full, complete with letterhead details, in the black and white booklet *Pmara Kutata*, available from the Sanctuary.

Those works I did in the Ashram were through wrong firing blown to pieces. So I am doing one big work again in the big porcelain works so I think it will be about the middle of December when I will be ready to show all here ...

Bangalore will speak out the truth in December ... Just wait until December and see the lovely flower with countless petals open out and all that was my people's Australia before the white man are those petals."

Bill had been introduced to Sri A. Samba Moorty, the Managing Director of the State owned Mysore Porcelains Ltd. The enterprise mainly made electrical insulators, but Moorty welcomed Bill with an assurance that the facilities of the factory were at his disposal.

I found no records to confirm whether or not Bill had his exhibitions in Bangalore. One letter survives which suggests that Bill accepted invitations from small groups to lecture and show his films around the city. It was also evidenced in later correspondence from an employee of Mysore Porcelains that Bill created works while visiting the factory—although how many and the themes expressed were not recorded. On the information available for this biography, the first five months of Bill's time in Bangalore remain somewhat a mystery.

By April 1972, the ICCR were again becoming restless over the fact that the time limit for the truck and works' re-export was approaching. To make sure that Bill was aware of the fact, the ICCR sent him a no-nonsense telegram, addressed to "C/- Choudappa Reddy, Deputy Director of Tourism". It read:

"TRUCK ALONG WITH SCULPTURAL WORKS MUST BE RE-EXPORTED BEFORE JUNE 1972. PLEASE PROCEED TO BOMBAY WITH ALL WORKS. INFORM TELEGRAPHICALLY TITLE AND PRICE OF SCULPTURE PRESENTED TO PONDICHERRY ASHRAM."

This sparked off another round of protest and pleading by Bill and his supporters. He contacted various Indian friends with the news, not necessarily to ask for their help, but to let them know of the outrage being committed against him in the hope that they would act.

Among the papers salvaged from Bill's "spare room" I found original first drafts and copies of several such pleas. None were dated, but all gave Bill's address as "C/- Mysore Porcelain" and referred to the ICCR reminding him of the re-export obligation. All except one showed evidence of outside help in compiling the pleas. They told of Bill's desire to take his message throughout *all* of India, in the hope that the Indian people as a whole would come to support his mission. By this method Bill speculated that India could lead the world in recognising his cause. Those helping Bill were certainly of the opinion that his mission was a worthy one.

One of the pleas, addressed to Indira Gandhi, listed five separate reasons why a further extension or a total lifting of time-limits altogether should be sanctioned. They were:

> *"1. India being a vast country it requires more time to traverse the whole length and breadth to meet the people of different regions.*
>
> *2. I have new themes to work on sculptures which I want to do here (to be the mother earth principle).*
>
> *3. I want to visit different regions where aborigines and ... tribes live and I would like to give the expression of their life in my work.*
>
> *4. Neither my work nor my mission is with any commercial or otherwise motivation. This should be very clear to people who have to decide about my extension of stay.*
>
> *5. Maybe if I get proper encouragement to my spiritual feeling to India I may contribute to the cultural richness of this country in my own humble way.*
>
> *I further request that my representation should be judged on its basic purpose and not on the trivialities of the rules and regulations."*

In other pleas Bill gave a potted history of his life and ideals, stretching over five typed pages. There was one, however, which indicated that other things were on Bill's mind. It was a very rough first draft of a letter to Dr Pai.[9] Through the hastily written scrawl and crossed-out or over-written words, there emerged a letter which, although incomplete, seemed to come from the heart of a man in turmoil. It read:

> *"Your letter to the Prime Minister Indira Gandhi is held close to my heart as a treasure deeply human. That co-operation you asked of the Prime Minister to make my mission all success now has become urgent. A telegram from Delhi advised me to proceed to Bombay ready to be exported as the time allowed you is up by June.*
>
> *The Customs Dep do not even know what my mission is except a truck loaded with sculptures. If the Prime Minister will not intervene then the Customs act will represent the greatest insult ever offered to any man in history, and it will as I am now placed destroy that which my life is dedicated to do and in which the deepest wisdom of India is involved. That low mentality in power in Australia would be only too happy to see my mission to India smashed to pieces …*
>
> *My mission to the Indian people needs to be taken very slow to allow time for my mission to take shape in Indian minds. On the road the truck went into a hole breaking three works. Six months it has taken me to do these three works again.*
>
> *From Bombay to Bangalore—I have so far just done this and now I am ready to proceed more on a quick scale and now I am to be exported as they crudely put it.*
>
> *In Australia the low mentality of government dep caused me to tell them that I shall not return to my sanctuary any more (my sanctuary was outraged).*
>
> *Before I abandon everything I ask of India's reply. If the reply is still in a straight-jacket of time set against spirituality then"*

It finished mid-sentence. Did Bill know what he would do? At that point I would say not. Whether or not the above draft version was ever rewritten and sent is not known to me.

A letter to the Atkinsons, post-marked May 13th, 1972, mentioned nothing of Bill's problems regarding the expiry of his time limit. He wrote that he had finished the works he'd been creating and that they were being fired "now" in the porcelain factory's kiln. Bill did not give any description of the pieces. Instead he told of how well he was being treated:

> *"… They are very good to me in this huge government works doing insulators mostly. It is a wonderful place. Just opposite is the Indian Science Institute—200 acres and it must be the most or one of the most finest places in the world. I go there every day to get my food. My health is good and the lovely climate here helps all.*
>
> *I would very much like it to be possible for me to go to the Himalayan Mountain. It is a long way from here but true success here could make all possible.*
>
> *I would like to make a journey back to Australia to do a few things—one is my teeth need attention. Speak the truth and one [tooth] is a goner …*
>
> *Over two thousand people are working here, The Director of this place is good to me. He refused to take any payment for all they have done for me. He just said money does not come into this you are doing. It is such unsuspected places like this that you meet with people of spiritual depth …*
>
> *Everywhere you go in India you see the Eucalyptus trees and it makes you feel better. Just imagine 500 or so million people. It means that about 300 million are not needed, they just sit on the earth and it is too much for the earth to bear.*

---

9 The Dr Pai who had written the October 21st, 1971, letter to Indira Gandhi.

Next time I write I hope I can tell you I am ready to show all in Bangalore city and to be the gateway to India for me."

This letter to the Atkinsons in no way reflected the concern Bill was experiencing over the re-export of his truck and works. Apart from the off-hand mention of Bill's thinking about going home "to do a few things", all appeared to be rosy. But it was not. When I tried to obtain the exact circumstances from Bill, he kept coming back to money, or a lack of it, as being his main worry. The Bombay office of the ICCR wrote to Bill on May 26th, 1972, heading their letter with a red "Most Immediate". The letter went through, step by step, the conditions and previous extension granted "as a special case" and then told Bill that he had to head for Bombay immediately to re-export his truck and works.

Another possible reason for confusion and uncertainty in Bill's mind is that he may have become aware of mechanical problems with the truck. Early in August, 1972, the truck was to be diagnosed as having clutch, gear box and steering problems. There is no evidence to suggest that the truck had been driven since May, so it must be assumed that even Bill, with no mechanical knowledge, would have known that there were potentially serious, and costly, problems somewhere under the truck's floor. Did he know that the truck was incapable of making it to Bombay? Even if he could get it there, he had no money to pay for shipping it out of the country. And even if he did have the money to ship it—*he didn't want to* because he hadn't finished what he'd gone to do! He needed time and space to think. It was getting too much for him—re-export problems, money problems and mechanical problems.

On June 4th Bill was in Madras where a doctor signed a form stating that Bill had been re-vaccinated against cholera. Bill later told me that he bribed the good doctor with ten rupees to simply sign the form—because Bill did not want a needle. In the Atkinson box of papers I found a copy of a telegram on which I could decipher neither the date of its despatch nor the sender or receiver. It read:

"RICKETTS MR W STRANDED MADRAS CONTACT COMMON-WEALTH TRADING BANK OF AUSTRALIA NO 8 ELIZABETH ST MELBOURNE RUSH ADVICE LATEST REMITTANCE AND AMOUNT SENT TO INDIA FAVOUR PASSENGER DETAILS OF PASSENGERS ACCOUNT TO BE OBTAINED FROM THE WARDEN WILLIAM RICKETTS SANCTUARY MOUNT DANDENONG."

Bill's recollection was that he had no money because *"the bank broke down"*. He told me that while he was waiting for the money to come through, he took a cheap room in Madras: *"A room, not very nice, in a poor part of the city—very poor."* Lou Atkinson forwarded money to Bill, unaware of what it would be used for. On June 20th, Bill's passport was stamped through the Madras Airport. On June 21st, the passport was stamped at the Perth Airport. Also at Perth, Bill suffered the indignation of being caught out. A medical official asked to see where he had been re-vaccinated for cholera in India. Unable to show any evidence satisfactory to the medical official, Bill was re-vaccinated. *"Yes, I got caught there"*, he recalled with a wry smile. *"So I asked him to take it light."*

A lady by the name of Betty Cromb was working at Churinga Restaurant for Dorothy and Lou Atkinson in June, 1972. Although she had never met Bill, she had heard all about him. One evening she was there alone, the Atkinsons having gone away. She told me the following:

"I had been working at Churinga all day, a very cold day in mid-winter, and I was locking up to go home at about 5.30. Being winter it should have been dark, but there was a very bright moon. It was one of those bright, frosty nights. Well, just as I happened to look up I saw this figure, running down the steps—and you know what

those steps are like.[10] *A vision in white it was. My God, I thought, it's Robert Helpmann!*

But when he came up it was Bill. Of course, he hadn't told anybody he was coming, he just sort of arrived. What he'd done is he'd got to Perth, got a plane from Perth to Melbourne, got into town and caught the train to Belgrave. Now can you imagine Bill sitting up in the train in this white tussore Indian suit, with a turban to go with it with gold braid around it? Sitting up there probably shivering in the middle of all the commuters going to Belgrave? Then he got a taxi from Belgrave.

It was a laugh thinking he was Robert Helpmann, though."

The Sanctuary was locked tight and Betty could not raise Ron Olver to let Bill in. So she took him back to her house, gave him a feed, then dropped him back at Churinga where he spent the night. The next morning when Olver came to work, there was a surprise, gift-wrapped in Indian silk, waiting at the front gate: Acharya Billy was home—safe on his beloved mountain.

---

10 Those steps are not the sort of steps which any normal person would choose to run down at night. When you go for the best Devonshire Tea in the Dandenongs, you'll see what Betty meant.

22 | Consolidation
[1972–1993]

The version generally told of the events which led to Bill's departure from India is that the Indian Government "kicked him out of the country" because of his disregard of the conditions placed upon him. I've also heard it said that he was actually held by authorities at the Madras Airport until his money came through for the air fare back to Australia. I do not believe that this was the case.

In no correspondence did I sight any reference to the Indian Government wanting Bill out of the country. The concern was only for the truck and works, which were subject to duty and for which bonds and sureties had been guaranteed. Bill had been directed to proceed to Bombay so that the truck and works could be re-exported. Bill's personal time limit was never mentioned. Then, as we will see, Bill slipped out of the country without informing anybody of his intentions. If Bill had been subject to a departure "supervised" by Government officials, surely such supervision would have been reported to the other concerned Government departments. Lastly, the Indian Government would not have "kicked Bill out" until after he had arranged for the removal of his truck and works. I am in no doubt that Bill came home because he wanted to.

Bill's euphoria at being home was interrupted when he saw the newly constructed studio adjacent to his home. Ron Olver recalled that he *"kicked up all bloody might"* when he realised that his objections and specific instructions that the studio not be built had been ignored. Fortunately Olver had an ace up his sleeve. It was winter, and typically, Mt Dandenong was cold and damp. An oil heater had been installed in the new studio and when Olver ushered Bill through the door, Bill suddenly realised that he was in the warmest room on the property. Not only did the objections cease immediately, but the next morning Olver found that Bill had moved his bed and few personal effects into the new studio—where he stayed for the rest of the winter.

The matter of the Indian tour was not so easily overcome. It became a mini-saga, wending its way through four years until late 1976. The ICCR breathed a sigh of relief in September, 1972, when Customs and other concerned Indian Government Departments granted a further three-year extension on the truck and works' re-export. I did not ascertain how the extension came about, but assume that it was again the result of collective lobbying on Bill's behalf. Nobody in India knew where Bill was until V. P. Patil, a security officer who had befriended Bill at the Mysore Porcelain factory, received a letter from Bill saying that although he had come back to Australia, he planned to return to India. No doubt Bill was planning to conduct another fund-raising campaign, after which he could return to India as a financially independent crusader. Somewhere along the way Bill's plans became side-tracked.

Almost one year after Bill's return, the Forests Commission became involved and began negotiating directly with the ICCR to have the truck and works returned. The reason that it did not flow smoothly was that Bill also involved several other people and organisations in trying to re-export the goods—resulting in an intricate conglomeration of disorganisation. The details are many and varied, even entertaining at times. Suffice to say, though, that it was the Forests Commission who eventually did the trick and found themselves with an Austin truck full of works which had been packed between bags of straw—the whole of which had sat out in the open through four full years of southern India's tropical climate. It was towed from the Melbourne docks up to the Olinda Commission depot, where the workers had to wear masks as they unloaded the works from a rotting mess. The truck, although it would not have had more than 16,000 km on the clock, was deemed a write-off. Getting the truck and works back to Australia had cost approximately $5,600.

The Indian tour proved to be Bill's last great adventure. Although there would be minor ones to come, the course of his life had been shaped and his battle would be for evermore fought on Australian soil—almost exclusively on Mt Dandenong.

Bad news awaiting Bill upon his return from India was that Leo Corbet had died in 1971. Bill had not kept in close contact with Leo, but there had been a strong, lasting bond forged many years previously. The man who was described in an *Age* article of August 14th, 1965, as **"garrulous, portly and dapper with a pair of glasses that just won't sit straight [who would] sooner talk about the outback and its people than collect 20 cent pieces at the gate"** was gone.

Reg Harris, a mate of Leo's, told me a yarn which, as much as any other, shows just what a character the Centre lost:

> *"You know he was a little portly fellow, certainly not a rough and tumble type. Anyhow, his bedroom was up on the first floor and one night he was woken up by these noises. It turned out there were a couple of young blokes going through his gear down below. He thought, 'Christ, what am I going to do about this?' He thought, well, he better face them up, so he went downstairs to these two.*
>
> *'What are you two buggers doing there?' he asked them straight. 'Why're you robbing a poor old man like me for when you can go and rob a bloody bank?' Well, these blokes were a bit nonplussed, standing there looking at him and saying nothing. So he said, 'Don't just stand there! Put the bloody kettle on and let's have a cup of tea while we're talking about this.'*
>
> *So these blokes put the kettle on and they make a cup of tea, and Leo chatted them saying things like, 'Now you've got to do the right bloody thing—you don't go robbing old people,' and that sort of thing. After they'd finished the cup of tea Leo got up and said, 'Now you can get off—but before you clear off you can go over there and wash the bloody dishes up'. With that he turned around and went upstairs.*
>
> *He told me that when he got up stairs he put his ear to the floor board and heard these blokes saying, 'Jesus—what are we going to do with the old bastard?' And the other one said, 'I don't know, let's just wash the bloody dishes and piss off'. And that's just what they did—washed up Leo's dirty dishes and pissed off! That was Leo."*

Leo had married several years before his death, and his wife, Elsa, was left to try and carry on. One of the first strokes of bad luck to hit her was the bore water going "sour". With no good water to keep Pitchi Richi green, things began to deteriorate—despite all of Elsa's efforts. Over the years Elsa brought in a progression of managers who kept Pitchi Richi alive, barely.

More recently, in line with Leo's wishes that Pitchi Richi ultimately be of benefit to Centralia's Aboriginal people, Frank and Janet Ansell have taken over the management responsibility. With funding from Alice Spring's Tangentyere Council, the Aboriginal and Torres Strait Islander Commission [ATSIC] and other bodies, it is hoped that the renamed *Pitchi Richi Aboriginal Cultural Experience* will become a cultural and interpretive centre of very high standards. The plans which original project manager, Tony McDonald, formulated have been downgraded after input from business consultants. McDonald's vision was grand, but definitely achievable, and it is hoped that the downgrading will only be temporary.

Ultimately, Pitchi Richi is planned to be a venue where visitors will be able to experience the history and spirituality of the Centre's original people, as well as learning of the history and impact of the new arrivals. Currently, emphasis is being placed on highlighting the pivotal role Aboriginal people played in establishing pastoral industries in the outback regions. There are also occasional performances by the Arrernte Posse Dancers. Greening Australia is assisting with the site's rehabilitation. Exotic weeds, mainly Tamarisk species, are being removed and indigenous flora, including various "bush tucker" plants, are being reintroduced.

The significance and level of interest in Bill's work has been fully recognised, ensuring that they will be preserved as a prominent feature in the overall venue. It may be some years before the project is complete, but when it is finished it should be something of which Leo, and Bill, would have been proud.

Bill was given the chance to relocate his Holy Mountain when he returned from India. A long-time supporter from Adelaide, Mary Wilding, knew that Bill was unhappy with certain aspects of the Mt Dandenong scene and was looking to move if a suitable mountain could be found.

While Bill was away, Mary and her husband, Fred, thought long and hard about it and finally came up with the idea that the 960 m high Mt Remarkable, near Melrose in South Australia's Flinders Ranges, would be suitable. Mary made an appointment to see the then Premier of South Australia, Don Dunstan, to discuss the possibilities. Not quite sure how to handle such a request, and more than a little nervous, Mary simply went in to Dunstan's office and stated her case for why Bill should be "given" Mt Remarkable. She recalled that Dunstan listened patiently, but gave her no hints during her speech as to what he was thinking about it all. Mary told me that when she'd finished, Dunstan slumped back in his chair and said: ***"Thank goodness—something real for a change."***

Dunstan had the Title of the land examined and found that it was then in the vicinity of two small reserves; Alligator Gorge and Mambray Creek. Unable to find any negatives in Mary's proposal, Dunstan gave instructions to the departments concerned to proceed with arrangements which would make such a development possible. Mary clearly remembers being called to the phone the day Don Dunstan personally rang to tell her the good news. ***"You've got your mountain"***, she heard. In disbelief, Mary made him say it again.

Mary wasted no time in telling Bill, but of course she had to wait for him to come back from India before she could show it to him. When Bill did finally catch the train over from Victoria, he was bubbling with joy and enthusiasm. They all drove up, with Bill's arms waving wildly while he described what would be done with his new Holy Mountain. His joy was understandable—it's not every day that you get given a mountain. On reaching the site the group walked over the mountain and admired its richness. Bill noted the many positives; fast-flowing creek, plentiful wild life and profuse vegetation. But it was steep with a relatively loose surface. It was, compared with Mt Dandenong, a much drier bush land. It was almost 300 km from Adelaide. There was no ready-made support base, as he had in Victoria—no Dorothy and Lou across the road. And there were no lyrebirds, his chosen totem. When finally faced with a choice, he had to admit that what he already had was hard to beat—and he declined the offer. The two small reserves were ultimately connected and expanded to become what is now the 8,584 ha Mt Remarkable National Park.

Bill would never refrain from kicking up a storm whenever he saw the need. For years he had been frantic about the open access which cats, foxes and dogs had to his forest home. All indigenous wild life suffered as a result of this, with his all-too-frequent discoveries of little piles of feathers or possum fur causing frightening displays of emotion. There was only one answer to such a problem—to completely fence the perimeter with a vermin-proof structure. The Forests Commission were constantly being asked by the Advisory Committee to fund such a fence. In pressing the point, Jim Westcott had written in a report to Head Office, dated March 13th, 1970:

"I might mention that a steadily increasing attraction at the William Ricketts' Sanctuary and adjoining purchased properties is the presence of tame lyre birds and, if the current trend continues, there will soon be more lyre birds to be seen at the Ricketts' Sanctuary than in Sherbrooke Forest Park."

Westcott went to no end of trouble in his attempt to find the right fence for the job, finally settling on a "T" shaped design similar to that used in the noted Healesville Sanctuary.[1] When the Commission finally authorised $4,400 for a fence in October, 1973, Bill found himself in a quandary.

Firstly, the authorised fence did not follow the entire perimeter of all the land which had been added. Bill also reasoned that when his Sanctuary was contained within a fence, the Commission would be much less likely to increase the total area to Bill's preferred minimum of 40.5 ha. The deciding factor came when Bill learned that a swathe of his precious forest would have to be cleared before the fence was erected. Bill kicked up such a stink over the matter that the whole project was dropped. It was ultimately a major blow for the Sanctuary. Nowadays no lyrebirds are to be seen at the Sanctuary. In late 1988 Bill had a quote prepared for a predator-proof fence to encompass the entire Sanctuary as it now is. It came to more than $60,000. It can only be hoped that one day the wonderful dance of the lyrebird will again be seen at the Sanctuary.

In the USSR, Ivan Ivashko continued his own fight for peace, human rights and wild life preservation, using Bill's example and works as the bait. Despite his serious illnesses, he was able to publish more stories about Bill, as well as to make more appearances on Soviet television. By 1973 it must have become obvious to Ivan that Bill would never travel to the USSR. Ivan, instead, made plans to come to Australia for the purpose of gaining material from Bill which he planned to publish in what appeared to be a biographical book. It must have been a great disappointment for them both when Ivan cancelled the trip on the grounds that he could not afford the price of air travel, nor the time of sea travel. Ivan broke the news to Bill in a letter of September, 1973. That letter was the last from Ivan which I found in the "spare room".

Letters from another Odessa resident, Victor Margulis, dating from the late 1970s, refer to Ivan's passing. Victor took up Ivan's role of promoting Bill. He achieved at least one success by having a story about Bill televised at 6.00 p.m. on the August 19th, 1979, "Traveller's Club" program. Victor wrote that it was shown on Central Television to an audience of some 100 million viewers. Even if that figure were halved, it still represents good publicity. Before too long, the letters from the USSR ceased completely.

The Atkinsons continued their seemingly tireless support of Bill in whatever capacity they could. While the Advisory Committee, of which they were principals, was meant to be the buffer between Bill and the Forests Commission, it was, in reality, Dorothy and Lou who took on the main responsibility. As Jim Westcott recalled:

"Dorothy Atkinson and her husband Lou—no book on Ricketts would be complete without them. The amount of help they gave and trouble they saved the Commission is beyond description. Nobody would have any idea how much they did—nobody."

By early 1974 the Atkinsons were considering retirement. By that time their Churinga Restaurant had become a healthy business and they recognised that much of their trade came as a result of their proximity to the Sanctuary. Their close association with Bill had meant that a substantial collection of Bill's works, including many "seconds", had found their way into the grounds of Churinga. In a strange sort of way, Churinga was a part of the Sanctuary. The Atkinsons also knew of Bill's objection to any blatant commercialisation at the Sanctuary. It was

---

1 A first class wild life reserve located in the township of Healesville, north-east of Melbourne.

one thing for Bill to sell his small works there in his efforts to raise funds for his projects, but quite another to see souvenirs, take away food and the like detract from the Sanctuary's integrity. When they had decided that it was definitely time for them to go, the Atkinsons informed the Forests Commission that Churinga could be purchased for $60,000. The purchase would have enabled the Commission to have a commercially oriented facility to fully capitalise on the huge number of visitors to the Sanctuary, while maintaining the Sanctuary's integrity. The Commission declined the offer.

Churinga was ultimately taken over by the partnership of Dorothy's son, Mr David Smith, and Mrs L. P. Webster. When Dorothy and Lou resigned from the Committee on July 14th, 1975, David Smith and Mrs Webster inherited the Committee positions. Mrs Webster took on the responsibility of Chairperson. Mrs Webster and David admirably filled the potential vacuum left by Dorothy and Lou, continuing their role until the Committee's disbandment at the end of 1983. But just as Dorothy and Lou were always there for Bill prior to the Committee's inception, David [who lived at Churinga and was, therefore, "on call" 24 hours per day] and Mrs Webster continued the tradition of being there whenever Bill needed them. The partnership has also turned Churinga into the only "5 scone" tea rooms in the Dandenongs.[2]

Mary Harris retained the title of Bill's greatest supporter until her death, at the age of eighty-seven years, on August 26th, 1978. Her dream for Bundilla's preservation as a sanctuary collapsed after her death when a nephew stepped in, split up the estate and sold it all. The Corporation of Walkerville were able to purchase a number of Mary's paintings, which are shown as a collection in the municipal offices. Mary's collection of Bill's work, twelve pieces in all, was purchased by an Adelaide dealer and sent to Melbourne for auction. Bill was most distressed by the affair, ultimately buying back three of the works himself for a reported $21,000.

Now Bundilla is a private home, and all that Mary had gathered is scattered. All that is left of her in that little part of Adelaide which she loved so dearly is a small brass plaque mounted on a small pile of rocks in Howie Reserve. It reads:

IN MEMORY OF

MARY P HARRIS
1891–1978

ARTIST FROM YORKSHIRE
WHOSE SANCTUARY "BUNDILLA"
ADJOINED THIS RESERVE.
"THEY SHALL NOT HURT OR DESTROY
IN ALL MY HOLY MOUNTAIN
SAYS THE LORD." ISAIAH 65:25

Just thirty-eight days after Mary Harris' death, Bill lost another whom he classed as a friend—Ted Strehlow. In the decade or so preceding Strehlow's death, Bill had come to feel an overwhelming empathy with the man. Strehlow had been falling out with the University of South Australia, the Australian Institute of Aboriginal Studies and many academics over his reluctance to share his treasure, his wealth of knowledge about Central Australia's human and spiritual history. Strehlow wanted to run his own show in preparing what he had for release to the academic and public world. To do that, though, he required substantial funding—funding which he could not secure. It was, more than anything else, Strehlow's inability to secure funding

---

2 In M. Civitella and P. Nugent's, *Off Our Scones: Devonshire Teas In The Dandenongs* [Bold Concept, 1988], tea rooms were awarded "scone points" as a measure of their overall standard. Churinga was the only establishment to receive their maximum five scone "Exceptional!" award, and the accompanying review positively dripped with the highest praise.

which induced Bill's empathy. Bill, too, had sought funding without success, and as far as Bill was concerned, both he and Strehlow deserved funding.

The pair, Strehlow and Bill, had been supportive of one another over the years. Strehlow provided essays, translations and photographs to help Bill's work; Bill provided major works for Strehlow's home and Research Foundation building. Strehlow had, in 1973, travelled to Mt Dandenong to speak at an Open Day which Bill had organised. It was supposed to be a day when the public could see the works that Bill had created while he was in India. Bill was, of course, a bit premature [by about three years!], but he used the day to talk of his revelations.

Strehlow did not mention Bill's Indian tour, but instead used the opportunity to review his relationship with Bill and trace Bill's progression through to what he referred to as an "unmistakeable maturity" of expression. Strehlow went on to relate to the gathering that Bill's talents had also been recognised by Norman Lindsay, to whom Strehlow had sent a copy of *A Living Voice of the Living Bush*. Strehlow claimed that Lindsay had written back to him in February, 1969, saying:

> *"The examples you have sent me of the sculptures of William Ricketts leave me breathless. He is a great master of his art, and has found a unique expression of it. The more I study it, especially the greatness of his technical achievement in modelling the human face, the more I am staggered by it. To think that all these masterly works were being created in the long years of my own struggle for self expression convinces me that there is a great future for this country as a world civilisation."*

As the years passed, though, Ted Strehlow found it increasingly difficult to find time for Bill while he was fighting for the safe-guarded survival of his collection. There was some correspondence, but Bill generally accepted that Strehlow was otherwise engaged in a crucial battle of his own. After Ted Strehlow's death, Kathy Strehlow kept up the correspondence with Bill, keeping him abreast with her own desperate struggle—which has now become legend itself in Australian anthropological history. In the August 28th, 1987, edition of the *Good Weekend* magazine, Janet Hawley's article, "The Strehlow Collection: Preserved in Vitriol", quoted Kathy as saying, in reference to Bertha Strehlow's [Ted's first wife] law suits for ownership of the collection: *"In the early 1980s, when I thought she might succeed, I personally snipped the labels off 400 objects in the collection, so it would be useless to her if she got it, a pyrrhic victory ..."* In that article there was a photograph of Kathy standing outside of the Strehlow Research Foundation building holding the life-size bust of what appeared to be old Tjinapatunka, although the piece was not acknowledged as Bill's work.

Towards the end of 1979, Bill, through his association with the Australian Conservation Foundation [ACF], struck upon the idea of creating a monumental sculpture to be placed at an entrance to Victoria's proposed Alpine National Park. As an indication of his complete distrust of the Forests Commission, Bill decided to neither create nor fire the work within the Sanctuary's boundaries. That distrust had been further strengthened, in Bill's mind, by the Commission producing some 16,000 post-cards, on the back of which Bill's work was described as "art". Convinced that the Commission did not understand his motives, Bill offered to buy the whole batch for their cost price of seven cents each.

Ever the patient neighbour, David Smith allowed Bill to set up a small studio within the grounds of Churinga. Bill proceeded to create the central section of what he proposed would be a monolithic sculptural group. Not surprisingly, it consisted of the Aboriginal man and Bill's "spiritual self" together, in harmony. After more than twelve months in creation, the work was ready to be fired.

Bill contacted his friend, Geoff Walker, of Walker Ceramics, and asked him to organise a kiln for Bill to purchase. Walker came up with a huge gas-fired model capable of taking the big works. After setting it up to suit Bill's firing cycles, replacing the burners and generally modifying it for Bill's needs, they transported it up the hill, hired two mobile cranes and had the kiln lifted down into place at Churinga. The work went through the firing beautifully with hardly a flaw. Then it sat down at Churinga, waiting. One morning David was woken by the sound of smashing from the vicinity of where the work was sitting. He raced out of his house to find Bill in the last stages of destroying the huge work. All that was left were fragments on the ground. Bill's reasoning was simple, as far as he was concerned—it was not in tune with his spiritual concept. Bill wanted nothing more to do with it.

Part of the work is now incorporated into a pond in the grounds of Churinga, thanks to David's patience in putting together the jig-saw puzzle. The rest was used as hard fill. Eventually Bill had Geoff Walker return, along with two more mobile cranes, and the kiln was taken away.

Bill still maintained a remarkable pace throughout the 1980s. One of his main fights was to have the Forests Commission removed as the managing authority. Disregarding all of the good work for which the Commission had been responsible, Bill maintained that there was a conflict of interests. Bill and the Sanctuary stood for total conservation and wild life preservation. He could not accept that the Government Department responsible for forest harvesting, which included their sanctioning of the clear-felling and wood chipping of vast tracts of native forest, should be responsible for the management of a Sanctuary which was designed to stop such activity. His letter writing campaign was continuous.

One of the most revealing letters [which I sighted as a draft dated August 20th, 1981] was to Lindsay Thompson, who was by that time occupying the position of Premier of Victoria. Bill began by requesting that the Sanctuary be handed over to the National Trust or Heritage Commission, which was by then not an unusual request. He went on to outline his plans and vision. The vision revolved around building up the Sanctuary and was in three parts. The first part was complete, but the second and third parts [building up the Sanctuary into an absolute spectacle—a true Holy Mountain] required time and money. Bill suggested that after the Sanctuary was handed over to a more conservation-oriented body, all clear profit produced by the Sanctuary should be put into a special Trust Account in Bill's name, to be used for the completion of his vision. Bill stipulated that the Trust Account had to be beyond the reach of State or Federal taxes. At the end of the letter, bearing in mind that he was almost eighty-three years old, Bill predicted that his vision would take eight years to fulfil—perhaps ten.

That letter was written just one month after Bill had been discharged from the William Angliss Hospital in Upper Ferntree Gully. His hospitalisation had been attributed to "just weakness". Three days after his discharge, *Age* reporter, Jane Cafarella, interviewed him. She wrote of an old man, *"as frail as a fledgling bird"*, who struggled through waves of giddiness. *"I've never been like this in my life"*, he told her: *"Forty-six years with the strength of a lion! But now I've been struck for a purpose and that purpose was awesome."* Bill had no thoughts that his month-long stay in hospital was a sign of the beginning of the end. He explained to Cafarella that it was just a lesson in weakness. Cafarella interpreted it as: *"He knew strength, now he had to know weakness, just as the Aboriginal man knew strength until the arrival of the white man—when he abruptly learned weakness."*

It was not until Ken Nienaber came to Bill's aid in 1983 that the Forests Commission were relieved of their management role at the Sanctuary. Through persistent and effective lobbying, Nienaber had management of the Sanctuary placed in the hands of the Victorian Conservation Trust [VCT]. Bill was unsuccessful, however, in raising the funds for the completion of his grand Holy Mountain ideal. While he never gave up on this ideal, it quite often took second place to his desires to again take his message to the world. Always Bill was planning for the future, planning for a victory.

The beginning of 1984 saw Bill begin what was to be his last major work. It consisted of a familiar theme—the Aboriginal and white man together, in harmony. Bill wanted to add dimensions of free thought, far-ranging vision and soaring hope. To this end he contacted the

Museum of Victoria and asked for a loan of a wedge-tailed eagle. They obliged and sent up a mature wedge-tail, mounted in an attitude of being perched, with its huge wings outstretched. Bill was not overjoyed at having the dead, mounted bird to use as a model, but it was a means to an end. Ultimately the spirit of the bird would be liberated into the Sanctuary to become an inspiration to all who viewed it. The eagle was supposed to sit above the two men in the sculpture, but when the piece was completed, Bill again had doubts about the way he had portrayed the men. The piece sat unfired in the studio, waiting.

Bill's lessons in weakness came more regularly. On December 12th, 1984, in the heat of summer, he "dropped dead" while walking up the path to his house. It was mid-week, normally a quiet time in the Sanctuary, but fate stepped in and had Bill drop at the feet of two qualified nurses. He had no heart beat and was not breathing, but he was revived by CPR. It resulted in another stay at the William Angliss Hospital. By February the following year, though, Bill returned to the Sanctuary after having had a check-up by his doctor, claiming that the doctor had told him he had the body of a thirty year old. His powers of recuperation were again put to the test in May, 1986. Walking down to the gatehouse he slipped and fell, fracturing his hip— a normally debilitating mishap for the usual eighty-eight year old. It took a couple of hours of persuasion before Bill would let the Sanctuary staff call an ambulance—after which he was whisked straight down to the Dandenong and District Hospital. At 6.00 p.m. the following evening he was put under general anaesthetic and operated upon, ultimately having a steel pin inserted to hold him together.

The after effects of the general anaesthetic were horrifying for him. Nightmares and hallucinations gave him two days of hell, but just ten days after the operation Bill was walking around the hospital with the aid of a frame, trying his best to convince the staff that a hospital was no place for a man such as him to recuperate. He needed to be at home, growing with his forest. Twenty-one days after the operation Bill was back at the Sanctuary.

Another project which kept Bill busy throughout these years was his preparation of a new publication, *Australiandia*. The title was drawn directly from Jean Sibelius' classic work of 1900, *Finlandia*. Bill said that it was *Finlandia* which roused the native Finns to **"kick the Russians out"** of Finland. He hoped that *Australiandia* would rouse Australians to kick the environmental destroyers out of Australia. During those mid-1980s, Bill's white hot passion was the damage being done by woodchipping and clear-felling of forests.

Australiandia, at thirty-eight pages, was largely a compilation of previously published texts, although it did contain two written works by Bill which I had not seen previously. "The Great Extermination", stretching over four A4 sized pages, became another vehicle for Bill's version of the history of Australia—the dispossession of the spiritually aware original inhabitants by the **"thinking, speaking creature"** which represented, as far as Bill was concerned, a great many non-Aboriginal people, and the subsequent rape of Australia. It is a relatively moderate piece of writing in which Bill also included brief recollections of his days in Central Australia. *Australiandia's* epilogue, occupying a single page, became an impassioned plea for people to stand up and stop the **"clearfelling woodchipping barbarian"**, which Bill identified as the greatest threat to Australia's forests and wild life.

The publication was launched at the Sanctuary on October 10th, 1986, by Dr Geoff Mosley, whose twenty-year-long association with the ACF had commanded Bill's sincere respect. A small crowd of between fifty and sixty people gathered for the occasion. Geoff Mosley's short speech revolved around Bill's fight to preserve the Australian environment and drew attention to Bill's method of placing the works *into* the Australian bush, which in turn made visitors experience the bush in a totally new way. After Dr Mosley launched *Australiandia*, Bill stepped up to the microphone.

The years he had spent dreaming of *Australiandia's* publication, and the impact which he hoped it would have, resulted in Bill being wound up like a spring. He had no prepared speech, and, after thanking Dr Mosley, began:

"So what I would like to say to you is in two parts. The first part is India, ancient India, and the second part is, and I would like you to have some little measure of—a peeping into—Aboriginal man at the most ancient dawn of his <u>Dreaming</u>. That word <u>Dreaming</u> has been put into books all over the world as Dream Time. That's another insult to Aboriginal man—it is <u>Dreaming</u>.[3] Perhaps the first part of my life is inter-related with Aboriginal man quite a bit."

Bill then tried to explain his journey to India and his being likened to the ancient Rishis. In doing so, the spring inside him was unleashed. He became visibly disturbed, trying to find the right words to explain to the gathering the mystery which had overtaken him. He got through telling of Dr Pai's writing to Indira Gandhi and referring to him as "the said Rishi", but then he tried to explain who the Rishis were, saying: *"Then the Rishis were holding and guarding the vibrations of the Earth—"* At that point Bill gasped for air and began crying. As a murmur of concern rippled through the gathering, two friends jumped to his aid, physically supporting him and trying to get him to sit down. He recovered, telling them *"It's all right"*, before being left to go on again. *"The Rishis were holding—"*, but again he gasped and was overcome with emotion. When he settled down again he said: *"—the Rishis were holding the vibrations of God, but how am I to know that I was here doing certain work, and yet, the Rishis without printing presses said everything I'd dreamed of here. Yes, a vision, a dream—call it what you like."*

Bill tried to explain it further, but the more he tried, the greater became his agitation. He wanted to say how the wisdom of ancient India, which he believed to be the wisdom of ancient Australia, came to him, but he stalled. *"I can't go on"*, he said, but then he shouted: *"and I won't talk about it! It reached me here—I can't talk about it—if I do I'll insult God, and I won't do that."* What was he holding back? What was it that he'd experienced that he longed to reveal—but couldn't reveal? What was this secret that he'd never shared, but which took his breath away at the very thought of sharing?

"Is it possible that the Aboriginal man could enter my innermost-to-all structure of what I am as a man?", he asked himself as much as the audience. *"And how could he enter me and lift me up into higher realms of consciousness and higher states of being?"* He continued to speak, but it was in circles and with much left unsaid—only Bill knew what the full content was. He spoke of the *"Aboriginal man's missionary attitude"* which had come to him. He again came close to revealing his personal mystery, but baulked: *"I can't put it into words—man at the ancient dawn of his Dreaming—at the feet of his true—"* This time the gasp was painful even to the audience. Bill put a hand to his chest and teetered, barely containing his tears, looking as if he were going to drop in a faint at any moment. *"I can't"*, he pleaded. *"If I put it into words I'll damn God—I won't do it!"* And he didn't do it.

Instead Bill launched into a swirling speech about everything that was dear to him. I recall at the time becoming lost in the haze of words, the sentences left unfinished, the anger which welled up. Looking at a transcript I made of the speech, though, I can piece his words together. Given time to re-read them, I can understand some of what he was trying to put across. But on the day it was lost to me. Bill was on a roll and the "talking machine" had become lord.[4] I was not alone in my confusion, for after some ten or fifteen minutes, applause drowned Bill out at the end of a sentence. He tried to go on, but the applause drowned him out again. As the applause died down, Bill started to speak again—only to be drowned out a third time. The "talking

---

3 Bill was of the opinion that The Dreaming was in a timeless past. When he heard people saying "Dream Time", he classed it as sacrilege—people putting a *time* on the spiritual dawning of a people. By sticking to "The Dreaming", Bill kept the matter as timeless.

4 Bill himself gave me this term—the "talking machine"—after viewing a home-made video tape of himself explaining the Sanctuary [not of the day in question]. Bill said that when he was wound up and set going, it was like a machine talking. Although he recognised the fact that when he was in "talking machine" mode, he was not at all clear in his speech, he was never able to control the "talking machine" cutting in and taking over.

machine" retired and Bill came back to present those who had helped put the day together with potted boronias.

I often tried to get Bill to reveal the mystery which had repeatedly caught in his throat during his speech, but to no avail. Whatever it was, Bill has taken it with him.

Just over one month after the launch, Bill had the opportunity to meet one of his few heroes: Tasmanian, Dr Bob Brown. Bob Brown had been a leading force in the environmental battle over the proposed damming of the Franklin River in south-west Tasmania in the early 1980s. Bill had followed Brown's steady rise in the public arena with interest and admiration. Brown was not only a doer, but a doer who inspired others to join him in battle. He was also a man of compassion.

On December 24th, 1985, Bill had been featured in an *Age* article titled, "All the Bush Should be a Sanctuary, Says an Old Man Who Founded One", written by Louise Bellamy. The accompanying photograph had caught Bill in a moment of sadness and seemingly ready to burst into tears [which he is prone to do whenever he thinks of the bush creatures being killed through forest fire or clear-felling]. It was not the picture of a staunch little fighter, but of a very frail, old man. Towards the end of the article it was reported that Bill was being paid $187.16 per fortnight by the VCT.

Bellamy wrote: *"Although Mr Ricketts is grateful for the money, he said he was used to being poor and if sacrificing the money would draw the public's attention to the issue of woodchipping then the exercise would be worthwhile."* Brown read the article and, on January 14th, 1986, wrote to Bill on a Wilderness Society letterhead. It was a letter which did not attempt to hide the seriousness of recent Federal Government decisions to open more National Estate forests to the woodchip industry, but it was also a letter of strong optimism. Brown assured Bill that the Wilderness Society would be fighting all the way and speculated that, just as it was with the Franklin dam battle, the Australian people would join in the fight. *"The odds of protecting our National Estate forests indeed look formidable"*, Brown concluded, *"but like water on a stone, we will win through"*. Bill drew strength from that letter for a long time.

The occasion for Bill to meet Brown came when a large rally was organised on November 22nd, 1986, to protest against the logging, woodchipping and clear-felling of south-east Gippsland's old-age forests. Brown had come to Melbourne to speak at the rally and arrangements were made for Bill to meet him after the rally had ended. Bill did not take part in the protest march, deciding instead to wait at the rally site in the King's Domain park. As he sat on a park-bench surrounded by pigeons eager to share his biscuits, people stopped in droves to say hello, wish him well and express their admiration for what Bill had done at the Sanctuary. When it came time for the speeches at the rally, it was Bill's turn, sitting on the ground at the front of the large crowd, to look on with admiration as speakers put their message across clearly and with great effect. Brown's rousing address was full of optimism that the fight could, indeed, be won. I recall wondering at the time if Bill was secretly envious of people such as Brown who could, with words alone, capture and inspire a crowd of thousands? Or did Bill accept that his was just a different form of capturing and inspiring?

The two men met after the rally for only a brief time—Bob Brown was very much in demand that day. Brown was given a copy of *Australiandia* to take back to the fight in Tasmania. I did not hear their conversation, but when it had concluded Bill was happy.

Less than a fortnight later Bill was again on a hospital operating table having a large hernia repaired. It had been present for some time, but his recent landscaping activities had aggravated the condition. This time the operation was done with local anaesthetic only. Bill was perfectly conscious during the complete procedure. He recalled no pain, but said that he was aware of quite a bit of pushing and shoving "down there" behind the separating sheet. At one point Bill couldn't help wondering when it was going to be finished. *"How're you going down there?",* he asked. *"All right"*, was the reply: *"How are you going up there?"* None the wiser, Bill contented himself with being patient. Again, his recovery was startlingly quick.

Bill's fervent push for wild life preservation eventually brought him in touch with the organisation, Animal Liberation—in particular their campaigning to stop completely the duck-hunting seasons. Bill began by having petitions kept at his house, to be signed by Sanctuary visitors who supported Animal Liberation's fight. Although he collected thousands of signatures, for him it was not enough. He had to do something more, and in 1987 he decided that money was what Animal Liberation needed to get their message across. Bill turned to his only fund-raising source, his sculpture. He chose one of the pieces which he purchased from the Mary Harris collection, of the theme which depicted his rebirth at the hands of the Aboriginal patriarch. He would sell the work and donate the proceeds to Animal Liberation. Bill first offered the piece to the Victorian Government, through the VCT, for $23,000. The theme was already expressed in another piece in the Sanctuary, and money was reportedly tight—and the offer was declined.

Bill found himself in a quandary regarding how to sell the work while maintaining his distance from the art world. He reasoned that if the work went through a recognised auction house, he would have great difficulty shunning the labels of "artist" or "sculptor", which he despised and rejected. At one point he relaxed his stance and virtually had the work booked into a Sotheby's auction, but he withdrew at the last minute. Ideas were floated for having an auction at an independent venue which was not related to the art world, or even at the Sanctuary, but just the idea of an auction disturbed Bill. His indecision stretched through until 1988 when the *Herald* interviewed him about his desire to sell the work to raise money for Animal Liberation. While he wanted to raise the money, he was reluctant to have a major work leave the Sanctuary. *"It's part of my heritage"*, he told reporter, Ann-Maree Moodie: *"I wish [a buyer] would come to me and say 'here's the money, you keep the sculpture and put it up in the bush'."*

Shortly after the article was published on February 8th, a cheque for $5,000 was anonymously sent to Bill with a message for him to put the work in the bush. Then a dealer approached Bill on behalf of a private client who was willing to pay $24,000 for the work. Bill ended up selling the work through the dealer, donating $19,000 to Animal Liberation and tracking the donor of the $5,000 back through the bank so that the money could be returned. The $19,000 reportedly funded the full Victorian anti-duck-hunting campaign for 1988.

Bill's eagle work, after expanding and contracting through the varying humidities of seven years in the studio, was finally put into the kiln in September, 1991. Only the eagle section was fired, after Bill's decision that the human components of the work were not to his liking. Fortunately the piece came through the firing process, but another problem arose in trying to decide where to place it within the Sanctuary. Several false starts were made, but something would interfere before the process was complete. Now, without Bill's creative direction, the eagle can never be liberated into the forest.

Early in 1992 Bill suffered renal failure, resulting in three operations and causing his prolonged hospitalisation. Upon his return from hospital, Bill developed a minor chest infection which could easily have overtaken his seemingly indomitable little body. Although Bill fought back and shook off the infection, he never quite regained a state of total good health. When asked how he was, he would give a slight grimace and wave a hand from his head down across his chest. He'd say he was fine—except that there was *something* not quite right in his body, *something* that he couldn't shake off. His spirit and strength of purpose remained as strong as ever. If people asked questions, he made sure that he gave them answers—even if it tired him so much that he would have to spend the remainder of the day resting. As far as promoting and explaining his Vision, he would not, and could not, slow down his pace.

At around 11.00 p.m. on Wednesday, June 9th, 1993, Bill was given a cup of tea in his bed at the William Angliss Hospital in Upper Ferntree Gully. He had been away from his Sanctuary for almost two weeks—not because he was desperately ill, but simply because he had reached a point where he could not look after himself effectively. He was upset and distressed about being away from his home, but no assistant had been provided to help him. Nor had his home been set up to accommodate him in his condition. At midnight, when next nursing staff checked him, Bill was dead.

One week later, on Thursday June 17th, a small group of people gathered in the Sanctuary to share the experience of uniting Bill's ashes with his Sanctuary. Bill had selected the ground at the base of a Mountain Ash tree to be the starting point for another journey. He had named the tree his "Sacred Tree of Life".

Close by, in another of the Sanctuary's alcoves, was a small plaque bearing the words:

> *"To melt and become as the Living Waters—Running and singing—a flow of life in my Dreaming."*

It is unlikely that Bill created the plaque with that day in mind, but it expressed perfectly what we were there to do. That was the day for Bill to be united with his Spiritual Mother, the Earth. Light rain fell during the night that followed. Bill's ashes mixed with the rain and were drawn into the Earth. Then, as the Living Waters, he flowed up through his majestic Mountain Ash—into the ferns and soil and through the earth to flow through the fountains of his creations.

He will truly remain a living part of his Sanctuary—a flowing of Life in his Dreaming.

Epilogue

Unquestionably, the course of William Ricketts' life was extraordinary. Early in his adulthood he identified what he perceived as wrongs in the way new Australia was treating the old Australia. He set himself a goal to rectify those wrongs and worked towards that end with zealous fanaticism. Not once during the rest of his long life did he waver from that course. While goal-setting and single-minded pursuit are not at all rare, most who have done it successfully have centred their goals on personal success through the accumulation of wealth and material possessions. Bill's goal, on the other hand, was totally altruistic. That is what set him apart. Any self-promotion he had entered into had been done to draw attention to his altruistic goal.

When Bill first started his campaign, his was a relatively lonely voice. Nowadays Bill's ideals are shared by many, although there are few who approach the issues with comparable long-term dedication. Human rights, wild life preservation and a respect for all Life and the Earth have become almost fashionable. The ancient "primitive" wisdoms are attracting more attention as an increasing number of the population lose faith in, or become disillusioned with, the "modern" wisdoms. Every corporation, it seems, has a public relations department trying desperately to convince their neighbours and clients that they really are "greener" than the rest. The primary reason for this contest to be the "greenest" of the "greens" is public pressure.

Society's swing to an increased awareness of the issues outlined above has only come about by individuals thinking about such issues and making their own decisions about them. Public opinion then dictates how the "decision makers" react. To start that thought process, though, there had to be something or someone to provide the impetus—to provide the spark that would ignite a flame in the individual's heart. Bill was one of those catalysts providing the spark. He was fortunate in that he had a talent which, with very little guidance, was able to attract attention. We have seen that Bill claimed that the talent came not from him, but from a higher source. He did not accept that something so powerful could come from an ordinary man alone—so he put it down to Divine intervention. Who can argue with him? Who really knows? It was his way of explaining what to him remained a mystery. Wherever it came from, Bill's talent was such that it could firstly arouse curiosity and admiration, then capture the imagination and hold it long enough to leave an impression.

While Bill had been the driving force at the head of his particular campaigns, he was in no way alone. From the beginning, he attracted a close group of loyal helpers from every walk of life. From otherwise hard-nosed business men and women to starry-eyed idealists, many have found something in Bill that inspired them to support him. The names mentioned in this volume represent a small percentage of the total. The vast majority gave their time and energy freely. In many instances they barely received a "thank you" for that effort. And as their energy and enthusiasm waned, more often than not through their "burning out" and not being able to keep pace with Bill, another would be there to fill the space. It is hard to pin down the quality in Bill which attracted such support. His own personal degree of devotion and commitment is often mentioned when supporters speak about him, as is the spiritual aspect he infused into the issues of human rights and environmentalism. Most often supporters shrug their shoulders and speak of Bill's whole personality.

Vijay Yogendra's feelings towards Bill are not confused:

> *"The one thing I always said in my lectures to people, that if there was one saint in Australia, it was William Ricketts. I always have revered him as a saint, because he has tremendous goodness and godliness in him. All right, you go after his bombardment of how he hates the white and all that—you let that pass and the rest is all beautiful. That's righteous anger. He has every reason to be angry about it because he sees the destruction of so many good things in life. So I respect him for his outbursts, which are not just outbursts—they are really genuine outbursts of care."*

Nitya Chaitanya Yati is another who had no doubts when he wrote "William Ricketts' Disarmament",[1] offering such extreme high praise as:

> *"I don't say he is the only man of his kind, but I believe that people like him are the only hope of mankind ...*
>
> *If the United Nations on the banks of the Hudson River, overshadowed by the great metropolis of New York, represents the mouth of the geodialectical[2] dragon of world civilisation, the dragon's tail-end is in Mount Dandenong. Even the slightest sting on the tail will make the mouth howl. William Ricketts is not a stinging scorpion; what he can infuse into the consciousness of world polity is good sense ..."*

The anomaly is that while Nitya, living almost 10,000 km away, endowed such high praise upon Bill, there are multitudes living less than 30 km from the Sanctuary who do not know who William Ricketts was. Many more living close by have heard of the Sanctuary, but have no idea about what is in there. Yet the Sanctuary attracts, on average, over 1,000 people per week through the gate.

The artistry of Bill's work is a major factor in the initial attraction of those large numbers of paying visitors—but Bill is barely, if at all, recognised in the "art world". Ainslie Roberts,[3] while Bill was still alive, gave me his thoughts on why that might be:

> *"Here we've got a living genius on our hands and he is still not recognised by the arts world ... I think it's the same old story that the art world are always clamouring for something different—'but let's get together and form a group so that we know we're not different at all'. Because Bill can't be classified—there's no precedent for his work, he doesn't fall into a sculpting class as in the convention of John Dowie and others—they feel uncomfortable because he doesn't conform. I know—I've been through that. People don't know how to treat it—there's no class to put it in. They either drool over it or say 'Well yes, that's very interesting, isn't it?' or 'It makes a firm statement, doesn't it?' or something innocuous like that.*
>
> *But the ordinary people in the street, they rave about [Bill's work]. To me that's significant, because Bill actually has done what art should do—and the art critics*

---

1 First publication unsighted; reprinted in *Australiandia*, 1986.
2 This is the spelling which appears in the *Australiandia* copy of the article.
3 Ainslie Roberts received much acclaim and reward for his paintings which accompanied Charles P. Mountford's collected myths in the extremely successful Dreamtime Series of four books [*The Dreamtime, The Dawn of Time, The First Sunrise* and *The Dreamtime Book*], and the *Dreamtime Heritage* book written by his wife, Melva Jean Roberts. The first of these books was published in 1965.

should do—and that's to bridge the gap between the ordinary populous and the artist. But [the art world] never does, you see—all they do is widen it. No, Bill's bridged it all by himself and they stream up there in their tens of thousands."

Over the years that Bill was at Mt Dandenong, many hundreds of thousands of people have visited the Sanctuary. Acclaimed Koorie artist, Lin Onus AM, has definite views about the contribution Bill has made to bridging gaps:

"I think he's Australia's greatest sculptor, there's just no two ways about that. But it goes further. If you consider the number of people who have passed through that place since it's been in existence—if only he touches one per cent of those people, he's done a pretty amazing job. The fact is that they get off a tourist coach and walk in there; it's just something to pass the day—something to see. They don't realise that they've gone through a learning process. I'd be inclined to say that in terms of public awareness, the Department of Aboriginal Affairs does something with a $23 million budget and it gets nowhere. Bill Ricketts is worth a dozen $23 million public awareness programs."

The personal impact Bill had on many of the visitors to the Sanctuary is also extraordinary. The visitors' books, which used to be available to any visitor who wished to enter their name and comments, overflow with praise, good wishes and love. One of the comments Bill picked out and held dear came from a young woman from the USA. *"Your sanctuary cannot be described in words"*, she wrote, *"it has to be felt in the heart"*. On March 3rd, 1982, Evan and Annita Melting Tallow, and Glen and Lema Eagle Speaker, all indigenous Americans, met and spoke with Bill. Before leaving they asked him for a pen and a piece of paper, on which they wrote:

"It was an honour meeting You,
Will always Remember You, as
A <u>Friend</u> and a true Spirit of
The Land.
From The Blood Tribe
of CANADA"

They each signed their name to the note before handing it to Bill.

Bill's greatest fear was that after he had gone the Victorian Government would step in and develop the Sanctuary into a more commercially orientated, and therefore more profitable, asset. Bill had heard rumours that such action may be undertaken. Unfortunately, nowhere in the original and only Agreement is there any provision to safeguard the Sanctuary against such development now that Bill is gone. It will be up to the supporters that Bill has left behind to carefully monitor the situation and ensure that it continues faithful to his vision.

Just one of the things Bill wanted to do before he went was to change the name of the Sanctuary. He felt that the present name was too much the "I am". Better to have a universal name, he said; one which reflected the underlying theme in the Sanctuary. He saw a phrase in 1979 which stuck with him; part of the title of an article about him written by Chris Canning and published in the *Simply Living* magazine. It contained a word which Bill believed to be the most powerful of all words—the one force, he said, that could engender the total respect for the Earth and all Life. Bill said it was the force that people brought to the Sanctuary—and which they could take away. Bill would have liked to have seen his Sanctuary renamed, *"The Forest of Love"*.

List of Plates

Index